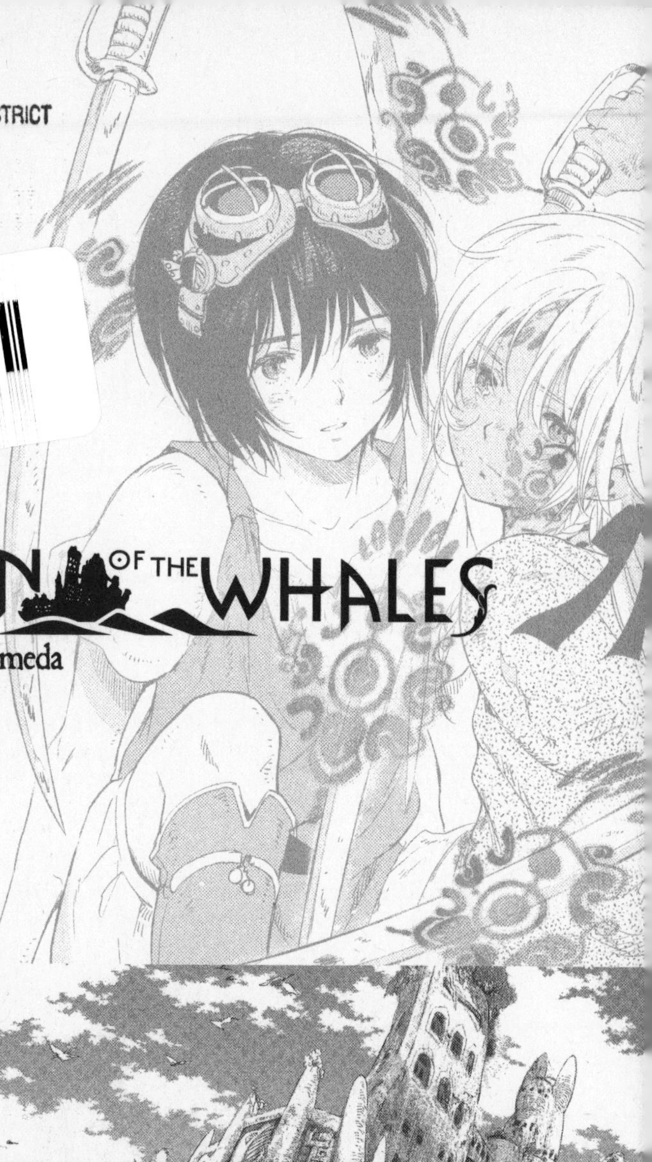

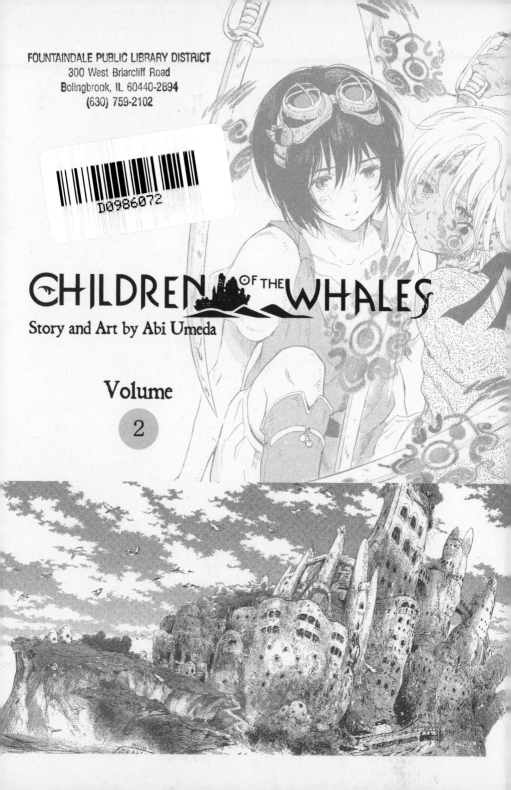

CHILDREN OF THE WHALES

Story and Art by Abi Umeda

Volume

2

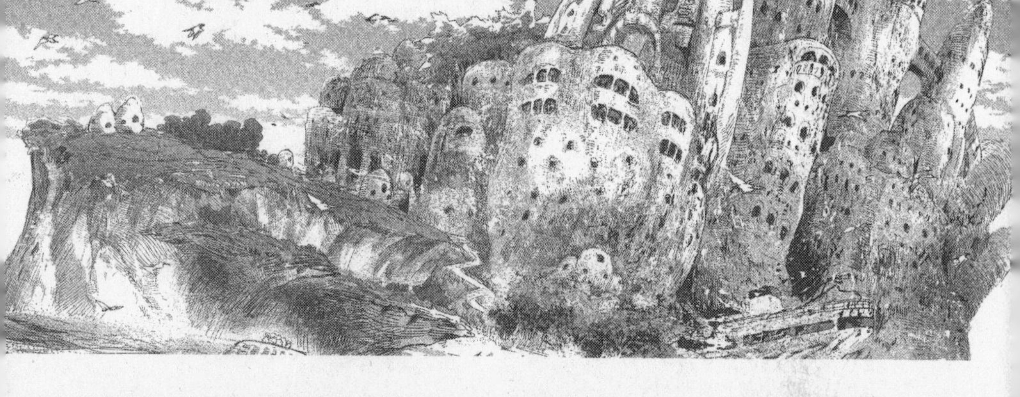

Characters

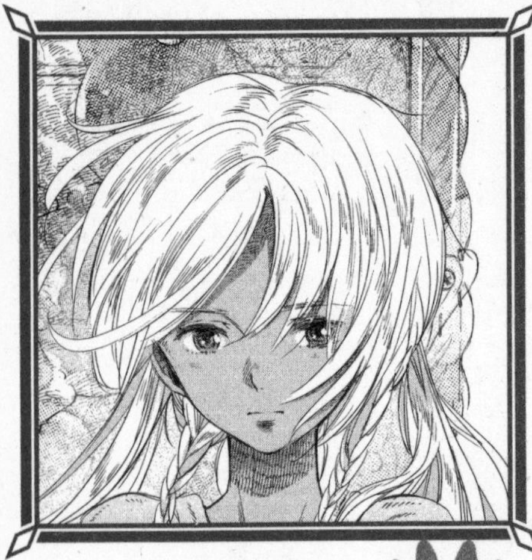

Lykos

The girl found aboard the abandoned ship drifting near the Mud Whale. An apátheia, one of the emotionless soldiers from the empire. But she feels close to Chakuro and his friends.

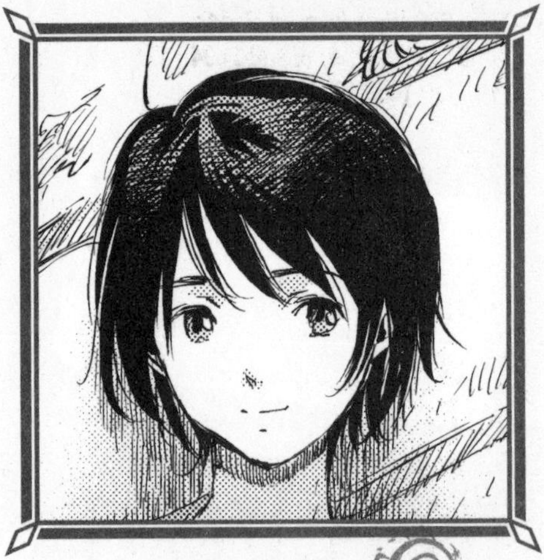

Chakuro

The young archivist of the Mud Whale. He has hypergraphia, a disorder that compels him to record everything.

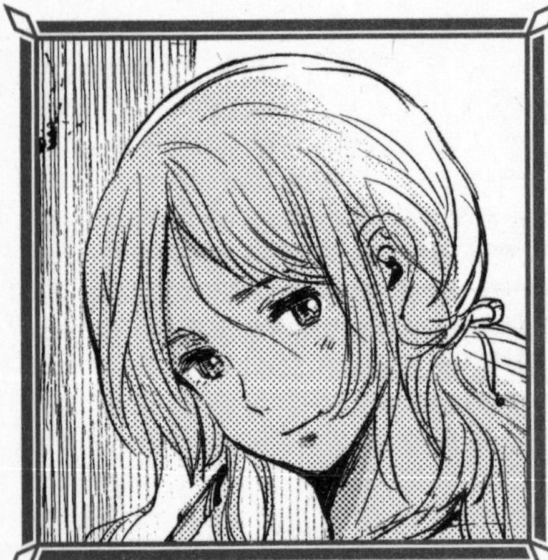

Suou

A candidate to be the next mayor of the Mud Whale. Chakuro and the other Marked trust him.

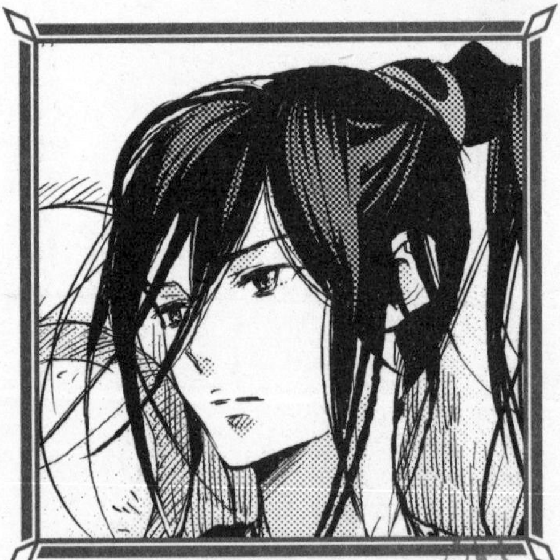

Ouni

The most accomplished thymia user on the Mud Whale. The leader of the moles, a group of troublemakers.

Taisha

Mayor of the Mud Whale, a figurehead. Died during the apátheia attack.

Neri

Caretaker of the tower where the Committee of Elders lives. She is kind to Lykos.

Sami

Chakuro's childhood friend. Died during the apátheia attack.

Thymia

Ninety percent of the inhabitants of the Mud Whale possess this psychic power, which allows them to move objects with their minds, but they have drastically shortened lives.

A Record of the Mud Whale and the Sea of Sand

Year 93 of the sand exile.

The Mud Whale drifts endlessly through the Sea of Sand, home to about 500 people who know nothing about the outside world.

The Marked are those who can wield thymia, a psychic power fueled by emotion. They die young, around the age of 30. Those who have no thymia are called the Unmarked.

Chakuro, the Mud Whale archivist, meets Lykos one day on an abandoned island-ship found floating near theirs. It's the first time he has met someone from the outside world, but Lykos doesn't share his excitement. As an apátheia, a soldier stripped of emotions, she is as cold as a doll.

After spending time with Chakuro and the others on the Mud Whale, Lykos begins to recover some of her emotions. She warns the Committee of Elders to flee, but it is too late and the Mud Whale is suddenly attacked by soldiers in harlequin masks.

The Mud Whale is instantly transformed from a paradise to a battleground, and many held dear are slain. All Chakuro can do is despair.

"The Mud Whale was our entire world."

Table of Contents

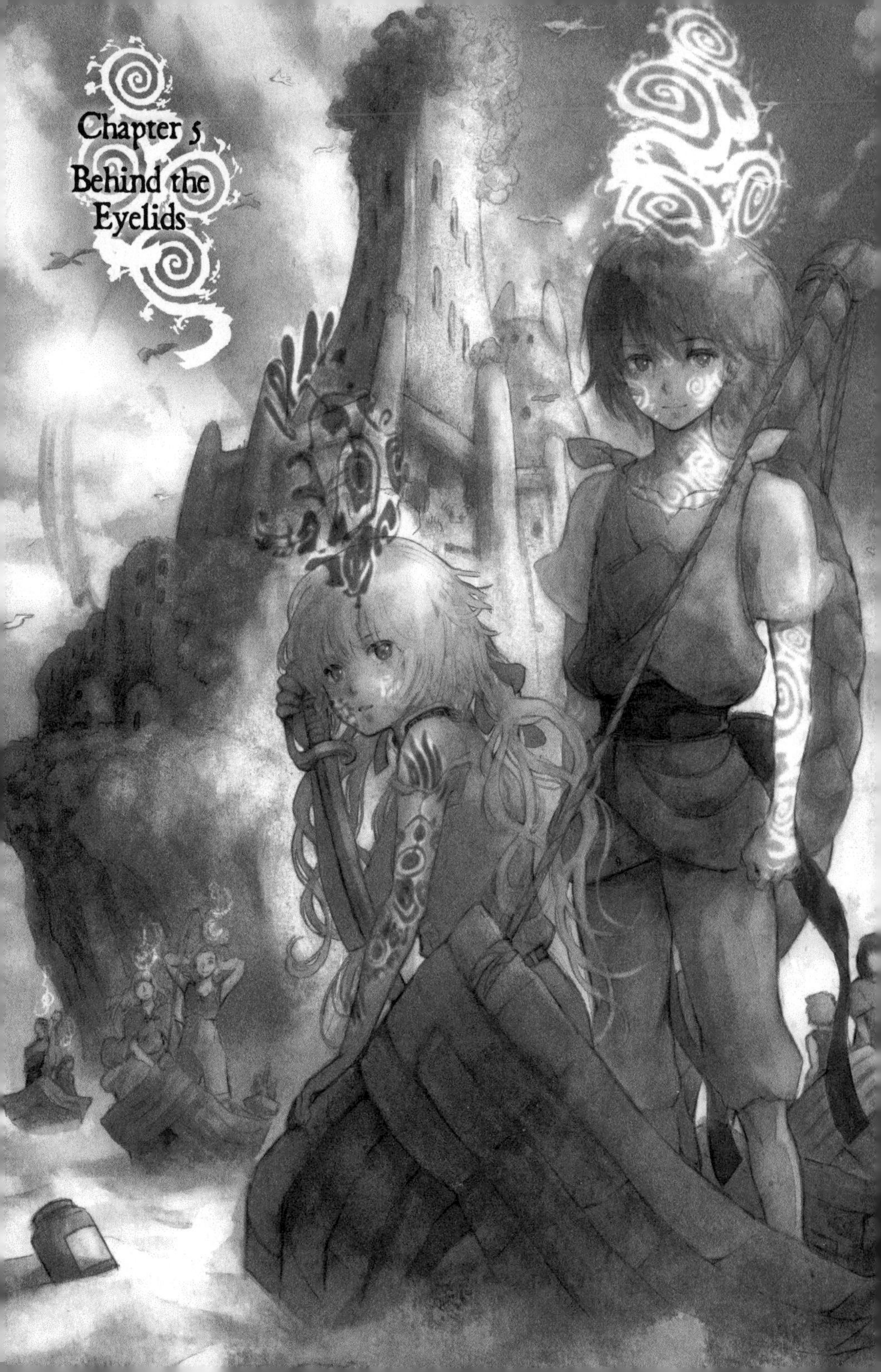
Chapter 5
Behind the Eyelids

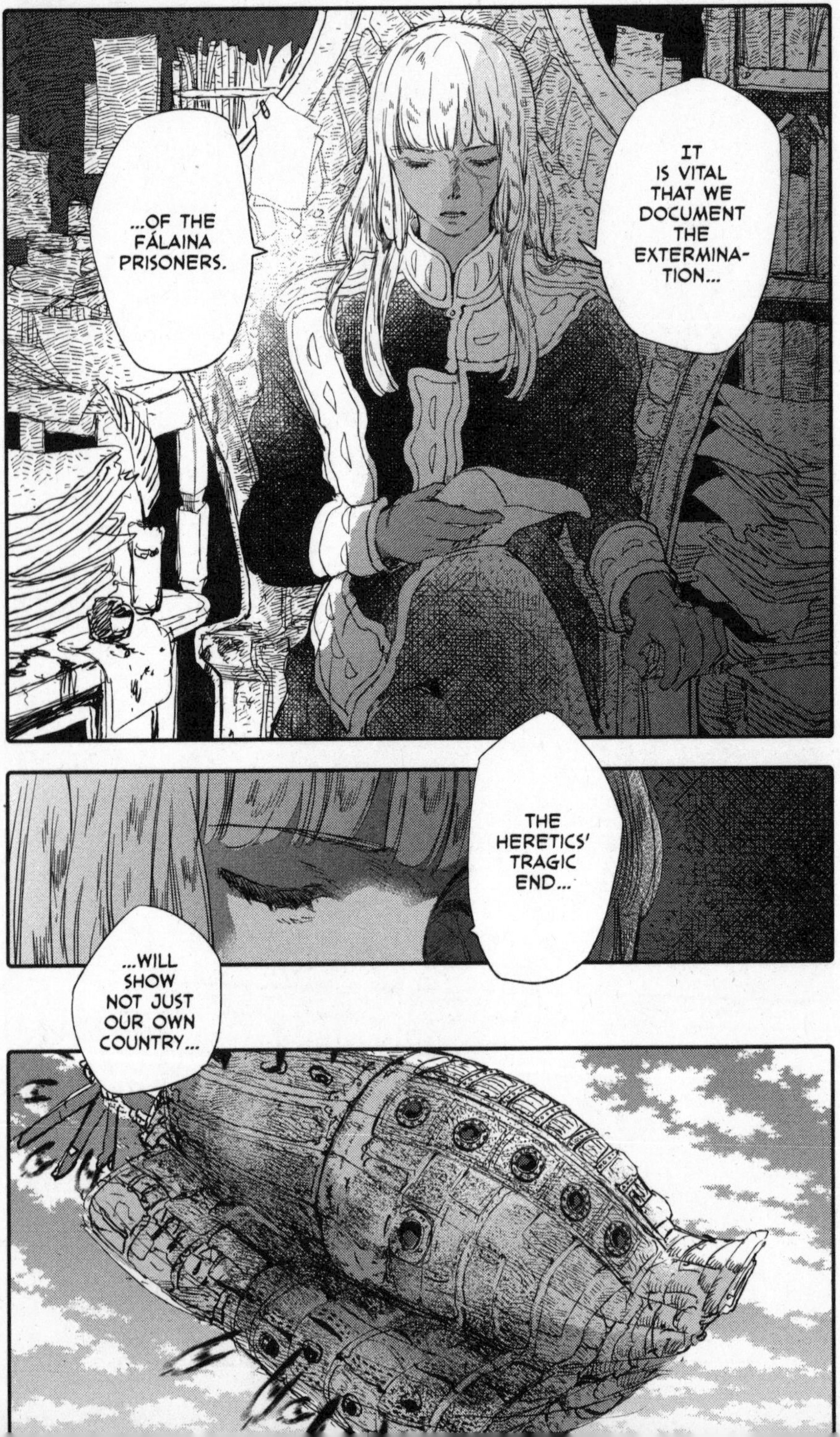
IT IS VITAL THAT WE DOCUMENT THE EXTERMINATION...
...OF THE FÁLAINA PRISONERS.
THE HERETICS' TRAGIC END...
...WILL SHOW NOT JUST OUR OWN COUNTRY...

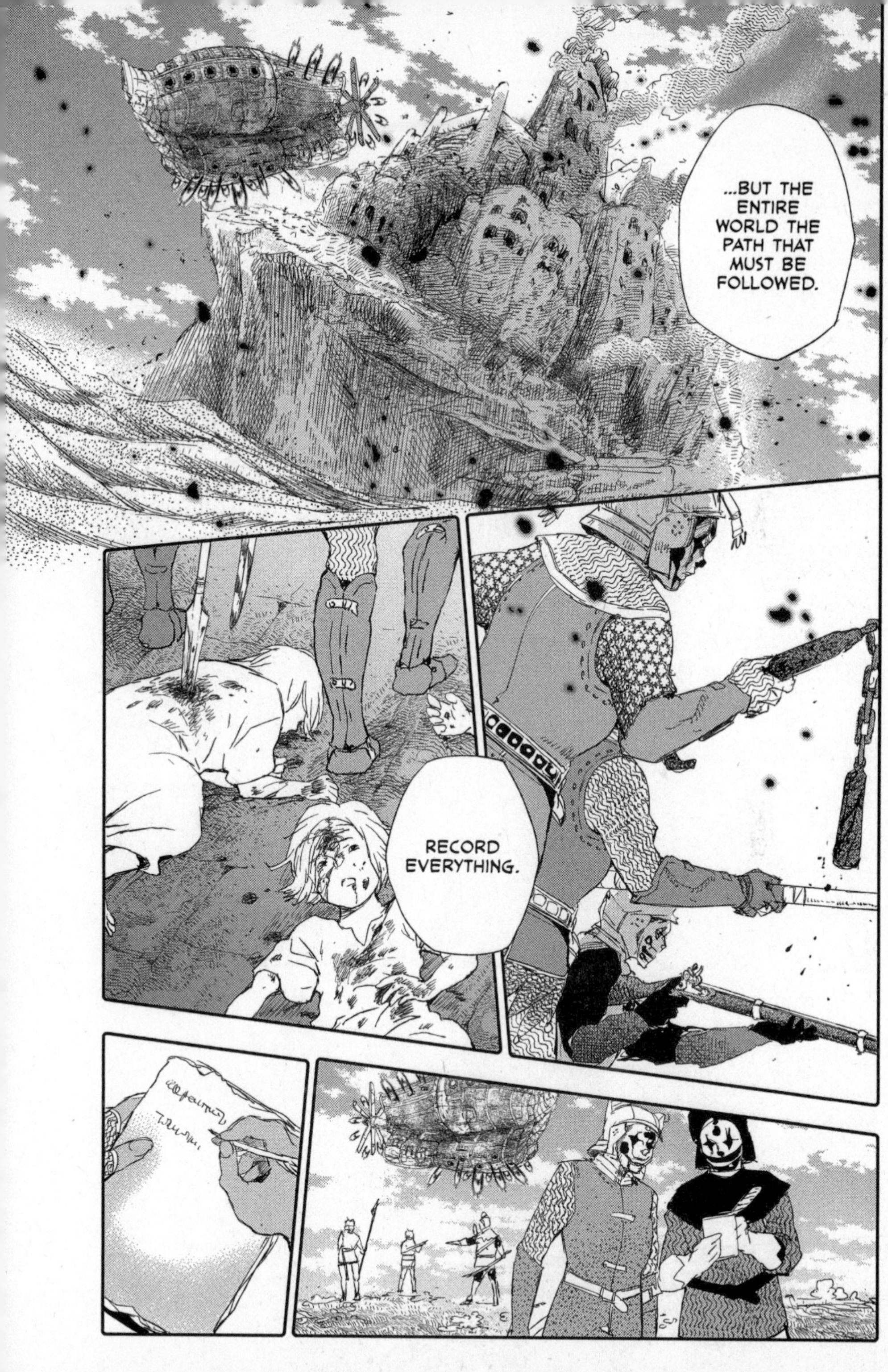
...BUT THE ENTIRE WORLD THE PATH THAT MUST BE FOLLOWED.
RECORD EVERYTHING.

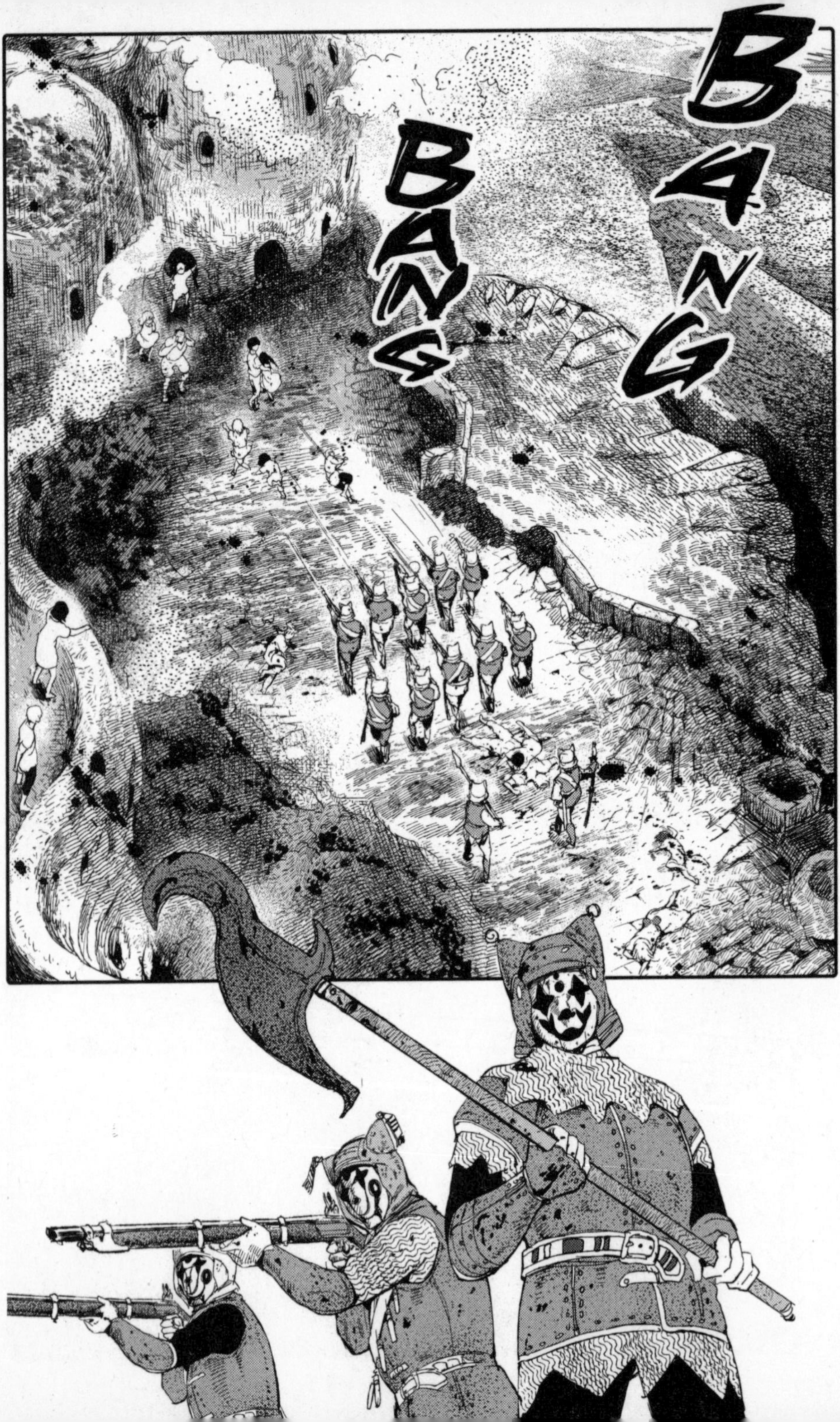
BANG
BANG

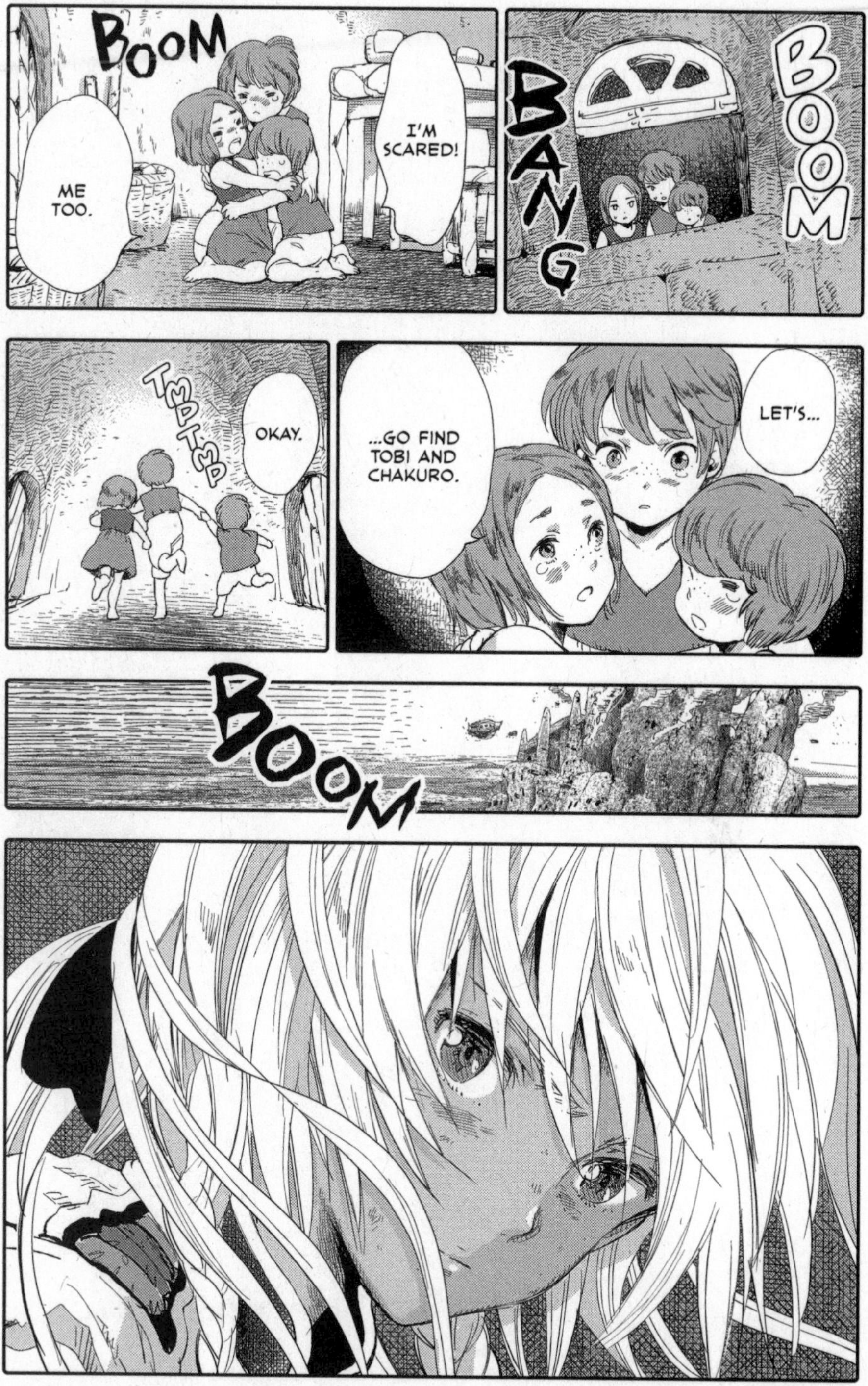
BOOM
BANG
I'M SCARED!
BOOM
ME TOO.
LET'S...
...GO FIND TOBI AND CHAKURO.
OKAY.
TMP TMP
BOOM

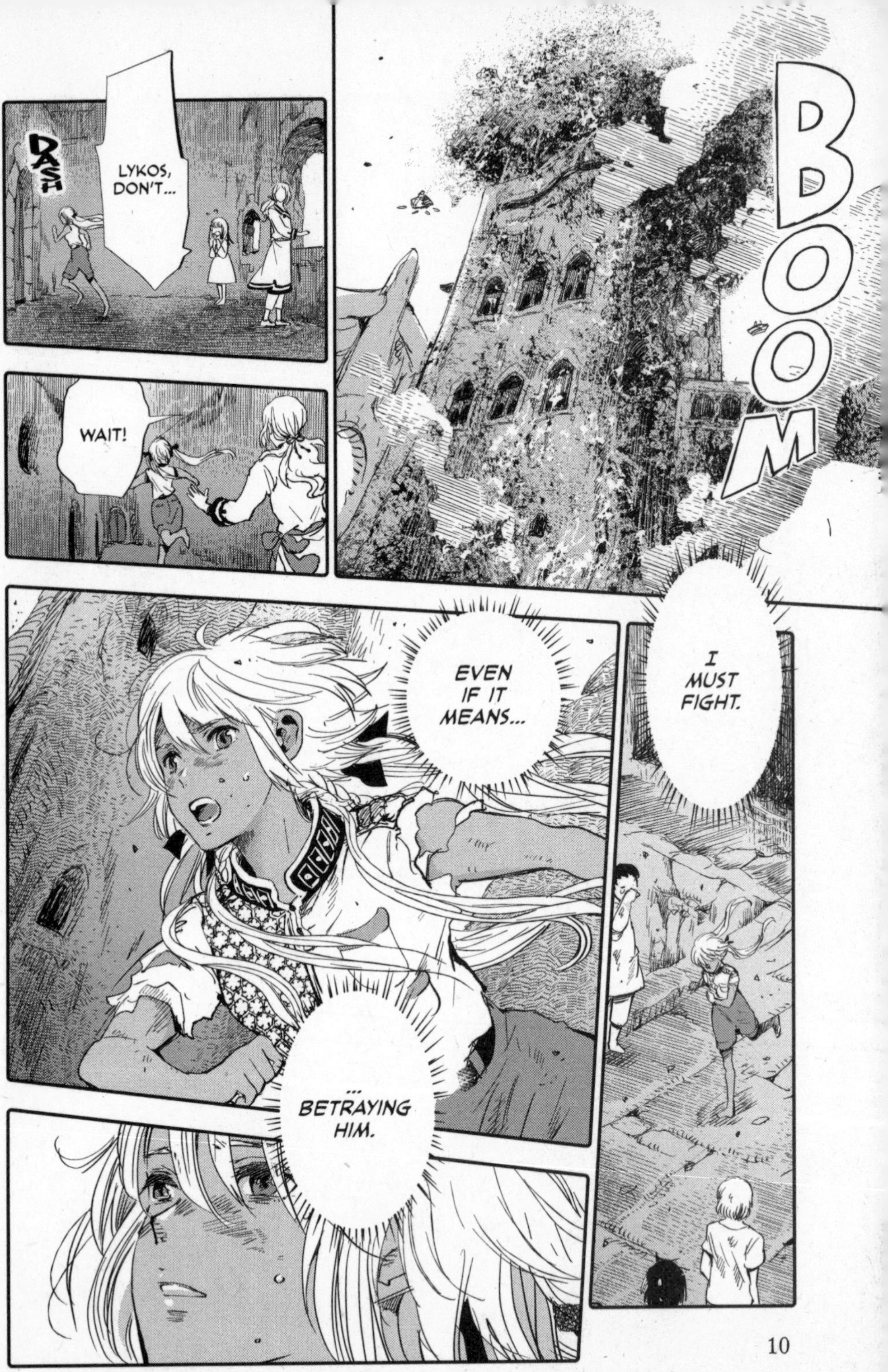
BOOM
LYKOS, DON'T...
DASH
WAIT!
I MUST FIGHT.
EVEN IF IT MEANS...
...BETRAYING HIM.

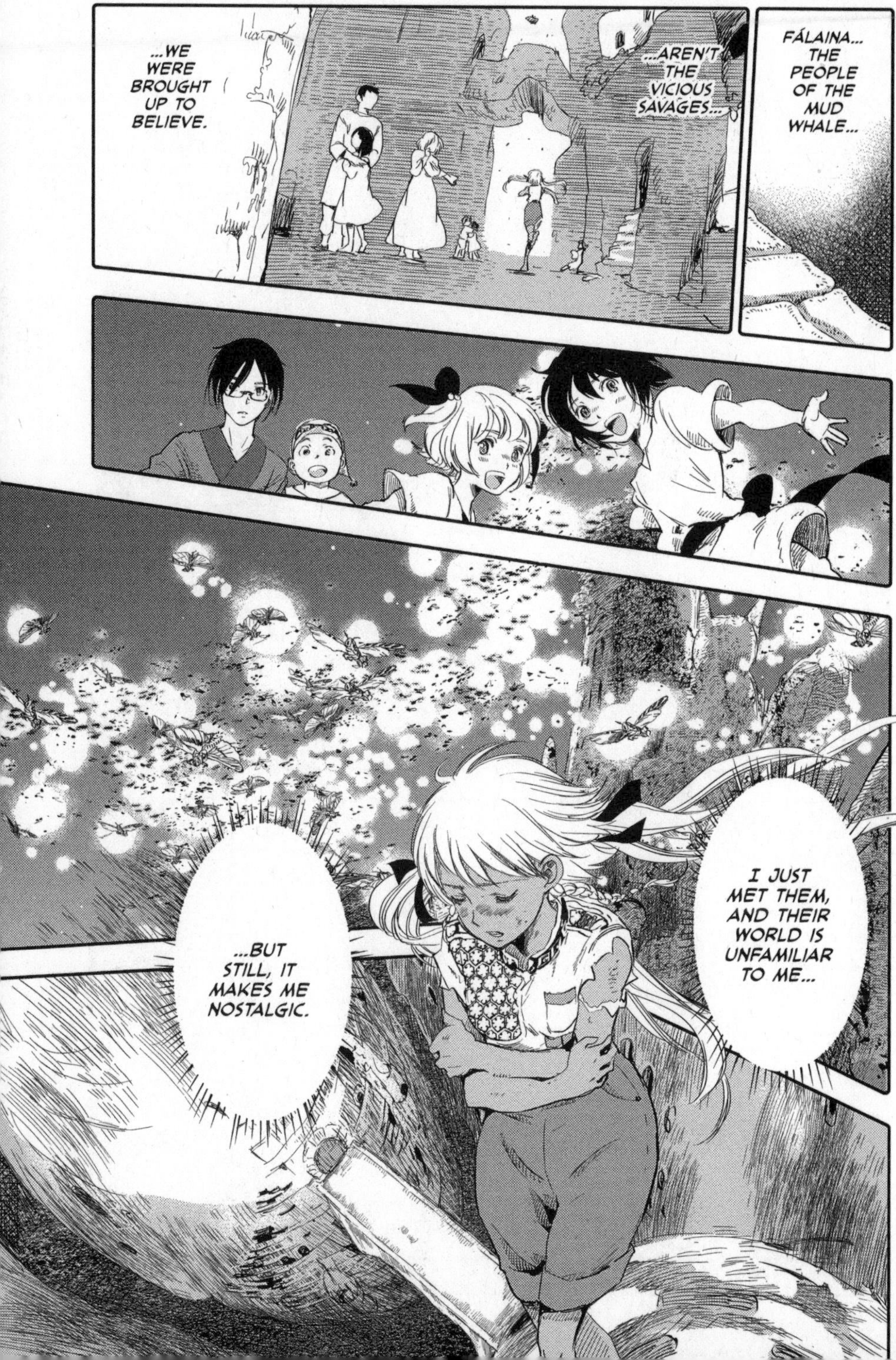
FÁLAINA... THE PEOPLE OF THE MUD WHALE...
...AREN'T THE VICIOUS SAVAGES...
...WE WERE BROUGHT UP TO BELIEVE.
I JUST MET THEM, AND THEIR WORLD IS UNFAMILIAR TO ME...
...BUT STILL, IT MAKES ME NOSTALGIC.

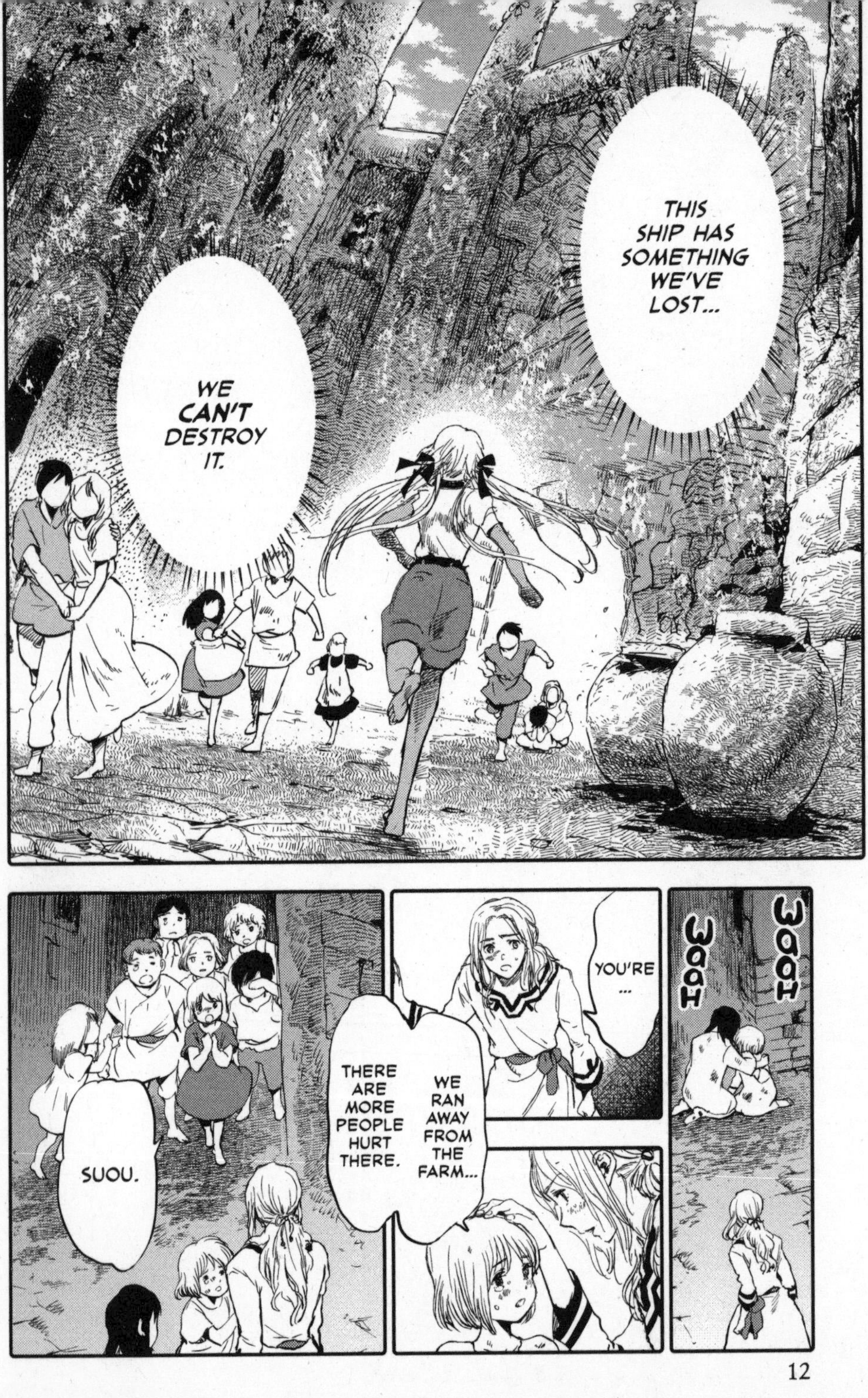
THIS SHIP HAS SOMETHING WE'VE LOST...
WE CAN'T DESTROY IT.
WAAH
WAAH
YOU'RE ...
WE RAN AWAY FROM THE FARM...
THERE ARE MORE PEOPLE HURT THERE.
SUOU.

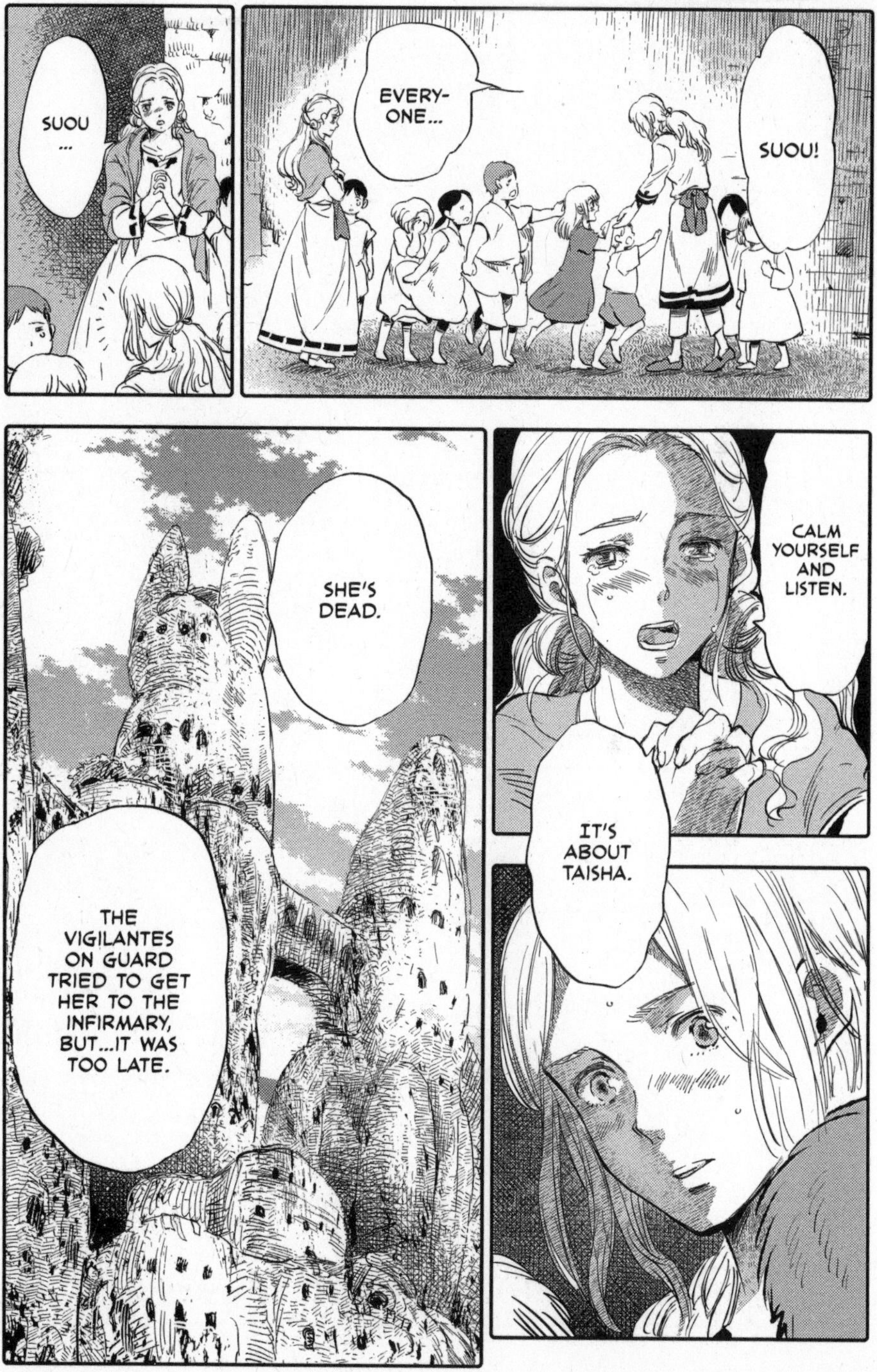
SUOU!
EVERY-ONE...
SUOU ...
CALM YOURSELF AND LISTEN.
IT'S ABOUT TAISHA.
SHE'S DEAD.
THE VIGILANTES ON GUARD TRIED TO GET HER TO THE INFIRMARY, BUT...IT WAS TOO LATE.

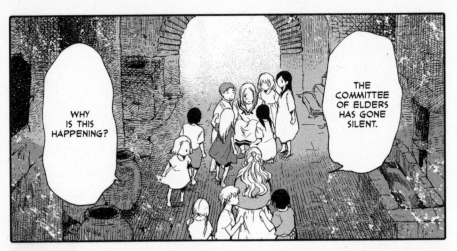

THE COMMITTEE OF ELDERS HAS GONE SILENT.
WHY IS THIS HAPPENING?
SHI-NONO.
SOB
...
TRMBL
CLENCH
GATHER EVERYONE IN THE CENTRAL PLAZA...
...AND HAVE THE VIGILANTES SURROUND THEM FOR PROTECTION.

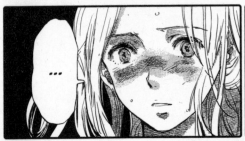

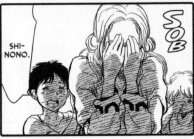

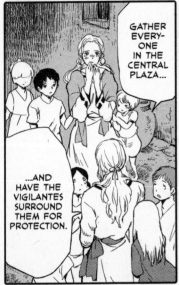

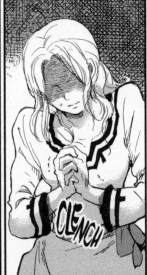

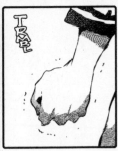

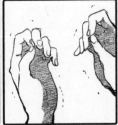

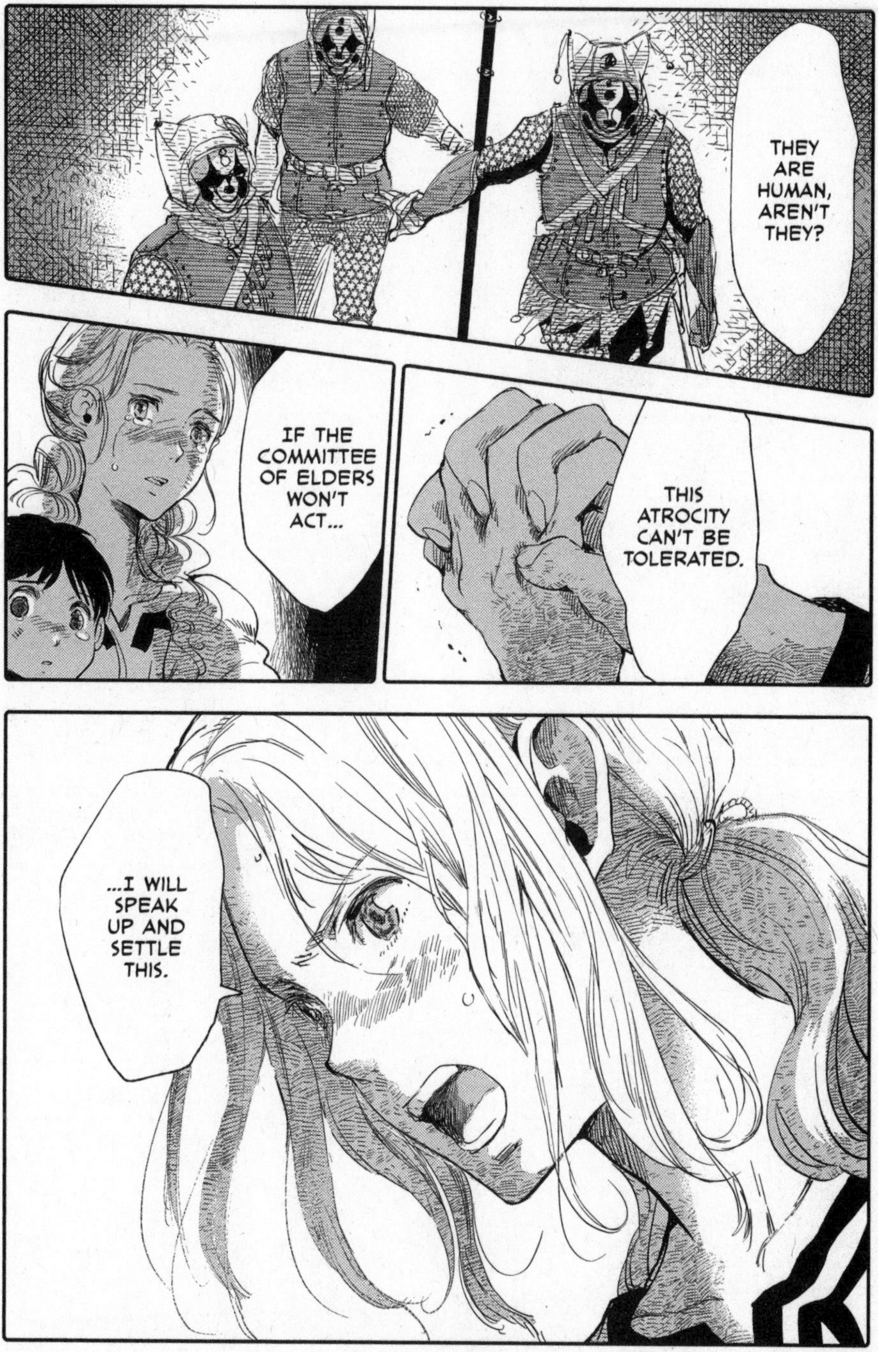
THEY ARE HUMAN, AREN'T THEY?
THIS ATROCITY CAN'T BE TOLERATED.
IF THE COMMITTEE OF ELDERS WON'T ACT...
...I WILL SPEAK UP AND SETTLE THIS.

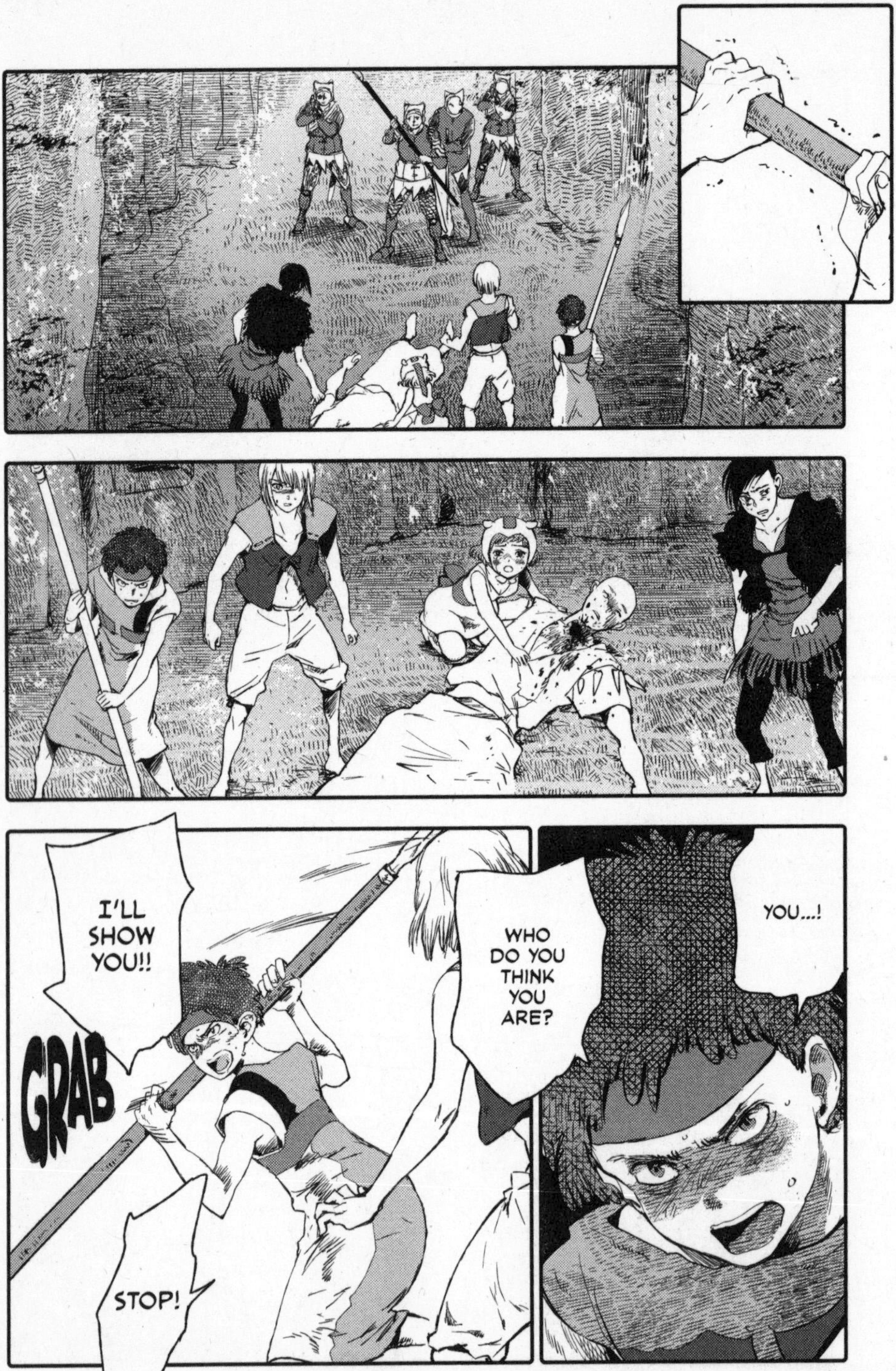
YOU...!
WHO DO YOU THINK YOU ARE?
I'LL SHOW YOU!!
GRAB
STOP!

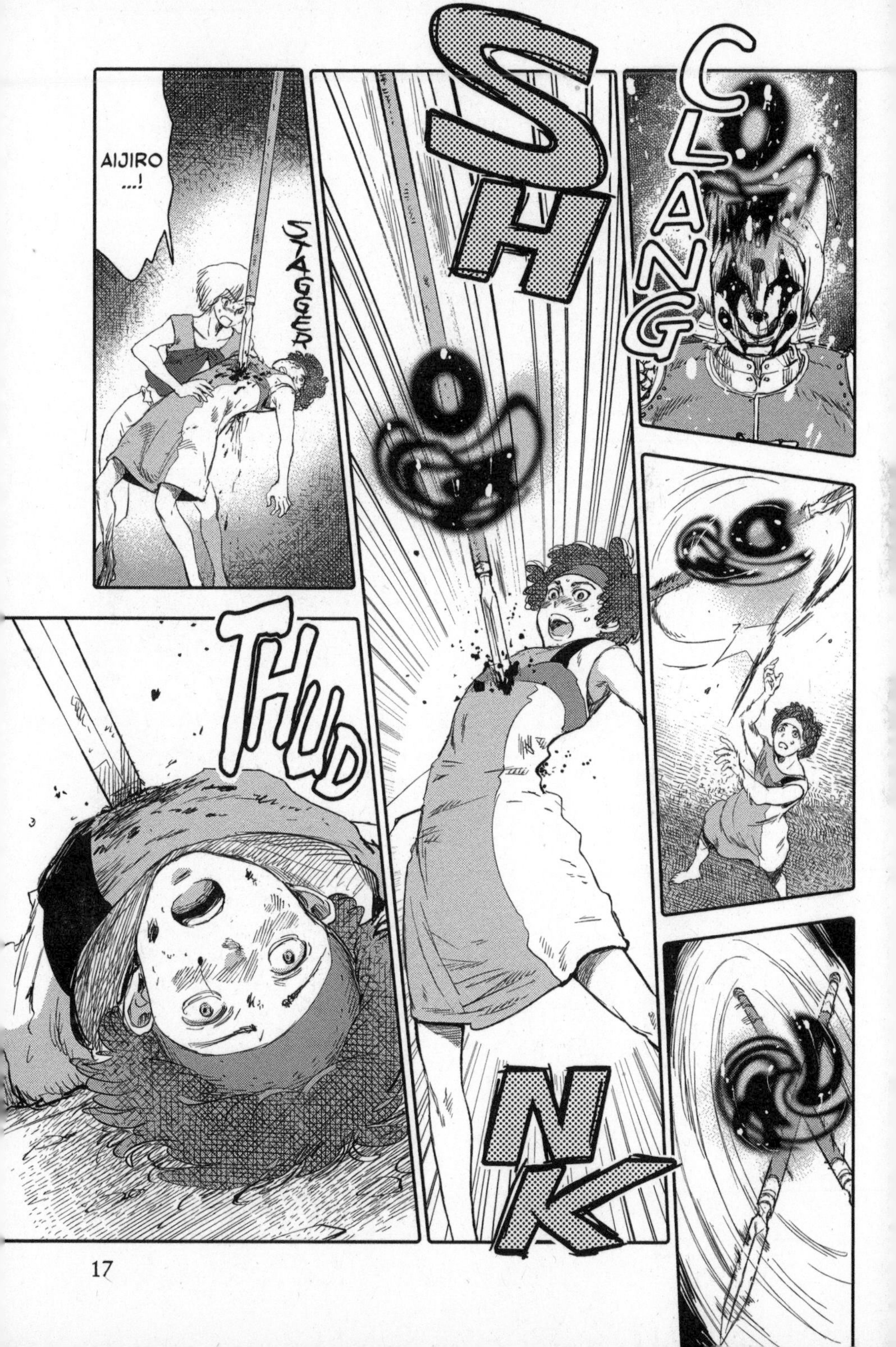
CLANG
SH
NK
AIJIRO ...!
STAGGER
THUD

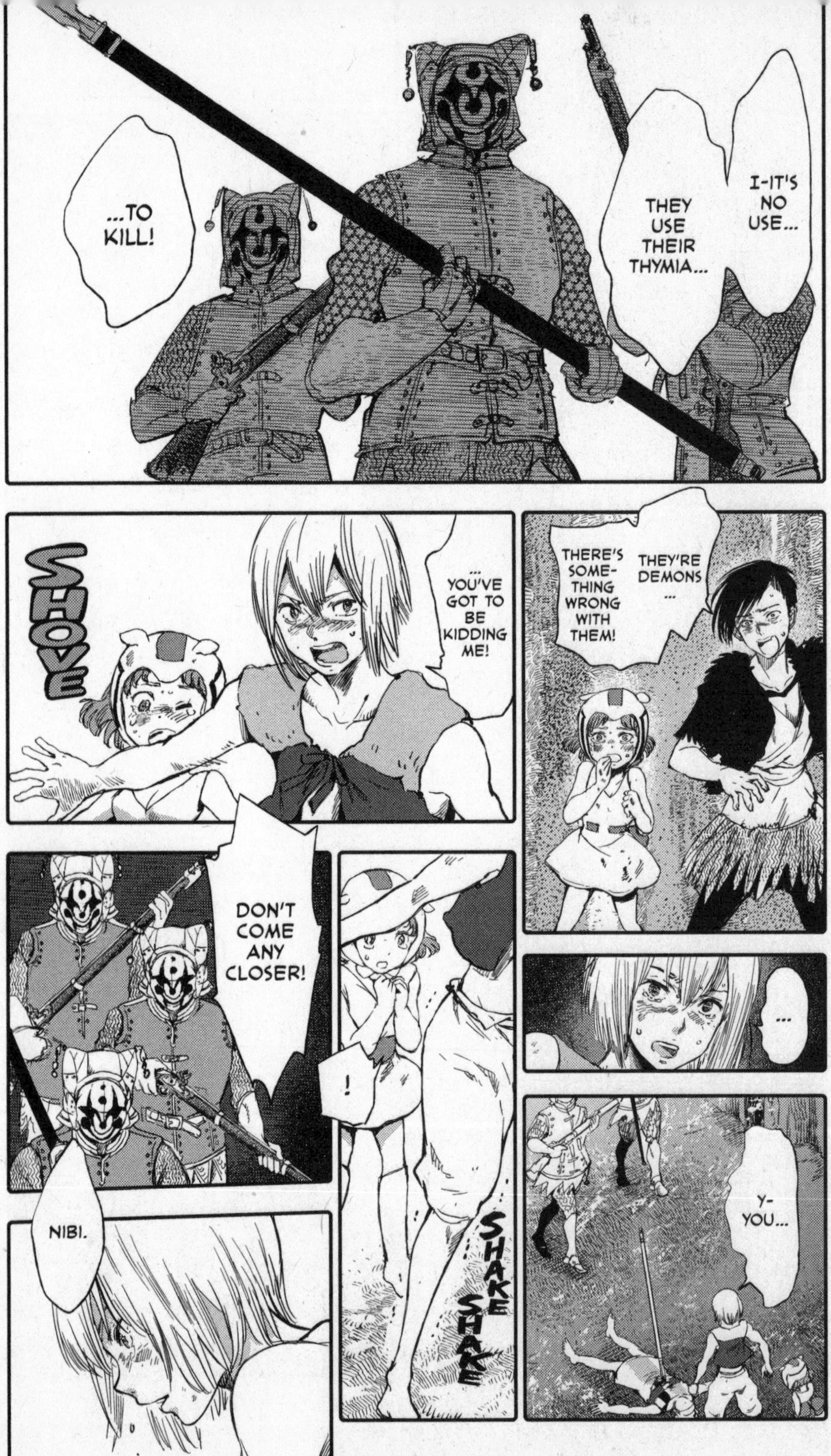
I-IT'S NO USE...
THEY USE THEIR THYMIA...
...TO KILL!
THEY'RE DEMONS...
THERE'S SOMETHING WRONG WITH THEM!
...YOU'VE GOT TO BE KIDDING ME!
SHOVE
...
Y-YOU...
!
SHAKE SHAKE
DON'T COME ANY CLOSER!
NIBI.

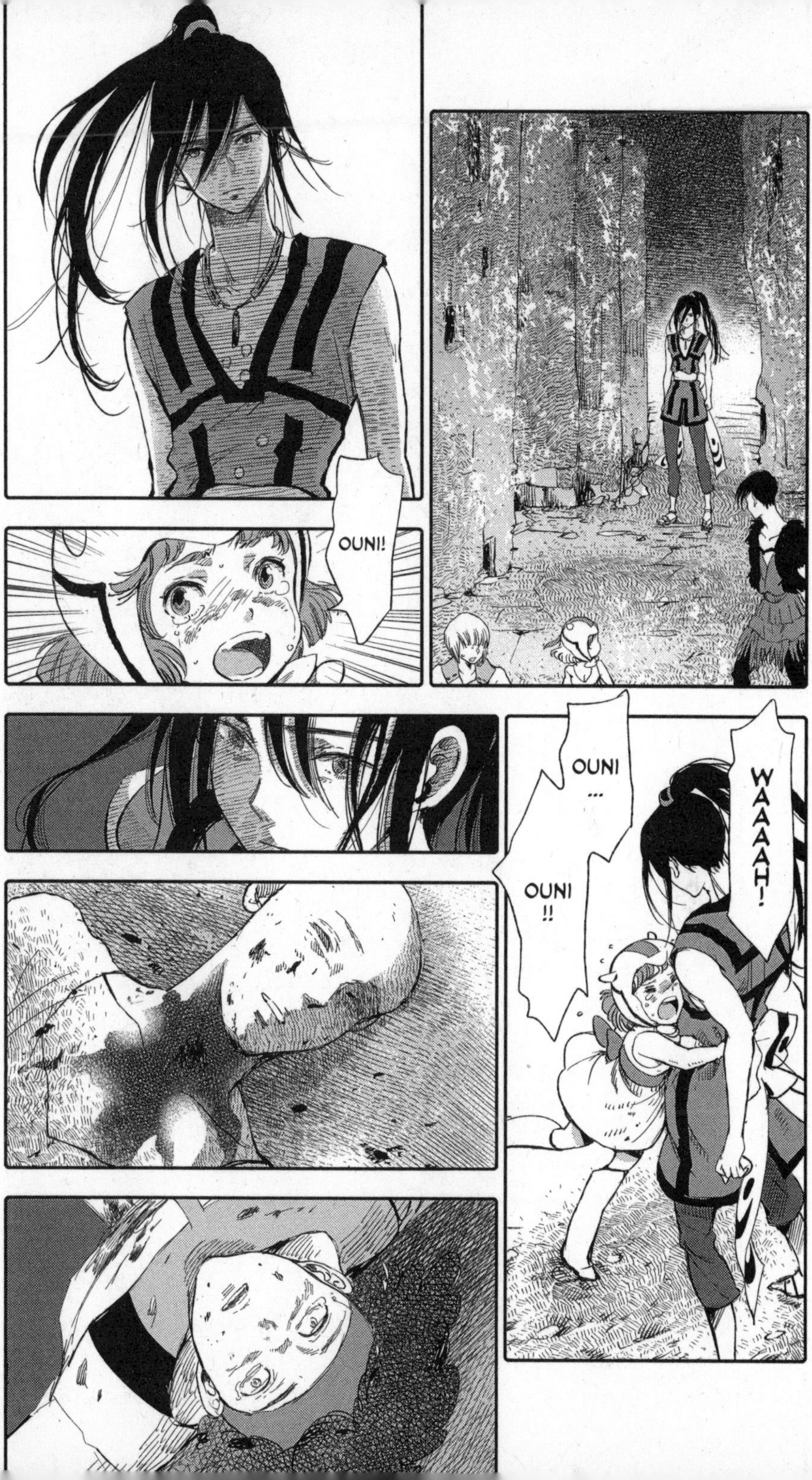
OUNI!
WAAAAH!
OUNI...
OUNI!!

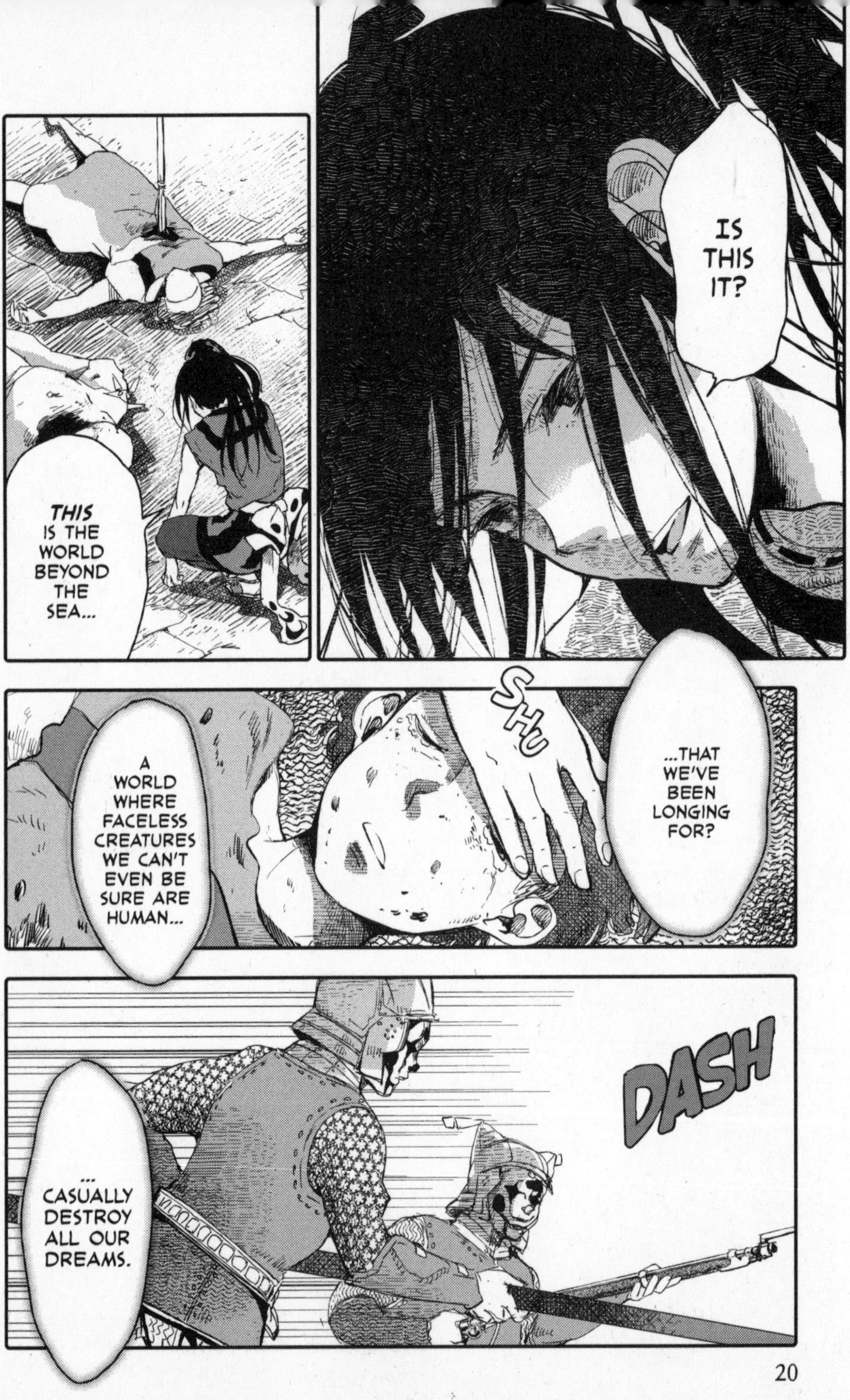
IS THIS IT?
THIS IS THE WORLD BEYOND THE SEA...
...THAT WE'VE BEEN LONGING FOR?
SHU
A WORLD WHERE FACELESS CREATURES WE CAN'T EVEN BE SURE ARE HUMAN...
DASH
...CASUALLY DESTROY ALL OUR DREAMS.

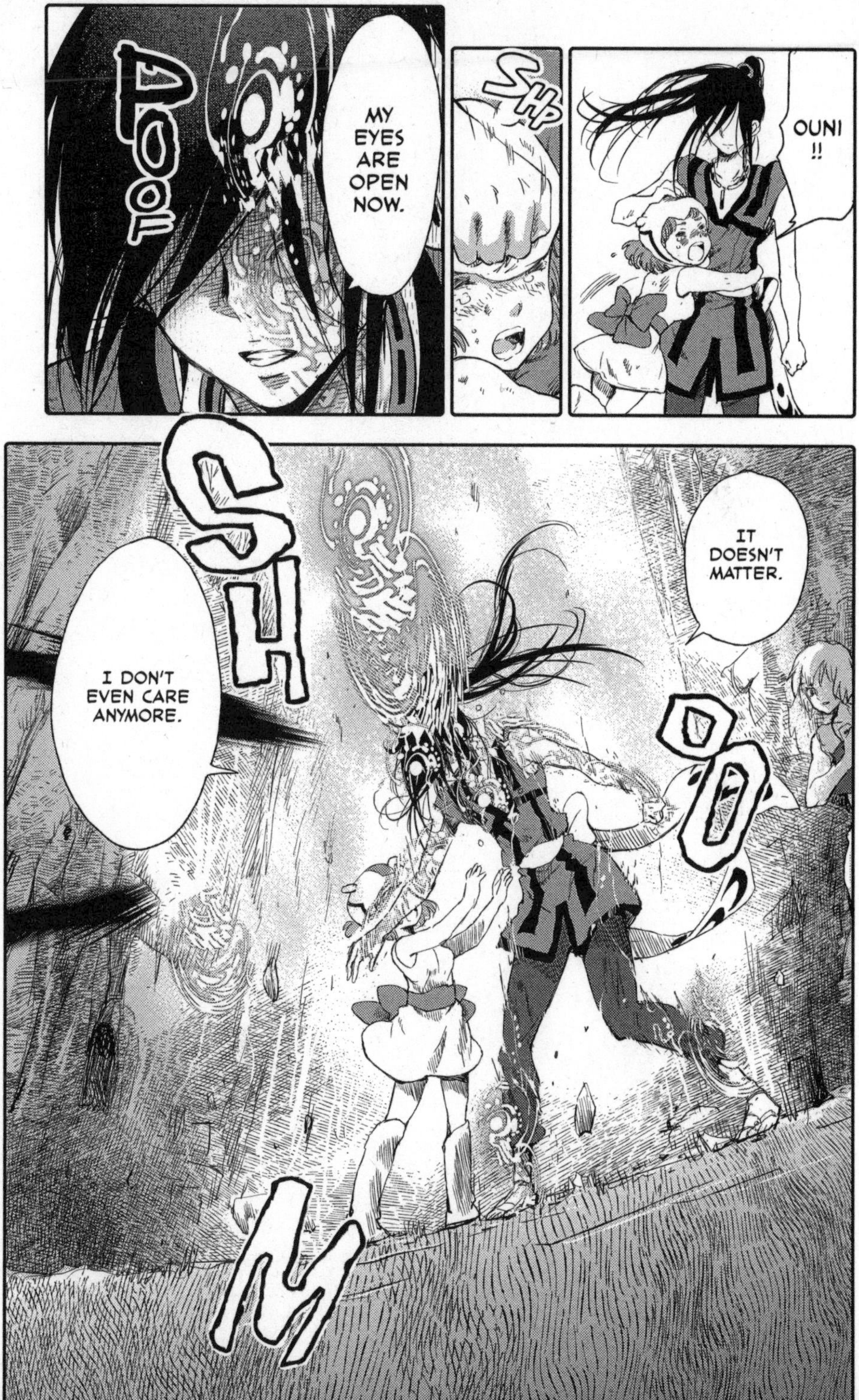
OUNI !!
SHP
POOF
MY EYES ARE OPEN NOW.
IT DOESN'T MATTER.
SH
I DON'T EVEN CARE ANYMORE.
M

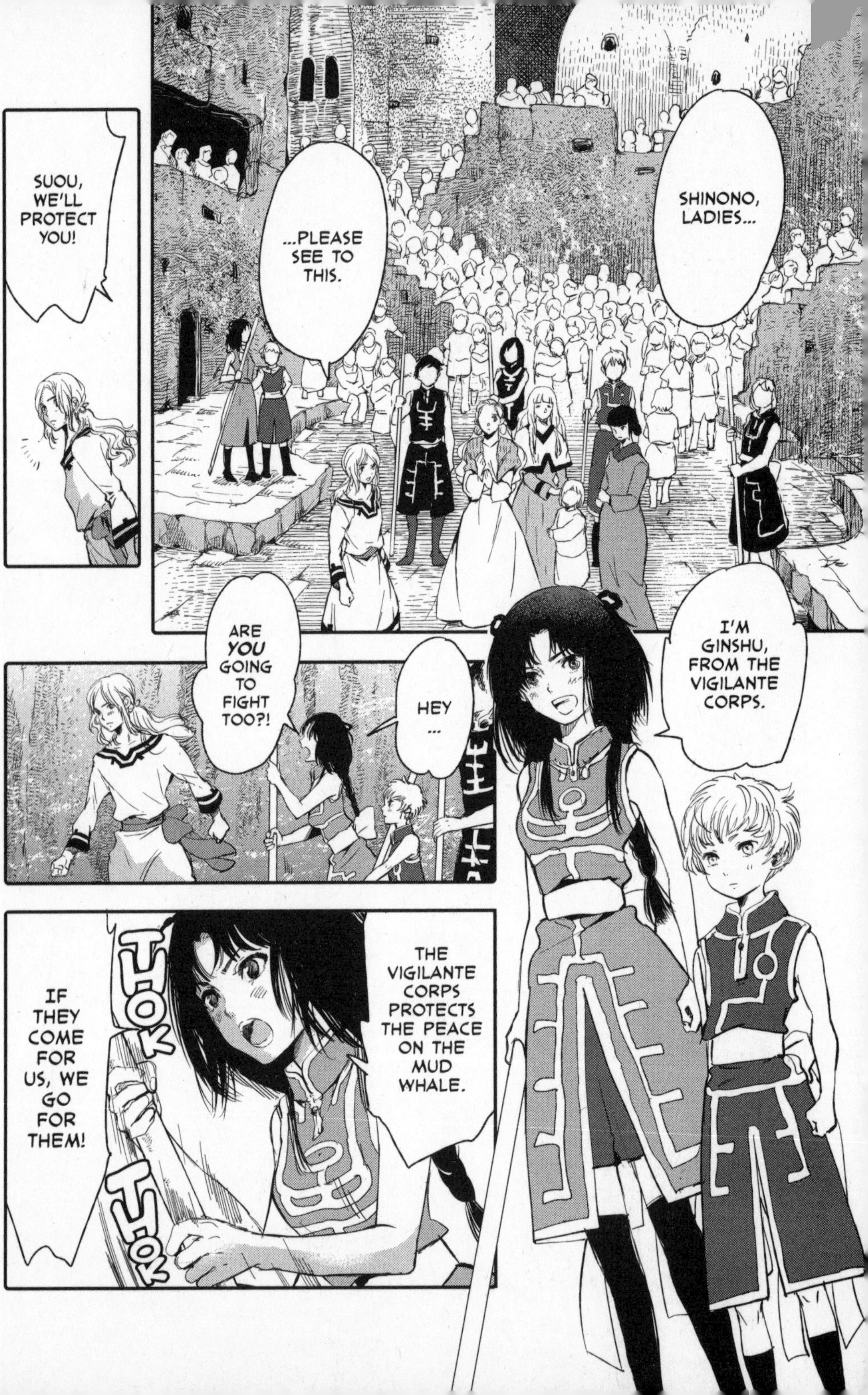
SHINONO, LADIES...
...PLEASE SEE TO THIS.
SUOU, WE'LL PROTECT YOU!
I'M GINSHU, FROM THE VIGILANTE CORPS.
THE VIGILANTE CORPS PROTECTS THE PEACE ON THE MUD WHALE.
HEY ...
ARE *YOU* GOING TO FIGHT TOO?!
IF THEY COME FOR US, WE GO FOR THEM!
THOK
THOK

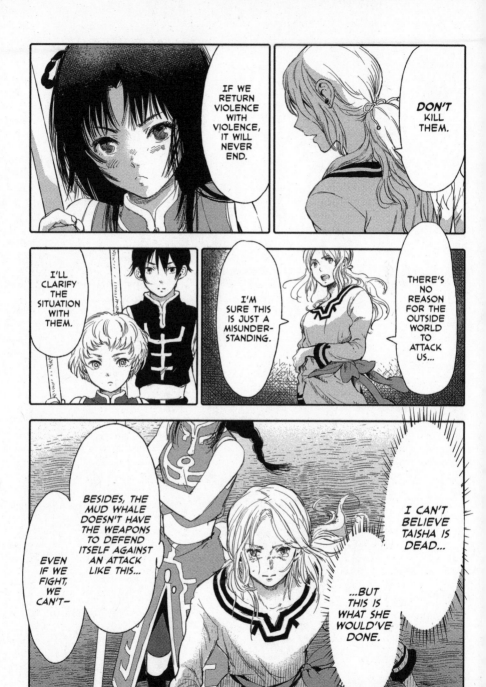

DON'T KILL THEM.
IF WE RETURN VIOLENCE WITH VIOLENCE, IT WILL NEVER END.
THERE'S NO REASON FOR THE OUTSIDE WORLD TO ATTACK US...
I'M SURE THIS IS JUST A MISUNDERSTANDING.
I'LL CLARIFY THE SITUATION WITH THEM.
I CAN'T BELIEVE TAISHA IS DEAD...
...BUT THIS IS WHAT SHE WOULD'VE DONE.
BESIDES, THE MUD WHALE DOESN'T HAVE THE WEAPONS TO DEFEND ITSELF AGAINST AN ATTACK LIKE THIS...
EVEN IF WE FIGHT, WE CAN'T–

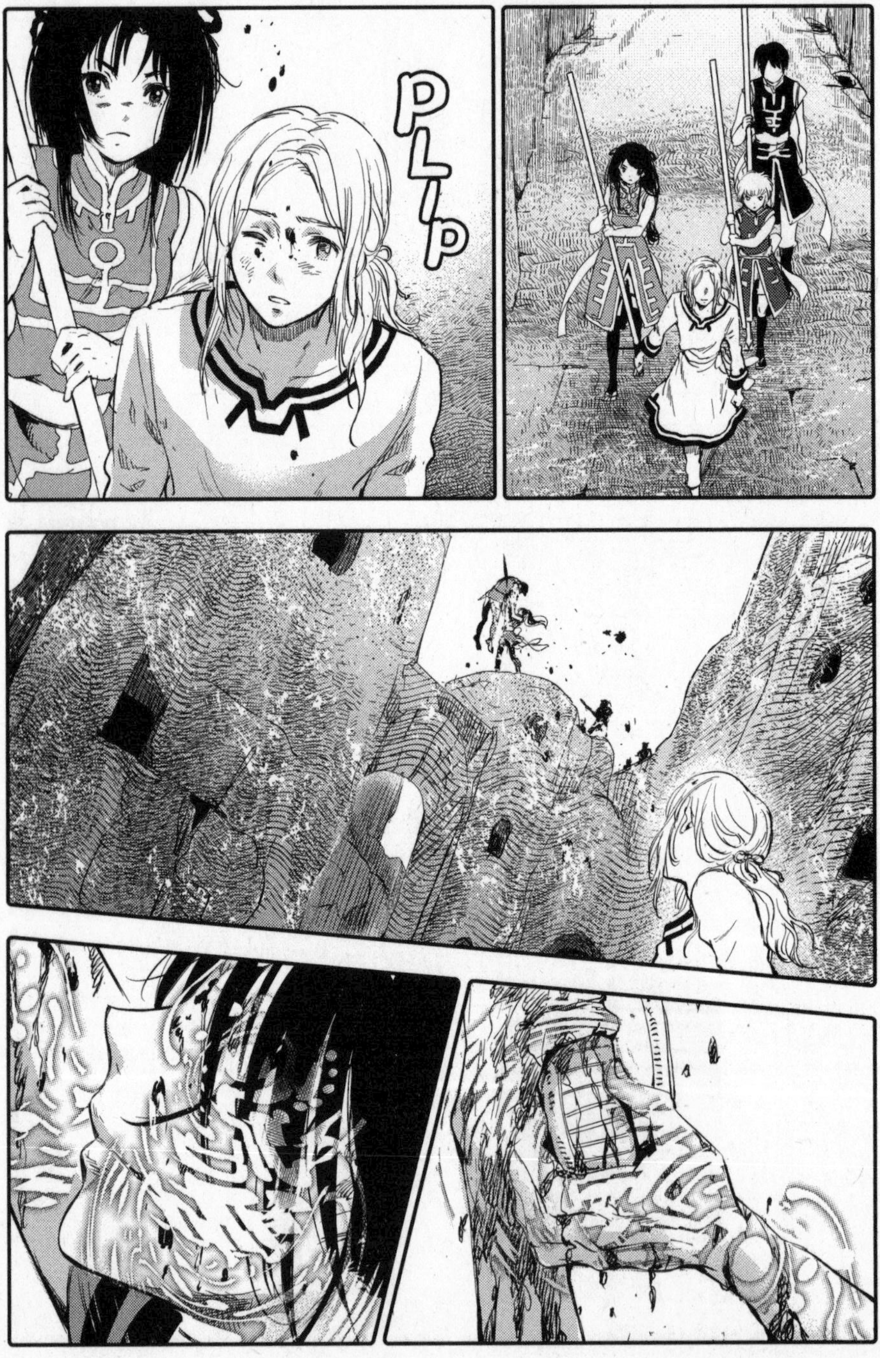
PLIP

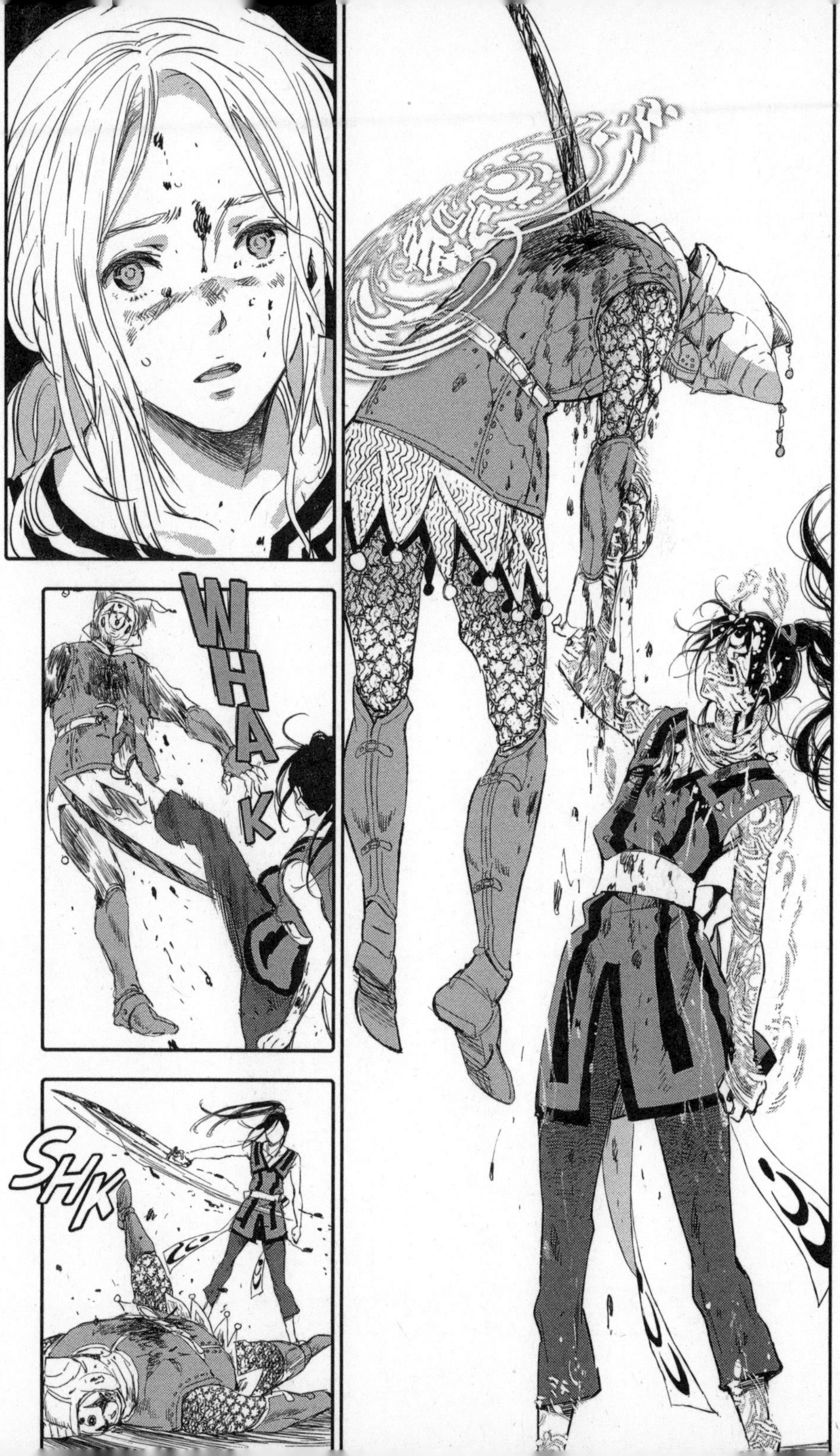
WHAK
SHK

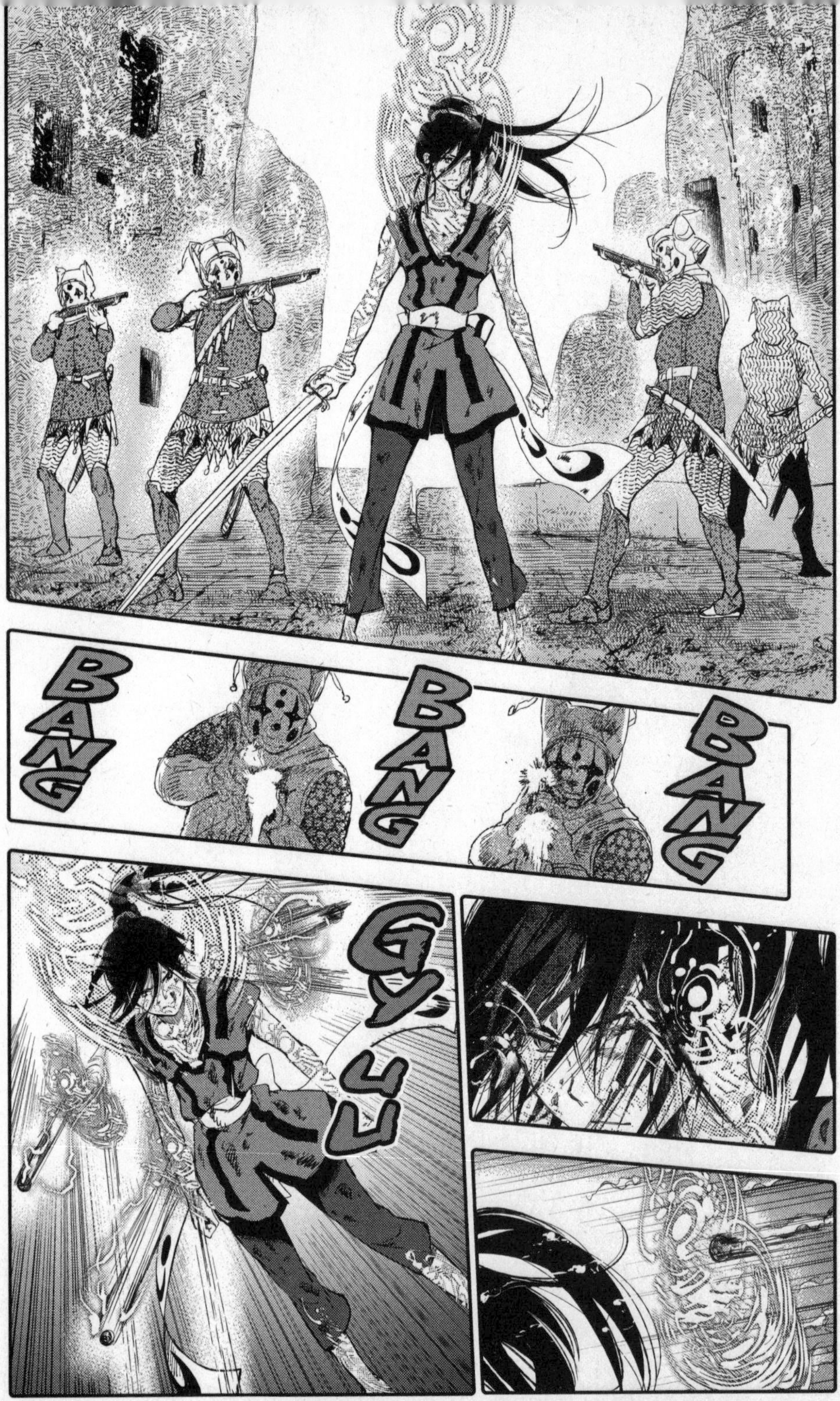
BANG
BANG
BANG
GYUU

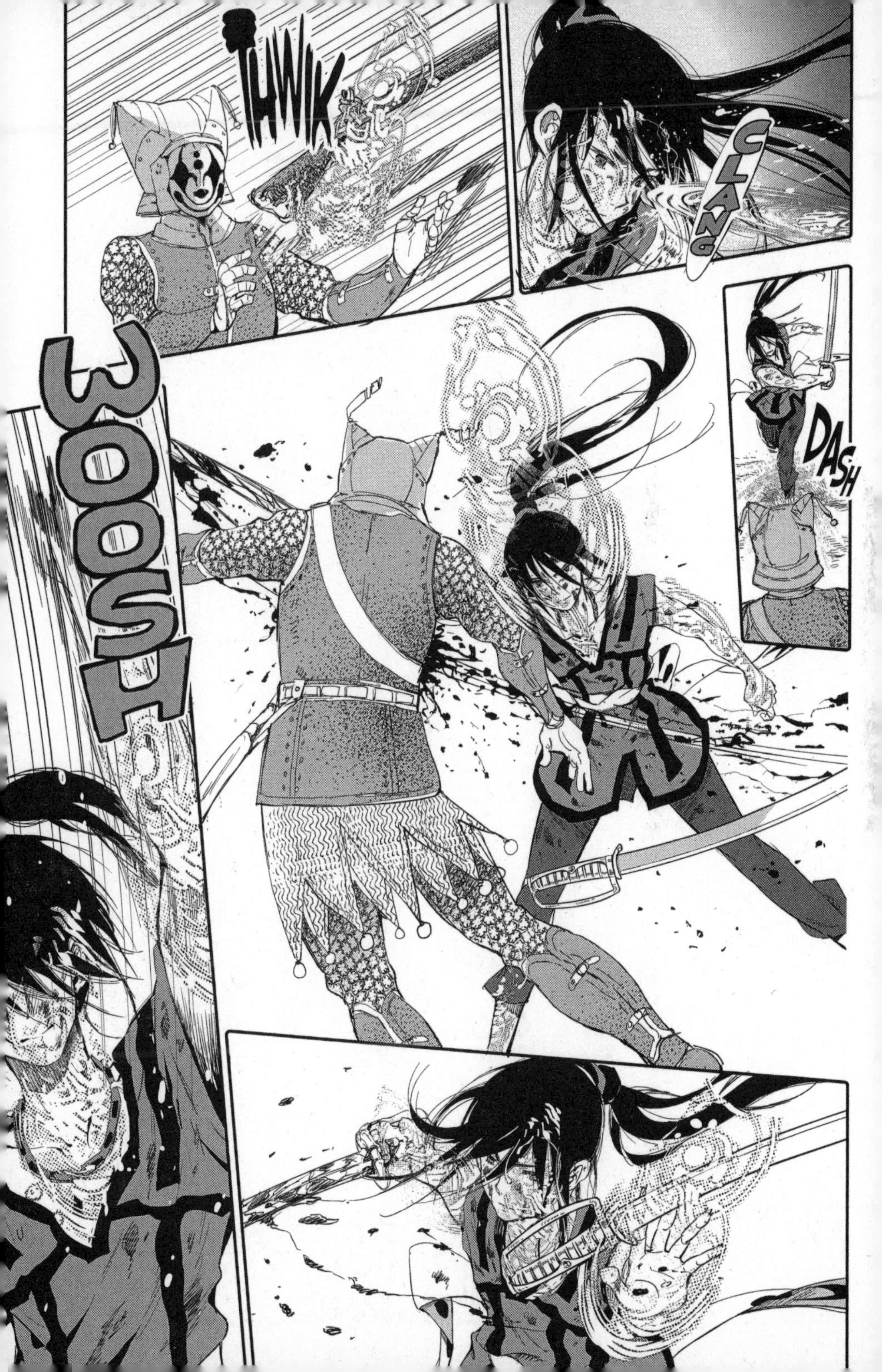
CLANG
THWIK
DASH
WOOSH

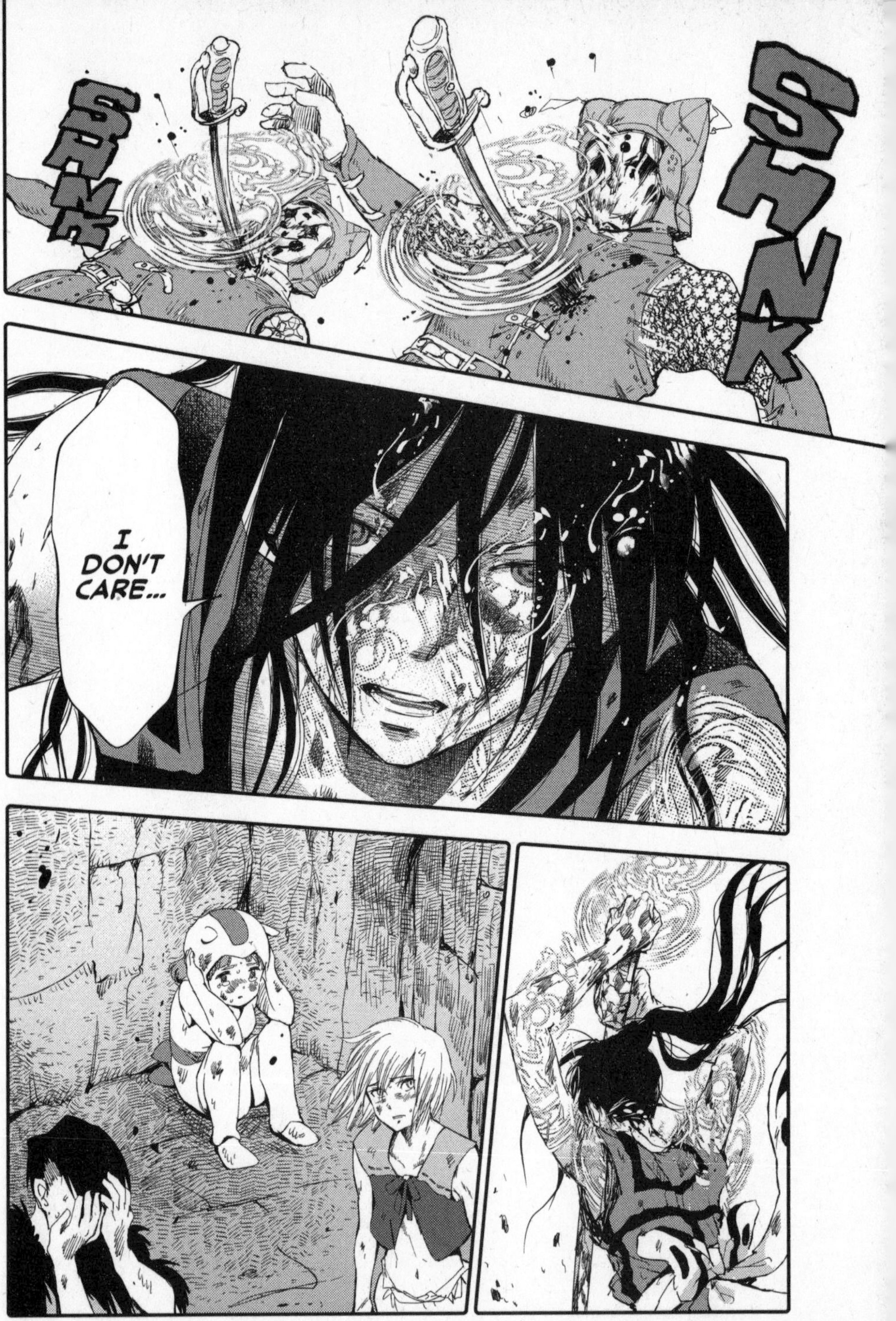
SHNK
SHNK
I DON'T CARE...

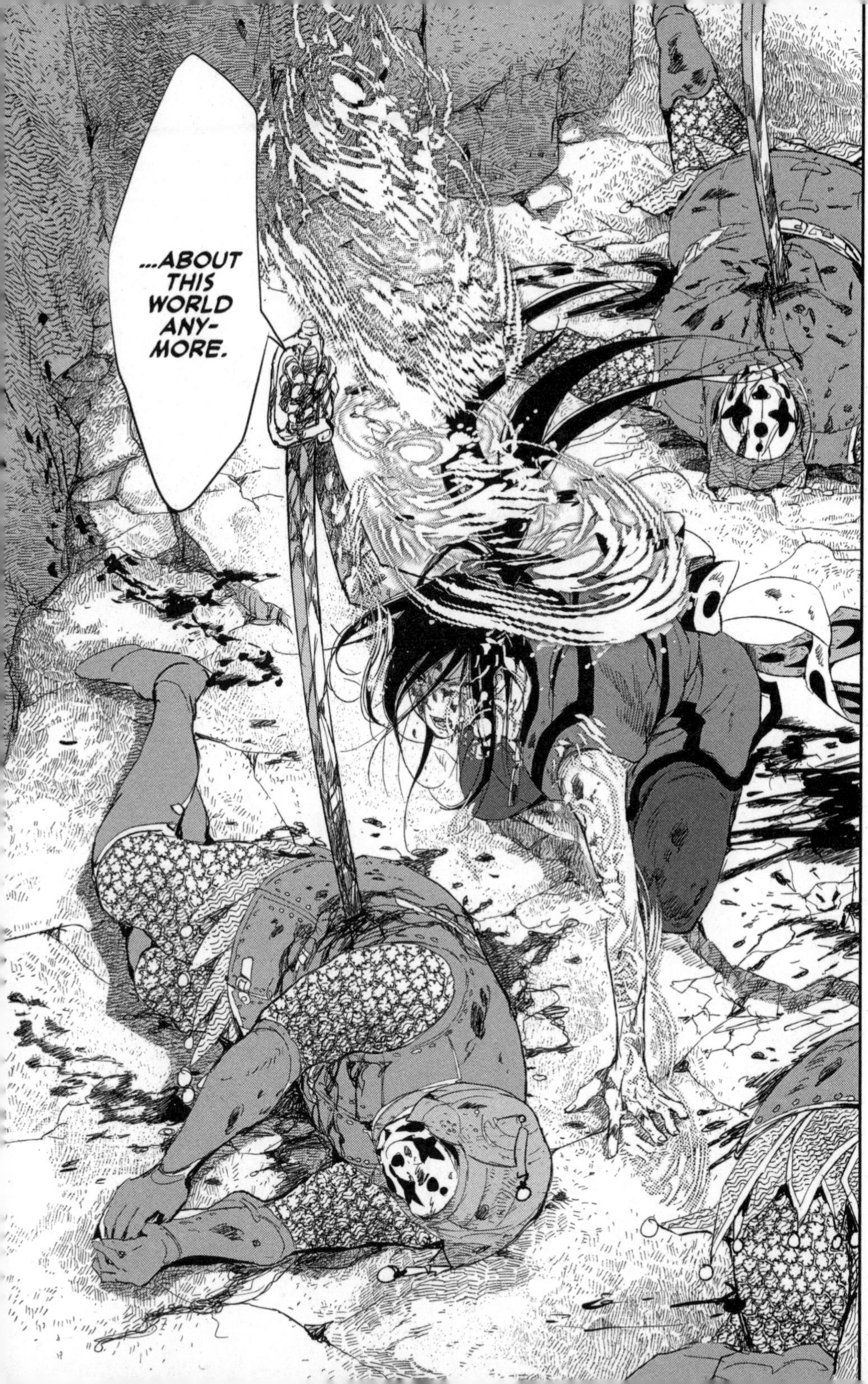
...ABOUT THIS WORLD ANYMORE.

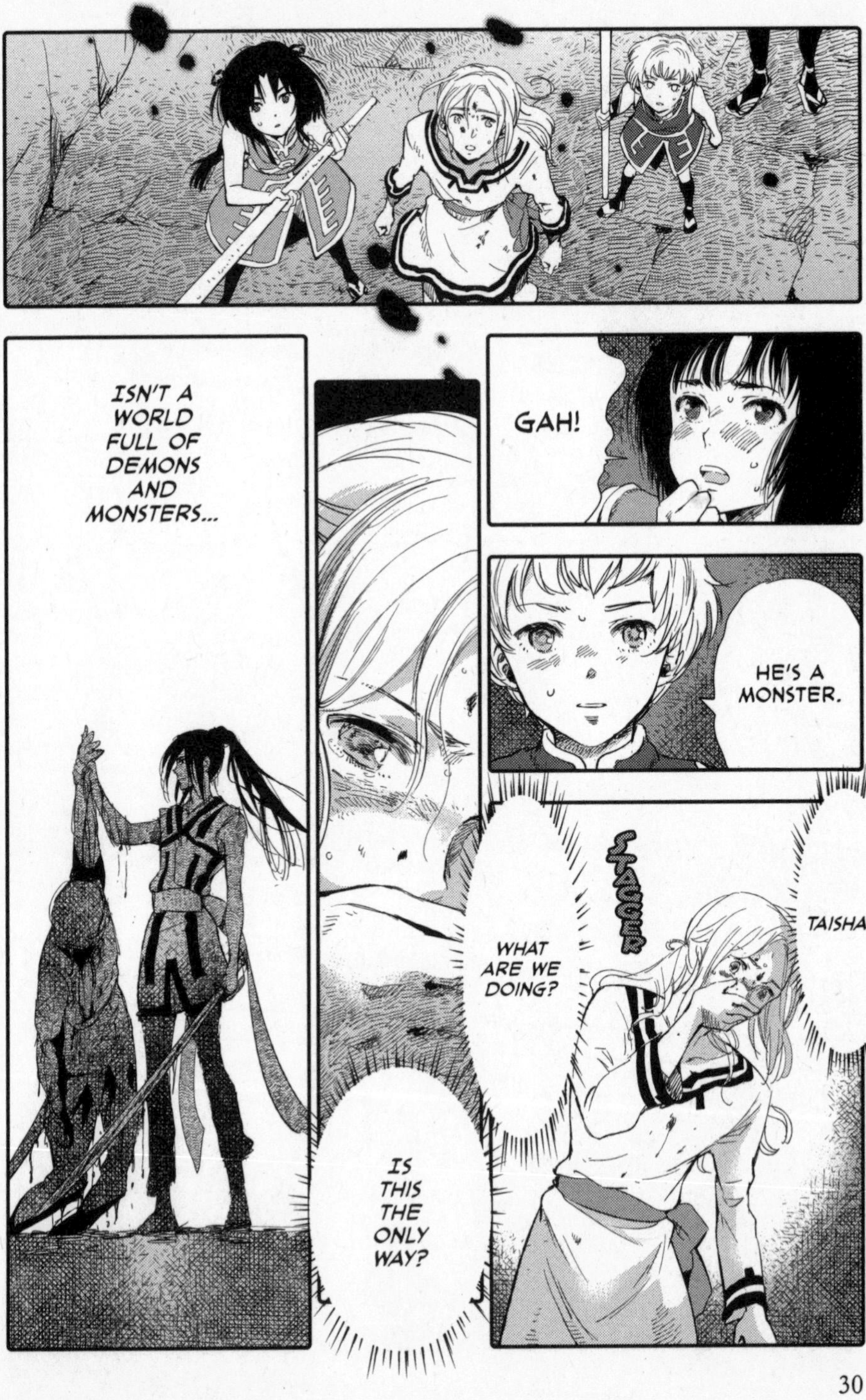
GAH!
HE'S A MONSTER.
TAISHA...
STAGGER
WHAT ARE WE DOING?
IS THIS THE ONLY WAY?
ISN'T A WORLD FULL OF DEMONS AND MONSTERS...

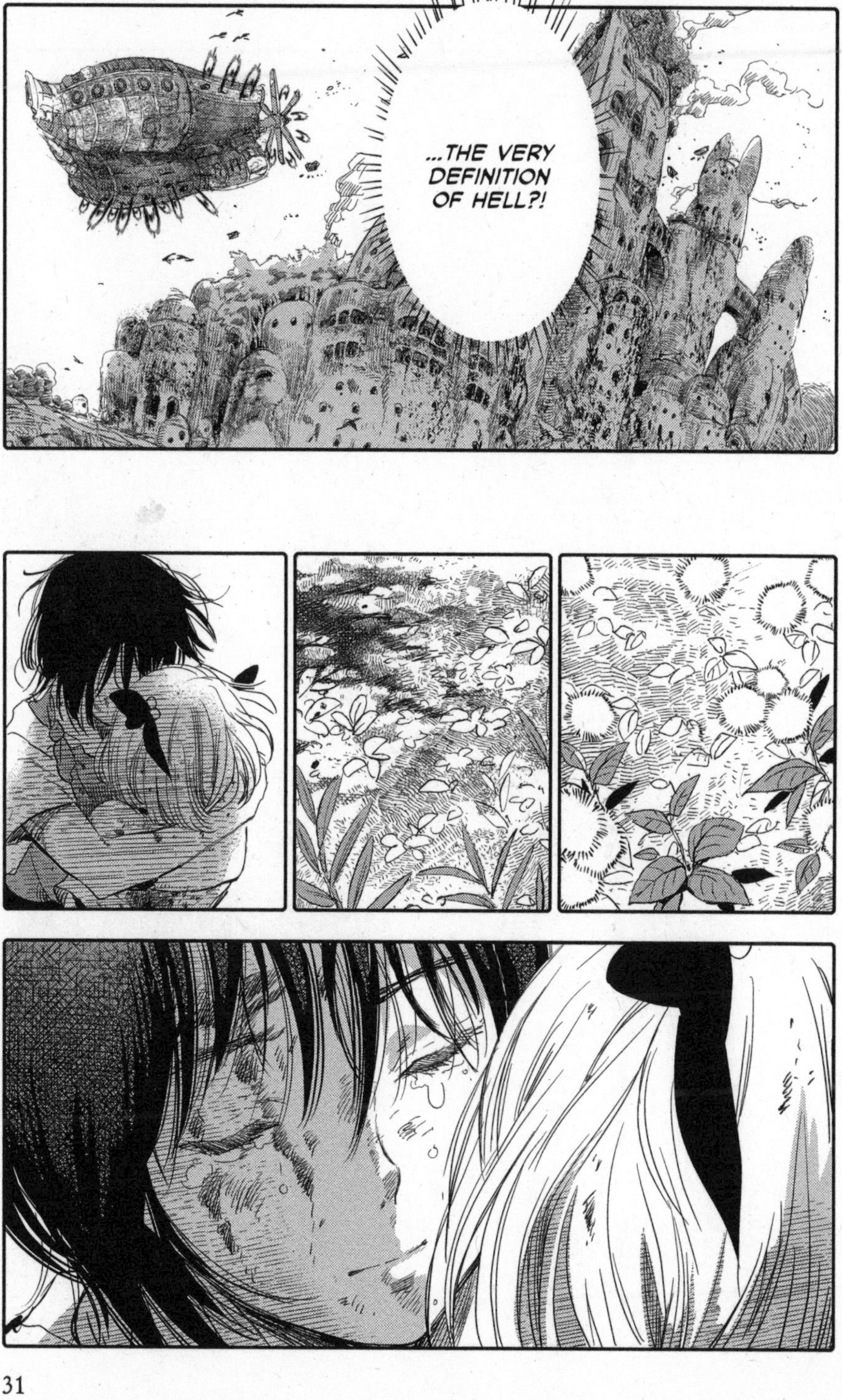
...THE VERY DEFINITION OF HELL?!

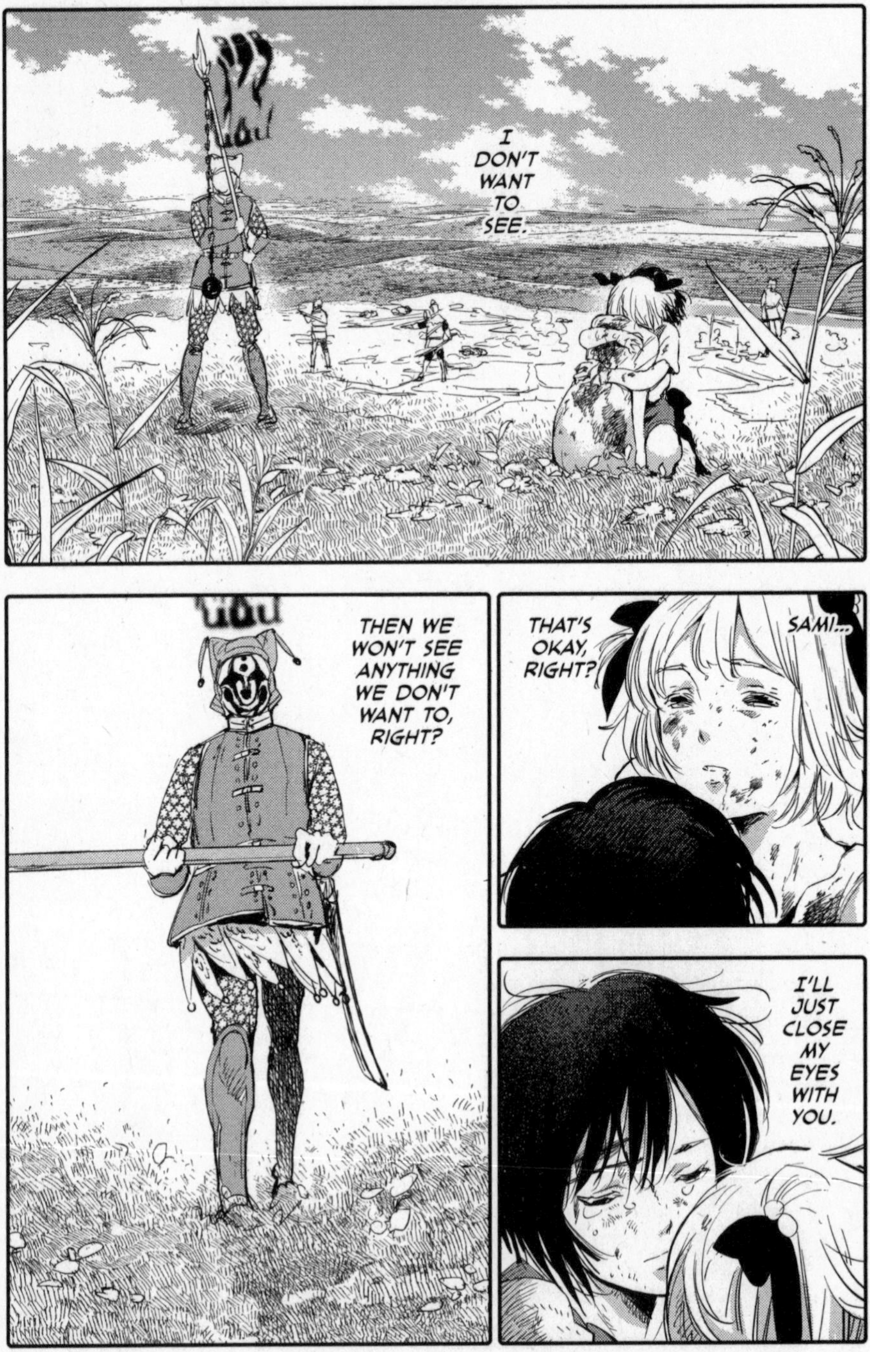
I DON'T WANT TO SEE.
SAMI...
THAT'S OKAY, RIGHT?
I'LL JUST CLOSE MY EYES WITH YOU.
THEN WE WON'T SEE ANYTHING WE DON'T WANT TO, RIGHT?

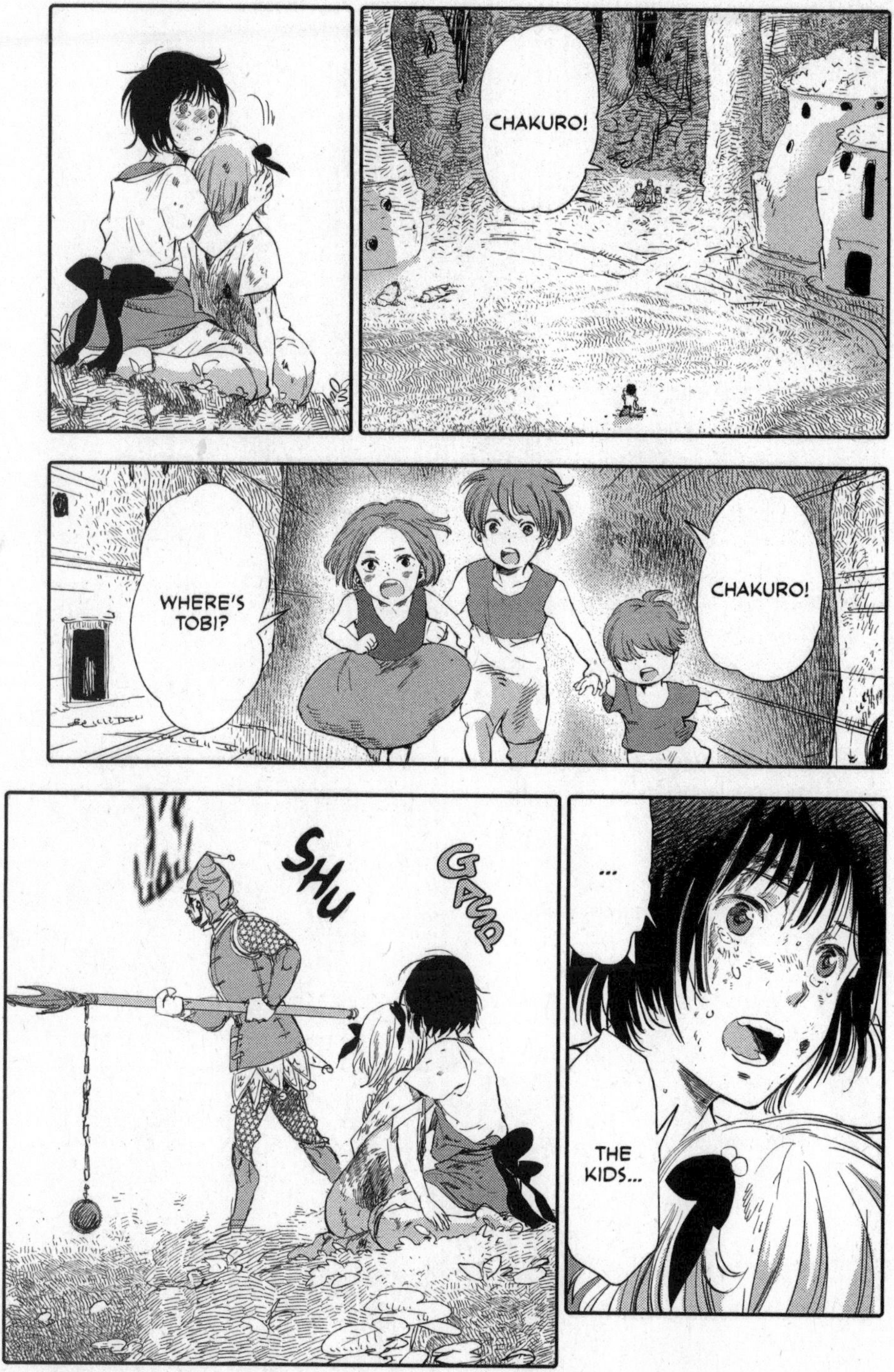
CHAKURO!
CHAKURO!
WHERE'S TOBI?
...
THE KIDS...
GAUA
SHU

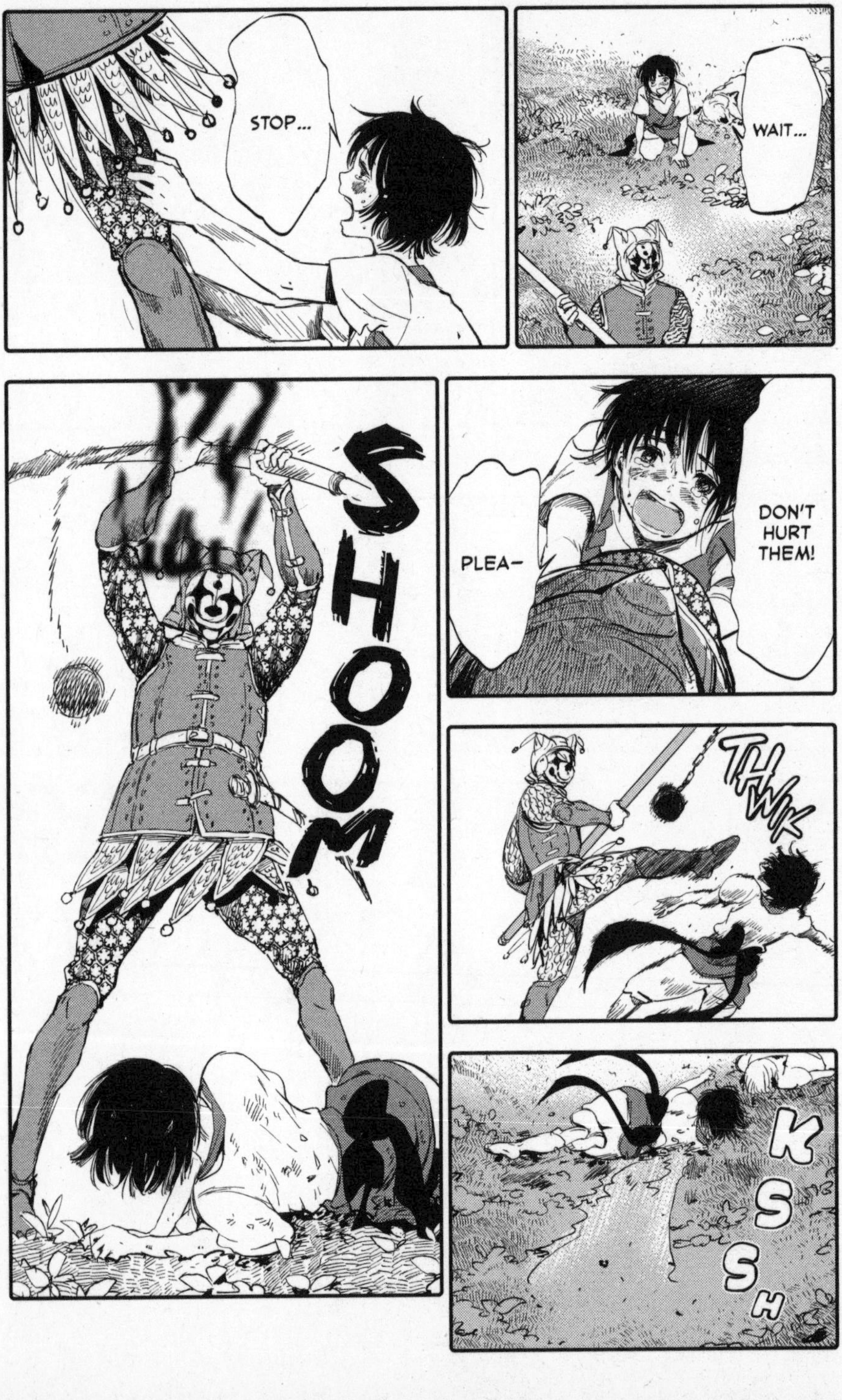
WAIT...
STOP...
DON'T HURT THEM!
PLEA-
THWK
KSSSH
SHOOM

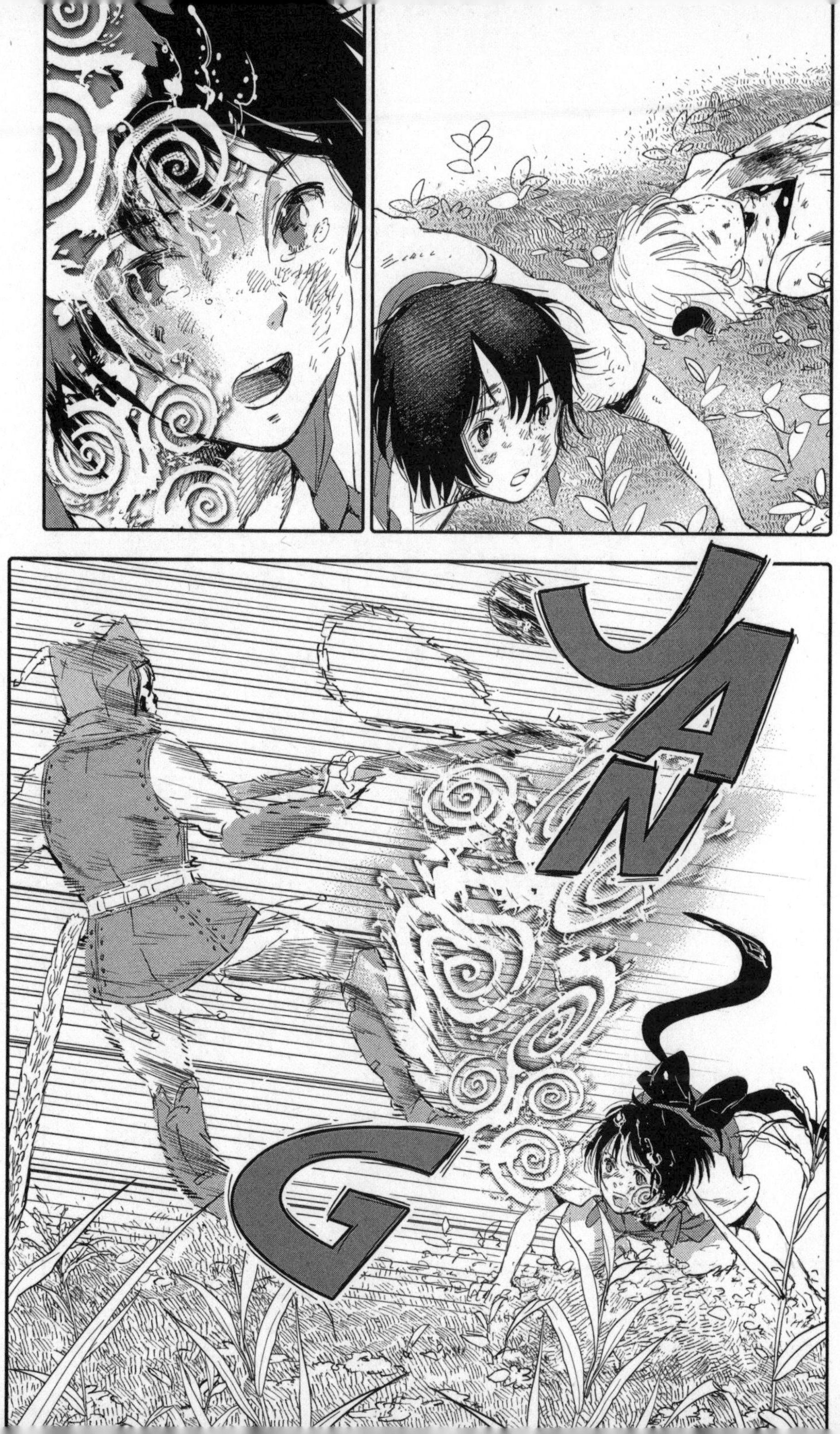
JANG

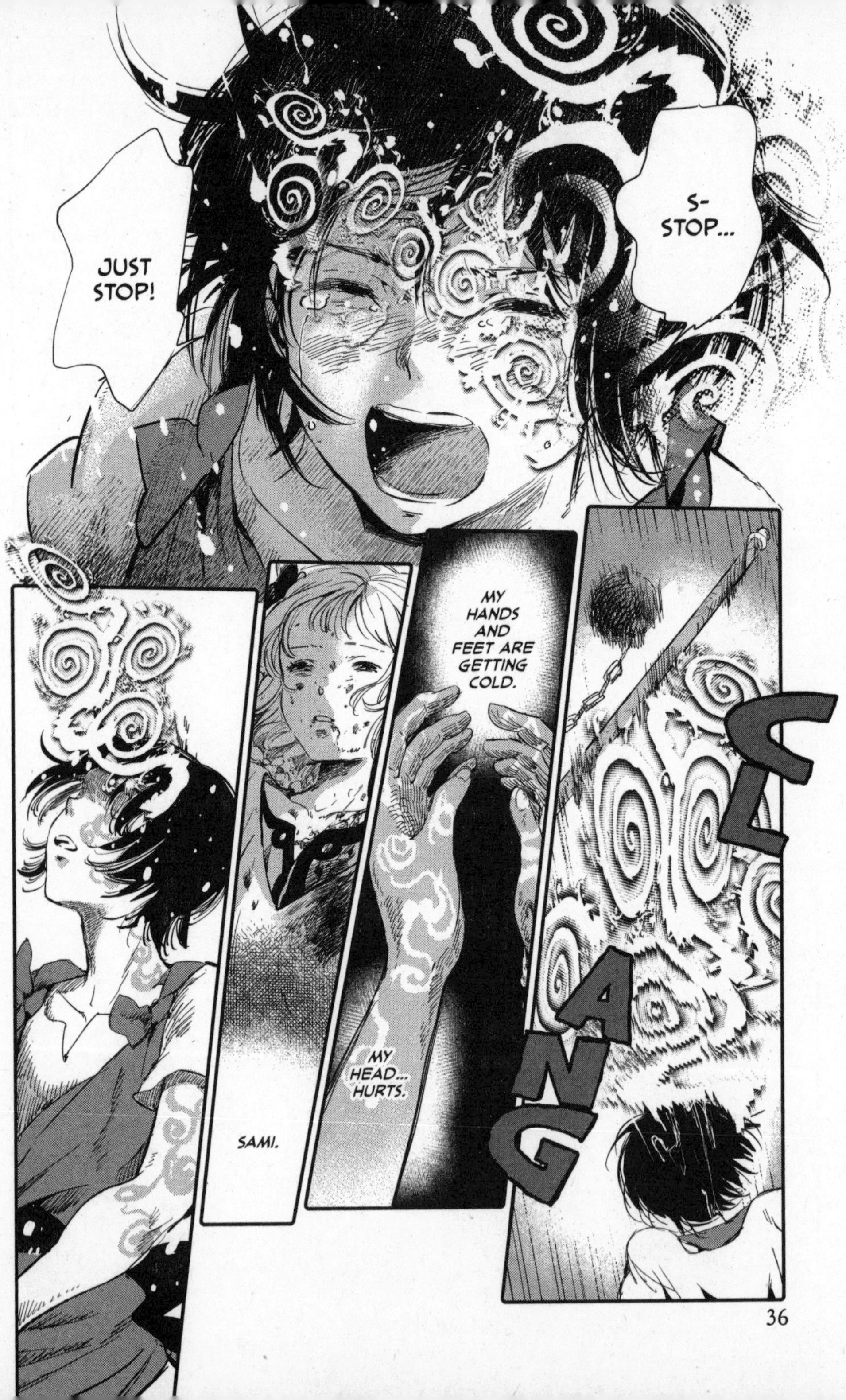
S-
STOP...
JUST
STOP!
CLANG
MY HANDS AND FEET ARE GETTING COLD.
MY HEAD... HURTS.
SAMI.

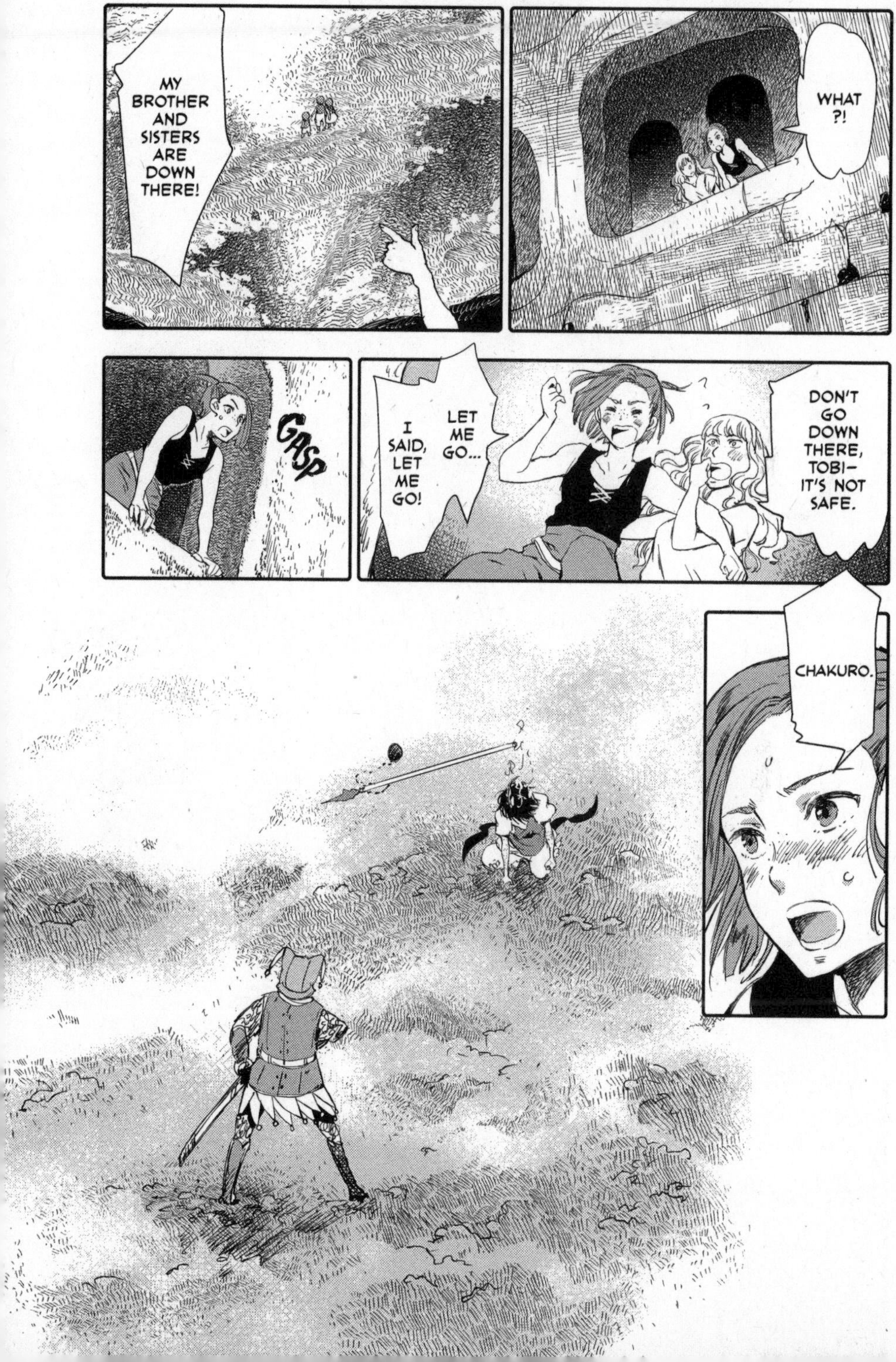
WHAT?!
MY BROTHER AND SISTERS ARE DOWN THERE!
DON'T GO DOWN THERE, TOBI—IT'S NOT SAFE.
LET ME GO...
I SAID, LET ME GO!
GASP
CHAKURO.

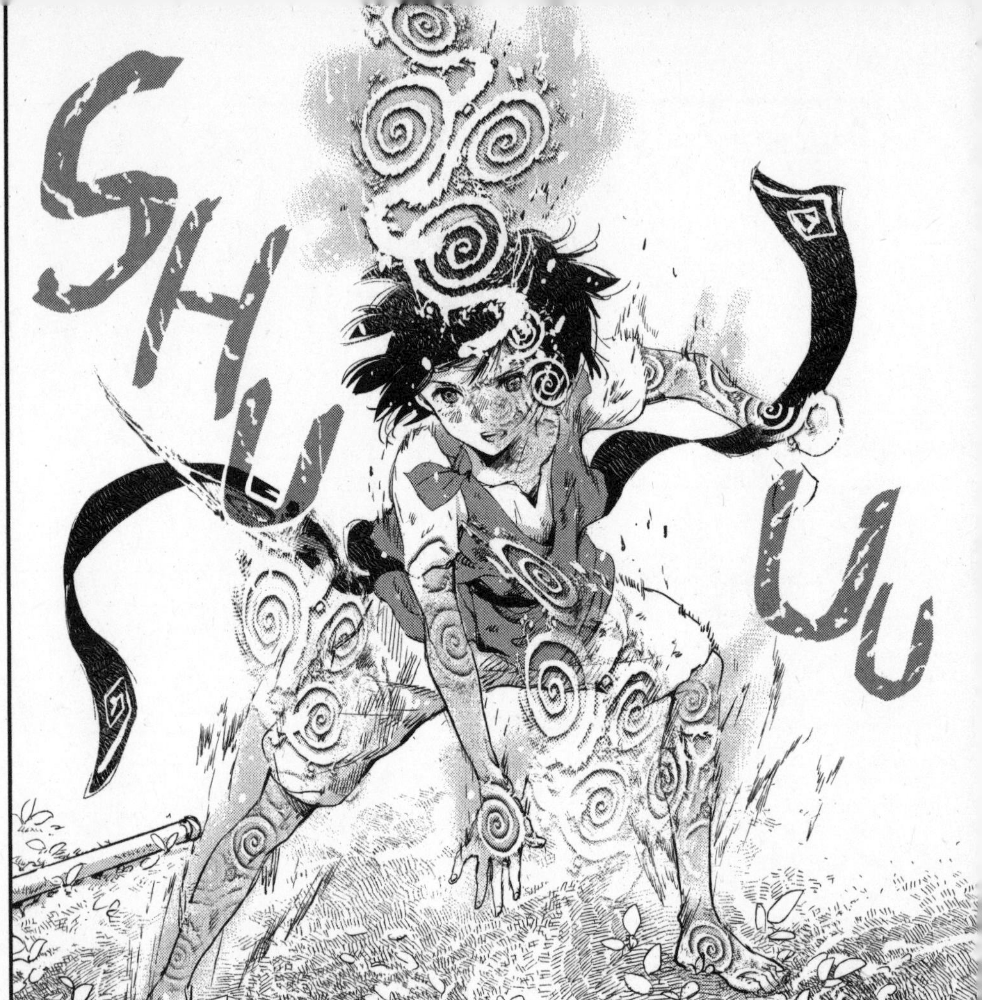
SHUUU
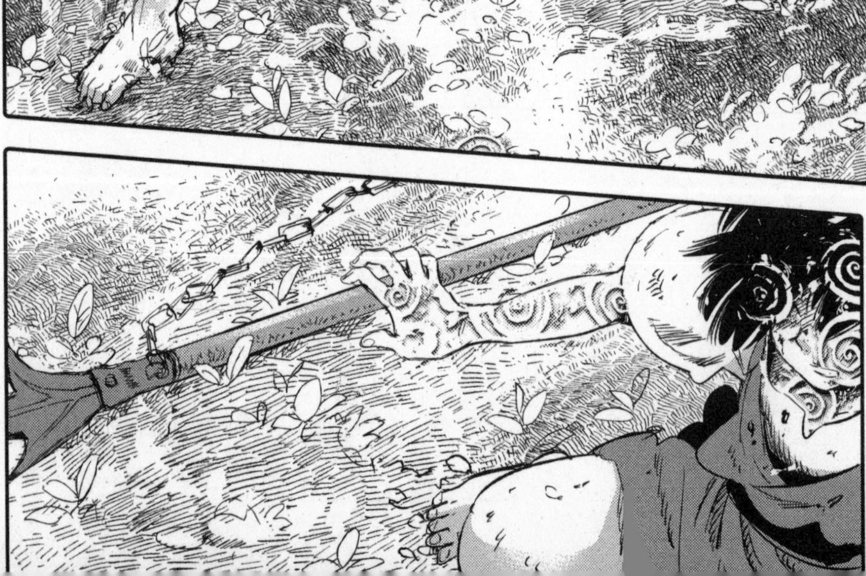

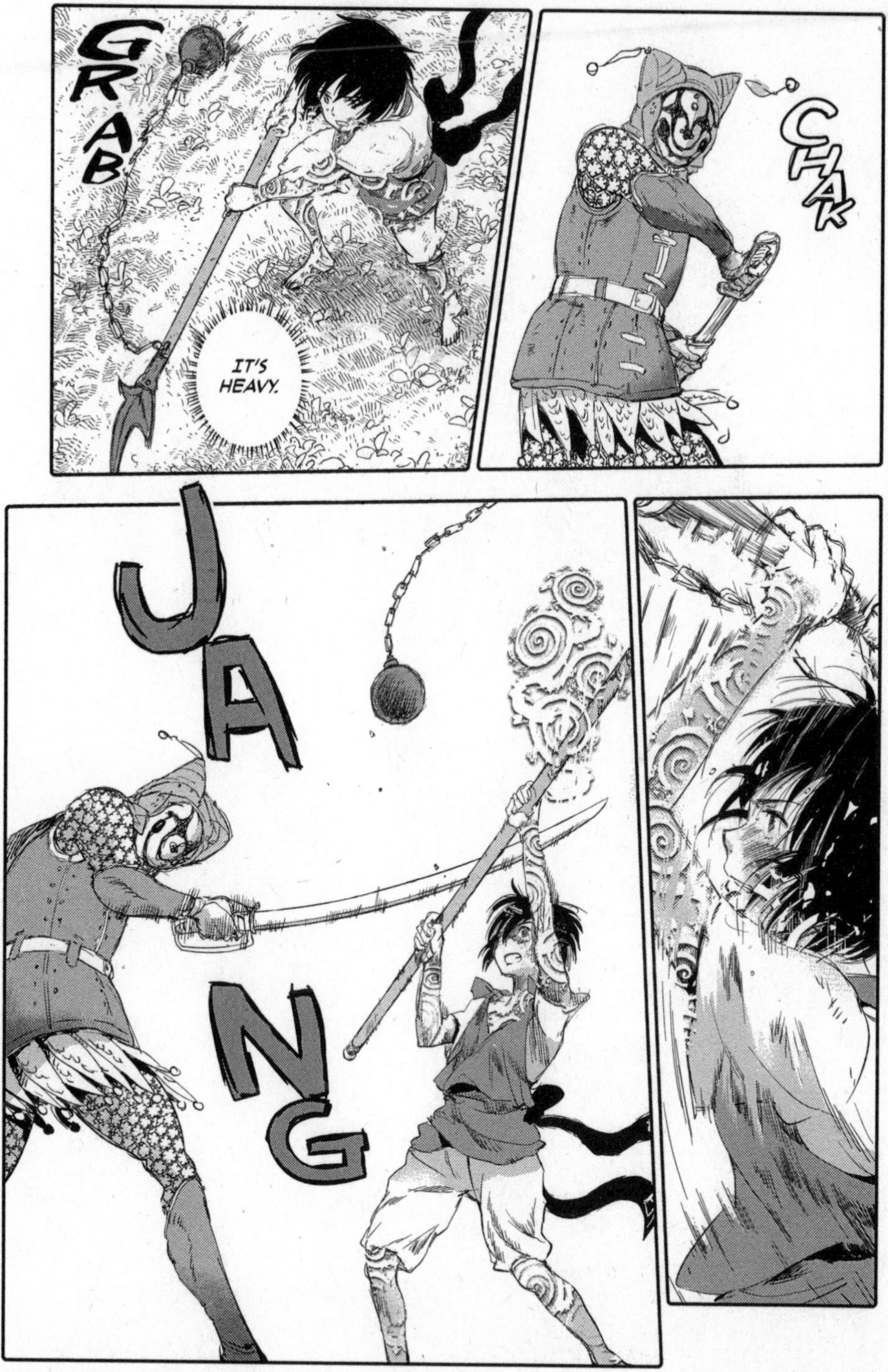
CHAK
GRAB
IT'S HEAVY.
JANG

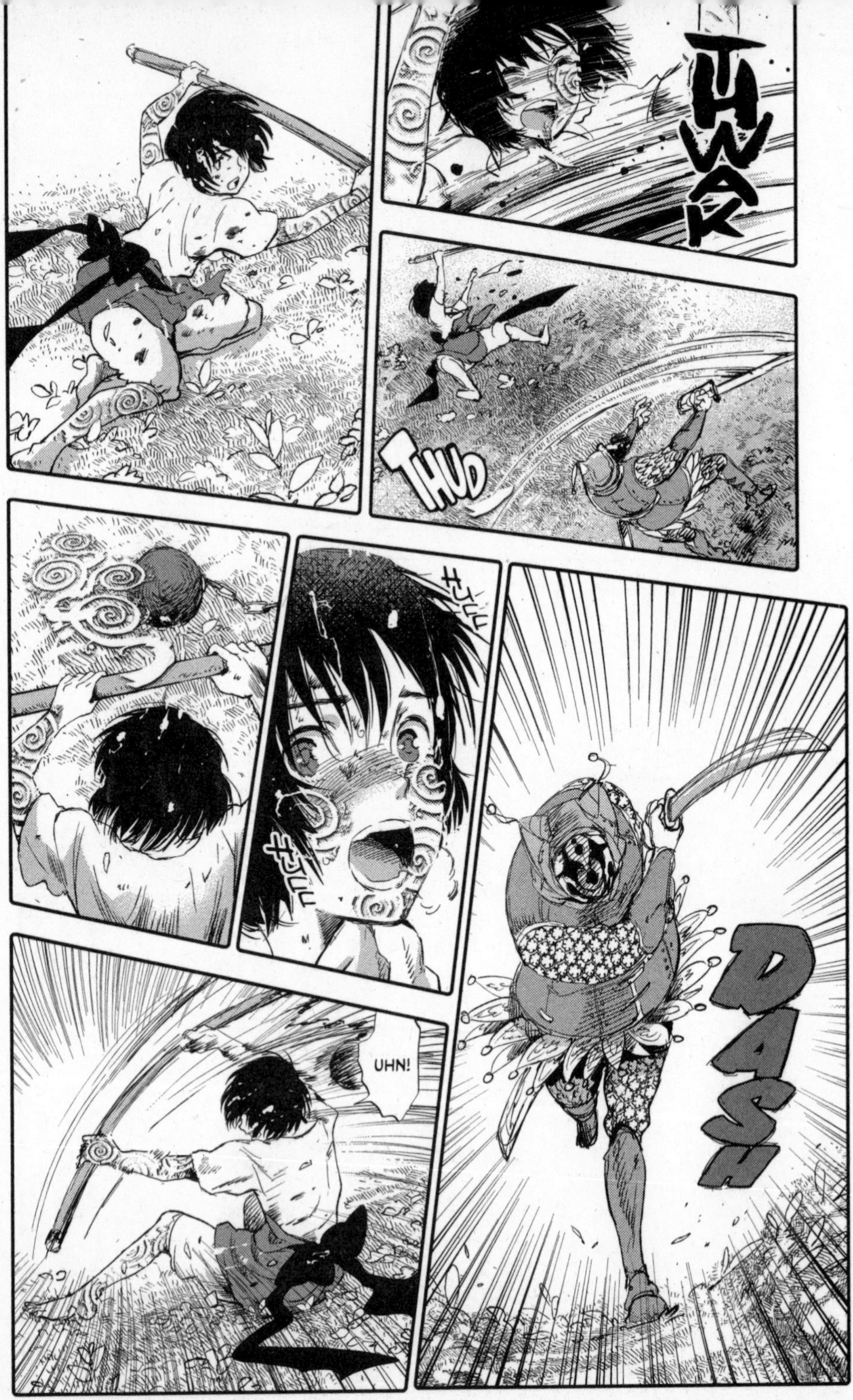
THWAK
THUD
DASH
UHN!

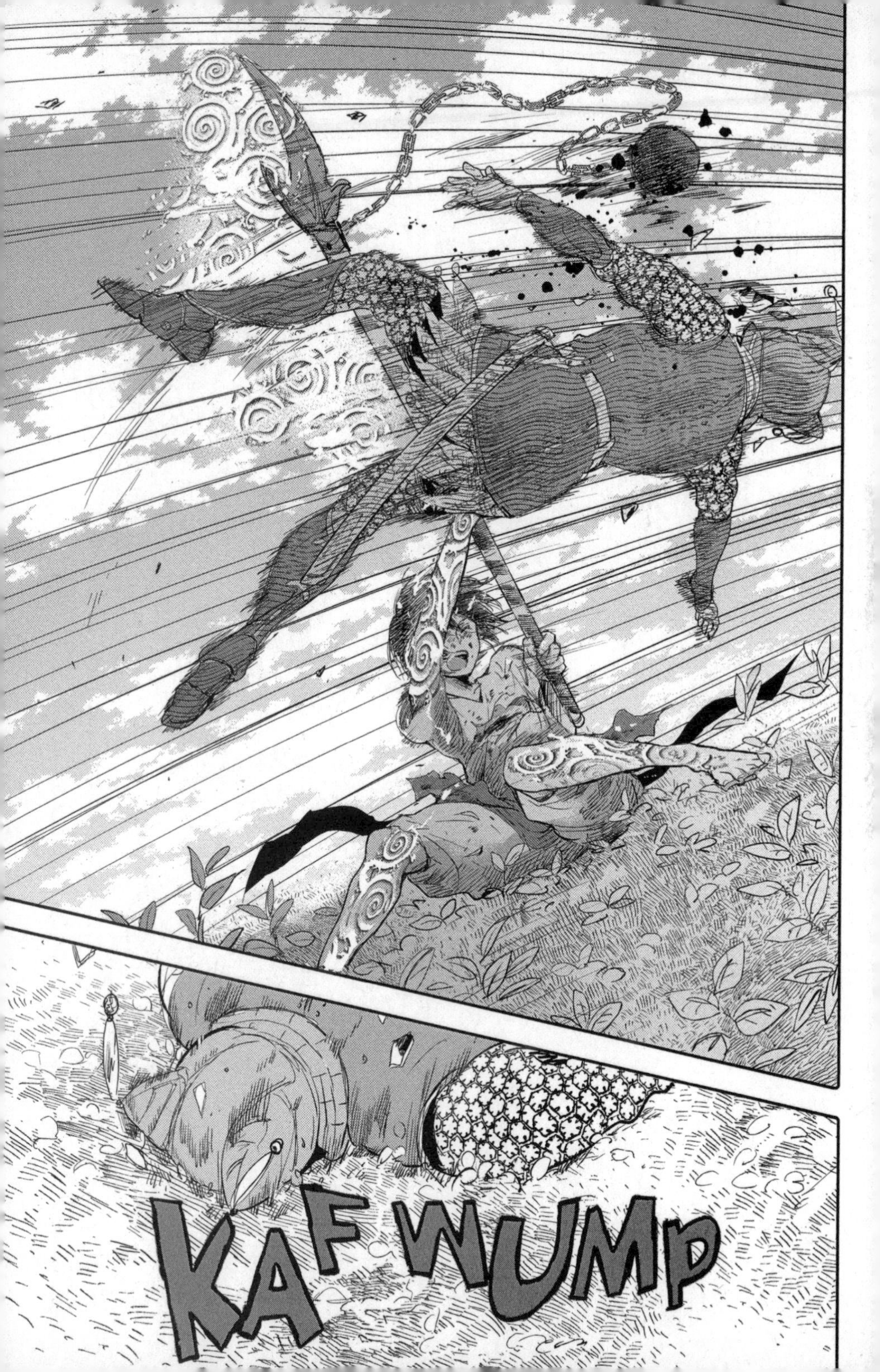
KAFWUMP

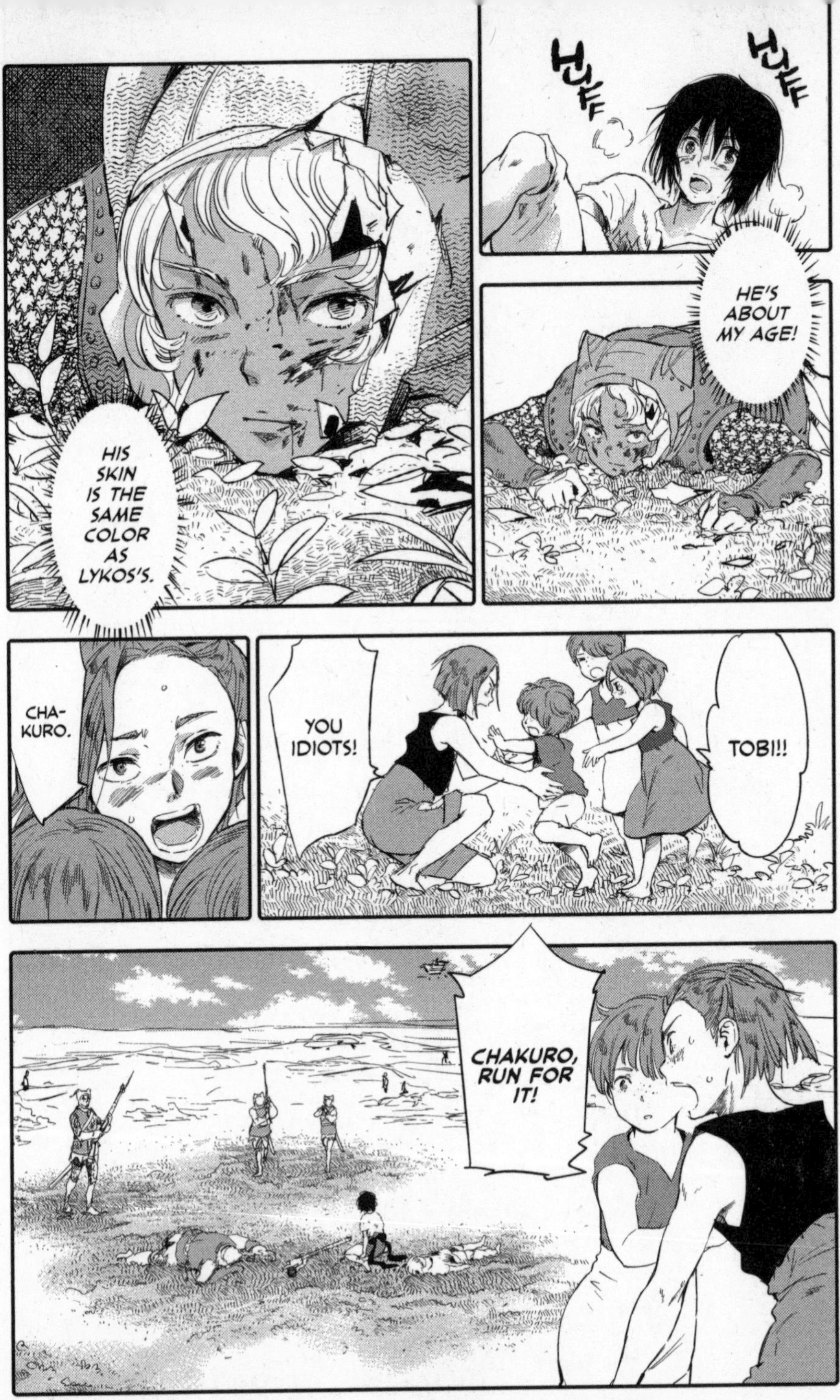
HUFF
HUFF
HE'S ABOUT MY AGE!
HIS SKIN IS THE SAME COLOR AS LYKOS'S.
TOBI!!
YOU IDIOTS!
CHA-KURO.
CHAKURO, RUN FOR IT!

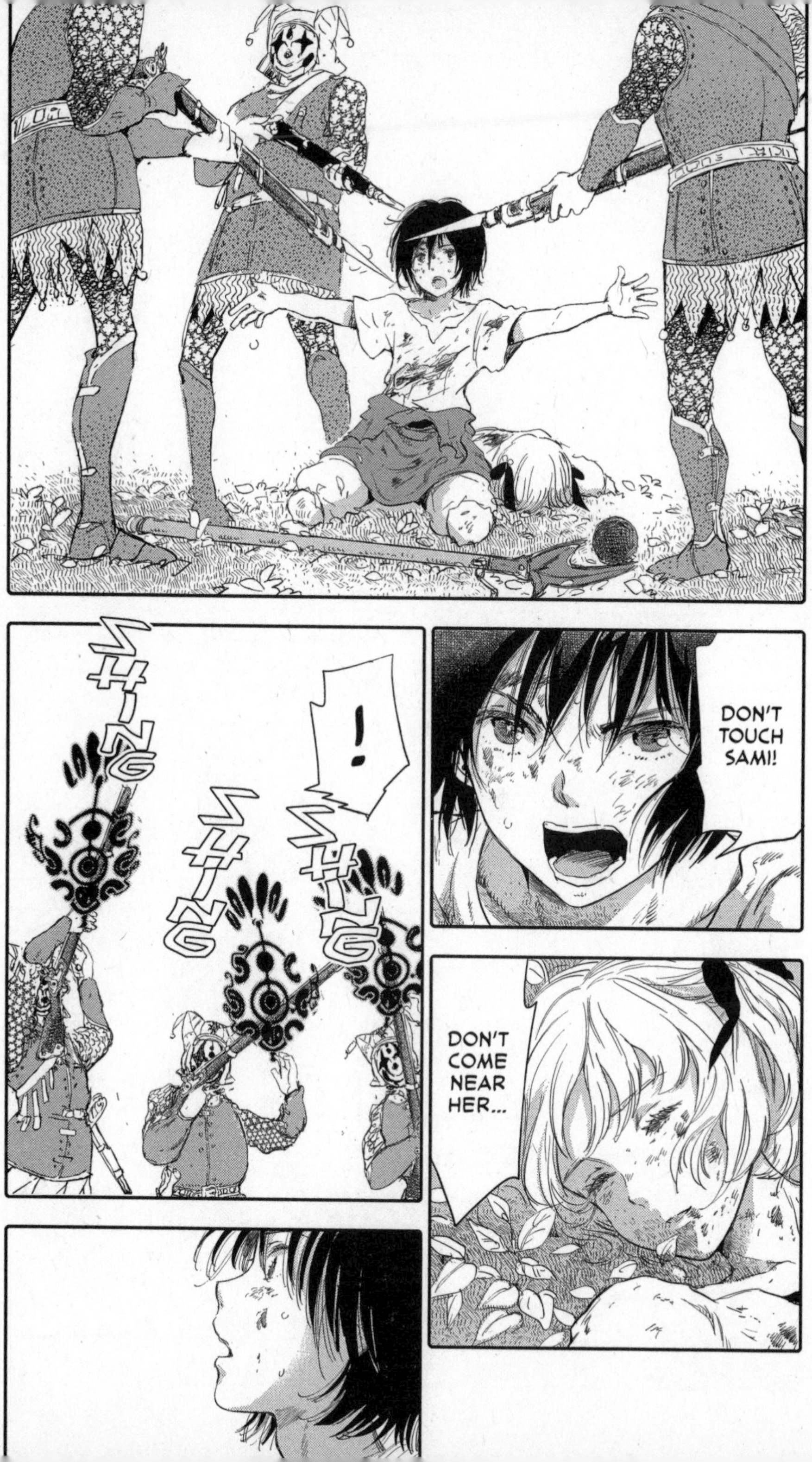
DON'T TOUCH SAMI!
!
SHING
SHING
SHING
DON'T COME NEAR HER...

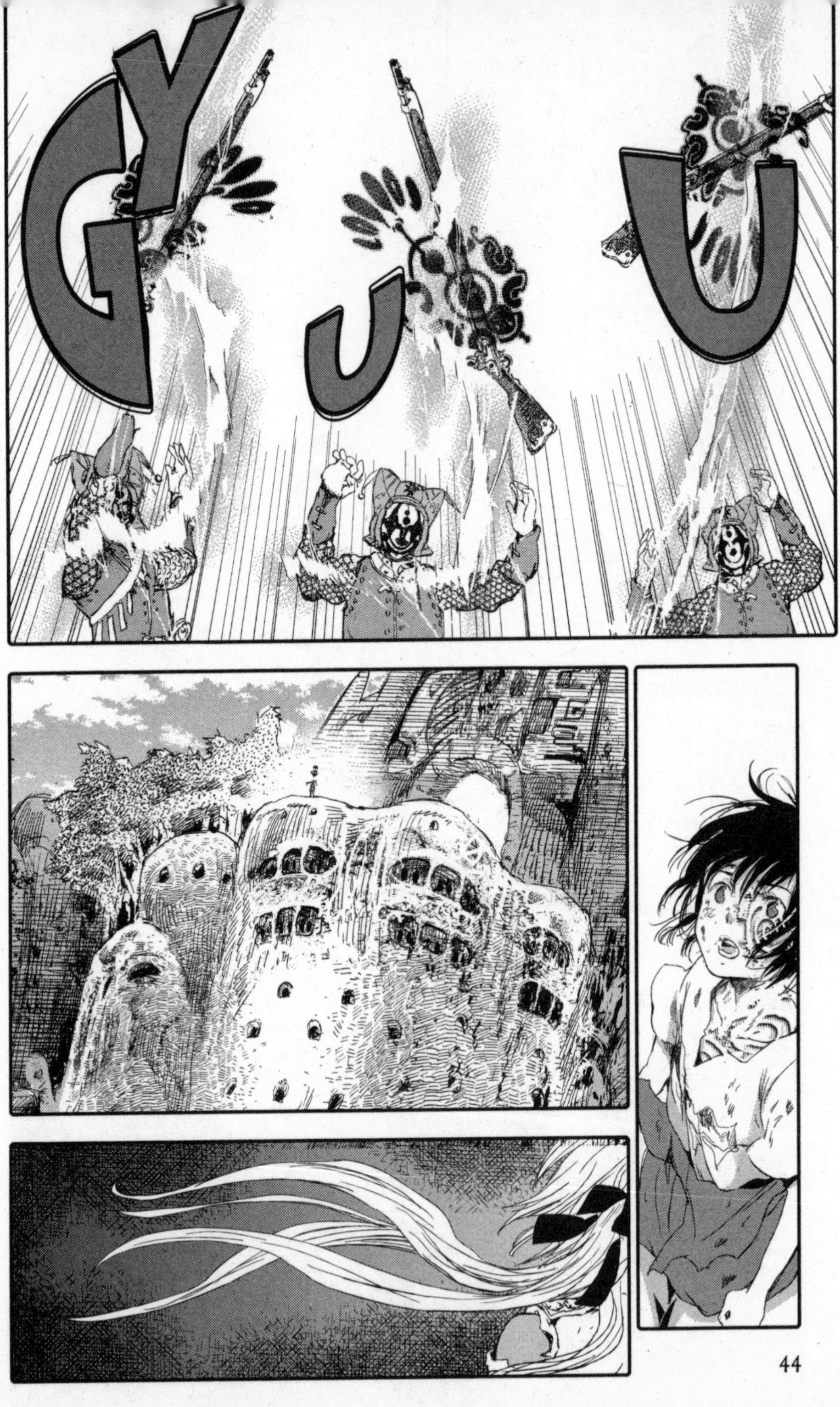
GYJU

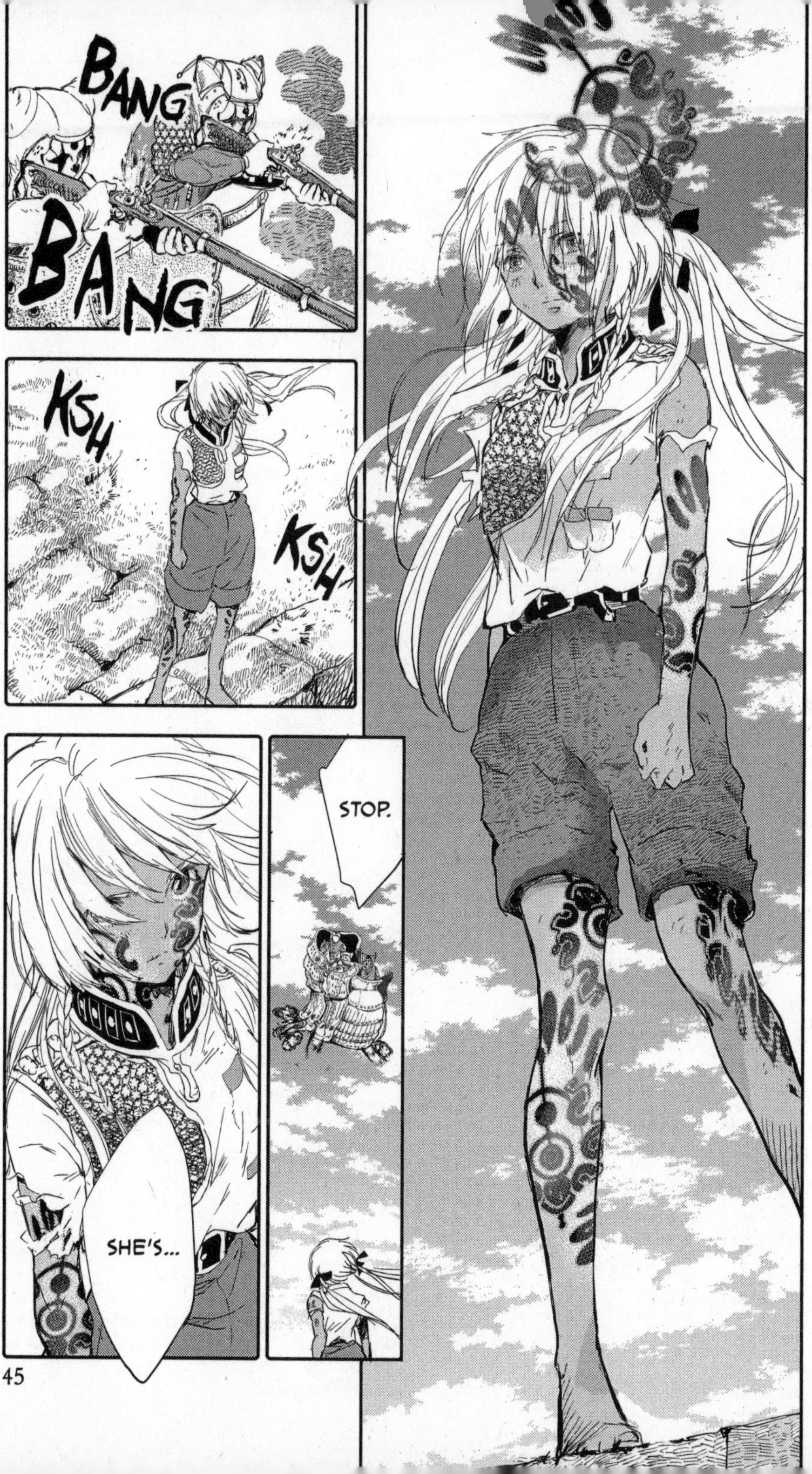
BANG
BANG
KSH
KSH
STOP.
SHE'S...

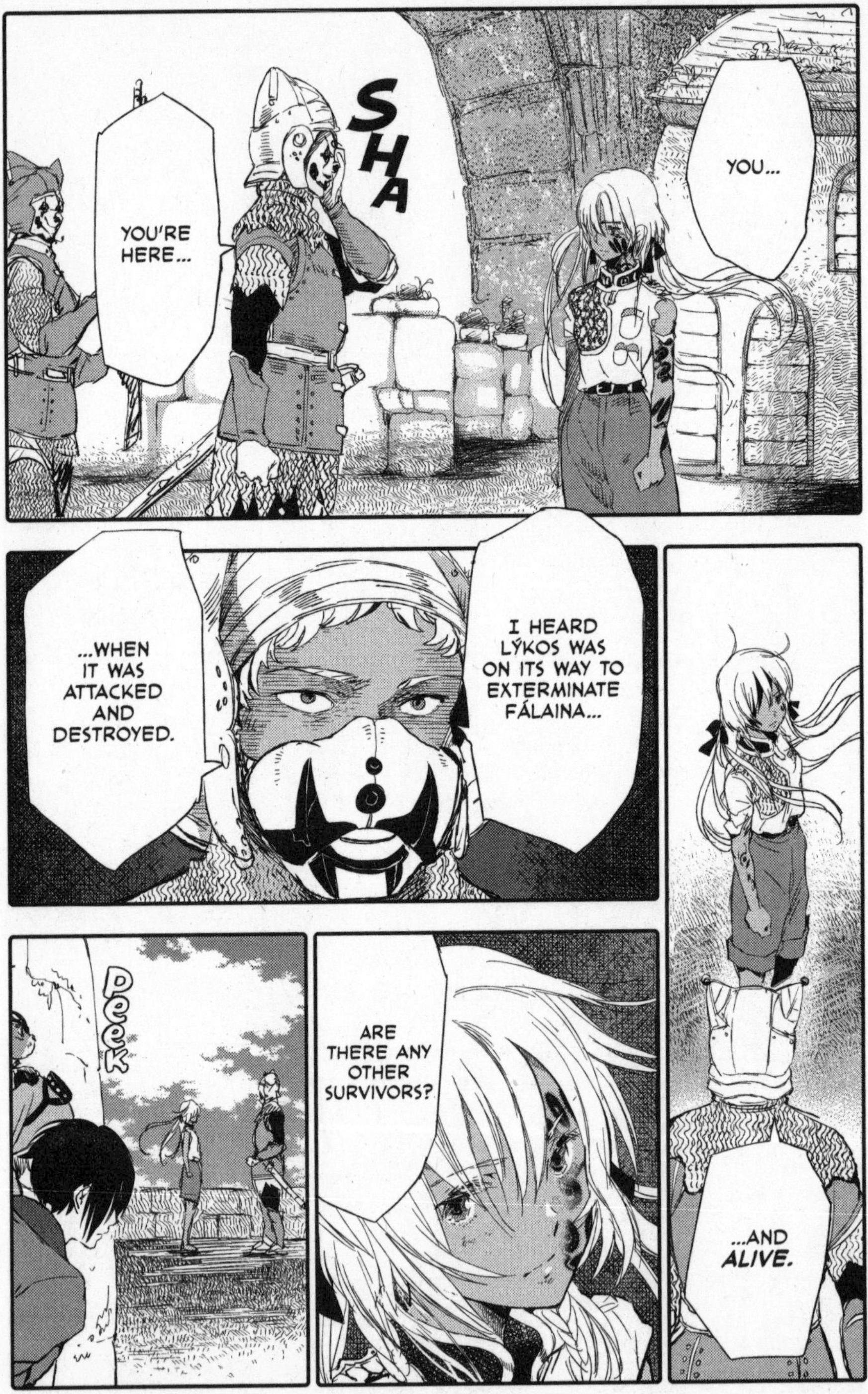
YOU...
SHA
YOU'RE HERE...
...AND ALIVE.
I HEARD LÝKOS WAS ON ITS WAY TO EXTERMINATE FÁLAINA...
...WHEN IT WAS ATTACKED AND DESTROYED.
ARE THERE ANY OTHER SURVIVORS?
Peek

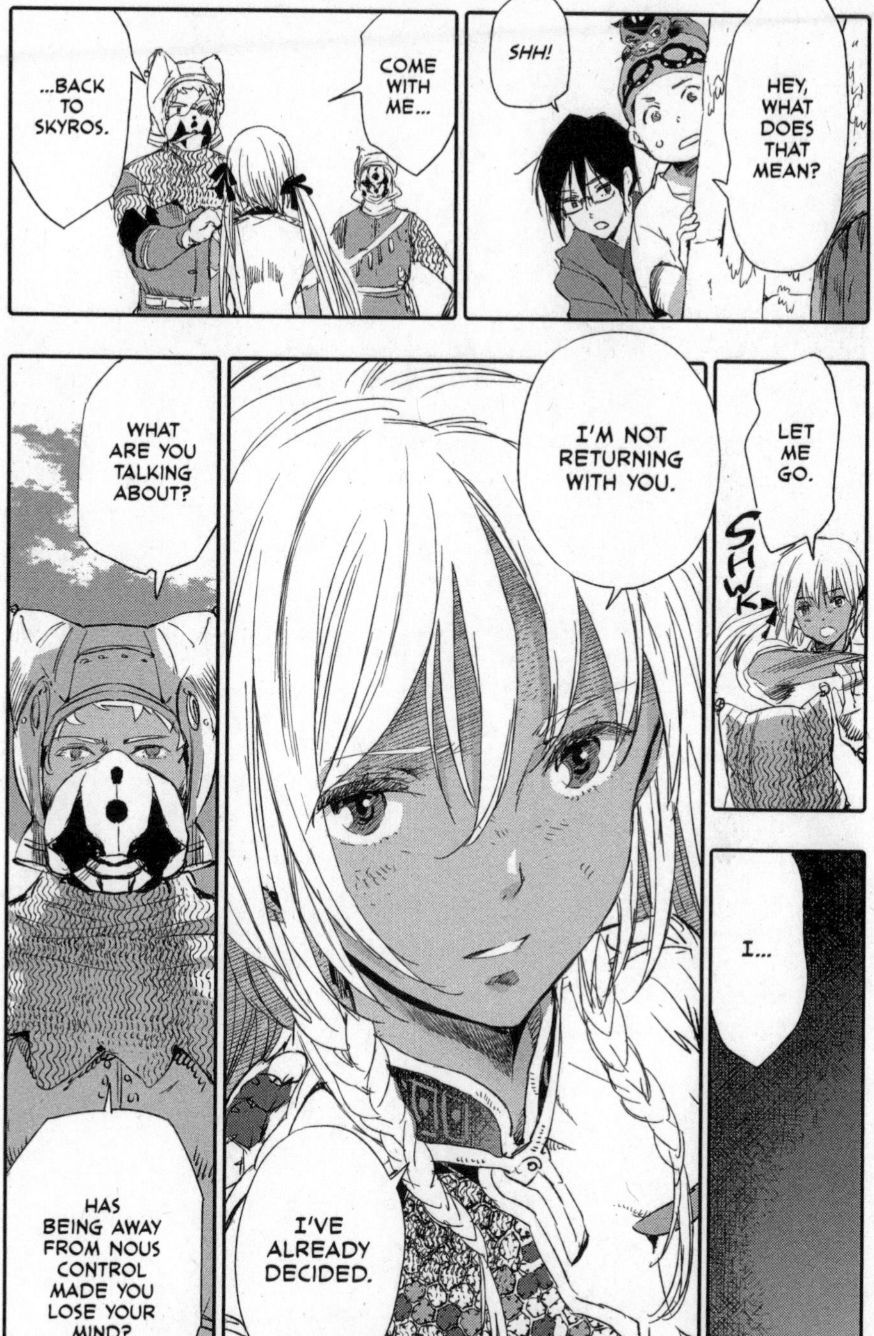
HEY, WHAT DOES THAT MEAN?
SHH!
COME WITH ME...
...BACK TO SKYROS.
LET ME GO.
SHWK
I...
I'M NOT RETURNING WITH YOU.
I'VE ALREADY DECIDED.
WHAT ARE YOU TALKING ABOUT?
HAS BEING AWAY FROM NOUS CONTROL MADE YOU LOSE YOUR MIND?

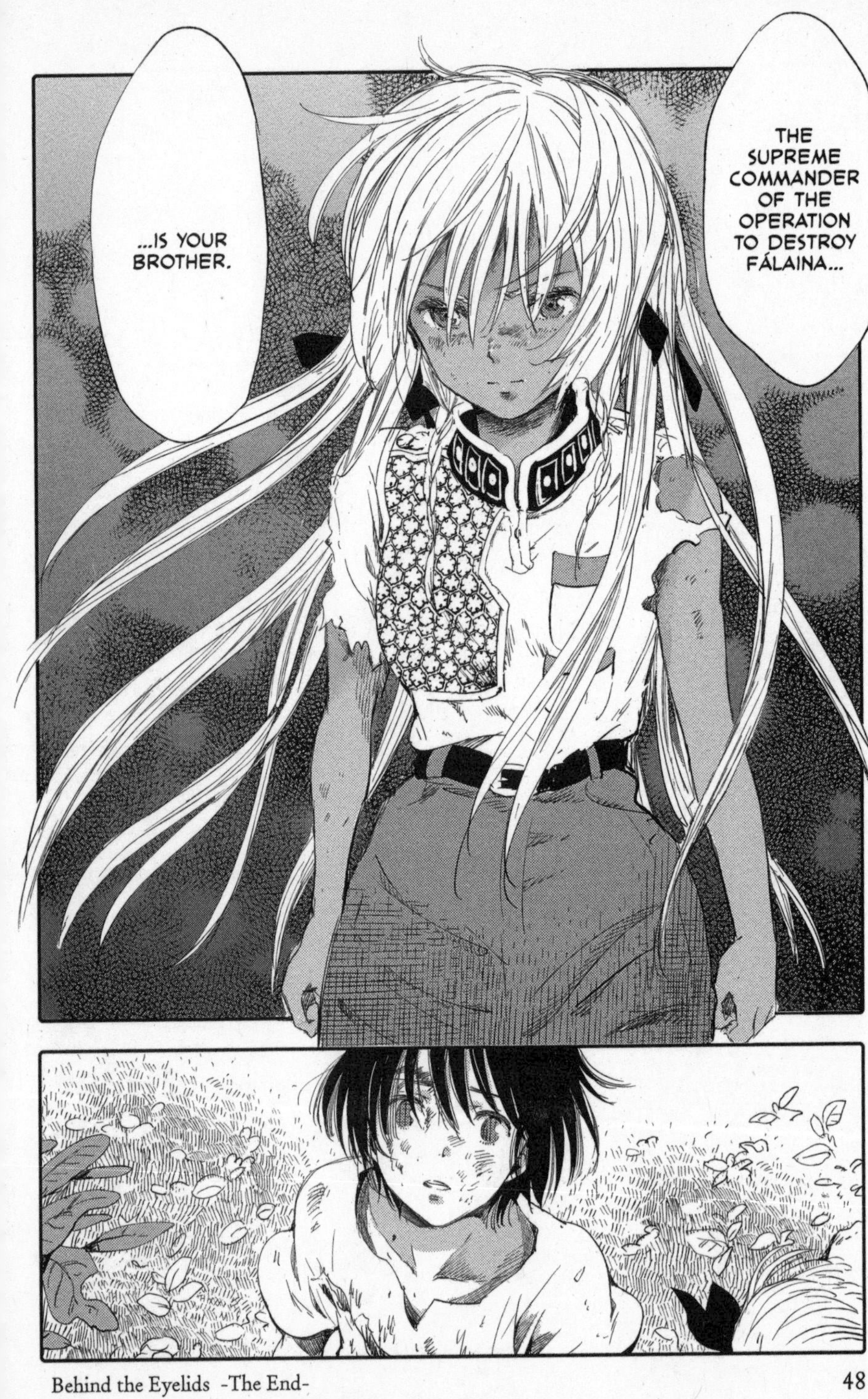
THE SUPREME COMMANDER OF THE OPERATION TO DESTROY FÁLAINA...
...IS YOUR BROTHER.

Sketch ④
Beliefs

It is said that the souls of those who are sent off in a sand burial dissolve into the Sea of Sand and concentrate around the Mud Whale, protecting it. The souls continue to exist in each grain of sand, but as time passes, they rise little by little toward the heavens.

The risen souls form a large blue canopy that keeps the sun and stars from falling down. The rain is the tears they shed. Stormy weather is considered lucky, but since it comes as a result of souls in pain, praying for it is prohibited.

The inhabitants of the Mud Whale direct their prayers to the bottom of the Sea of Sand and to the souls in the heavens.

The Archivist's Notes

Sketch 5

Education

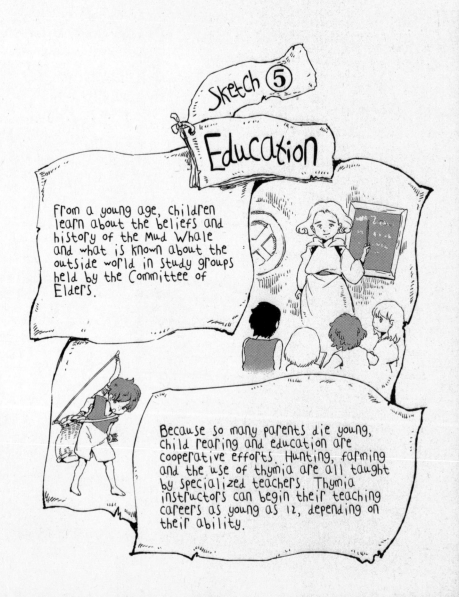

From a young age, children learn about the beliefs and history of the Mud Whale and what is known about the outside world in study groups held by the Committee of Elders.

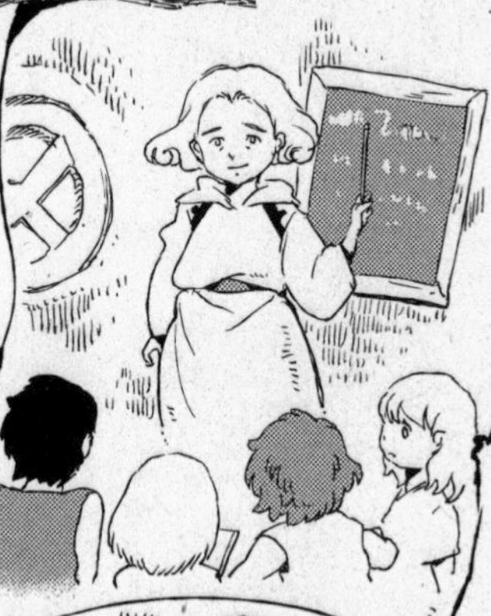

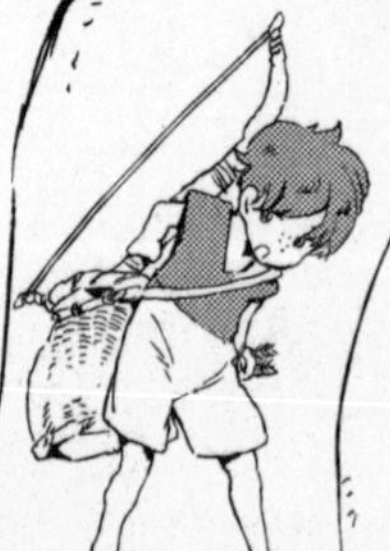

Because so many parents die young, child rearing and education are cooperative efforts. Hunting, farming and the use of thymia are all taught by specialized teachers. Thymia instructors can begin their teaching careers as young as 12, depending on their ability.

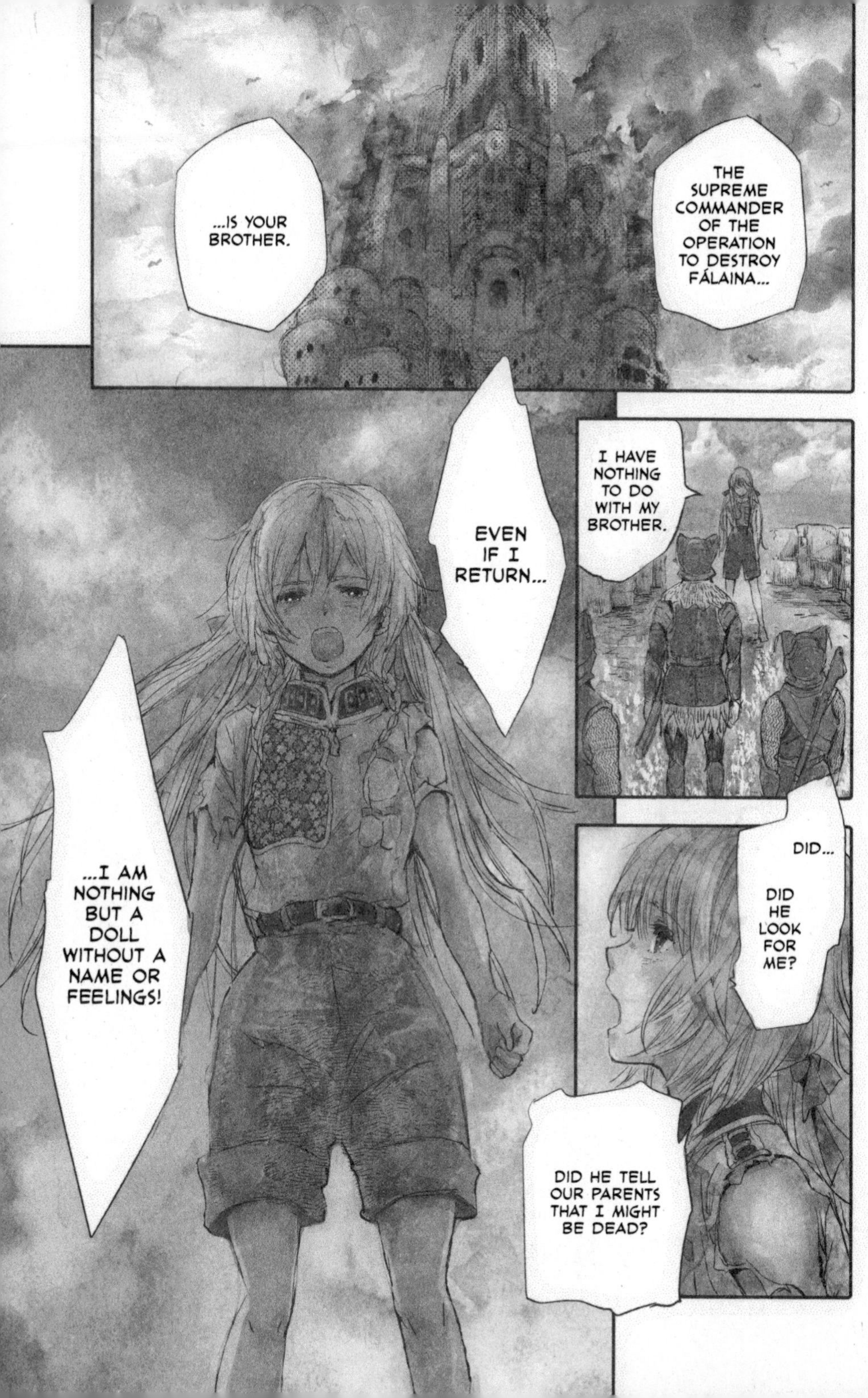
THE SUPREME COMMANDER OF THE OPERATION TO DESTROY FÁLAINA...
...IS YOUR BROTHER.
I HAVE NOTHING TO DO WITH MY BROTHER.
DID...
DID HE LOOK FOR ME?
DID HE TELL OUR PARENTS THAT I MIGHT BE DEAD?
EVEN IF I RETURN...
...I AM NOTHING BUT A DOLL WITHOUT A NAME OR FEELINGS!

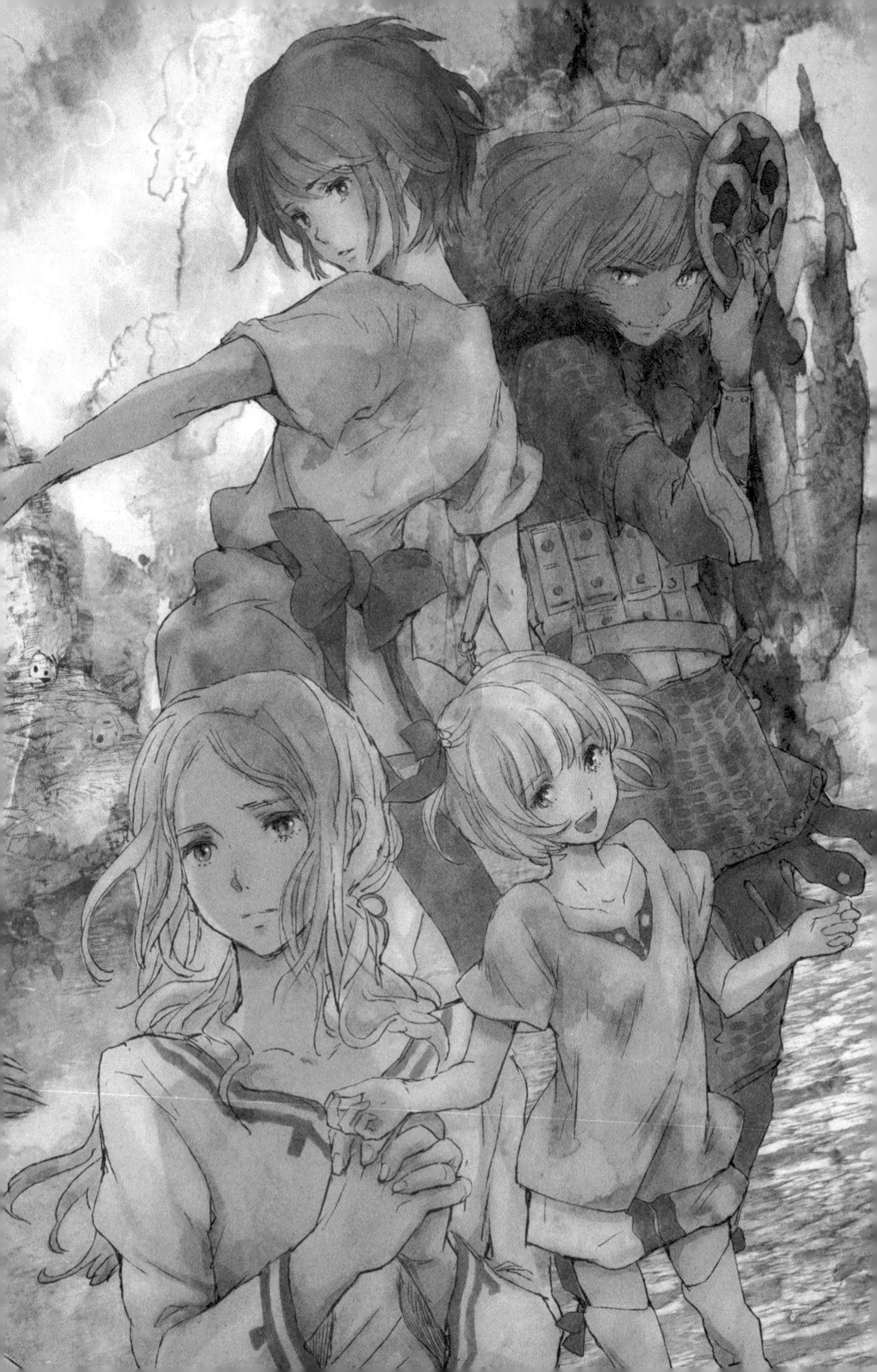

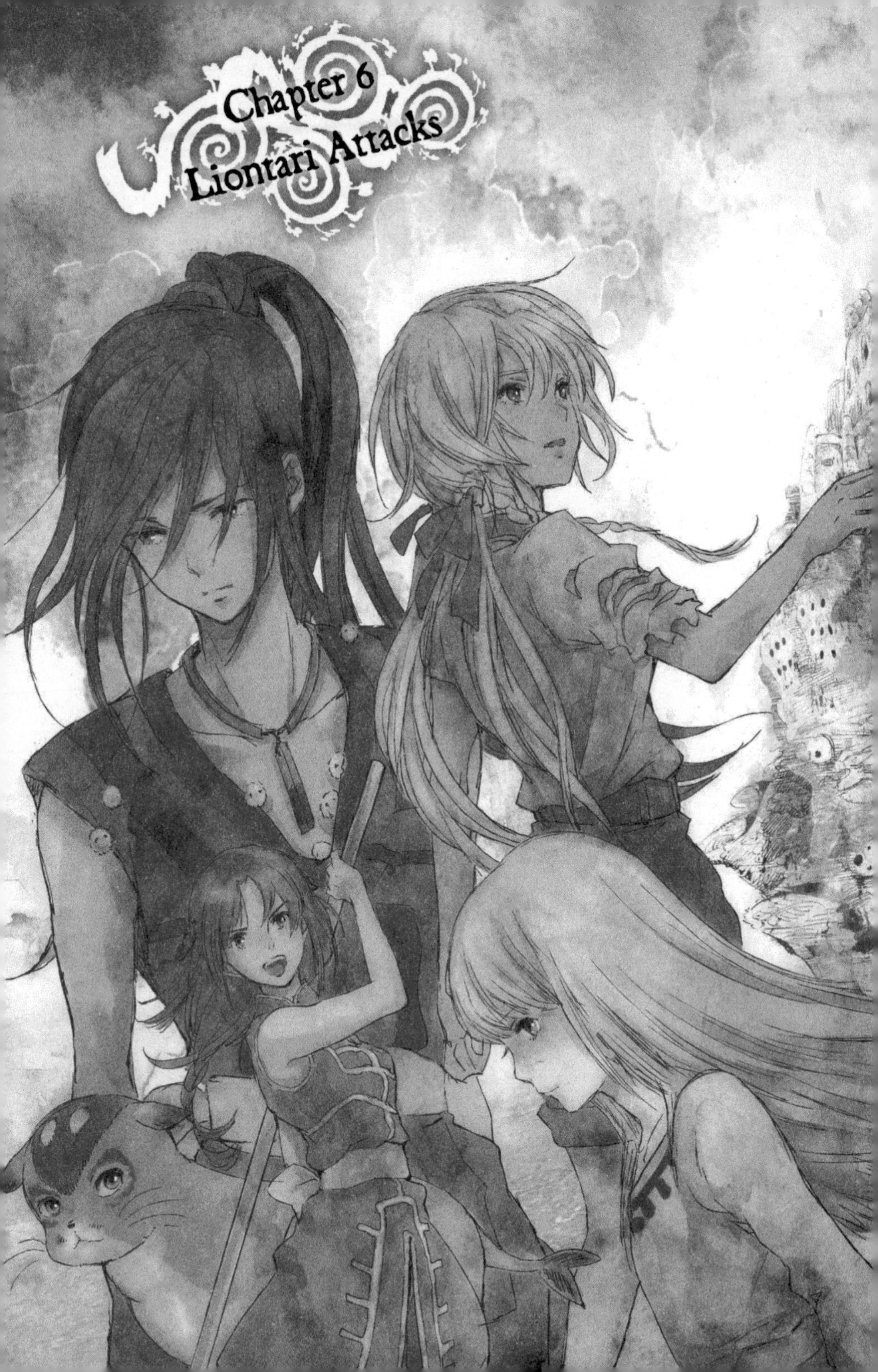
Chapter 6
Liontari Attacks

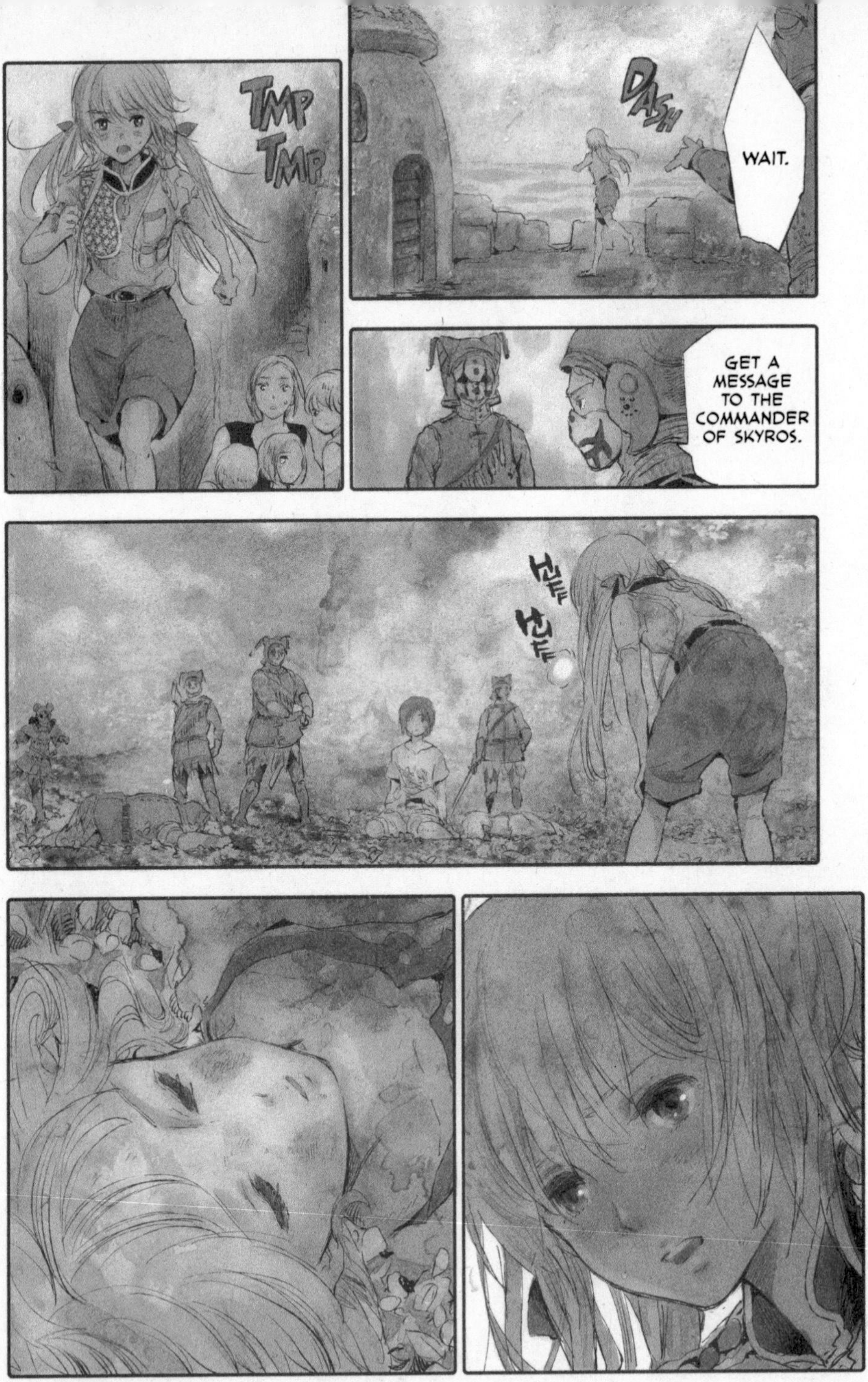
DASH
WAIT.
GET A MESSAGE TO THE COMMANDER OF SKYROS.
TMP TMP
HUFF HUFF

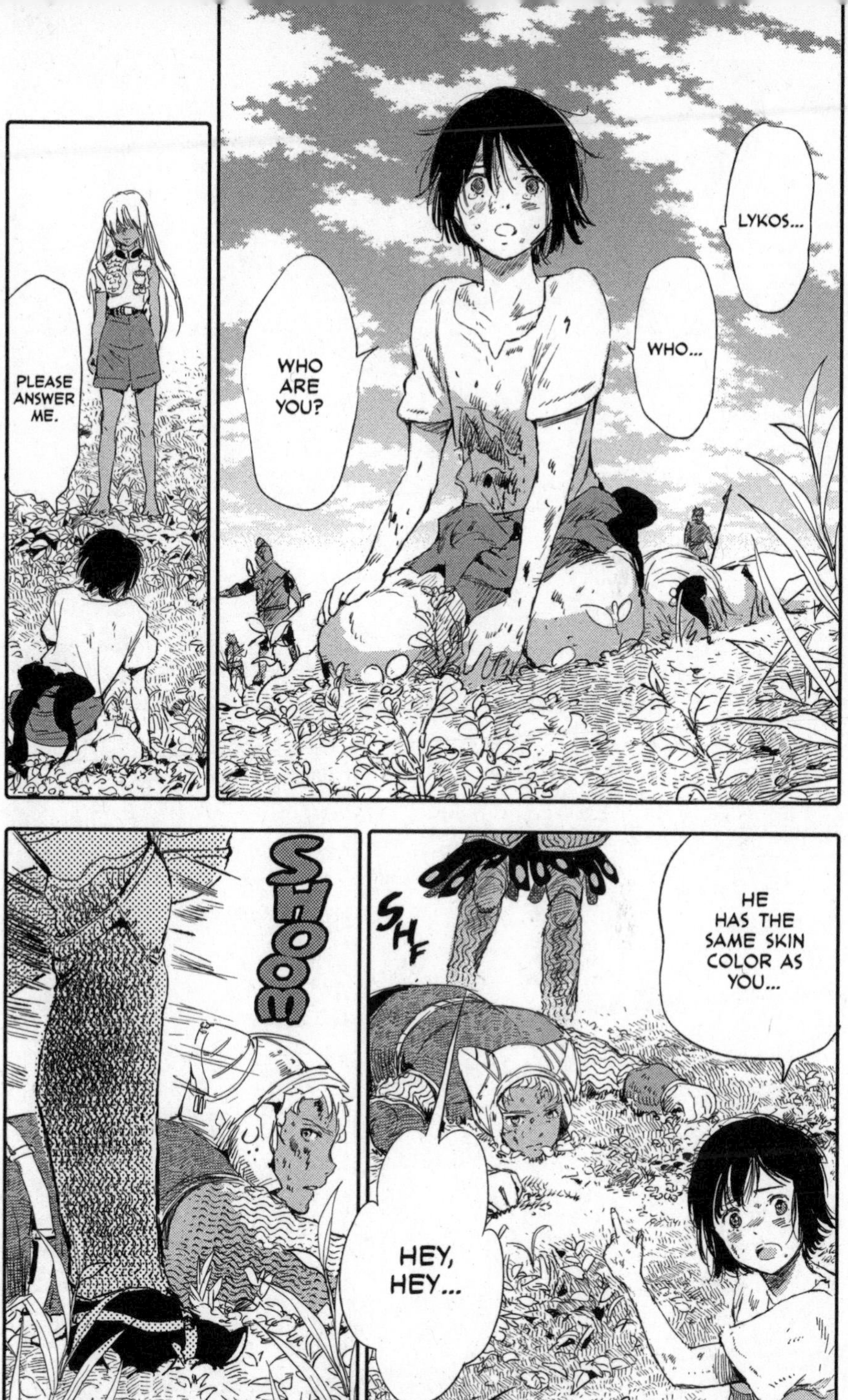
LYKOS...
WHO...
WHO ARE YOU?
PLEASE ANSWER ME.
HE HAS THE SAME SKIN COLOR AS YOU...
SHF
HEY, HEY...
SHOOM

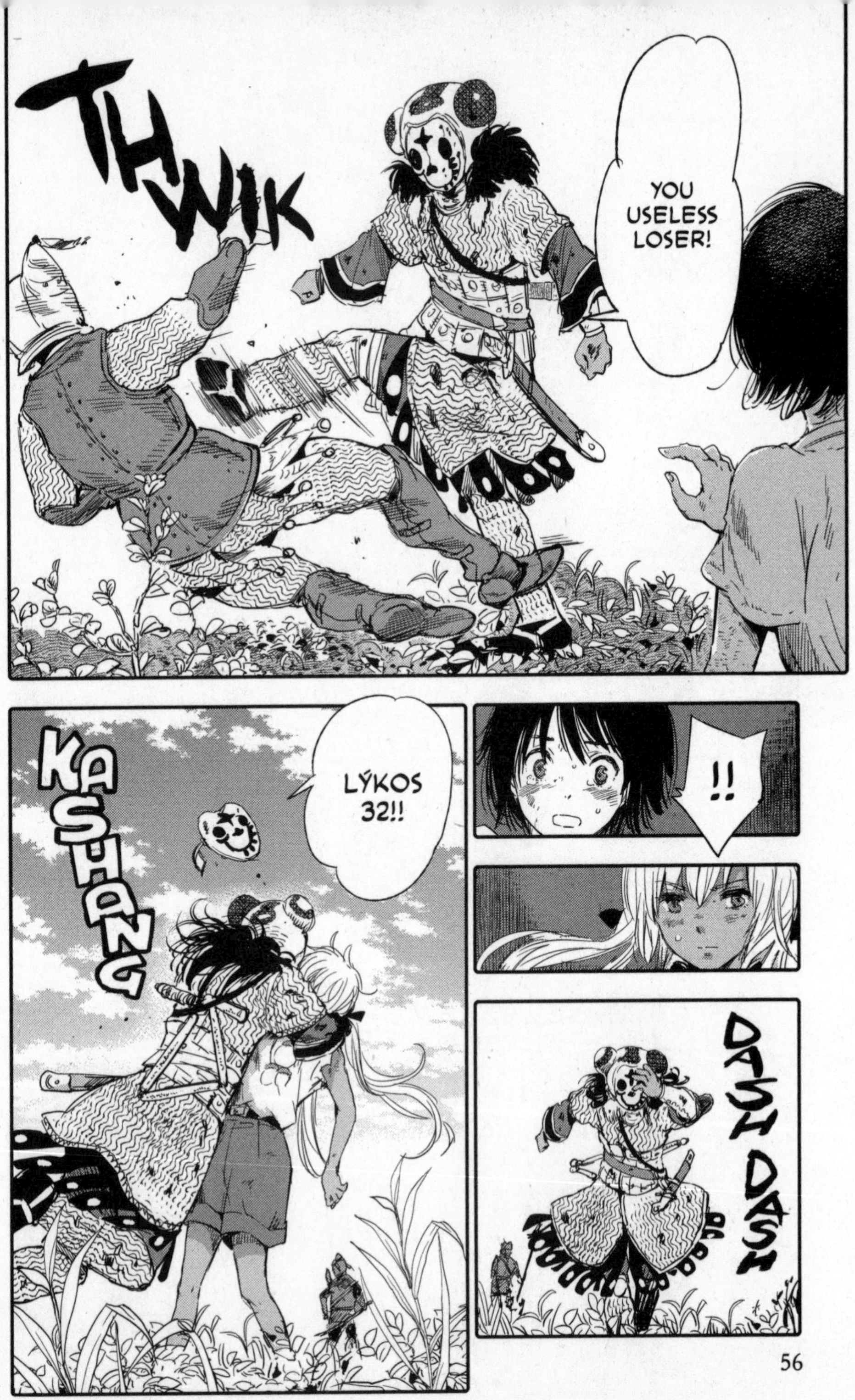
YOU USELESS LOSER!
THWIK
!!
DASH DASH
LÝKOS 32!!
KASHANG

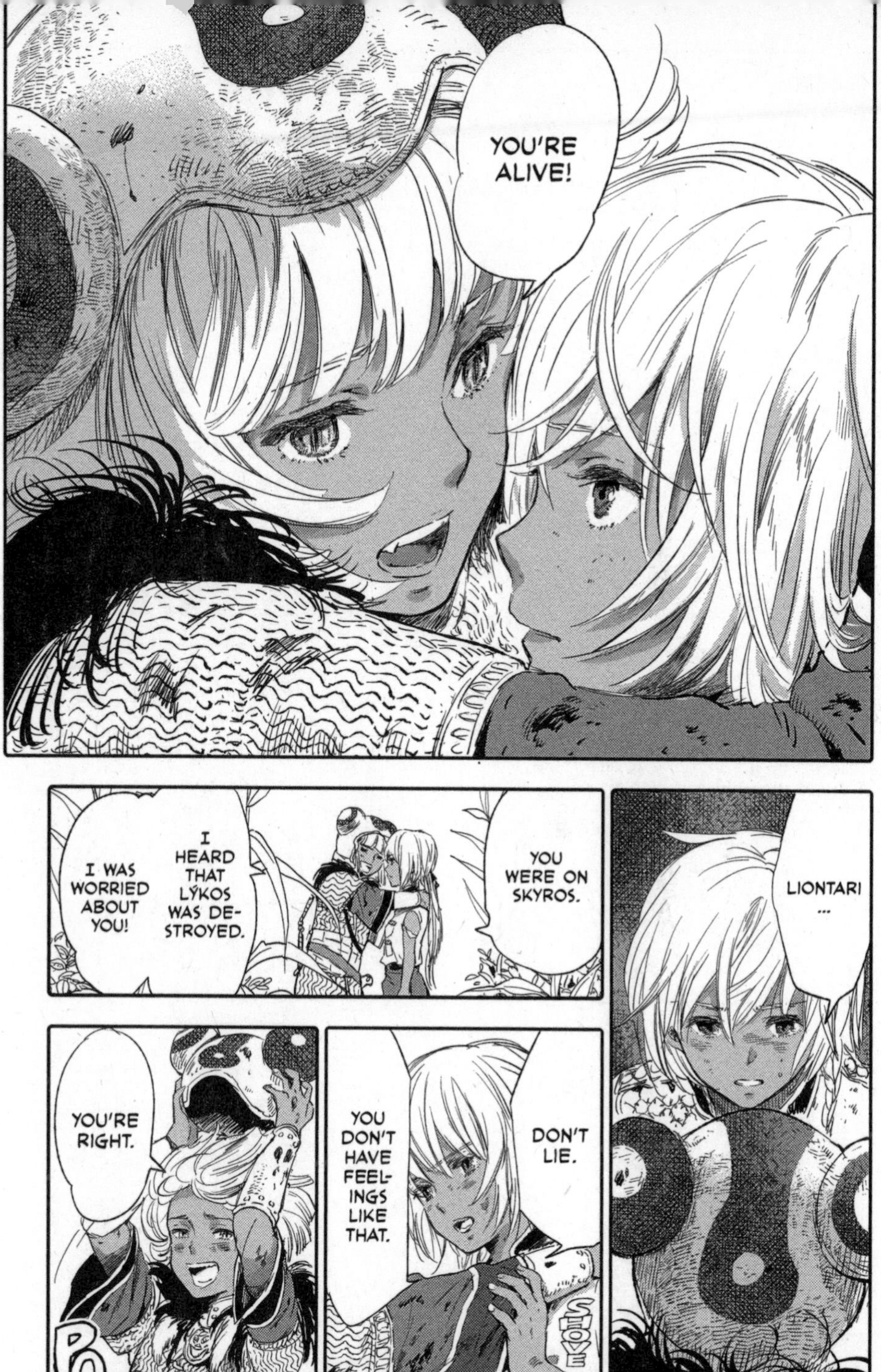
YOU'RE ALIVE!
LIONTARI ...
YOU WERE ON SKYROS.
I HEARD THAT LÝKOS WAS DESTROYED.
I WAS WORRIED ABOUT YOU!
DON'T LIE.
YOU DON'T HAVE FEELINGS LIKE THAT.
SHOVE
YOU'RE RIGHT.
POP

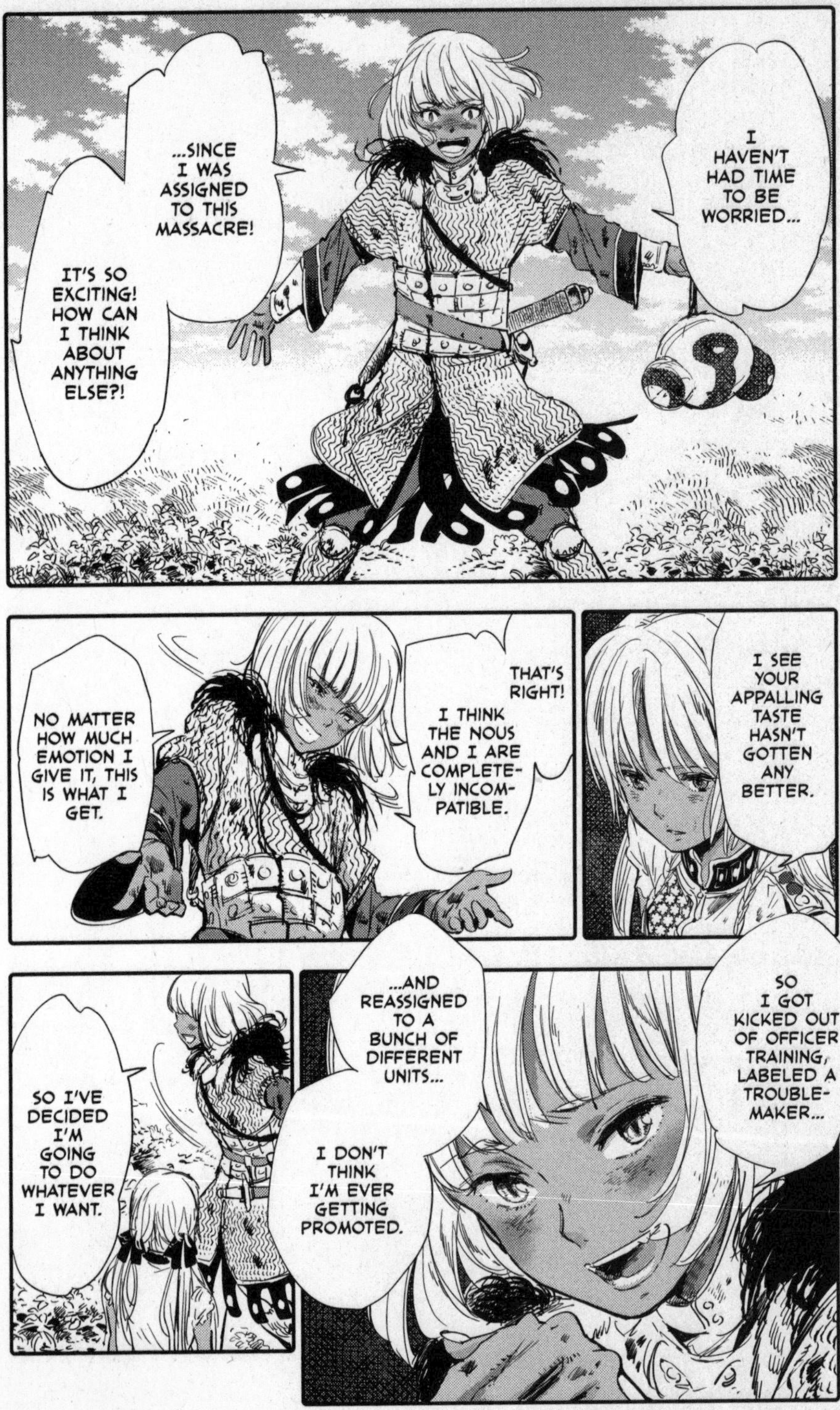
I HAVEN'T HAD TIME TO BE WORRIED...
...SINCE I WAS ASSIGNED TO THIS MASSACRE!
IT'S SO EXCITING! HOW CAN I THINK ABOUT ANYTHING ELSE?!
I SEE YOUR APPALLING TASTE HASN'T GOTTEN ANY BETTER.
THAT'S RIGHT!
I THINK THE NOUS AND I ARE COMPLETELY INCOMPATIBLE.
NO MATTER HOW MUCH EMOTION I GIVE IT, THIS IS WHAT I GET.
SO I GOT KICKED OUT OF OFFICER TRAINING, LABELED A TROUBLEMAKER...
...AND REASSIGNED TO A BUNCH OF DIFFERENT UNITS...
I DON'T THINK I'M EVER GETTING PROMOTED.
SO I'VE DECIDED I'M GOING TO DO WHATEVER I WANT.

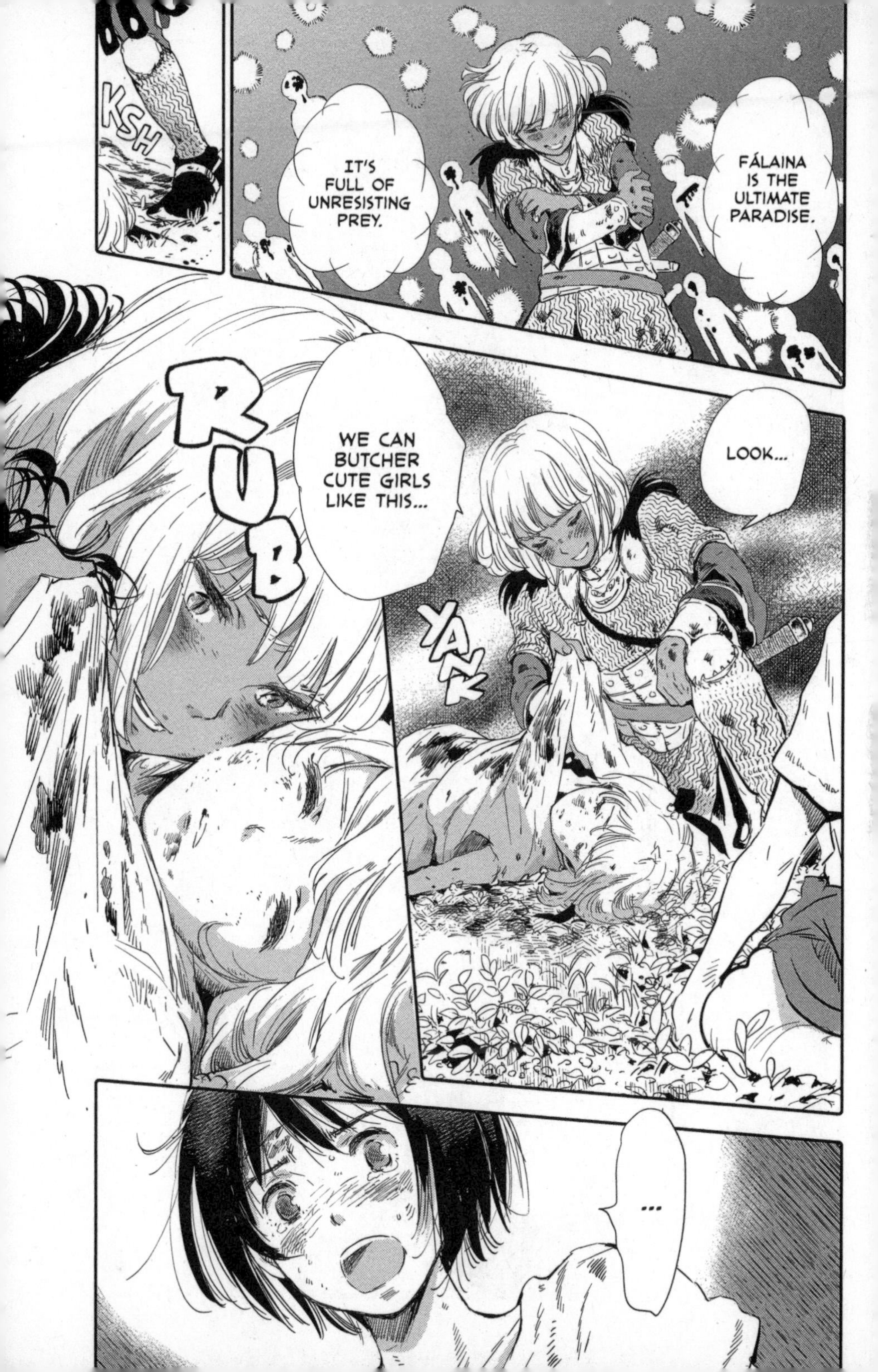
FÁLAINA IS THE ULTIMATE PARADISE.
IT'S FULL OF UNRESISTING PREY.
KSH
LOOK...
YANK
WE CAN BUTCHER CUTE GIRLS LIKE THIS...
RUB
...

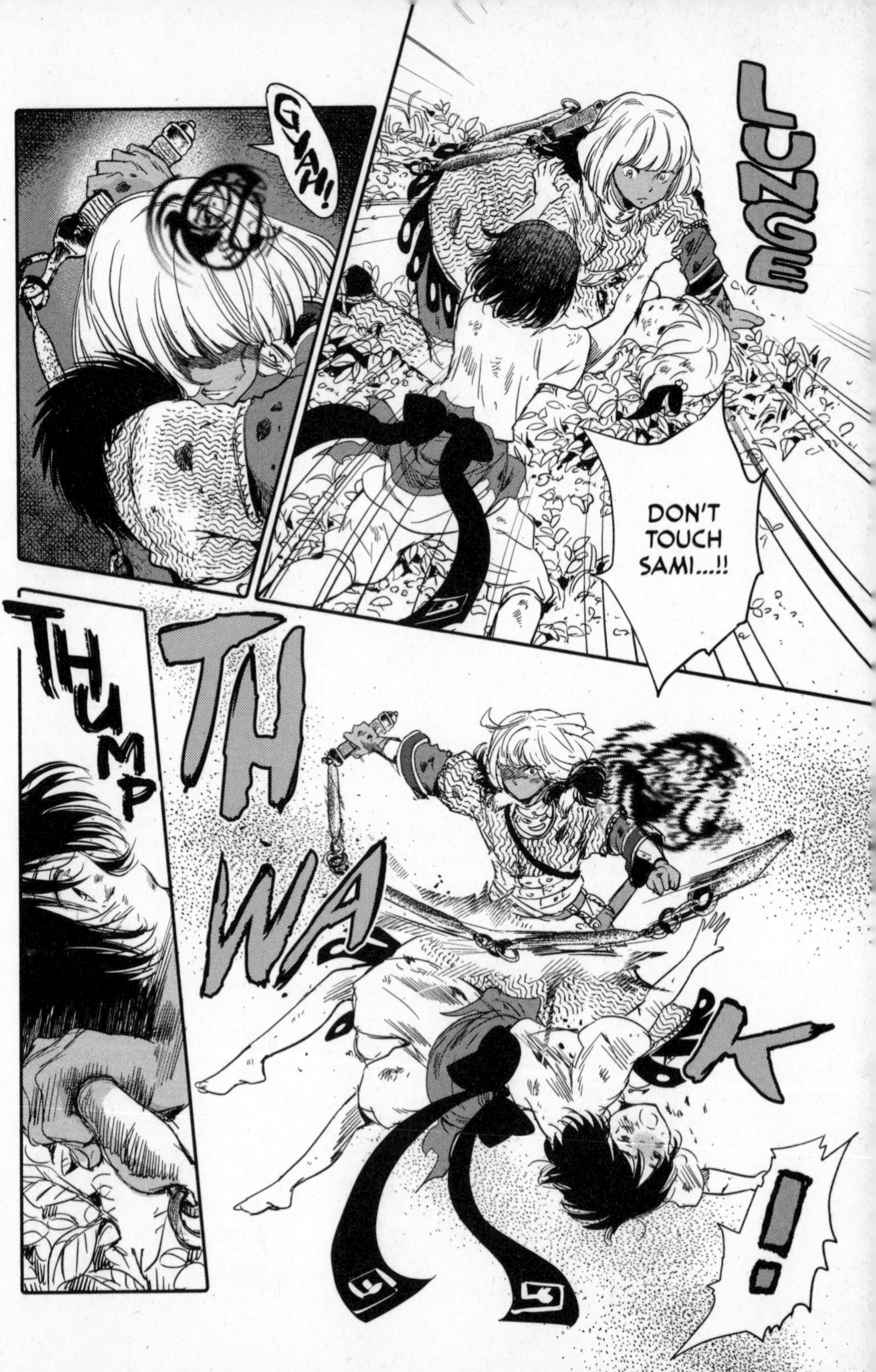
LUNGE
DON'T TOUCH SAMI...!!
GRAH!
THWACK
!
THUMP

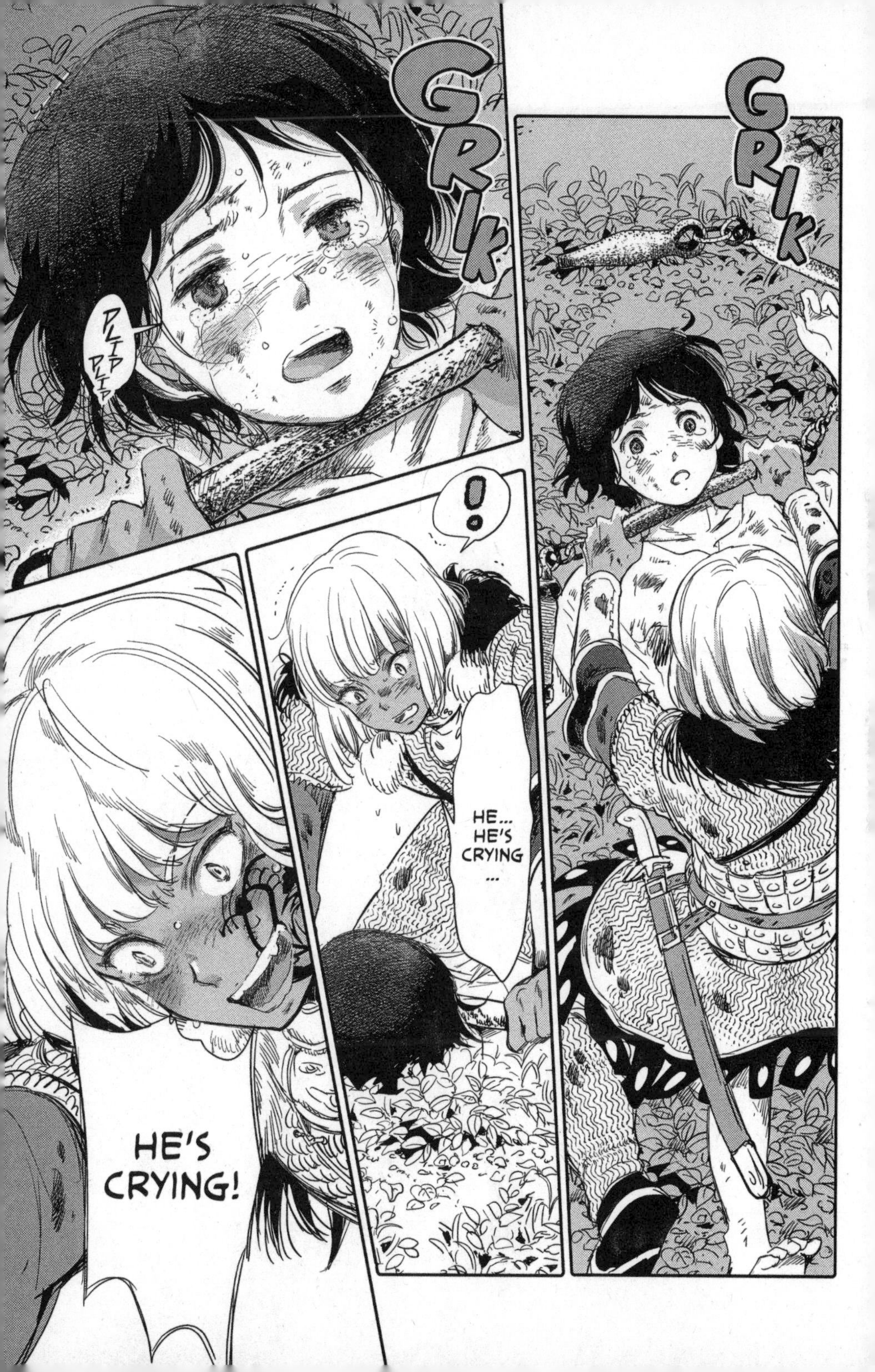
GRIK
GRIK
PLIP PLIP
!
HE... HE'S CRYING ...
HE'S CRYING!

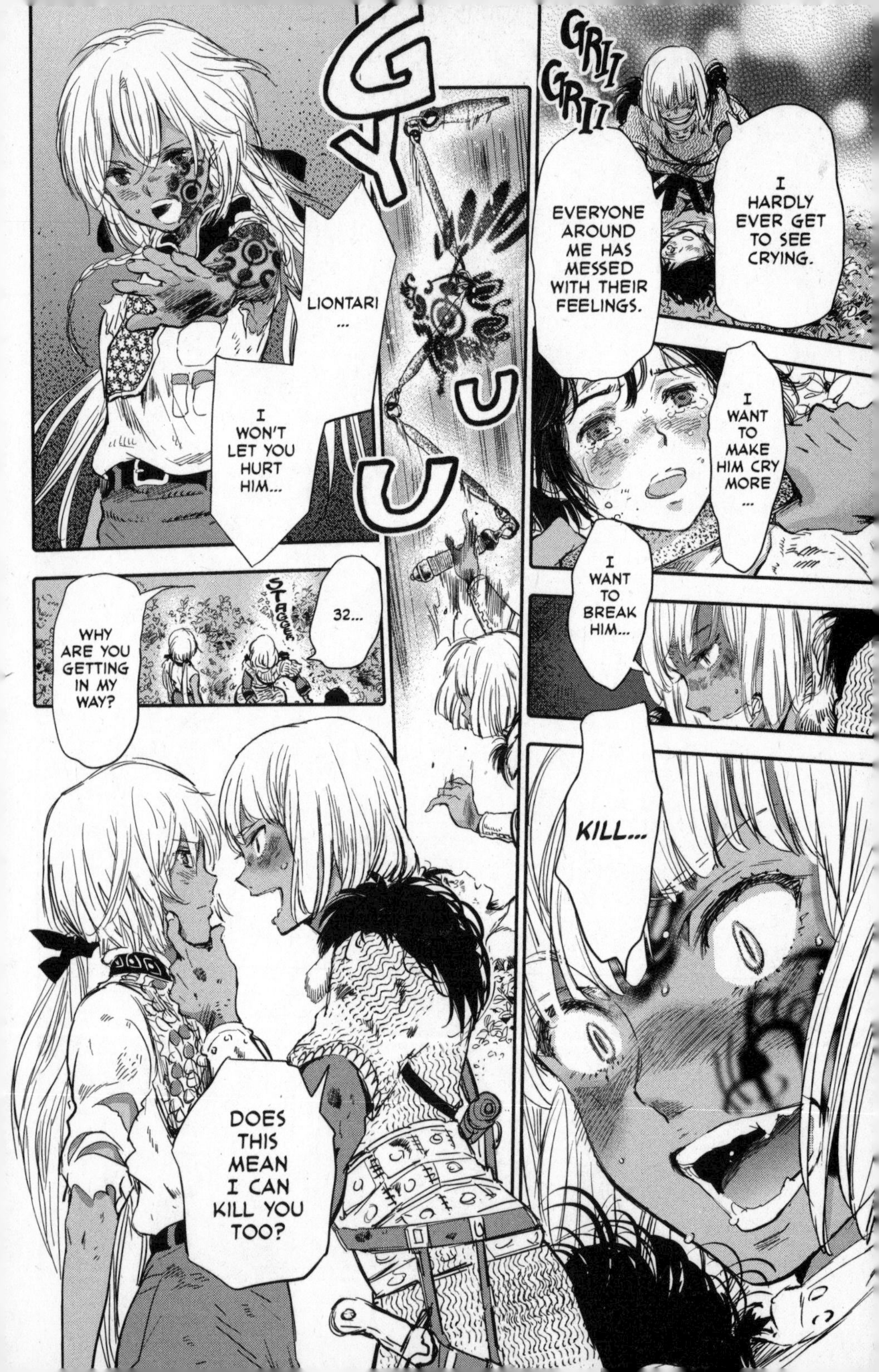
GRII GRII
I HARDLY EVER GET TO SEE CRYING.
EVERYONE AROUND ME HAS MESSED WITH THEIR FEELINGS.
I WANT TO MAKE HIM CRY MORE ...
I WANT TO BREAK HIM...
KILL...
GYUU
LIONTARI ...
I WON'T LET YOU HURT HIM...
32...
STAGGER
WHY ARE YOU GETTING IN MY WAY?
DOES THIS MEAN I CAN KILL YOU TOO?

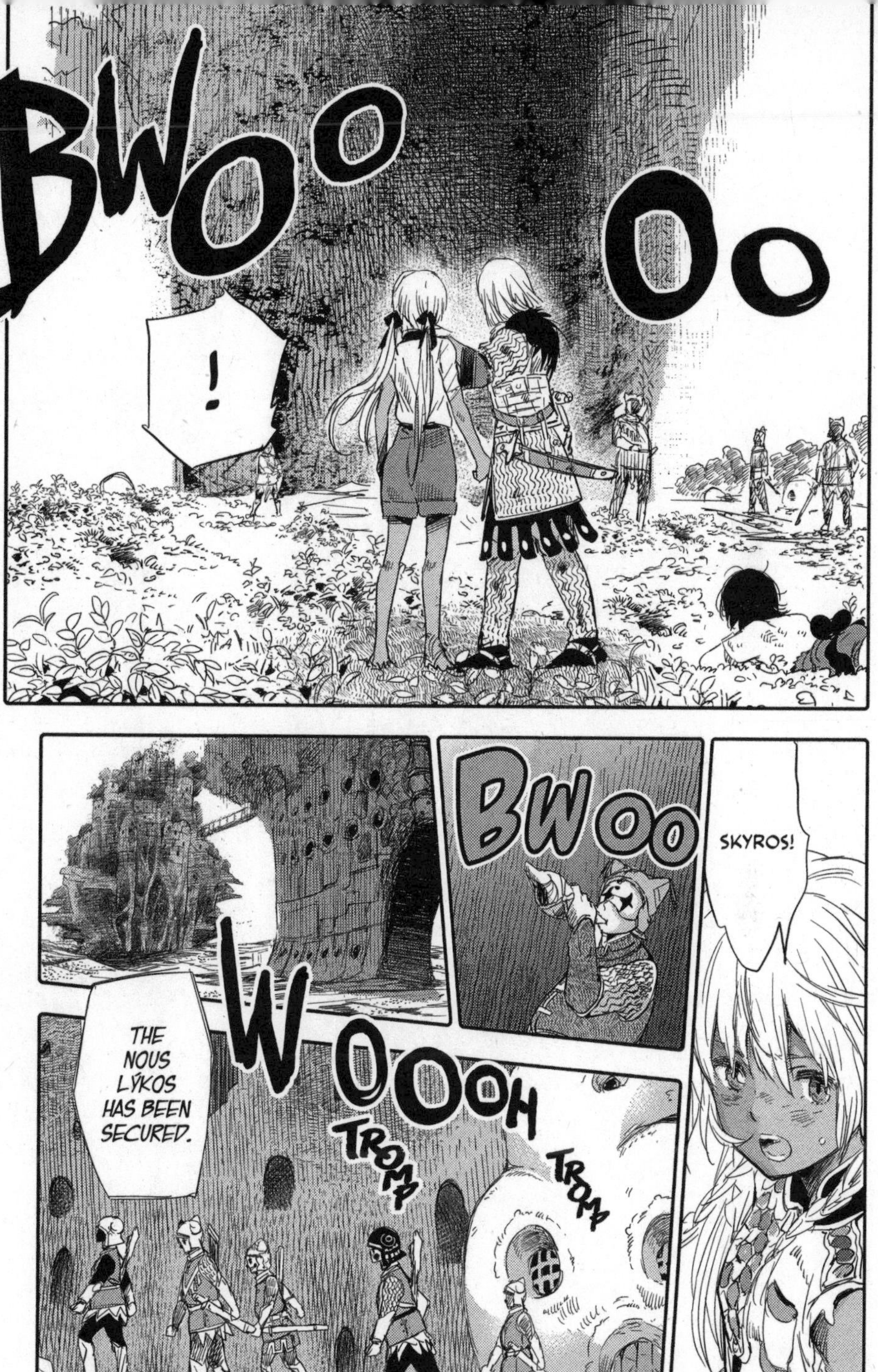
BWOOOO
!
SKYROS!
BWOO
WOOOOH
THE NOUS LÝKOS HAS BEEN SECURED.
TROMP
TROMP

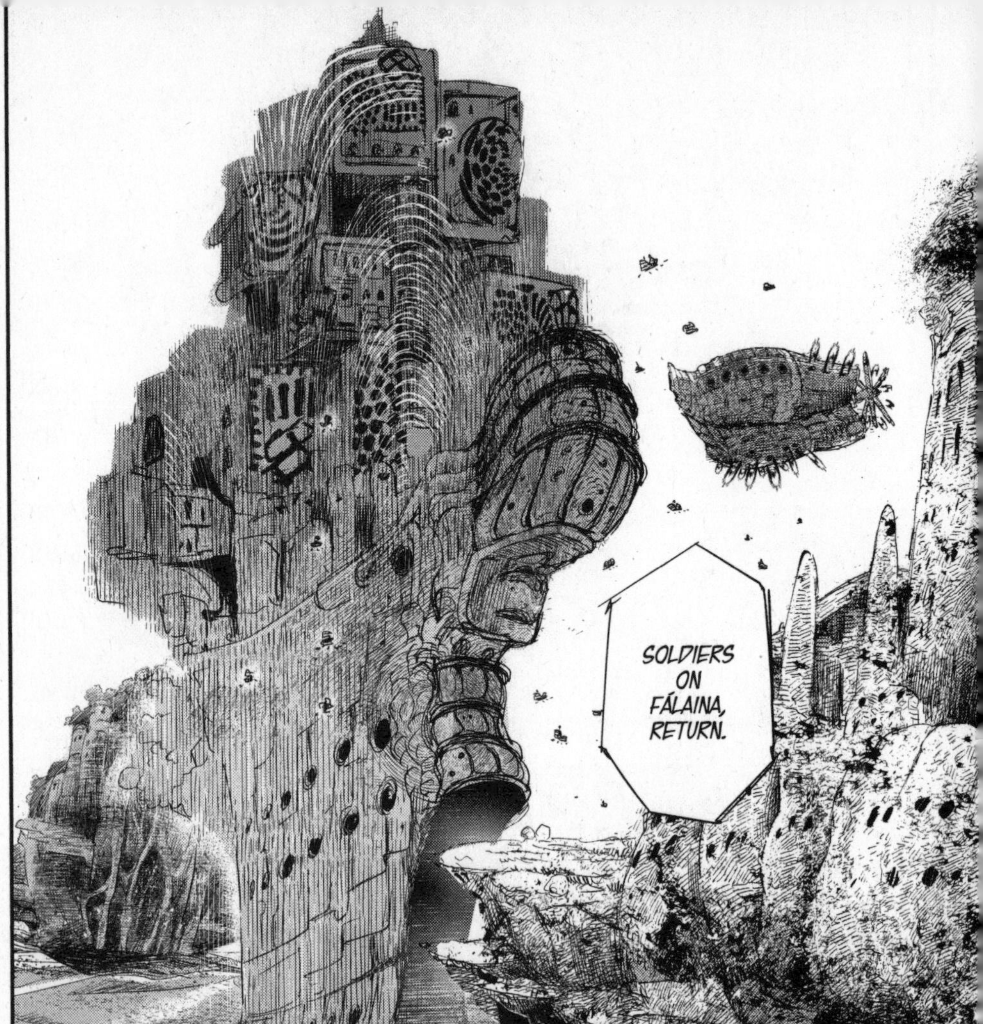
SOLDIERS ON FÁLAINA, RETURN.
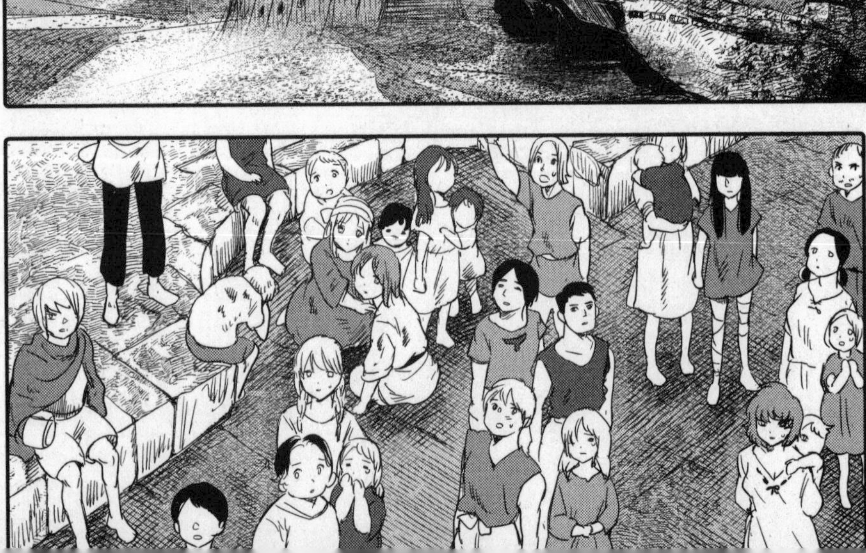

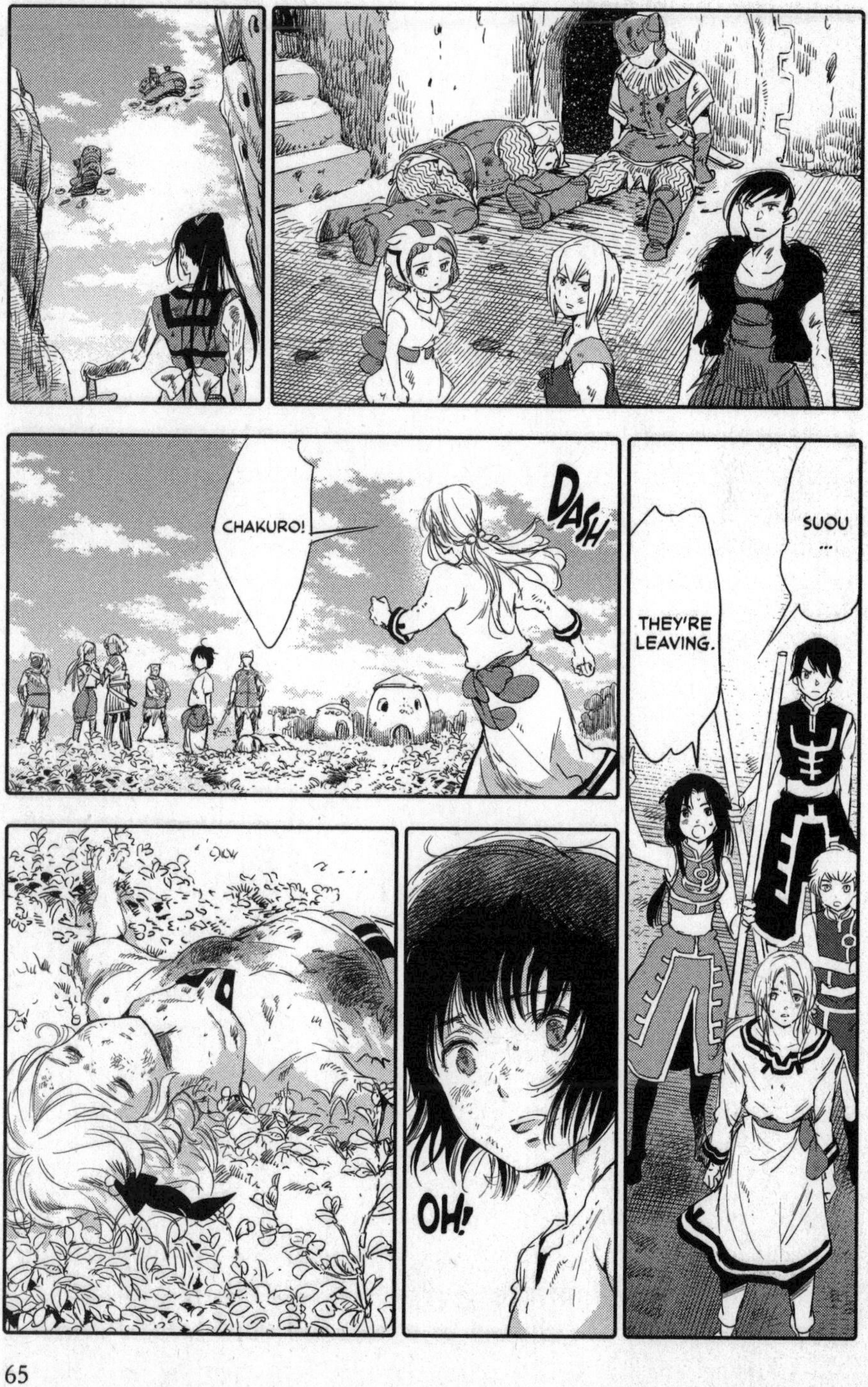
SUOU ...
THEY'RE LEAVING.
CHAKURO!
DASH
OH!

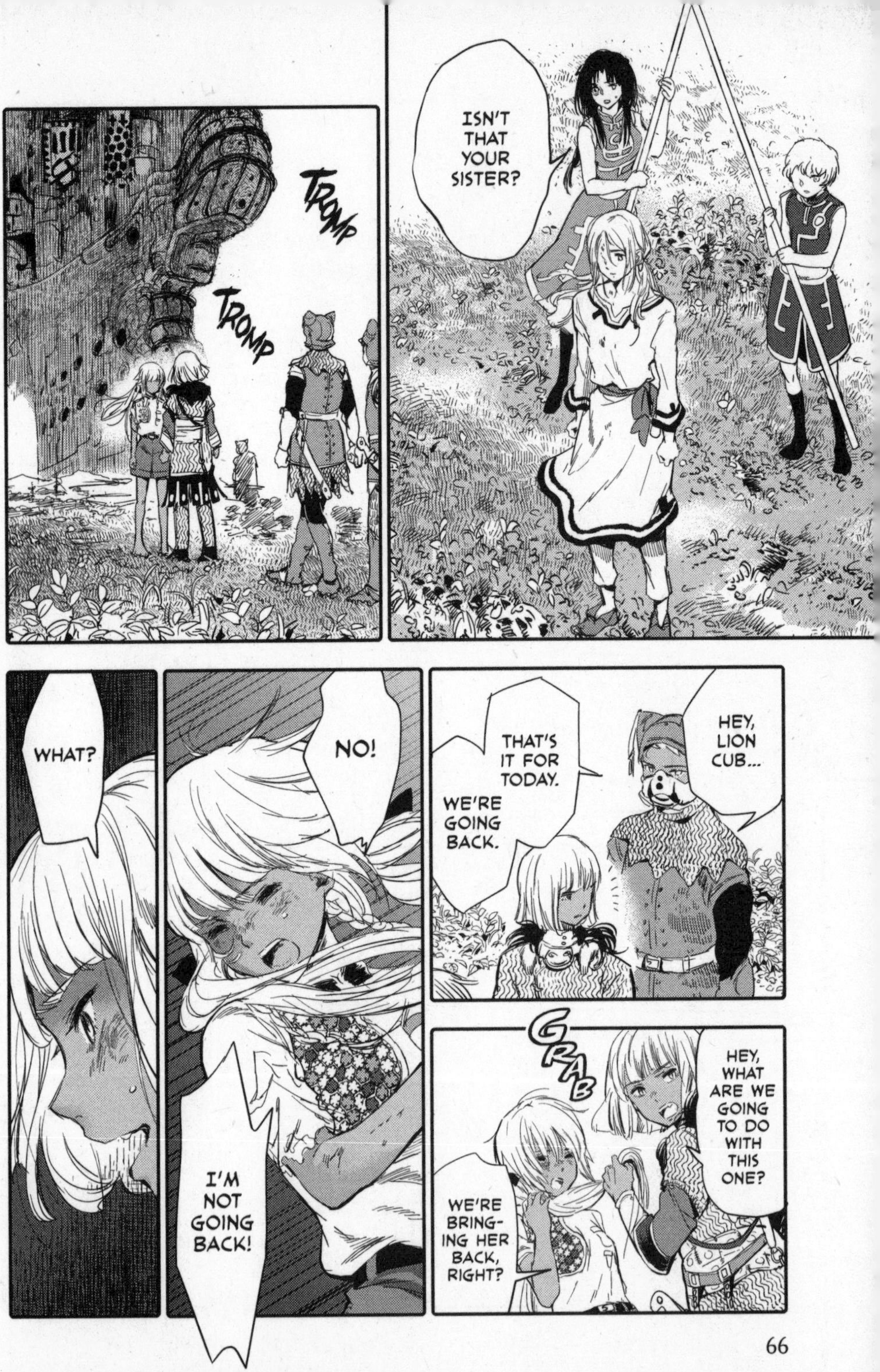
ISN'T THAT YOUR SISTER?
TROMP
TROMP
HEY, LION CUB...
THAT'S IT FOR TODAY. WE'RE GOING BACK.
GRAB
HEY, WHAT ARE WE GOING TO DO WITH THIS ONE?
WE'RE BRINGING HER BACK, RIGHT?
NO!
I'M NOT GOING BACK!
WHAT?

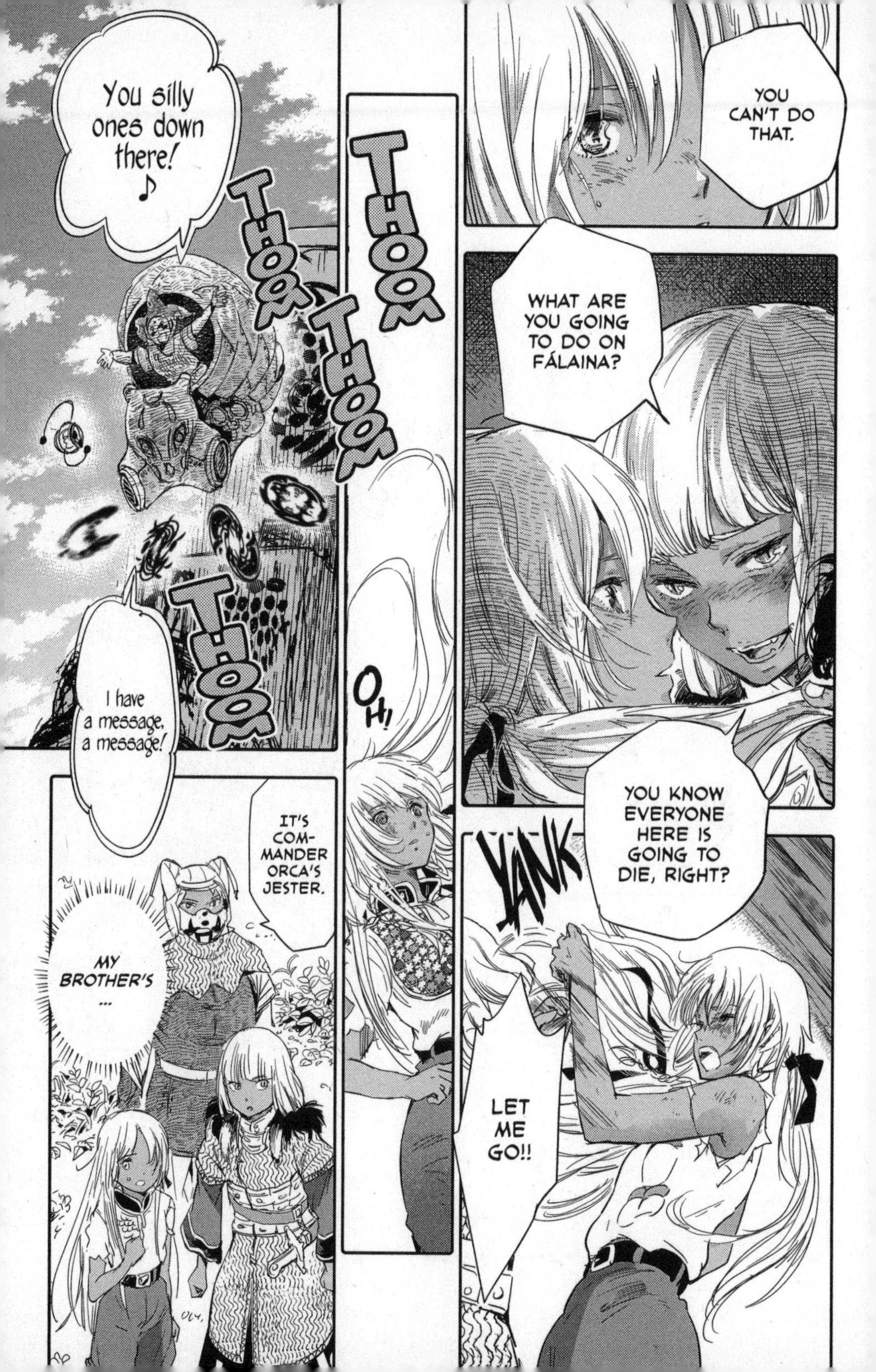
YOU CAN'T DO THAT.
WHAT ARE YOU GOING TO DO ON FÁLAINA?
YOU KNOW EVERYONE HERE IS GOING TO DIE, RIGHT?
YANK
LET ME GO!!
THOOM
THOOM
OH!
You silly ones down there! ♪
THOOM
THOOM
I have a message, a message!
IT'S COMMANDER ORCA'S JESTER.
MY BROTHER'S...

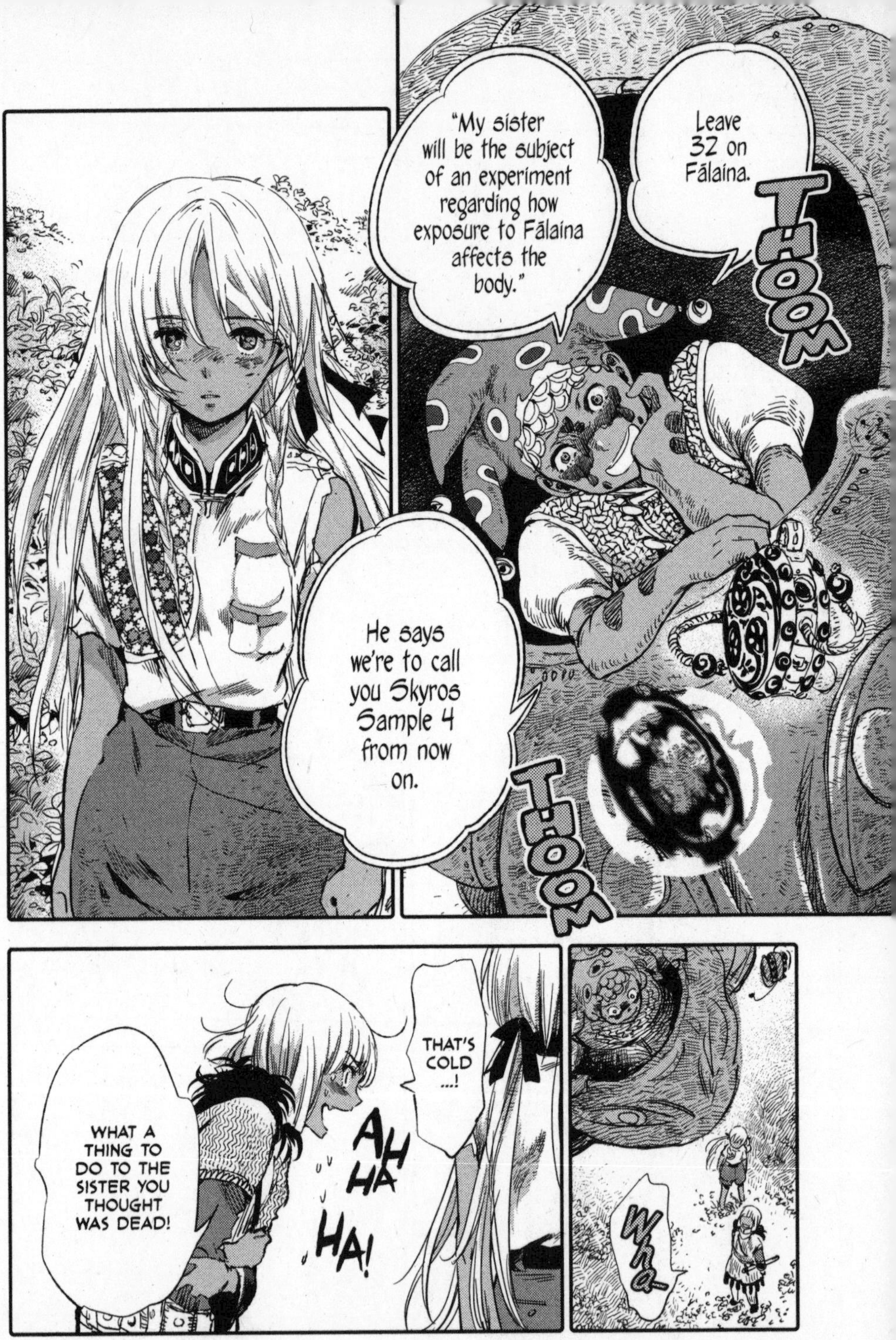
Leave 32 on Fālaina.
"My sister will be the subject of an experiment regarding how exposure to Fālaina affects the body."
THOOM
He says we're to call you Skyros Sample 4 from now on.
THOOM
Wha–
THAT'S COLD ...!
WHAT A THING TO DO TO THE SISTER YOU THOUGHT WAS DEAD!
AH HA HA!

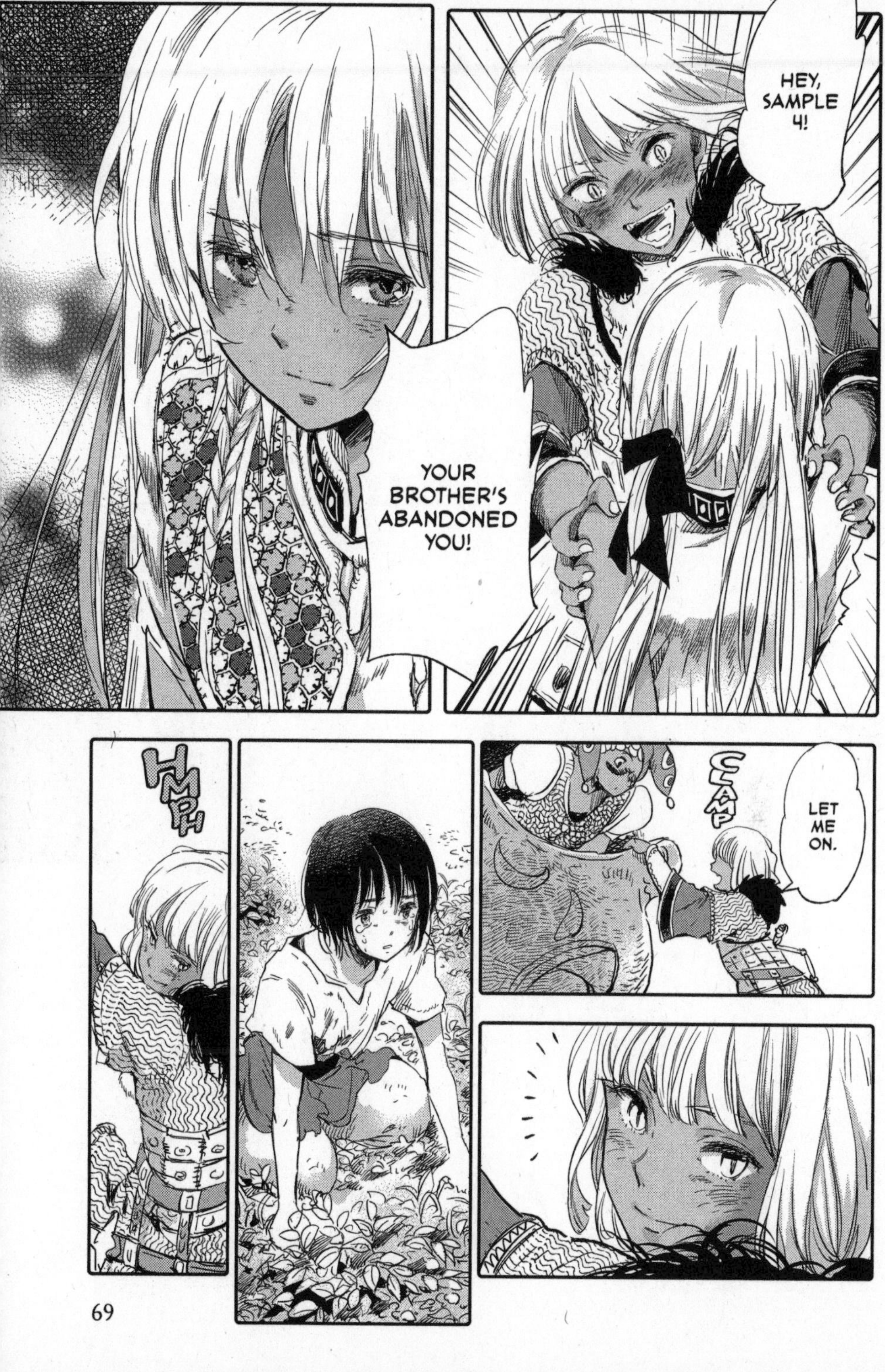
HEY, SAMPLE 4!
YOUR BROTHER'S ABANDONED YOU!
CLAMP
LET ME ON.
HMPH

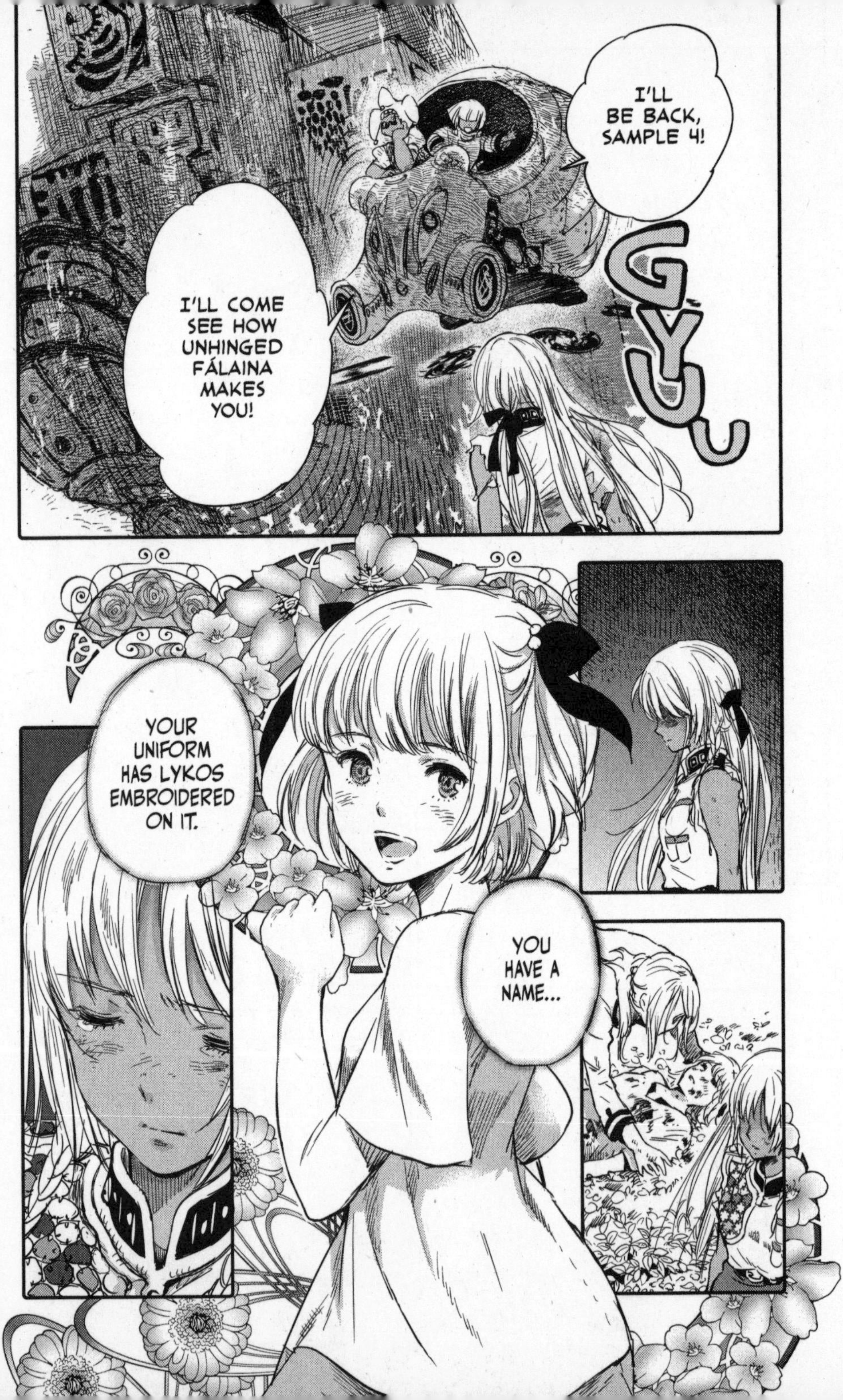
I'LL BE BACK, SAMPLE 4!
GYUU
I'LL COME SEE HOW UNHINGED FÁLAINA MAKES YOU!
YOUR UNIFORM HAS LYKOS EMBROIDERED ON IT.
YOU HAVE A NAME...

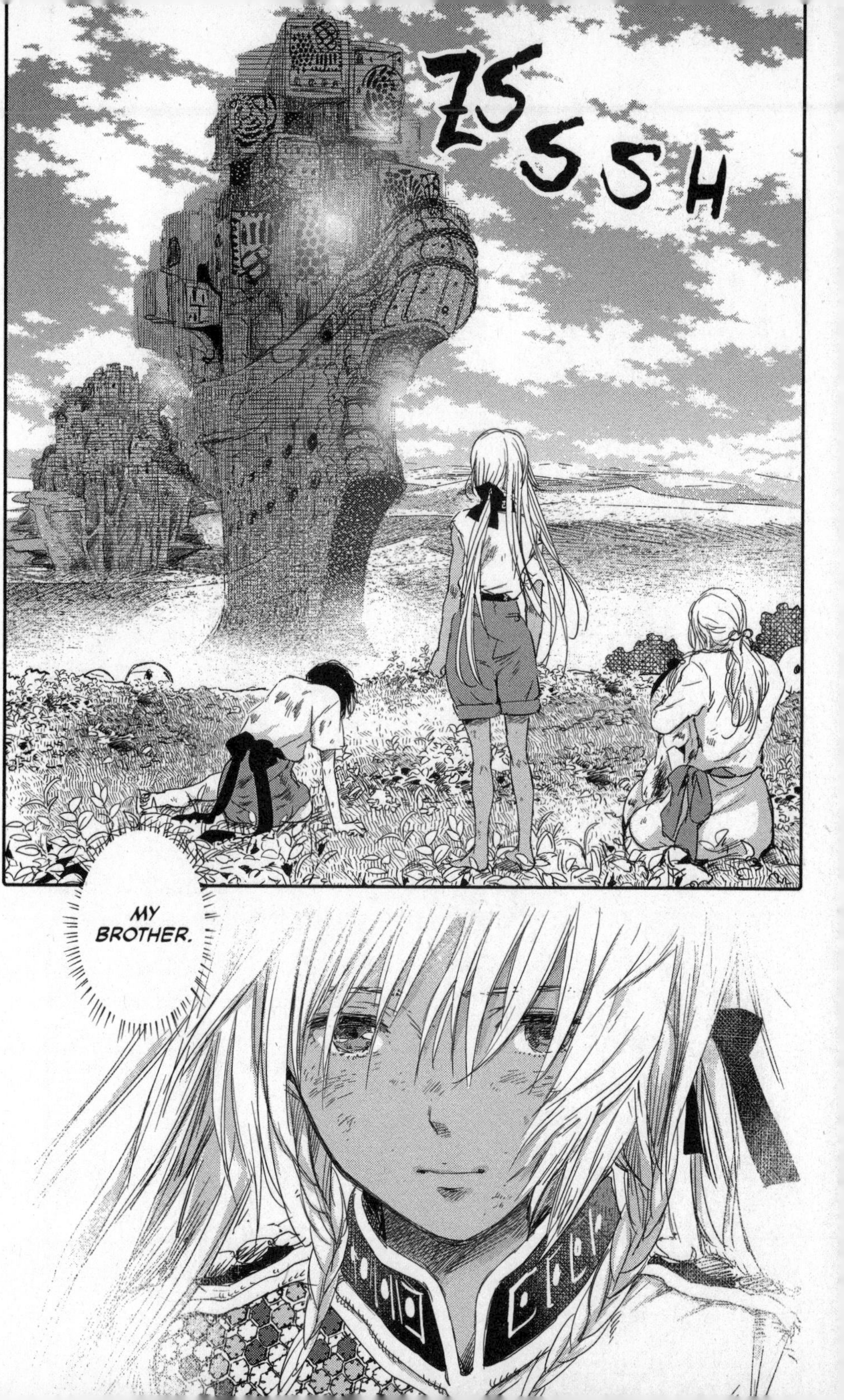
ZSSSH
MY BROTHER.

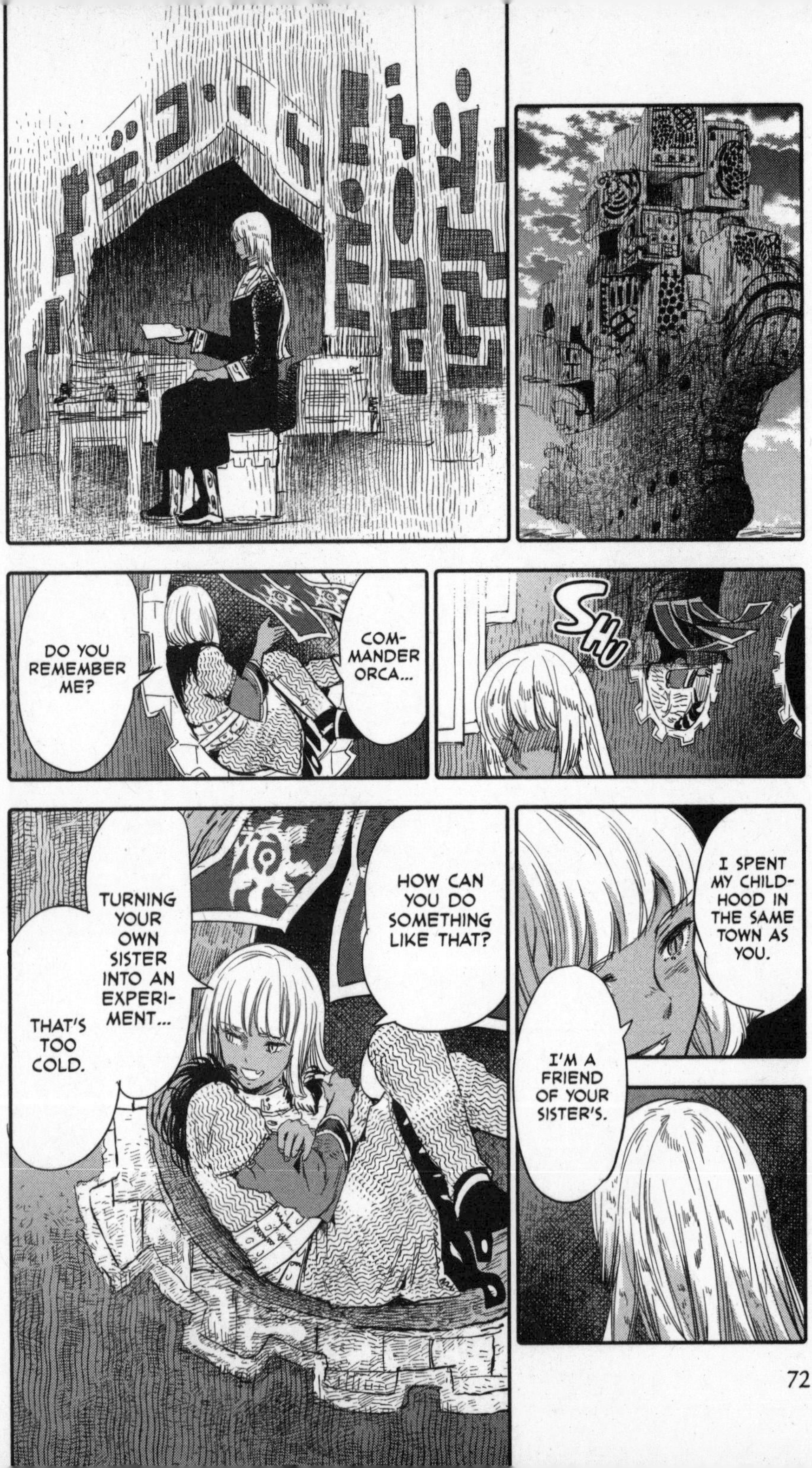
SHU
COM-MANDER ORCA...
DO YOU REMEMBER ME?
I SPENT MY CHILD-HOOD IN THE SAME TOWN AS YOU.
I'M A FRIEND OF YOUR SISTER'S.
HOW CAN YOU DO SOMETHING LIKE THAT?
TURNING YOUR OWN SISTER INTO AN EXPERI-MENT...
THAT'S TOO COLD.

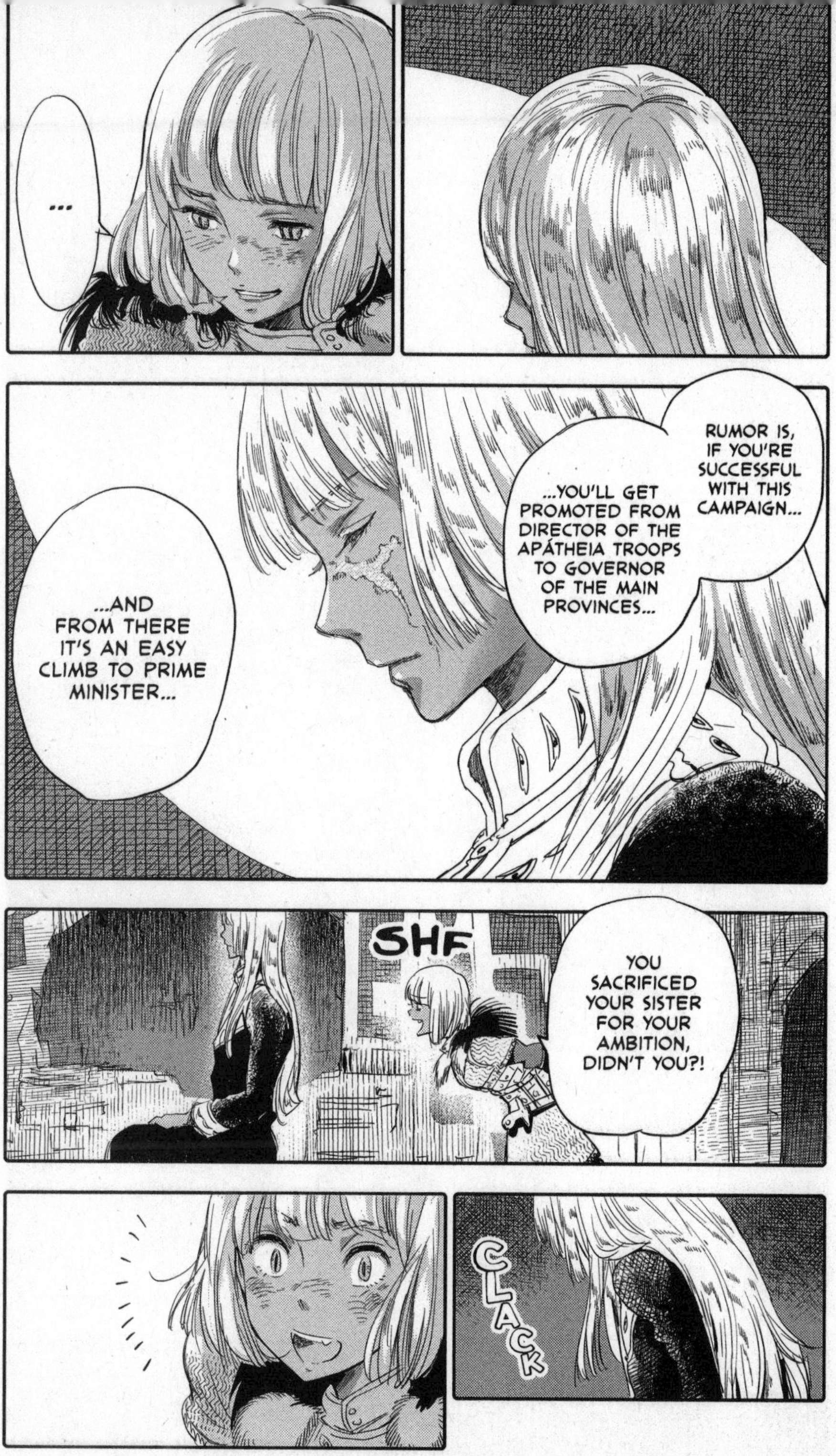
...
RUMOR IS, IF YOU'RE SUCCESSFUL WITH THIS CAMPAIGN...
...YOU'LL GET PROMOTED FROM DIRECTOR OF THE APÁTHEIA TROOPS TO GOVERNOR OF THE MAIN PROVINCES...
...AND FROM THERE IT'S AN EASY CLIMB TO PRIME MINISTER...
YOU SACRIFICED YOUR SISTER FOR YOUR AMBITION, DIDN'T YOU?!
SHF
CLACK

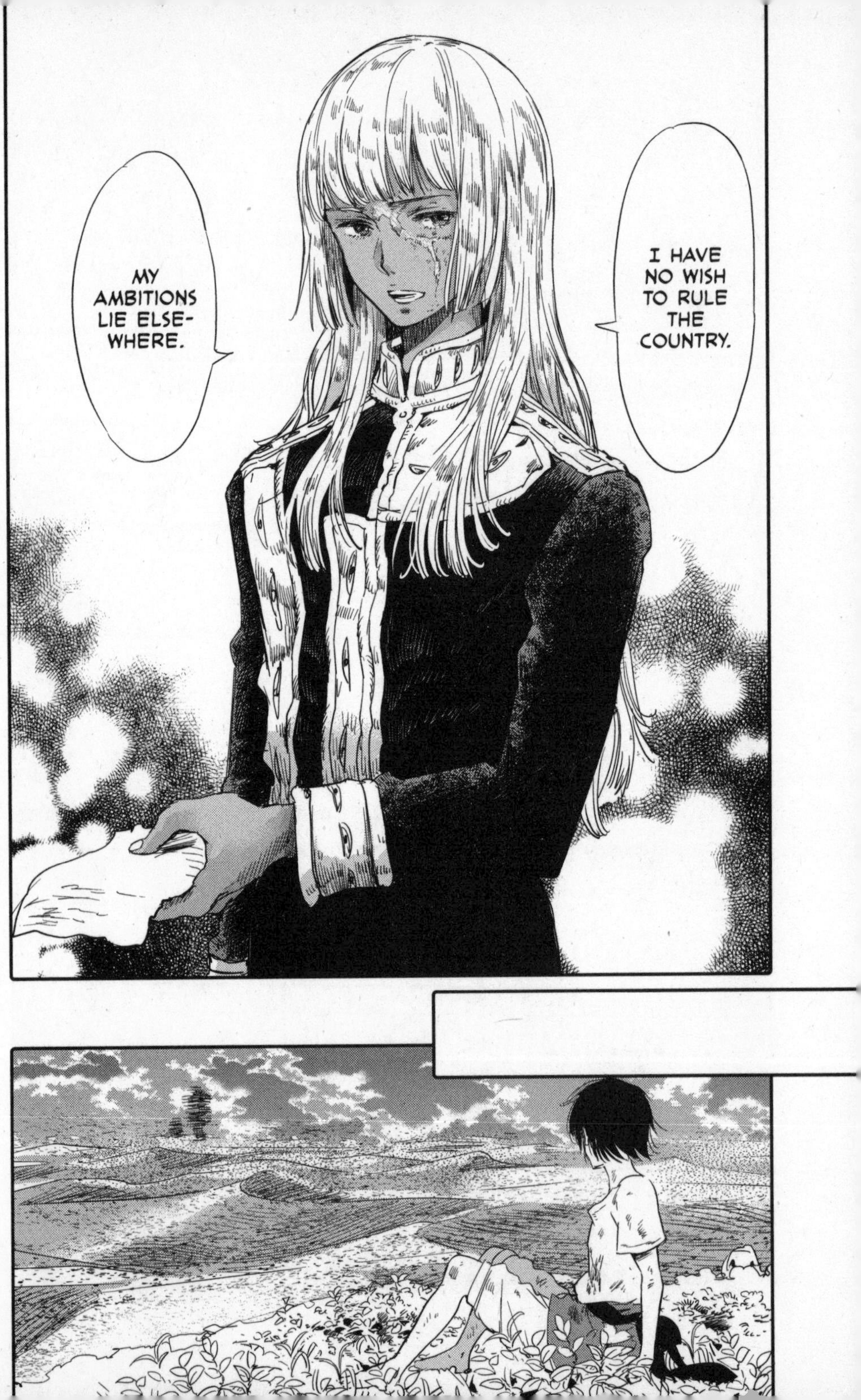
I HAVE NO WISH TO RULE THE COUNTRY.
MY AMBITIONS LIE ELSE-WHERE.

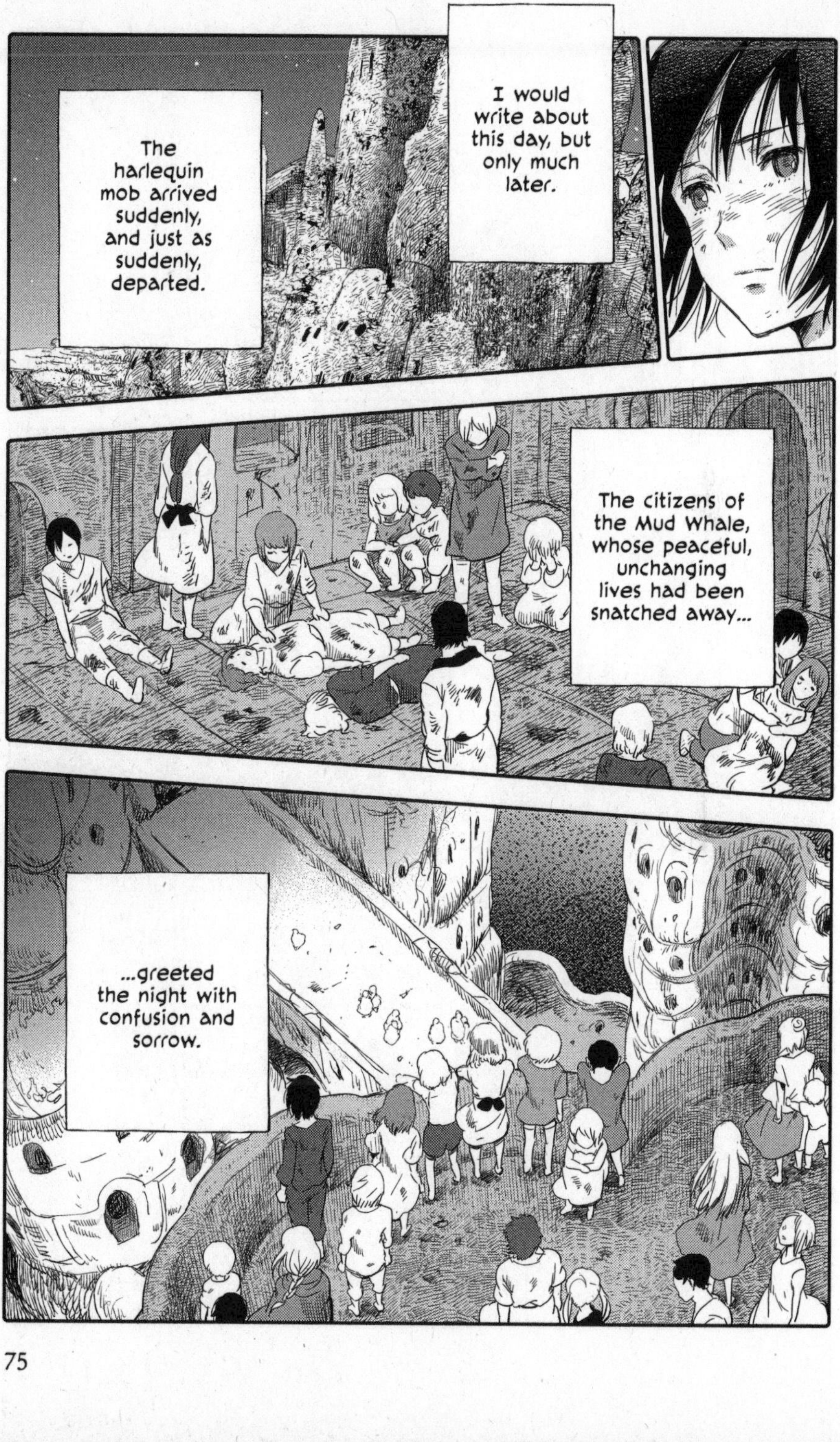
I would write about this day, but only much later.
The harlequin mob arrived suddenly, and just as suddenly, departed.
The citizens of the Mud Whale, whose peaceful, unchanging lives had been snatched away...
...greeted the night with confusion and sorrow.

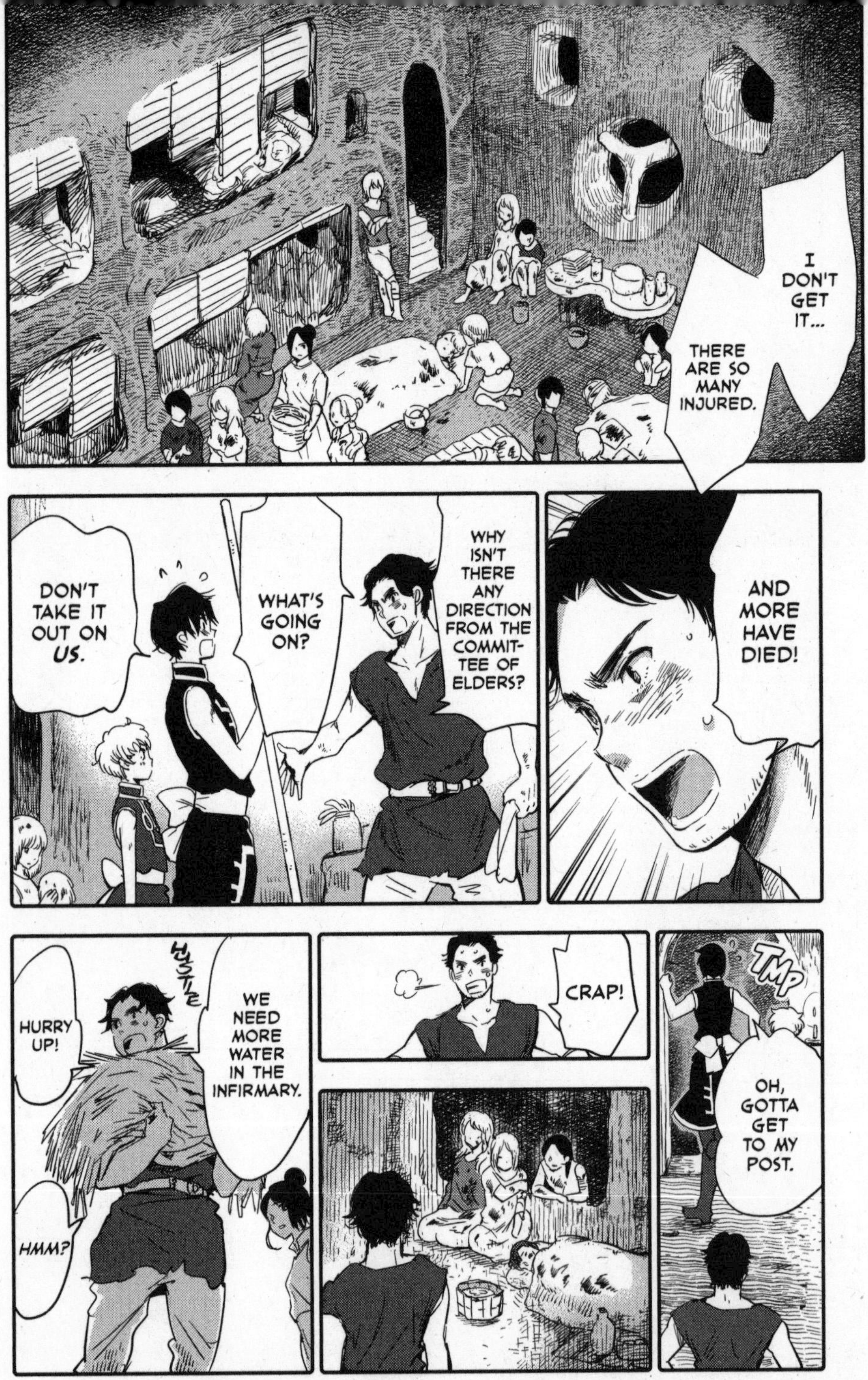

I DON'T GET IT...
THERE ARE SO MANY INJURED.
AND MORE HAVE DIED!
WHY ISN'T THERE ANY DIRECTION FROM THE COMMITTEE OF ELDERS?
WHAT'S GOING ON?
DON'T TAKE IT OUT ON US.
TMP
OH, GOTTA GET TO MY POST.
CRAP!
HUSTLE
WE NEED MORE WATER IN THE INFIRMARY.
HURRY UP!
HMM?

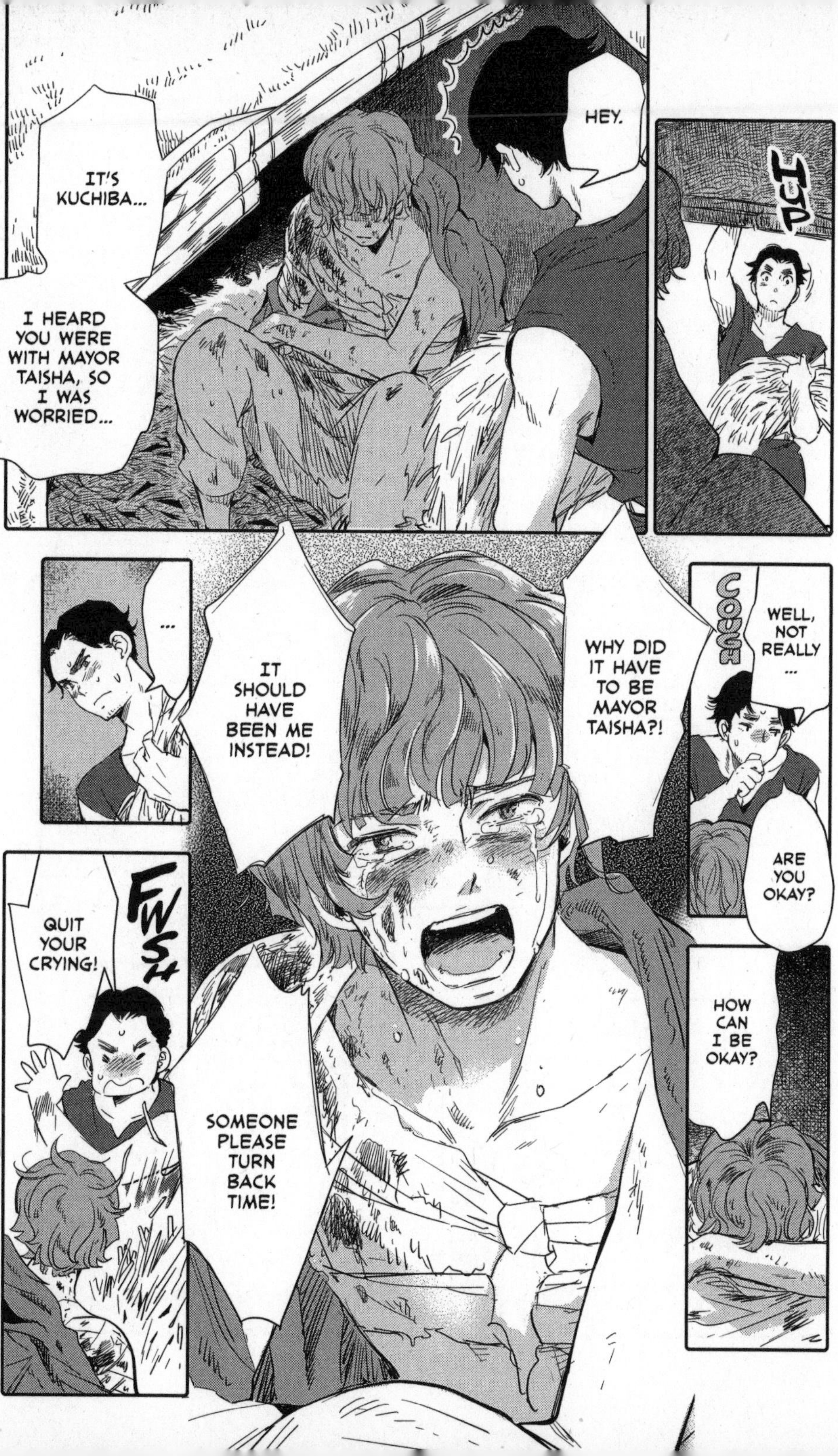
HUP
HEY.
IT'S KUCHIBA...
I HEARD YOU WERE WITH MAYOR TAISHA, SO I WAS WORRIED...
COUGH
WELL, NOT REALLY...
ARE YOU OKAY?
HOW CAN I BE OKAY?
WHY DID IT HAVE TO BE MAYOR TAISHA?!
IT SHOULD HAVE BEEN ME INSTEAD!
SOMEONE PLEASE TURN BACK TIME!
...
QUIT YOUR CRYING!
FWSH

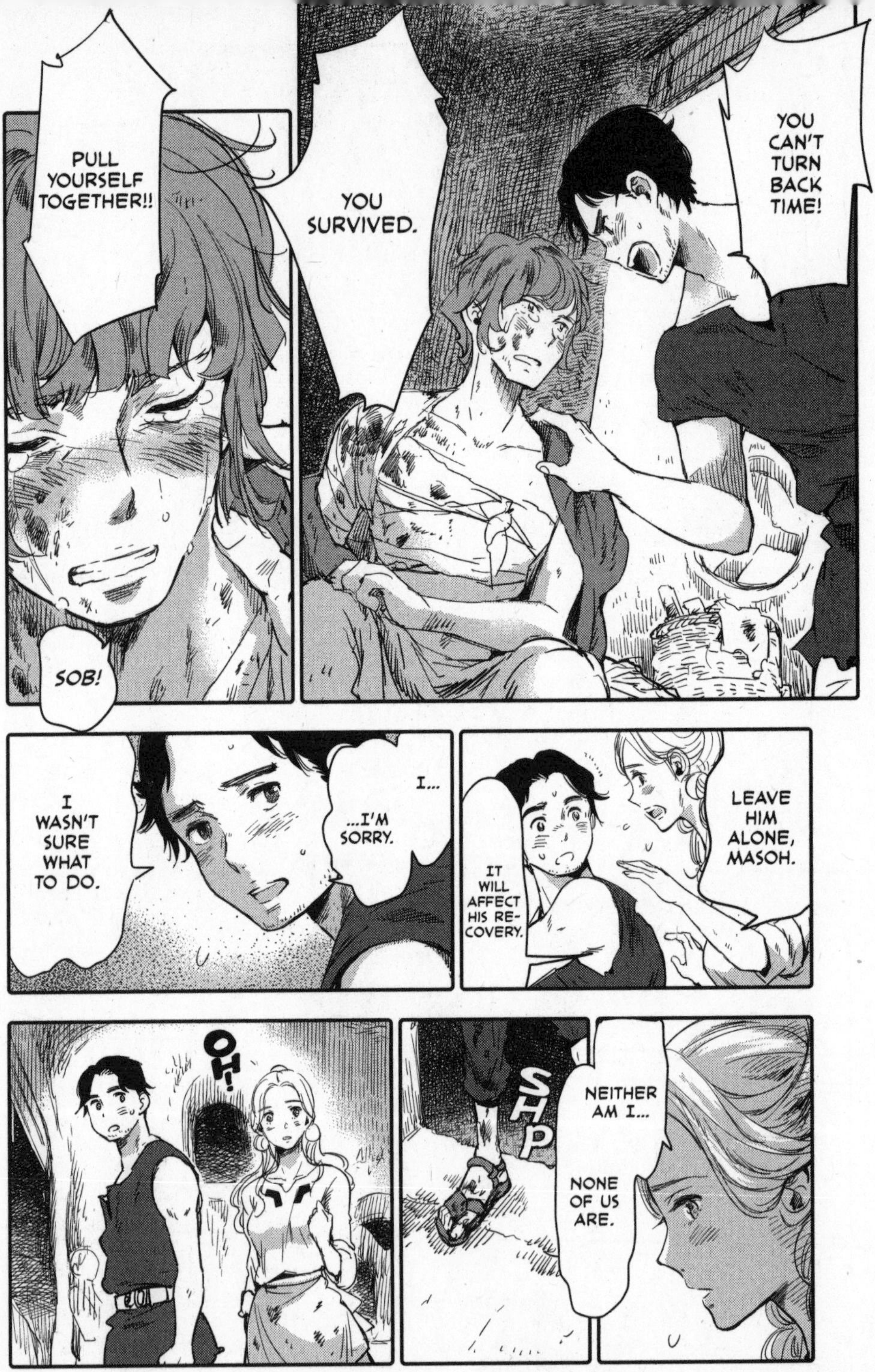
YOU CAN'T TURN BACK TIME!
YOU SURVIVED.
PULL YOURSELF TOGETHER!!
SOB!
LEAVE HIM ALONE, MASOH.
IT WILL AFFECT HIS RE-COVERY.
I...
...I'M SORRY.
I WASN'T SURE WHAT TO DO.
NEITHER AM I...
NONE OF US ARE.
SHP
OH!

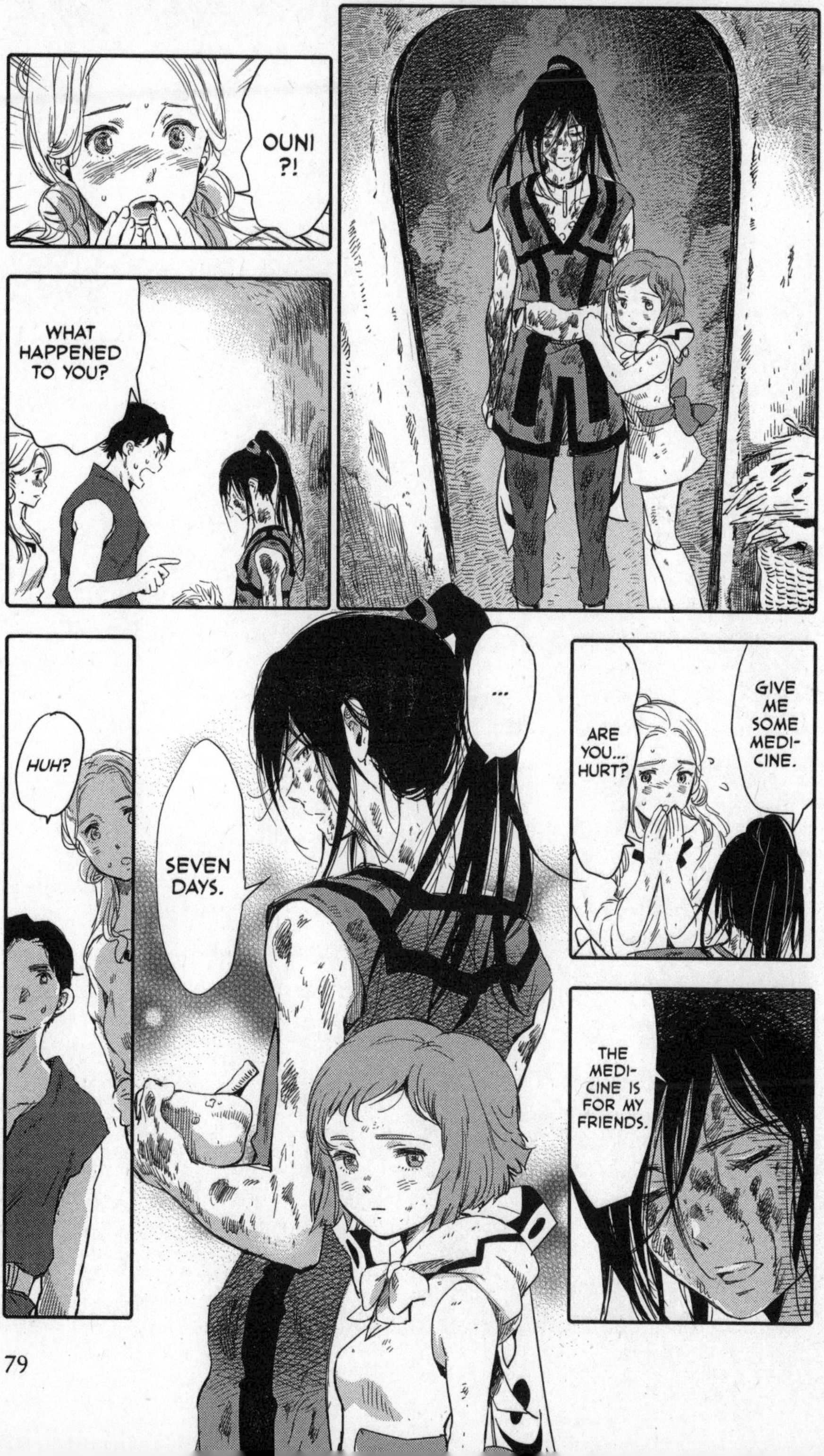
OUNI ?!
WHAT HAPPENED TO YOU?
GIVE ME SOME MEDI-CINE.
ARE YOU... HURT?
THE MEDI-CINE IS FOR MY FRIENDS.
...
SEVEN DAYS.
HUH?

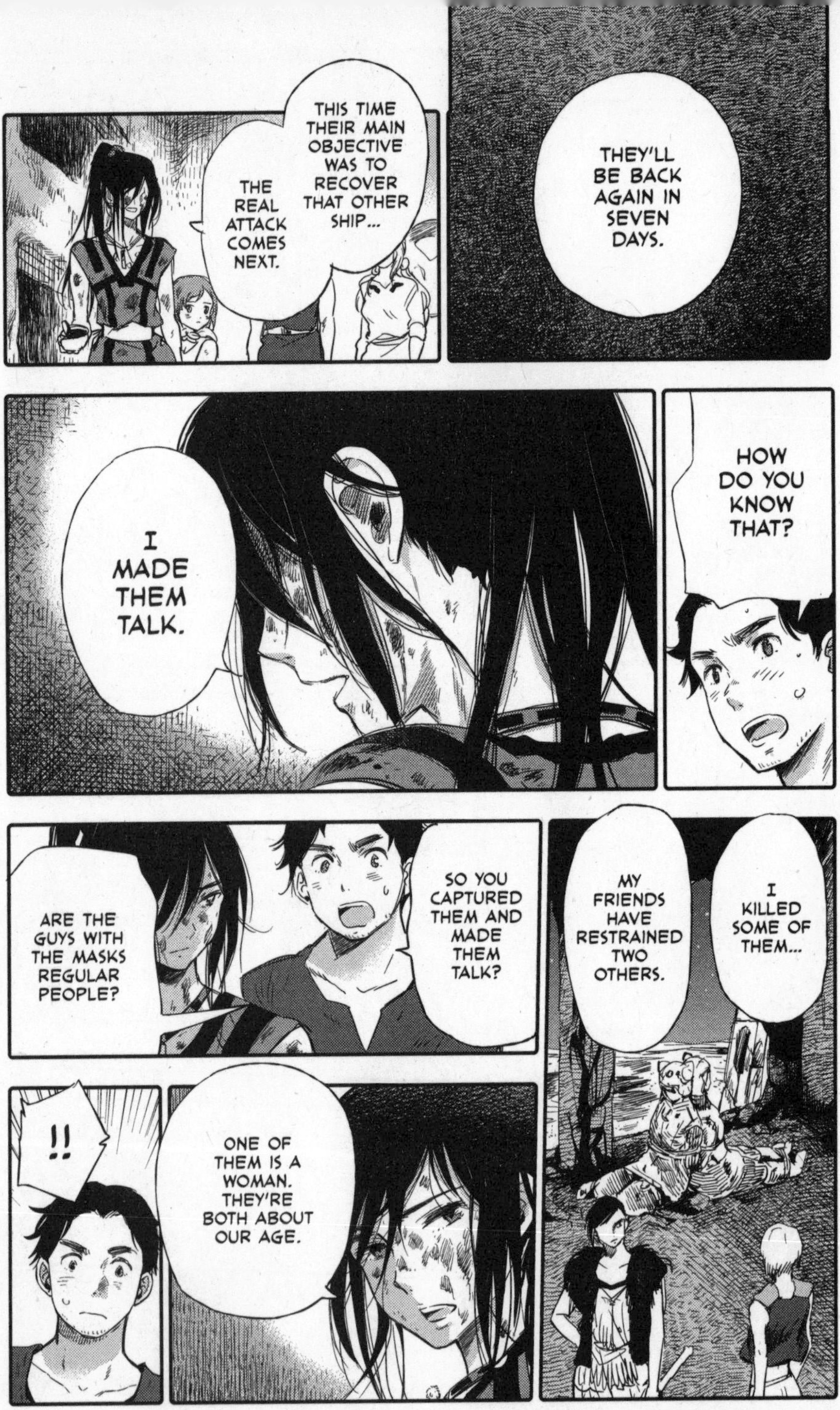
THEY'LL BE BACK AGAIN IN SEVEN DAYS.
THIS TIME THEIR MAIN OBJECTIVE WAS TO RECOVER THAT OTHER SHIP...
THE REAL ATTACK COMES NEXT.
HOW DO YOU KNOW THAT?
I MADE THEM TALK.
I KILLED SOME OF THEM...
MY FRIENDS HAVE RESTRAINED TWO OTHERS.
SO YOU CAPTURED THEM AND MADE THEM TALK?
ARE THE GUYS WITH THE MASKS REGULAR PEOPLE?
ONE OF THEM IS A WOMAN. THEY'RE BOTH ABOUT OUR AGE.
!!

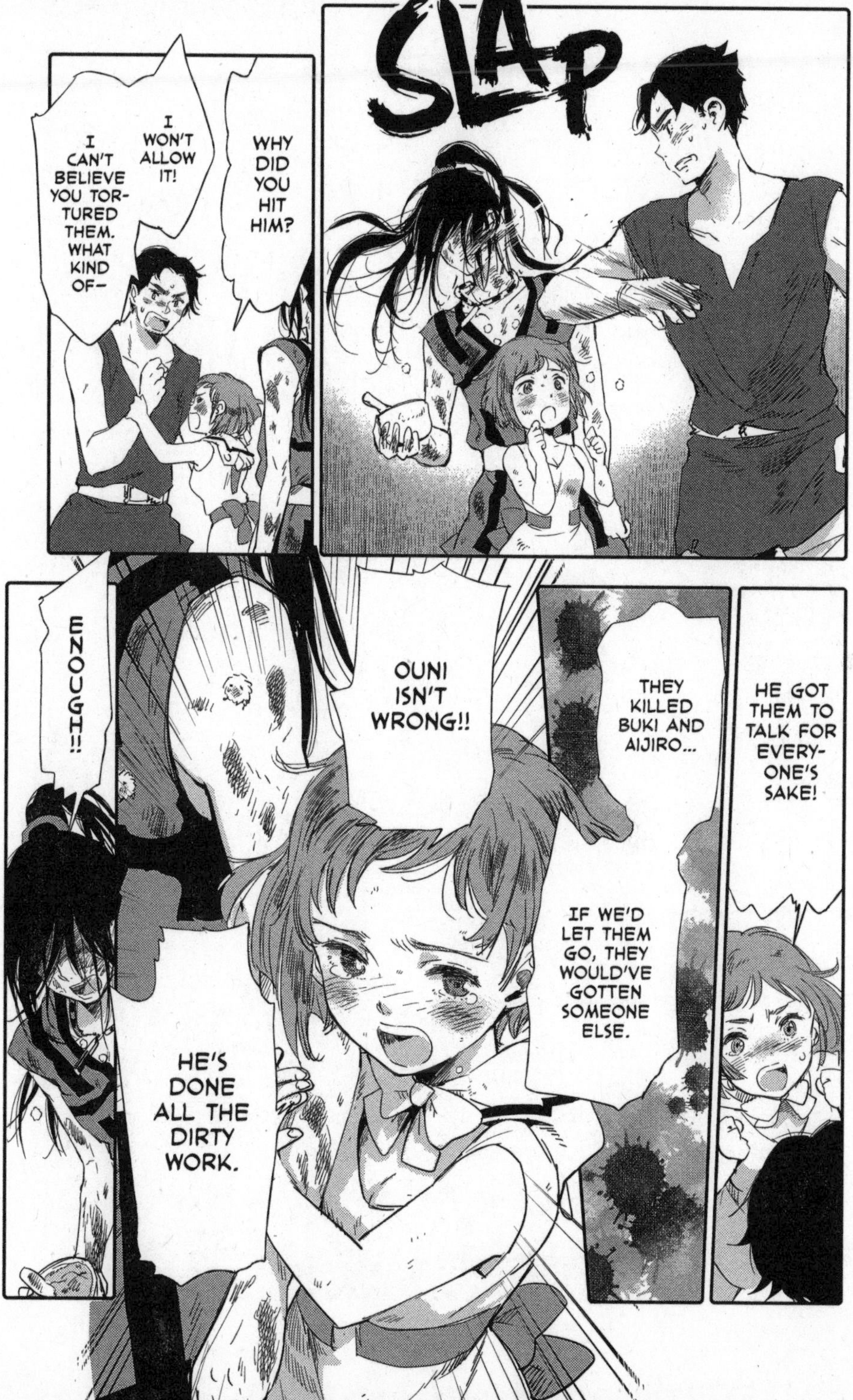
SLAP
WHY DID YOU HIT HIM?
I WON'T ALLOW IT!
I CAN'T BELIEVE YOU TORTURED THEM. WHAT KIND OF—
HE GOT THEM TO TALK FOR EVERYONE'S SAKE!
THEY KILLED BUKI AND AIJIRO...
IF WE'D LET THEM GO, THEY WOULD'VE GOTTEN SOMEONE ELSE.
OUNI ISN'T WRONG!!
HE'S DONE ALL THE DIRTY WORK.
ENOUGH!!

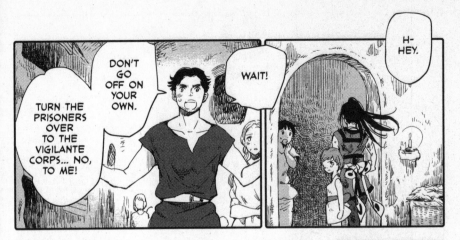

H- HEY.
WAIT!
DON'T GO OFF ON YOUR OWN.
TURN THE PRISONERS OVER TO THE VIGILANTE CORPS... NO, TO ME!
I ONLY TRUST MY FRIENDS.

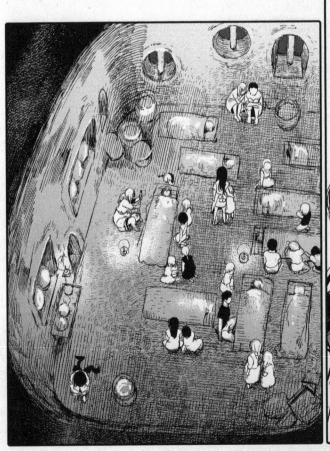

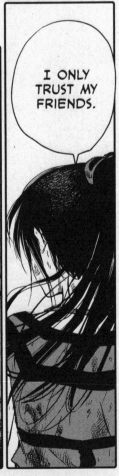

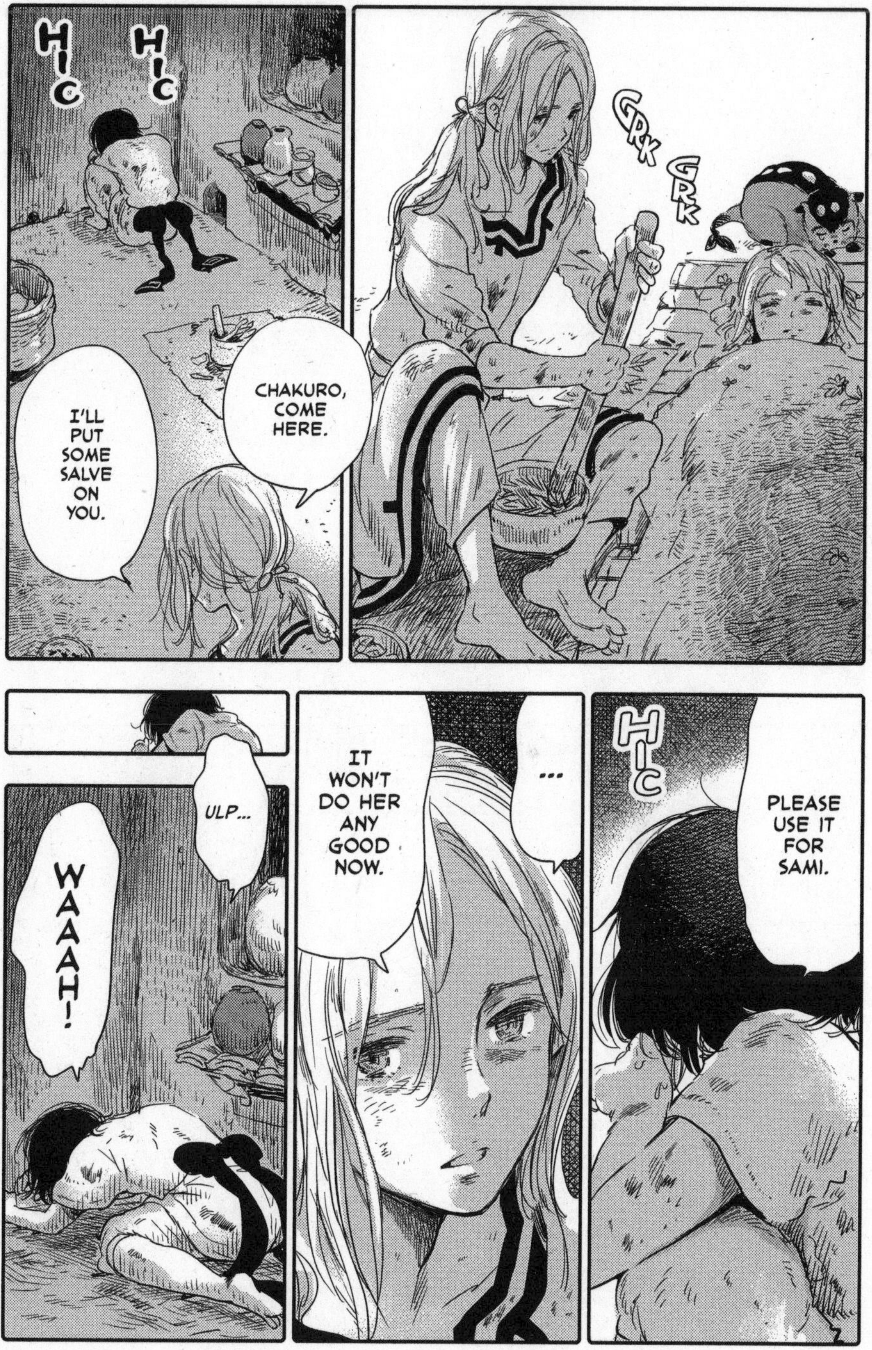
GRK GRK
HIC HIC
CHAKURO, COME HERE.
I'LL PUT SOME SALVE ON YOU.
HIC
PLEASE USE IT FOR SAMI.
...
IT WON'T DO HER ANY GOOD NOW.
ULP...
WAAAH!

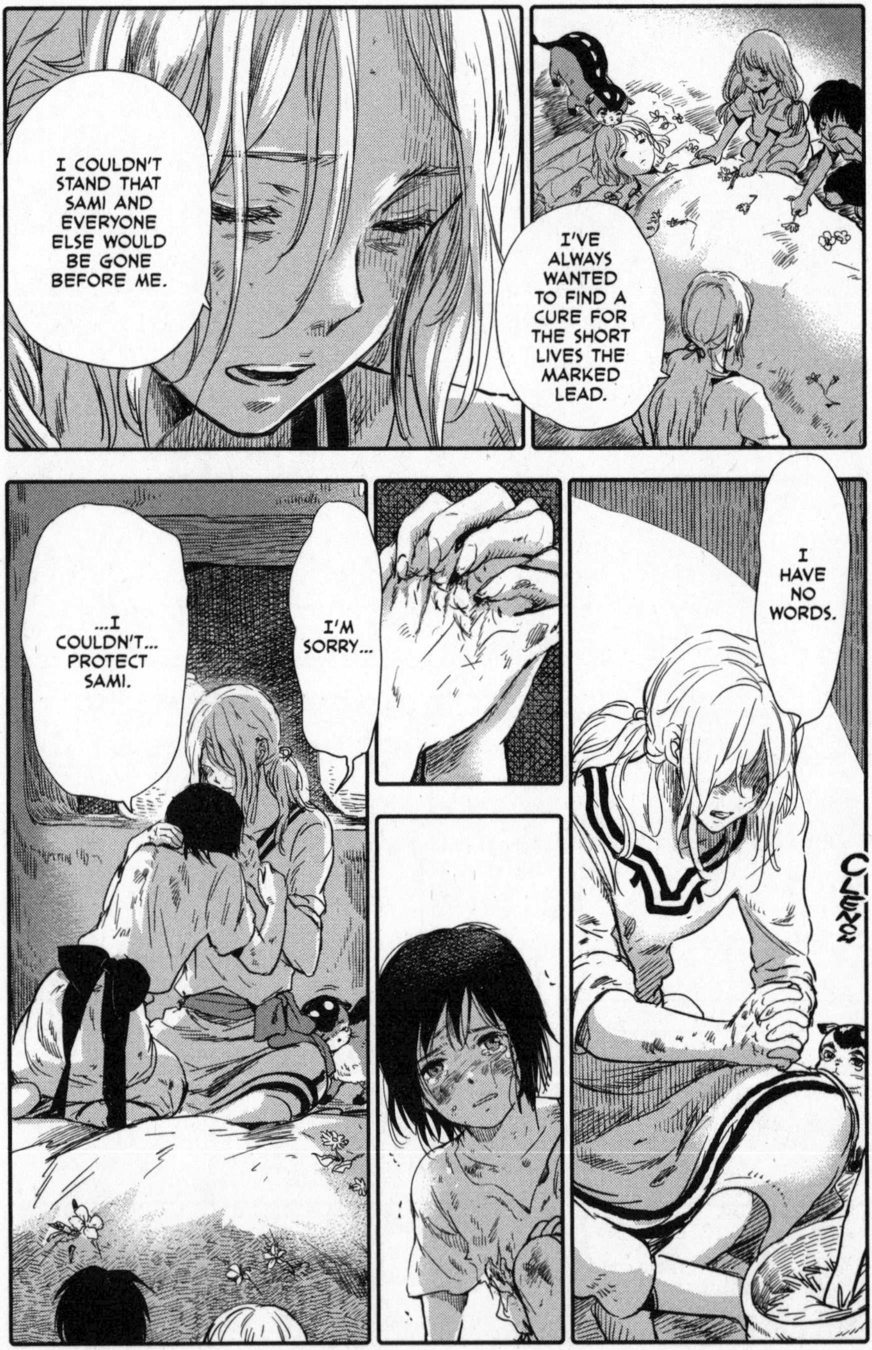
I'VE ALWAYS WANTED TO FIND A CURE FOR THE SHORT LIVES THE MARKED LEAD.
I COULDN'T STAND THAT SAMI AND EVERYONE ELSE WOULD BE GONE BEFORE ME.
I HAVE NO WORDS.
CLENCH
I'M SORRY...
...I COULDN'T... PROTECT SAMI.

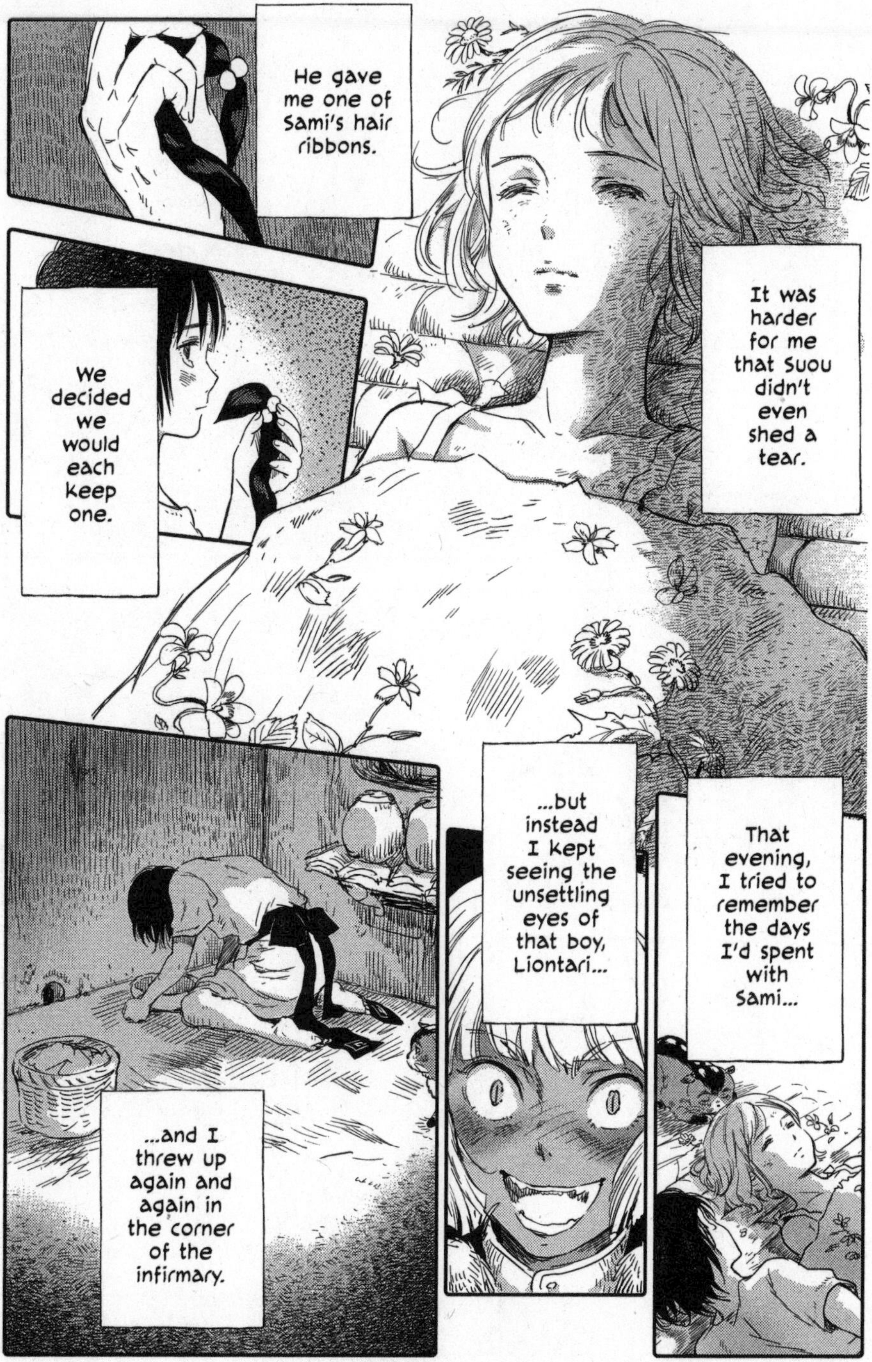
It was harder for me that Suou didn't even shed a tear.
He gave me one of Sami's hair ribbons.
We decided we would each keep one.
That evening, I tried to remember the days I'd spent with Sami...
...but instead I kept seeing the unsettling eyes of that boy, Liontari...
...and I threw up again and again in the corner of the infirmary.

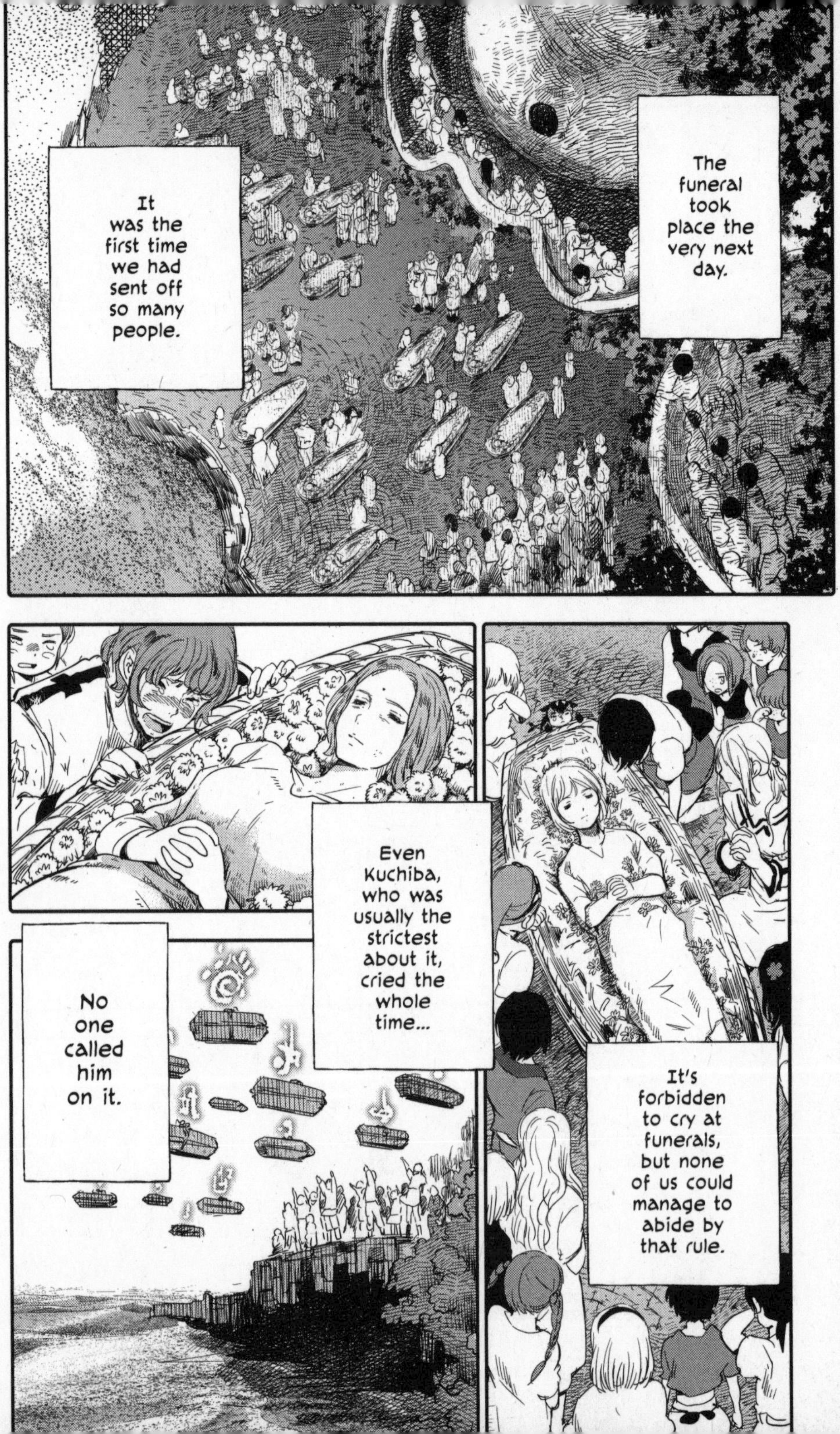
The funeral took place the very next day.
It was the first time we had sent off so many people.
It's forbidden to cry at funerals, but none of us could manage to abide by that rule.
Even Kuchiba, who was usually the strictest about it, cried the whole time...
No one called him on it.

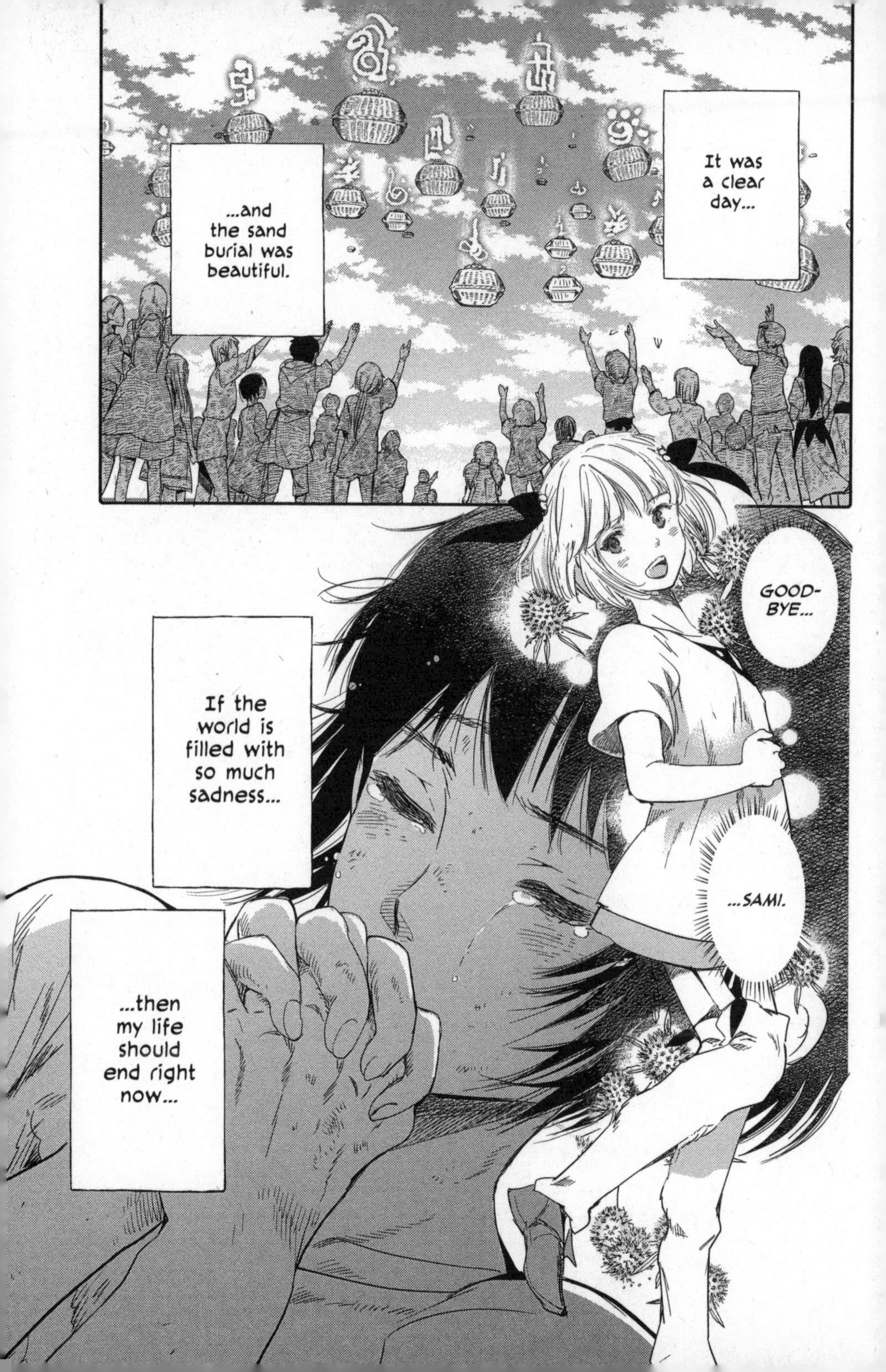
It was a clear day...
...and the sand burial was beautiful.
GOOD-BYE...
...SAMI.
If the world is filled with so much sadness...
...then my life should end right now...

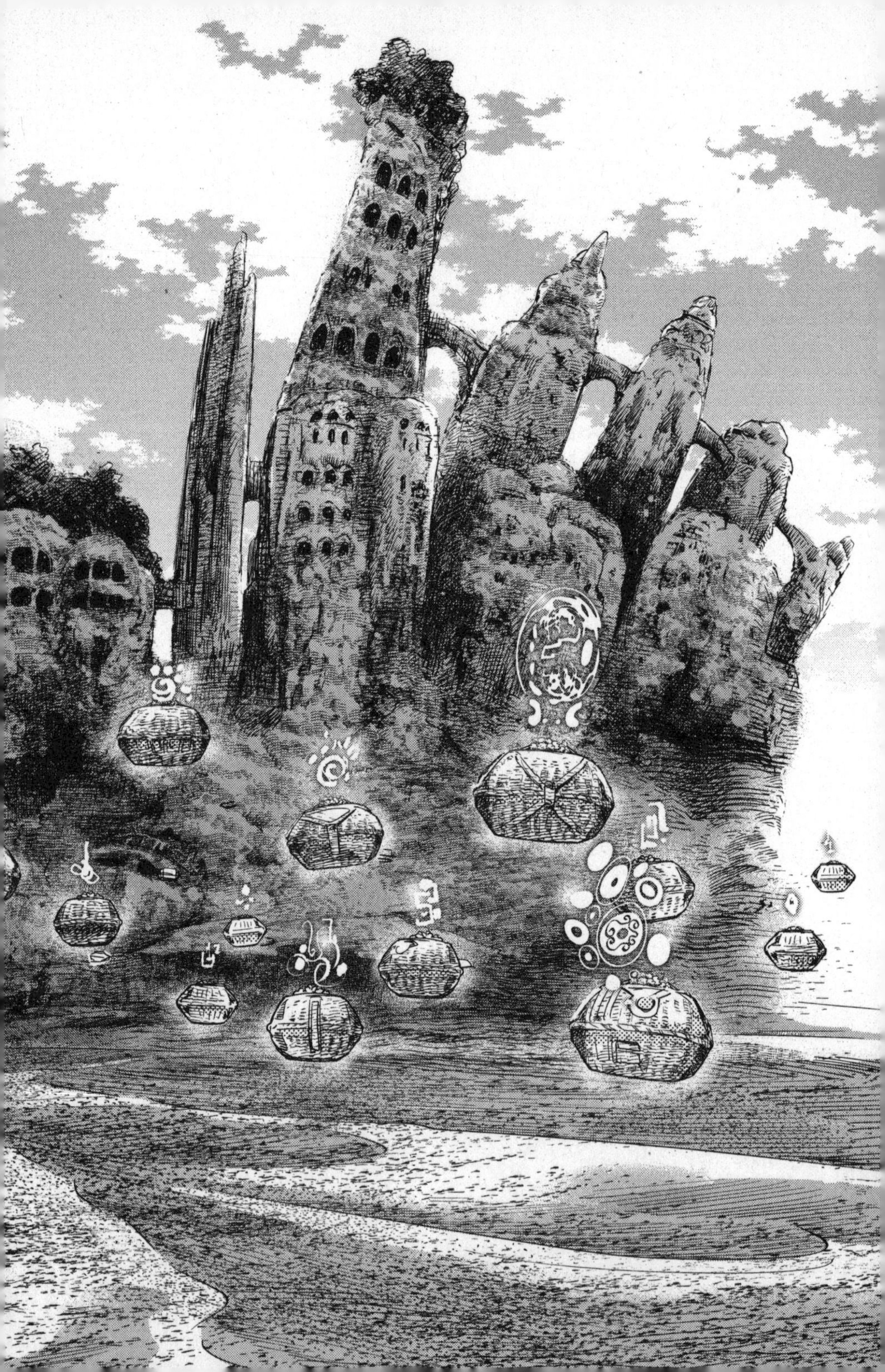

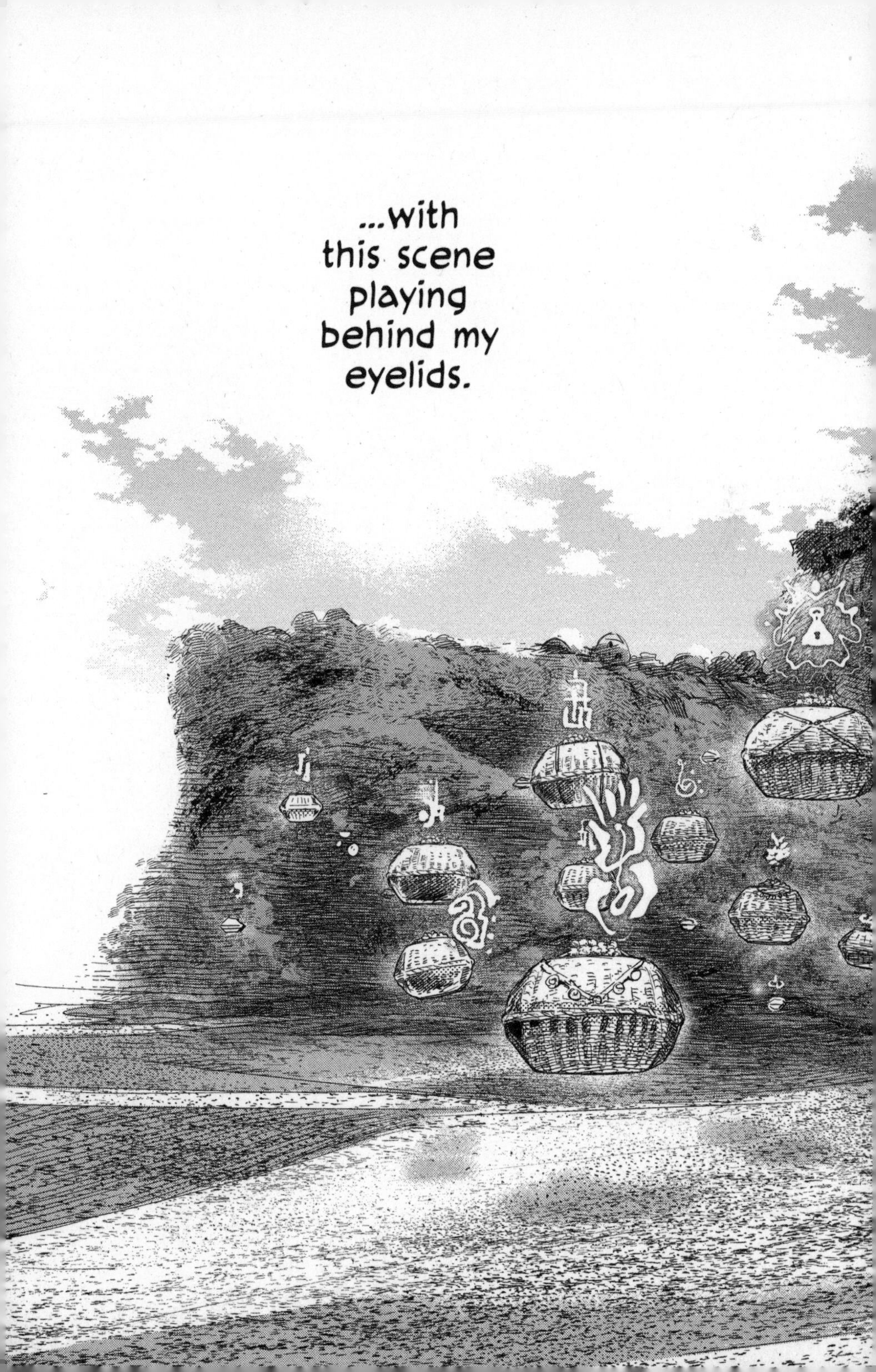
...with this scene playing behind my eyelids.

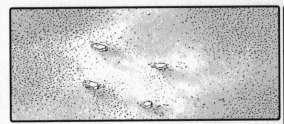

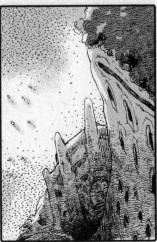

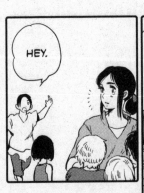

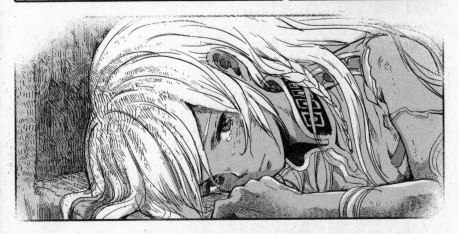

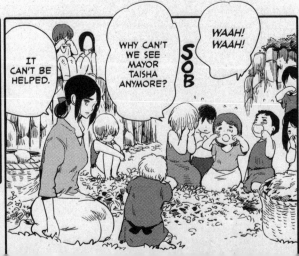

WAAH! WAAH!
SOB
WHY CAN'T WE SEE MAYOR TAISHA ANYMORE?
IT CAN'T BE HELPED.
HEY.

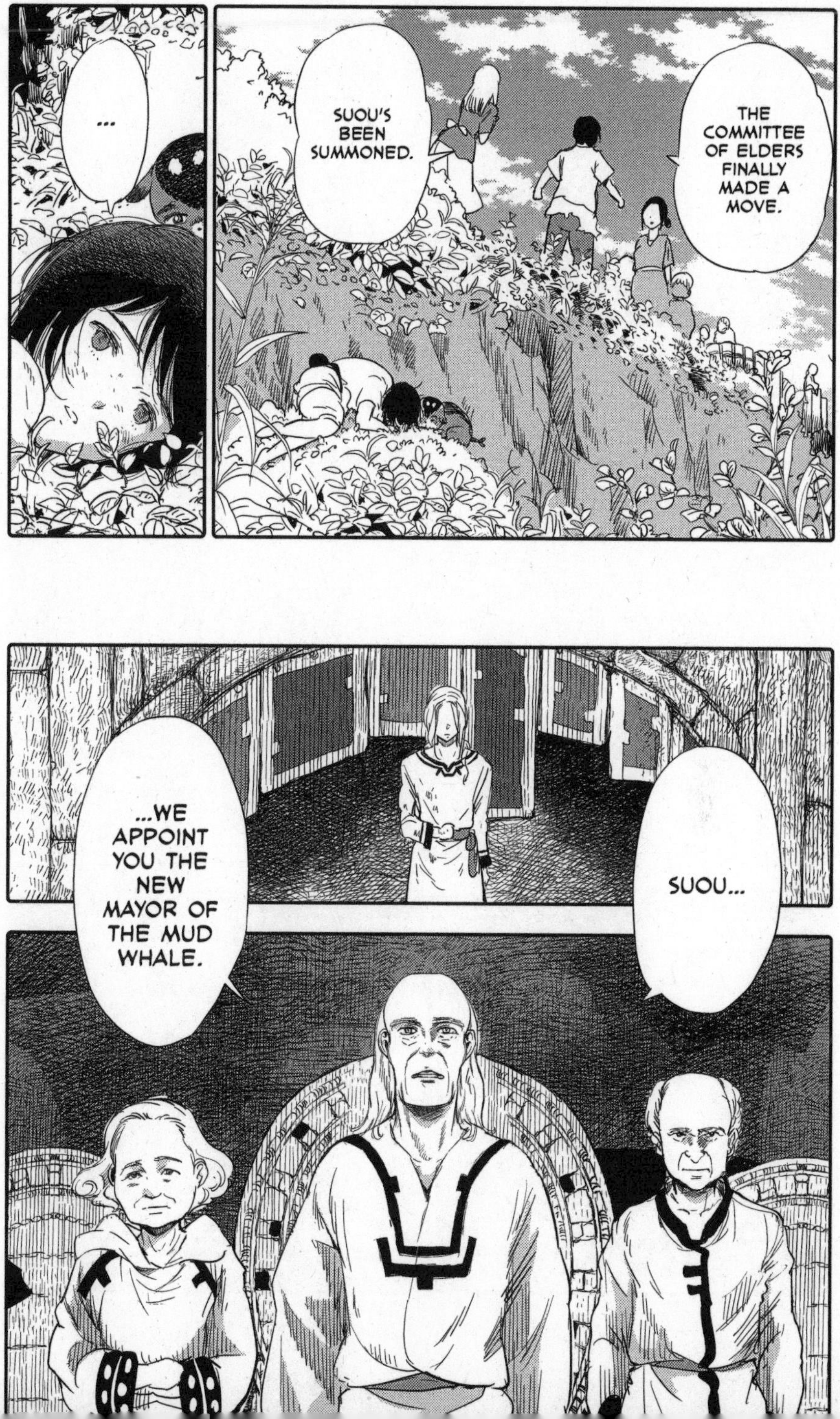
THE COMMITTEE OF ELDERS FINALLY MADE A MOVE.
SUOU'S BEEN SUMMONED.
...
SUOU...
...WE APPOINT YOU THE NEW MAYOR OF THE MUD WHALE.

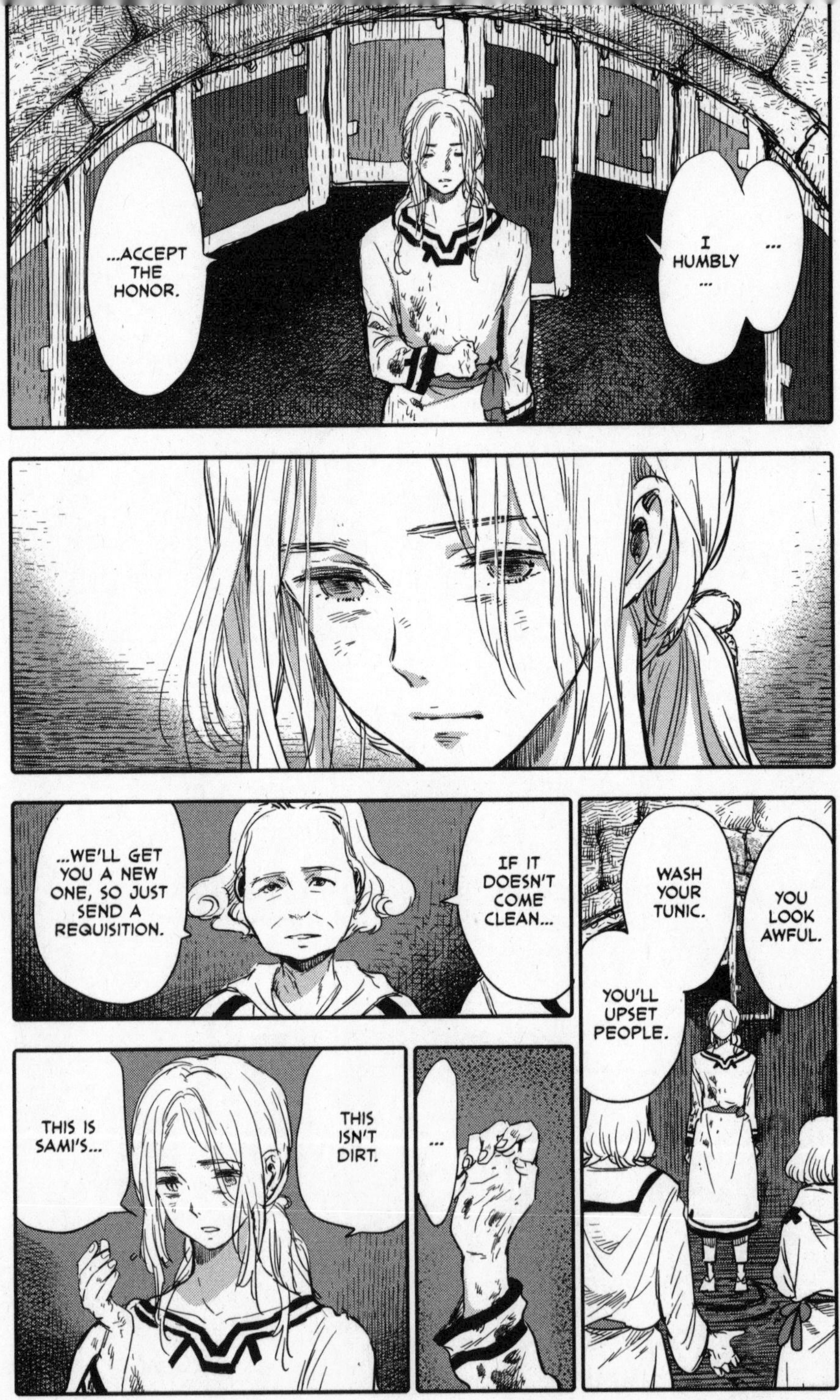
... I HUMBLY ...
...ACCEPT THE HONOR.
YOU LOOK AWFUL.
WASH YOUR TUNIC.
YOU'LL UPSET PEOPLE.
IF IT DOESN'T COME CLEAN...
...WE'LL GET YOU A NEW ONE, SO JUST SEND A REQUISITION.
...
THIS ISN'T DIRT.
THIS IS SAMI'S...

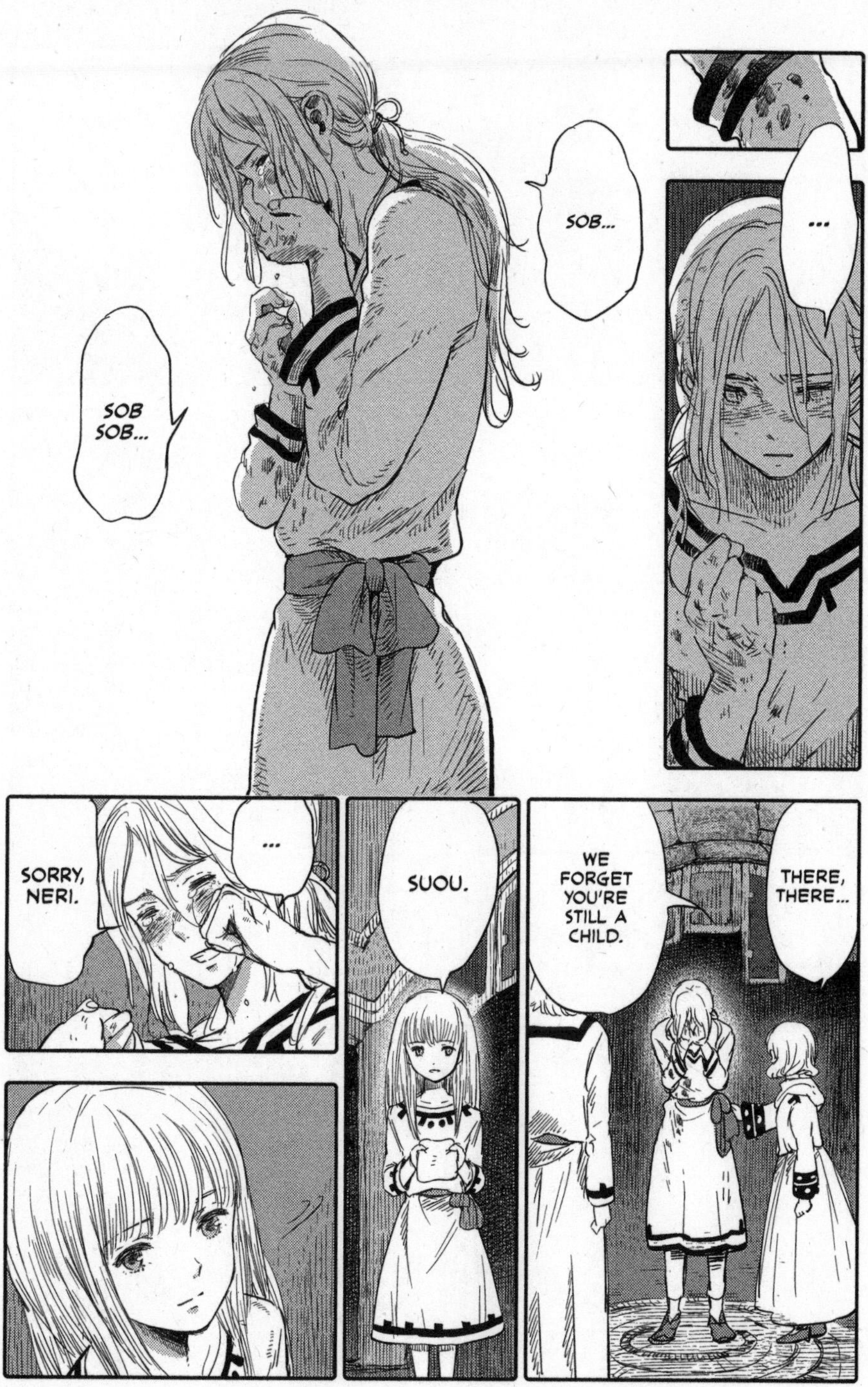
...
SOB...
SOB SOB...
THERE, THERE...
WE FORGET YOU'RE STILL A CHILD.
SUOU.
...
SORRY, NERI.

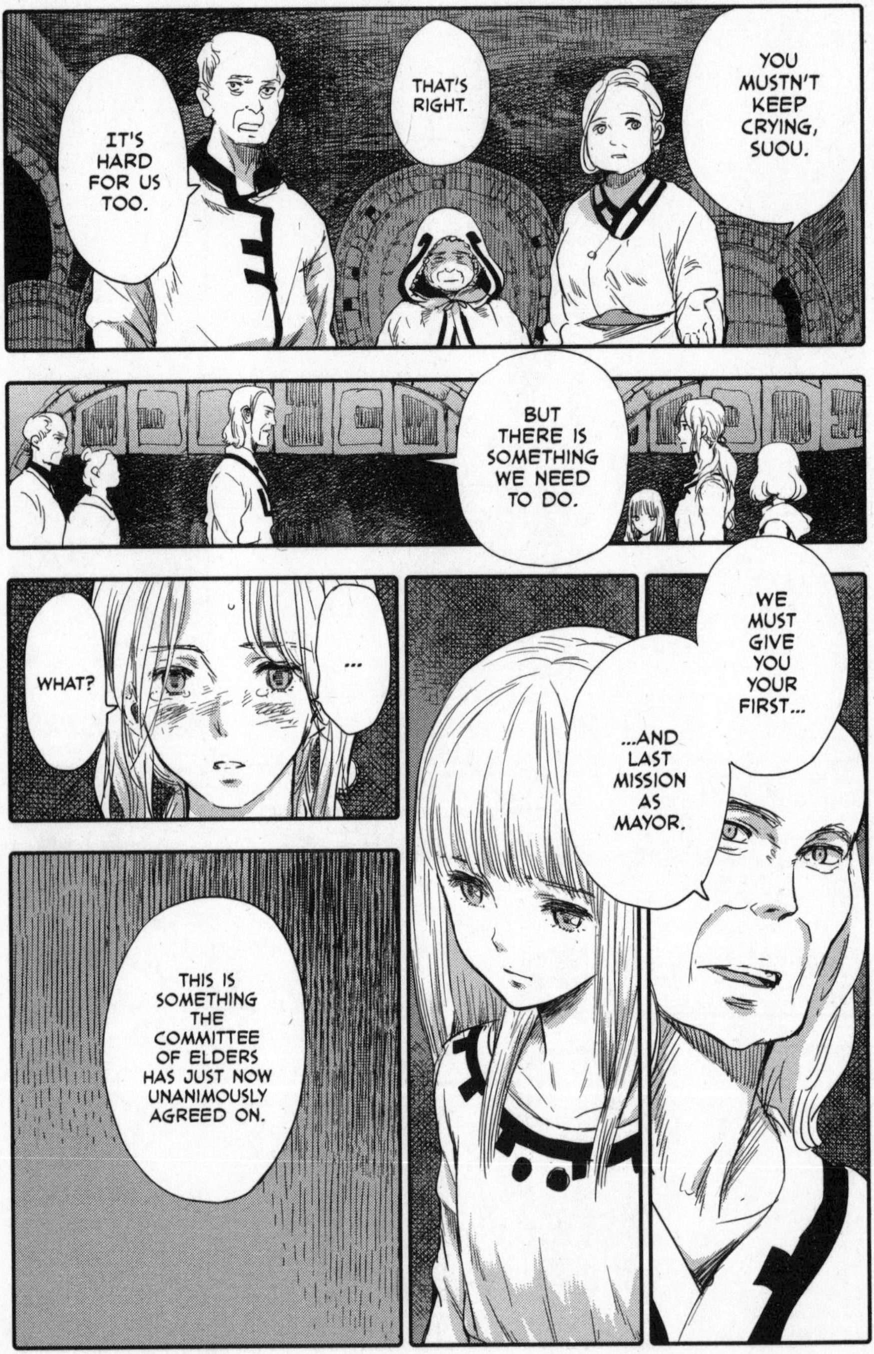
YOU MUSTN'T KEEP CRYING, SUOU.
THAT'S RIGHT.
IT'S HARD FOR US TOO.
BUT THERE IS SOMETHING WE NEED TO DO.
WE MUST GIVE YOU YOUR FIRST...
...AND LAST MISSION AS MAYOR.
...
WHAT?
THIS IS SOMETHING THE COMMITTEE OF ELDERS HAS JUST NOW UNANIMOUSLY AGREED ON.

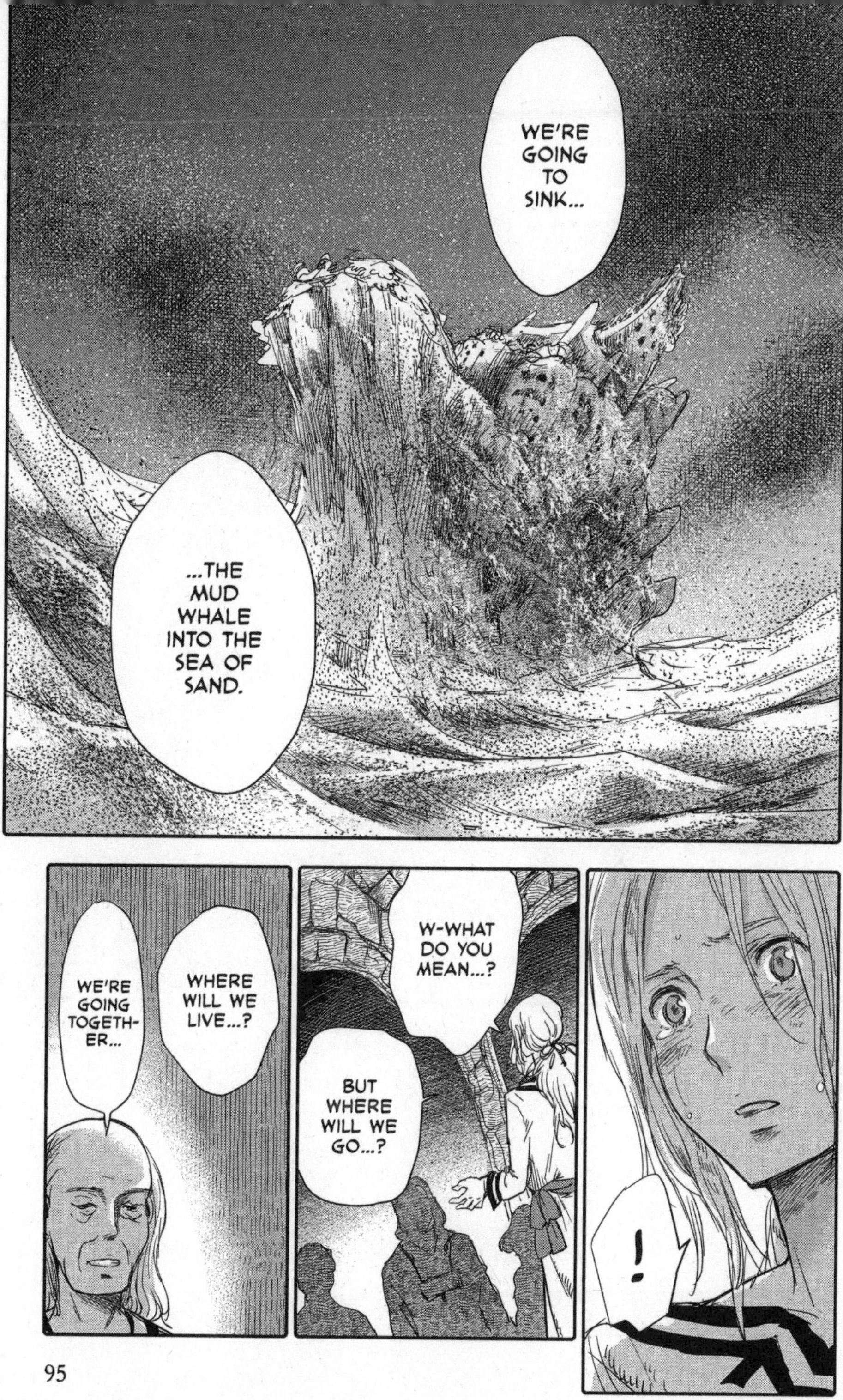
WE'RE GOING TO SINK...
...THE MUD WHALE INTO THE SEA OF SAND.
!
W-WHAT DO YOU MEAN...?
BUT WHERE WILL WE GO...?
WHERE WILL WE LIVE...?
WE'RE GOING TOGETH-ER...

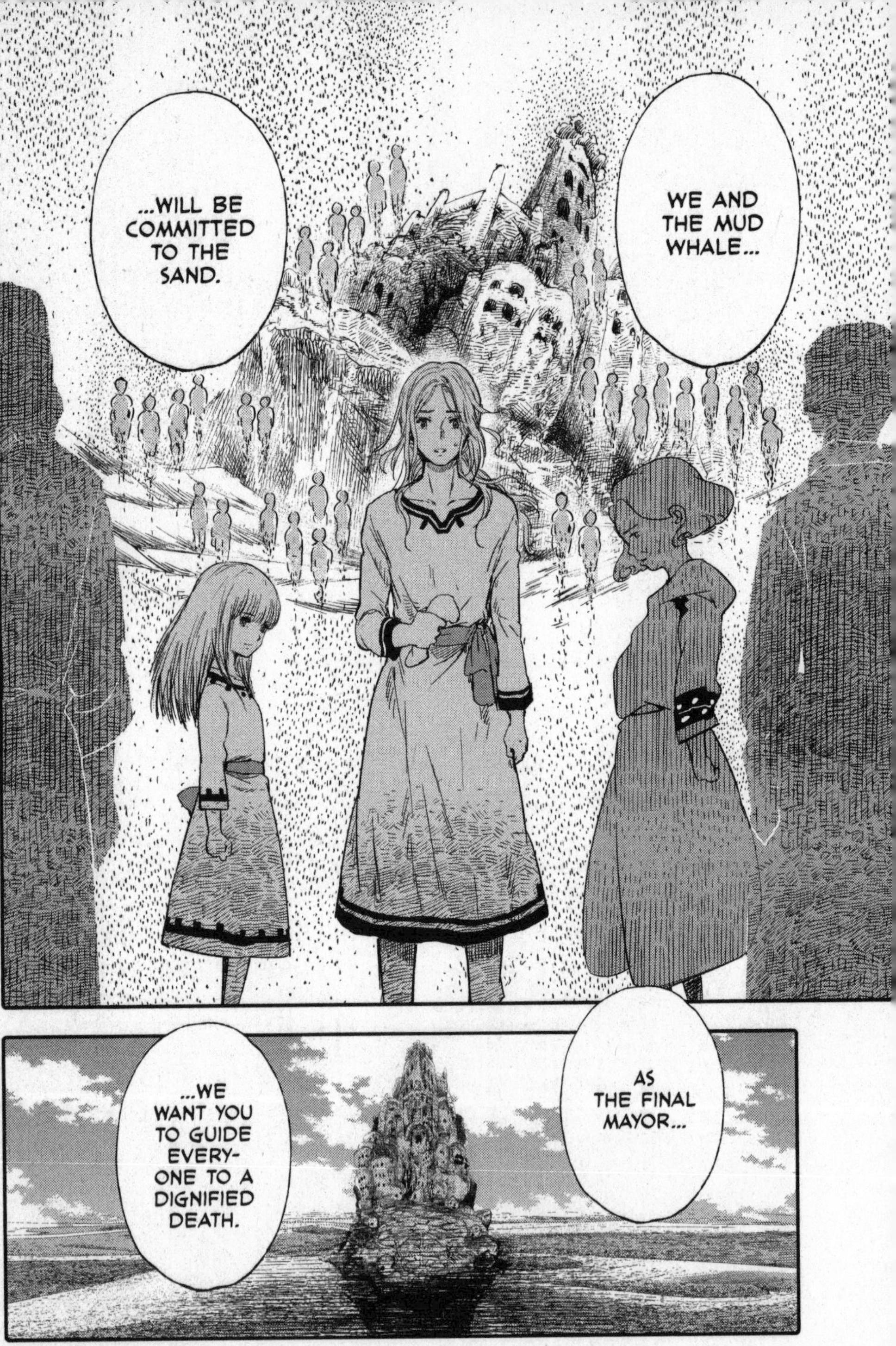
WE AND THE MUD WHALE...
...WILL BE COMMITTED TO THE SAND.
AS THE FINAL MAYOR...
...WE WANT YOU TO GUIDE EVERY-ONE TO A DIGNIFIED DEATH.

Liontari Attacks -The End-

Chapter 7
This World Is Beautiful Because...

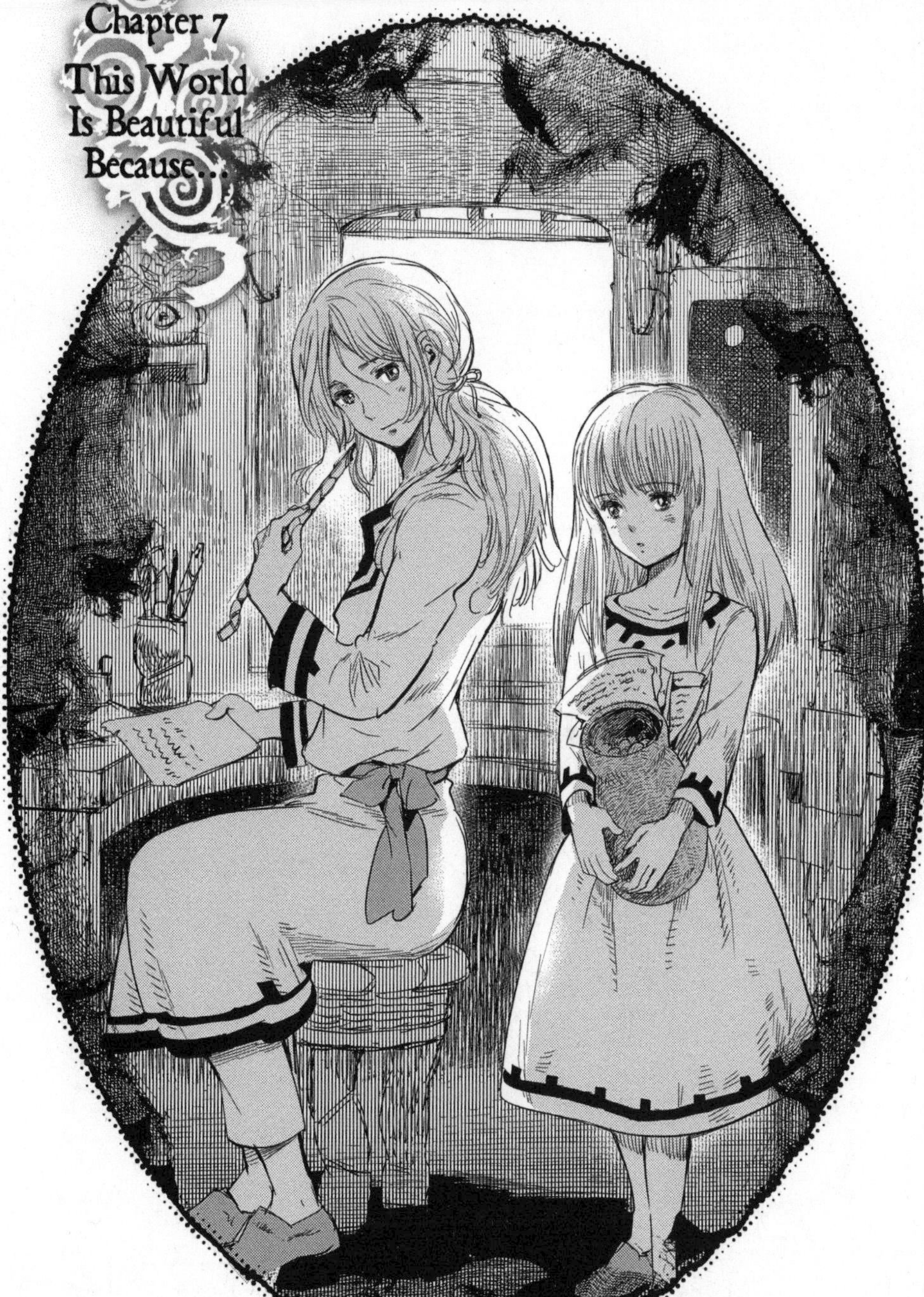

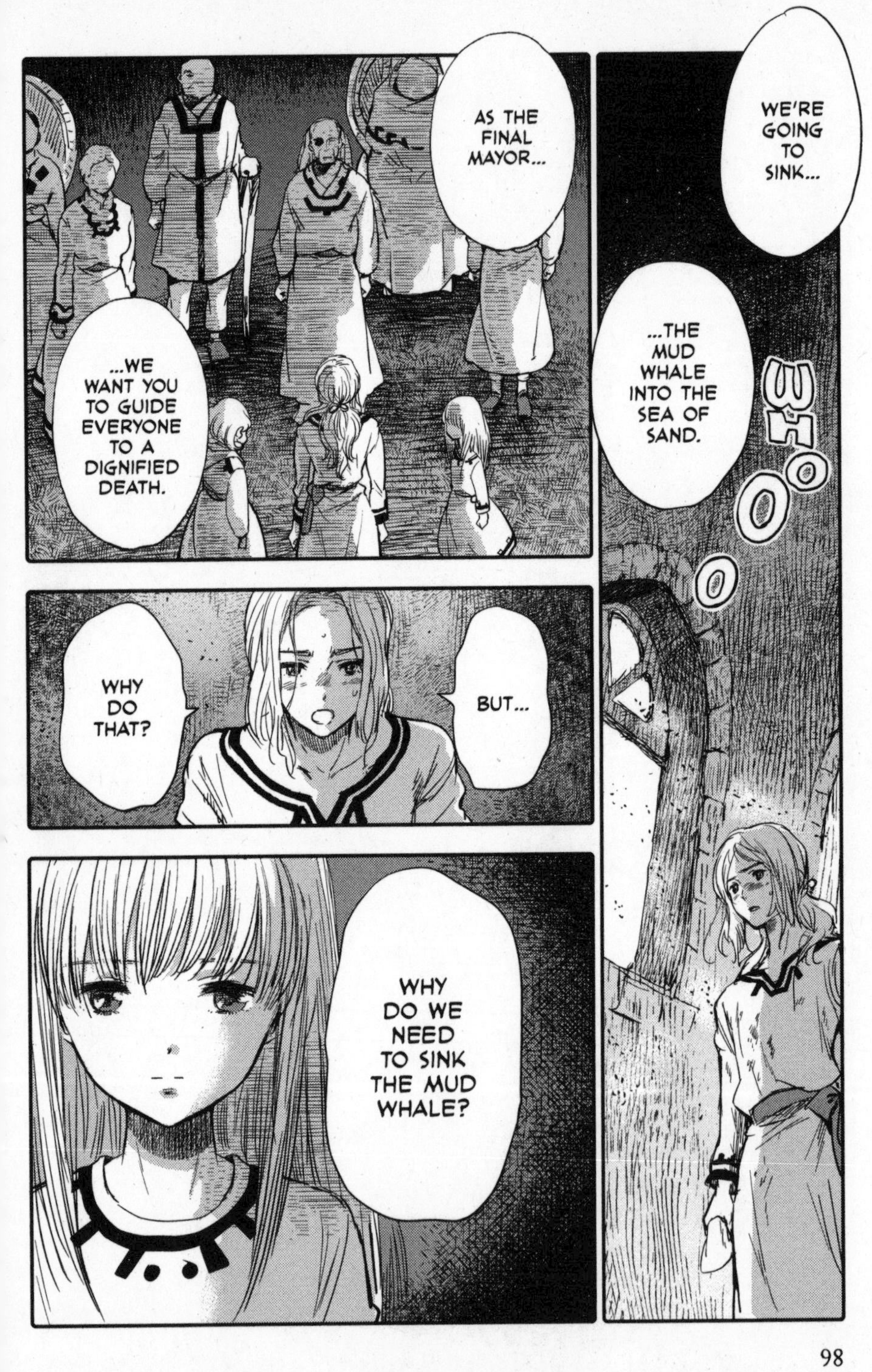
WE'RE GOING TO SINK...
...THE MUD WHALE INTO THE SEA OF SAND.
SHOOO
AS THE FINAL MAYOR...
...WE WANT YOU TO GUIDE EVERYONE TO A DIGNIFIED DEATH.
BUT...
WHY DO THAT?
WHY DO WE NEED TO SINK THE MUD WHALE?

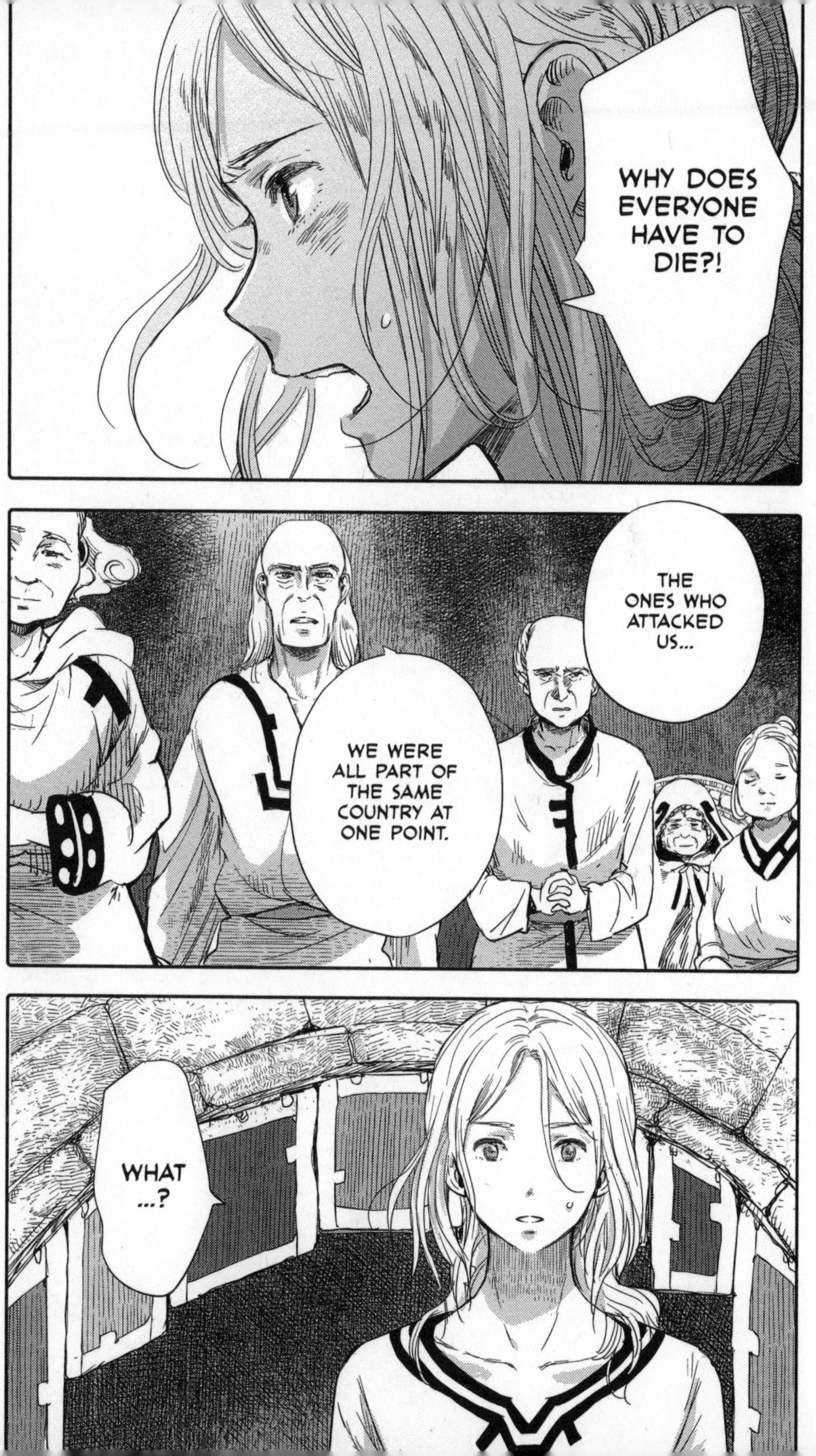
WHY DOES EVERYONE HAVE TO DIE?!
THE ONES WHO ATTACKED US...
WE WERE ALL PART OF THE SAME COUNTRY AT ONE POINT.
WHAT ...?

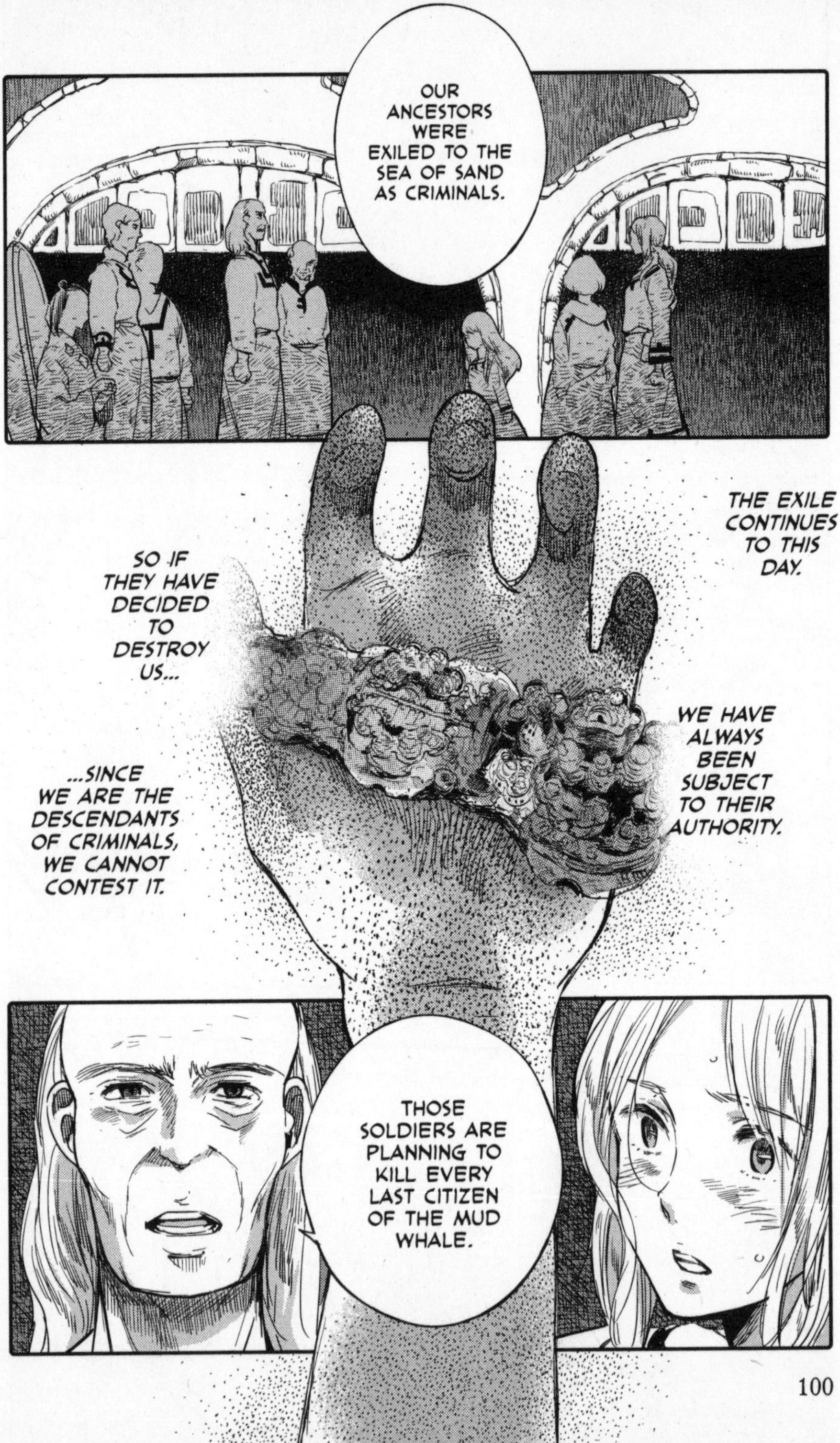
OUR ANCESTORS WERE EXILED TO THE SEA OF SAND AS CRIMINALS.
THE EXILE CONTINUES TO THIS DAY.
WE HAVE ALWAYS BEEN SUBJECT TO THEIR AUTHORITY.
SO IF THEY HAVE DECIDED TO DESTROY US...
...SINCE WE ARE THE DESCENDANTS OF CRIMINALS, WE CANNOT CONTEST IT.
THOSE SOLDIERS ARE PLANNING TO KILL EVERY LAST CITIZEN OF THE MUD WHALE.

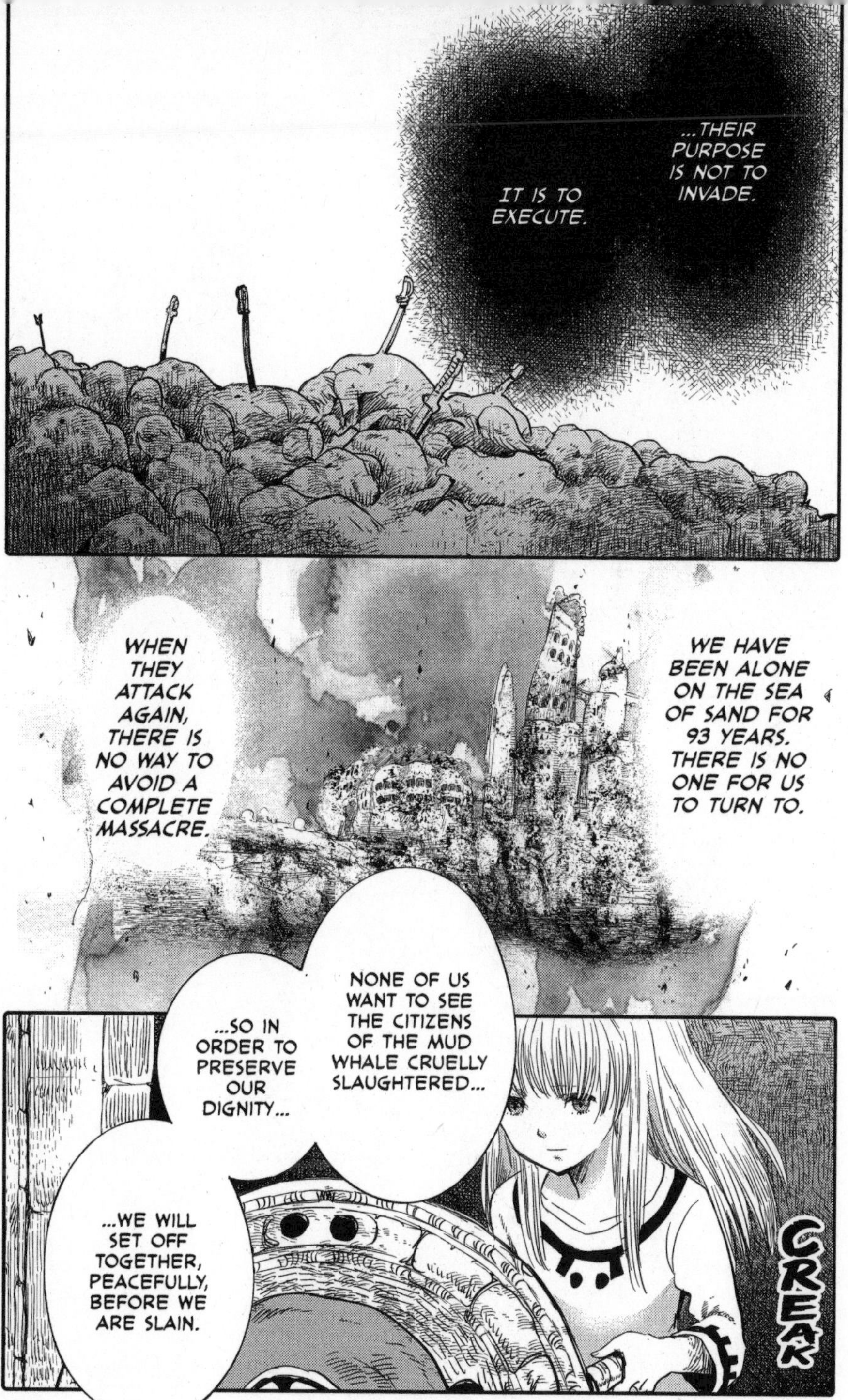
...THEIR PURPOSE IS NOT TO INVADE.
IT IS TO EXECUTE.
WE HAVE BEEN ALONE ON THE SEA OF SAND FOR 93 YEARS. THERE IS NO ONE FOR US TO TURN TO.
WHEN THEY ATTACK AGAIN, THERE IS NO WAY TO AVOID A COMPLETE MASSACRE.
NONE OF US WANT TO SEE THE CITIZENS OF THE MUD WHALE CRUELLY SLAUGHTERED...
...SO IN ORDER TO PRESERVE OUR DIGNITY...
...WE WILL SET OFF TOGETHER, PEACEFULLY, BEFORE WE ARE SLAIN.
CREAK

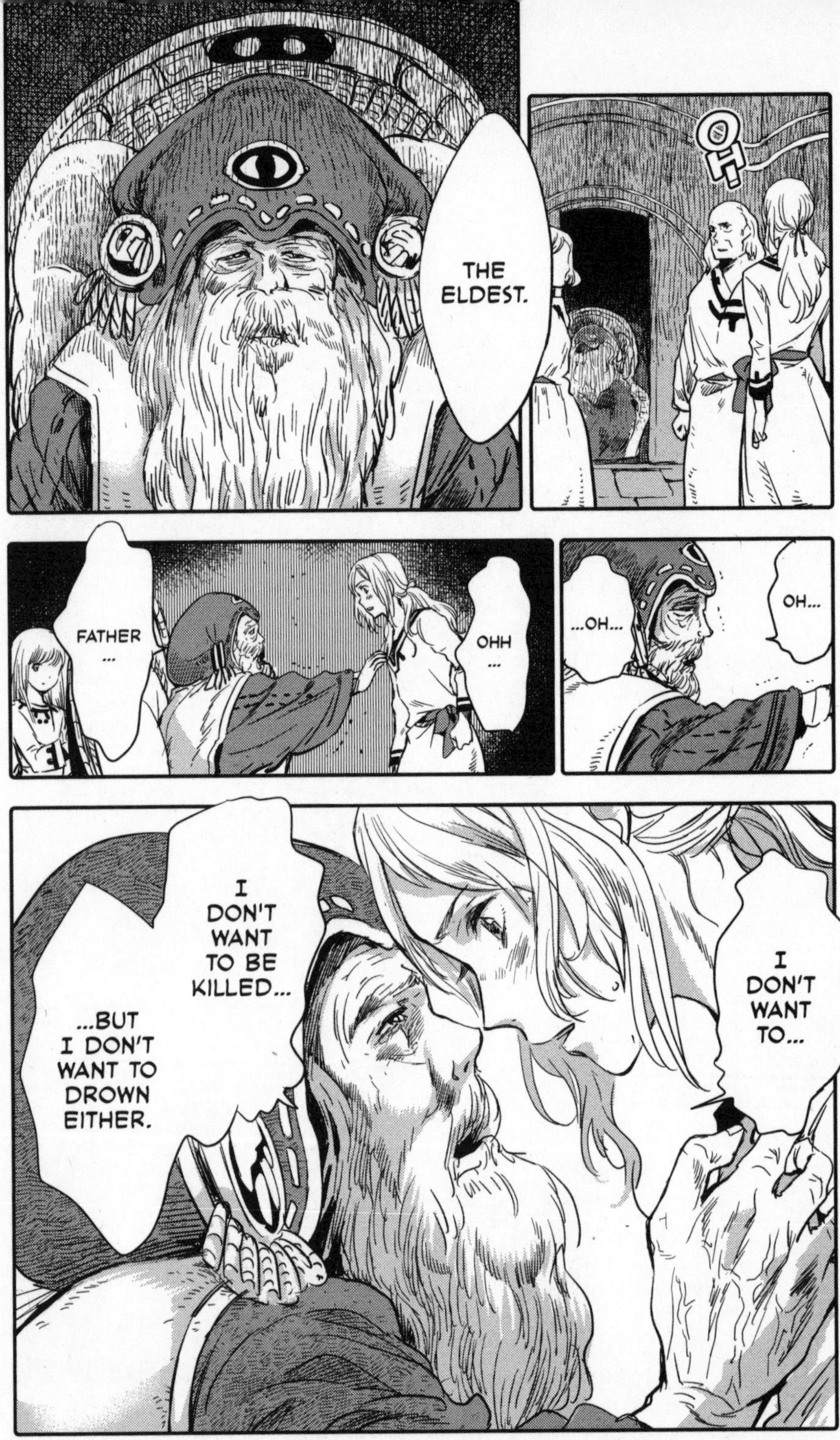
OH!
THE ELDEST.
OH...
...OH...
OHH ...
FATHER ...
I DON'T WANT TO...
I DON'T WANT TO BE KILLED...
...BUT I DON'T WANT TO DROWN EITHER.

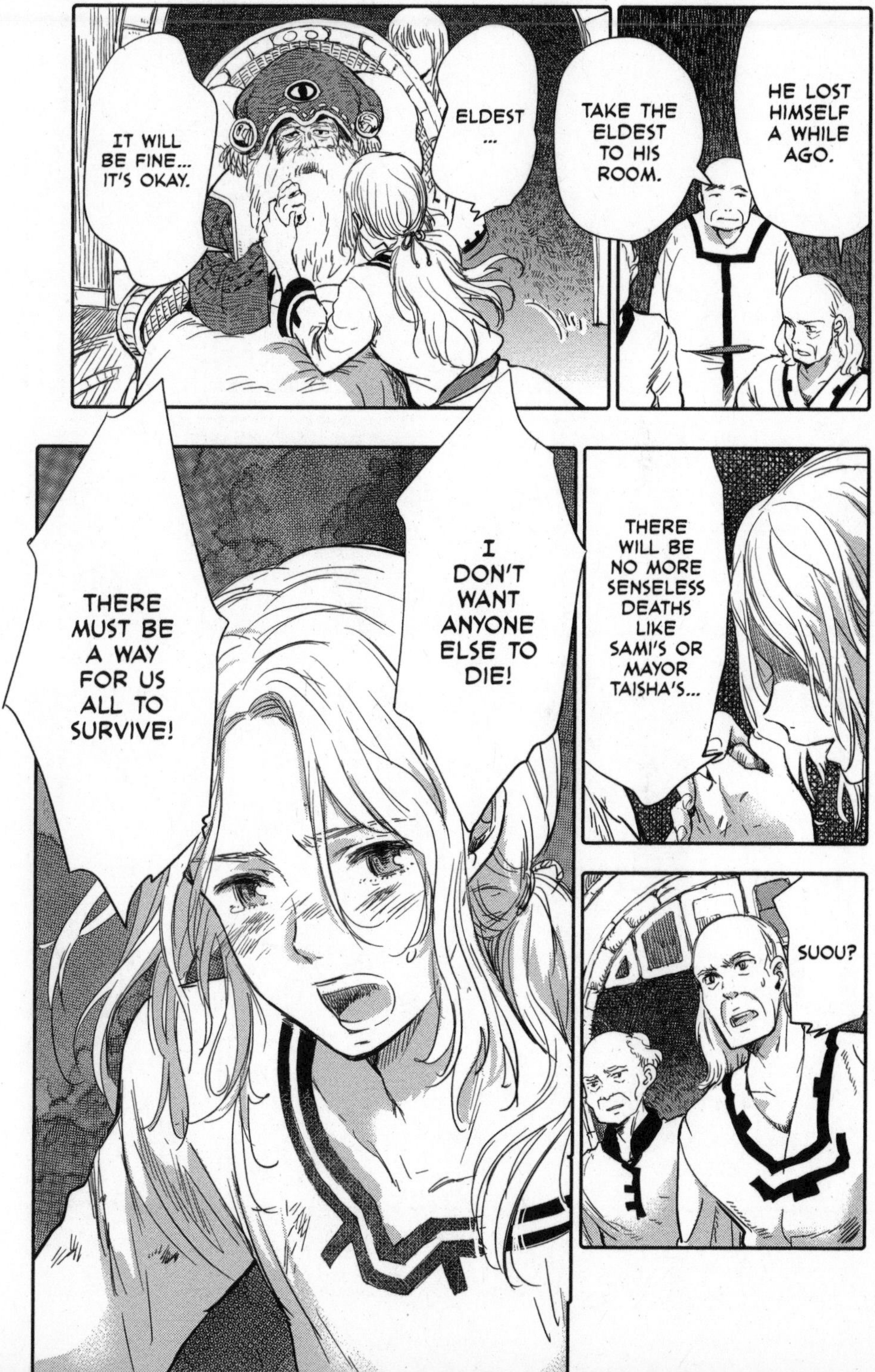
HE LOST HIMSELF A WHILE AGO.
TAKE THE ELDEST TO HIS ROOM.
ELDEST...
IT WILL BE FINE... IT'S OKAY.
THERE WILL BE NO MORE SENSELESS DEATHS LIKE SAMI'S OR MAYOR TAISHA'S...
SUOU?
I DON'T WANT ANYONE ELSE TO DIE!
THERE MUST BE A WAY FOR US ALL TO SURVIVE!

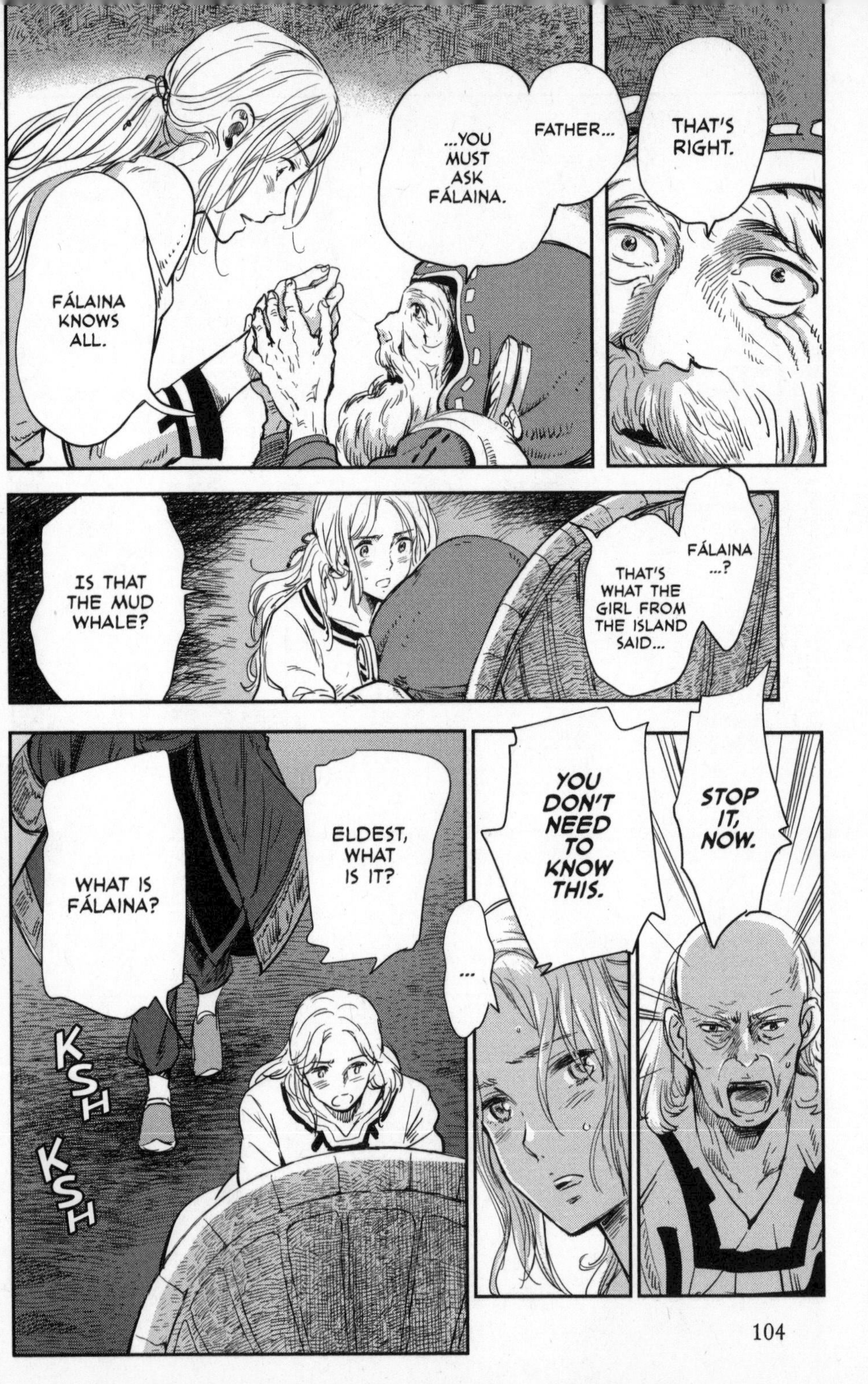
THAT'S RIGHT.
FATHER...
...YOU MUST ASK FÁLAINA.
FÁLAINA KNOWS ALL.
FÁLAINA ...?
THAT'S WHAT THE GIRL FROM THE ISLAND SAID...
IS THAT THE MUD WHALE?
STOP IT, NOW.
YOU DON'T NEED TO KNOW THIS.
...
ELDEST, WHAT IS IT?
WHAT IS FÁLAINA?
KSH
KSH

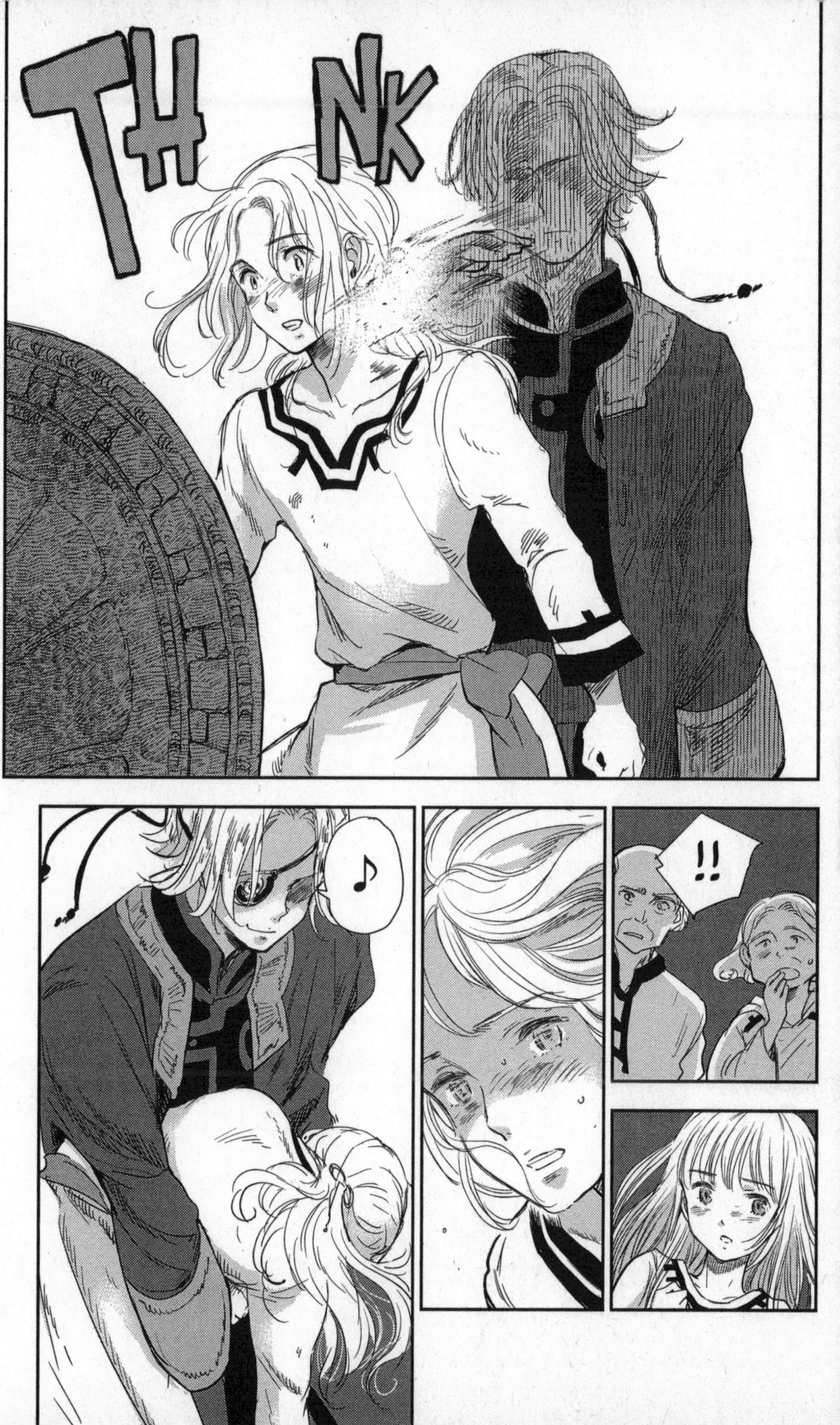
TH NK
!!
♪

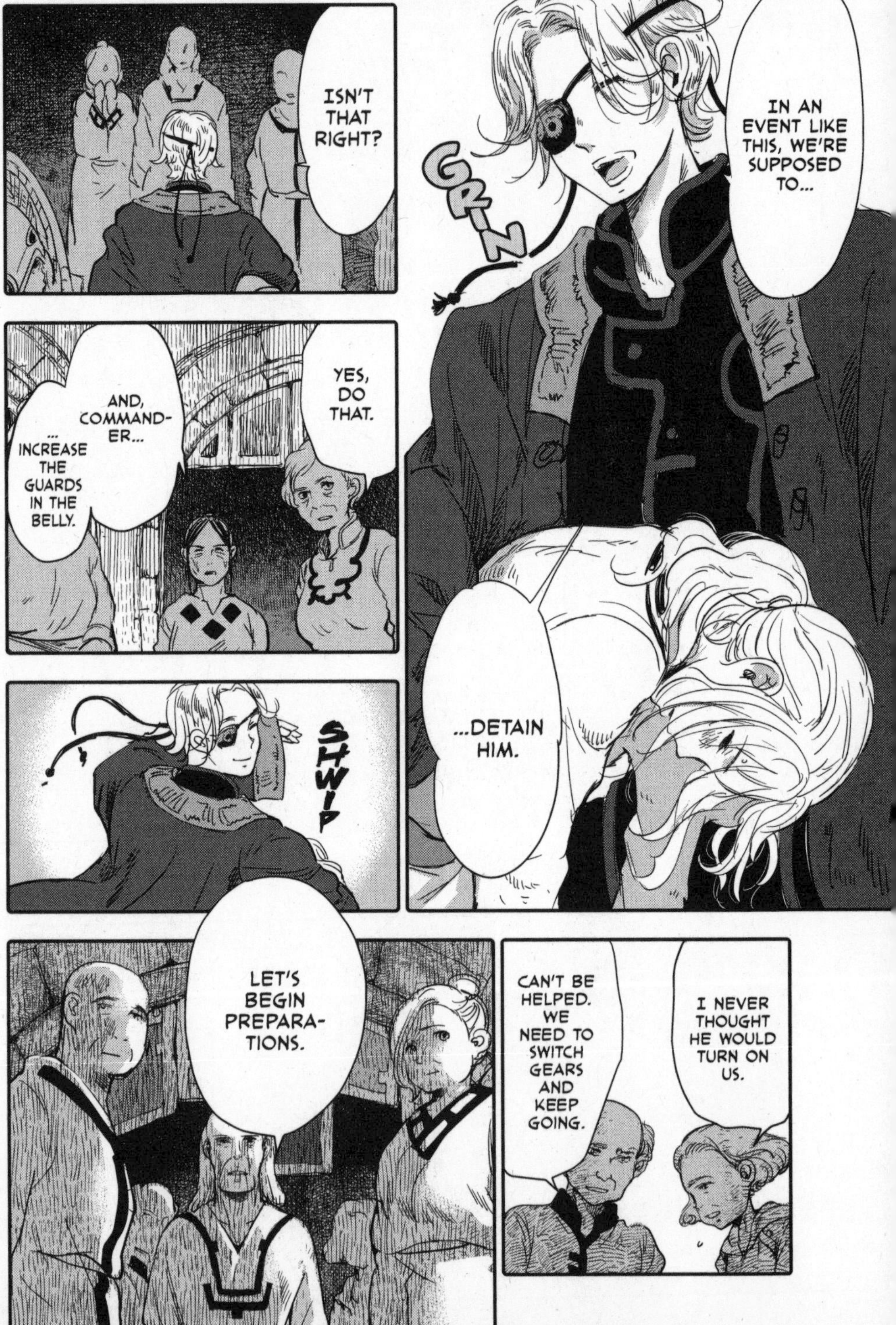
IN AN EVENT LIKE THIS, WE'RE SUPPOSED TO...
GRIN
...DETAIN HIM.
ISN'T THAT RIGHT?
YES, DO THAT.
AND, COMMANDER... ...INCREASE THE GUARDS IN THE BELLY.
SHWIP
I NEVER THOUGHT HE WOULD TURN ON US.
CAN'T BE HELPED. WE NEED TO SWITCH GEARS AND KEEP GOING.
LET'S BEGIN PREPARATIONS.

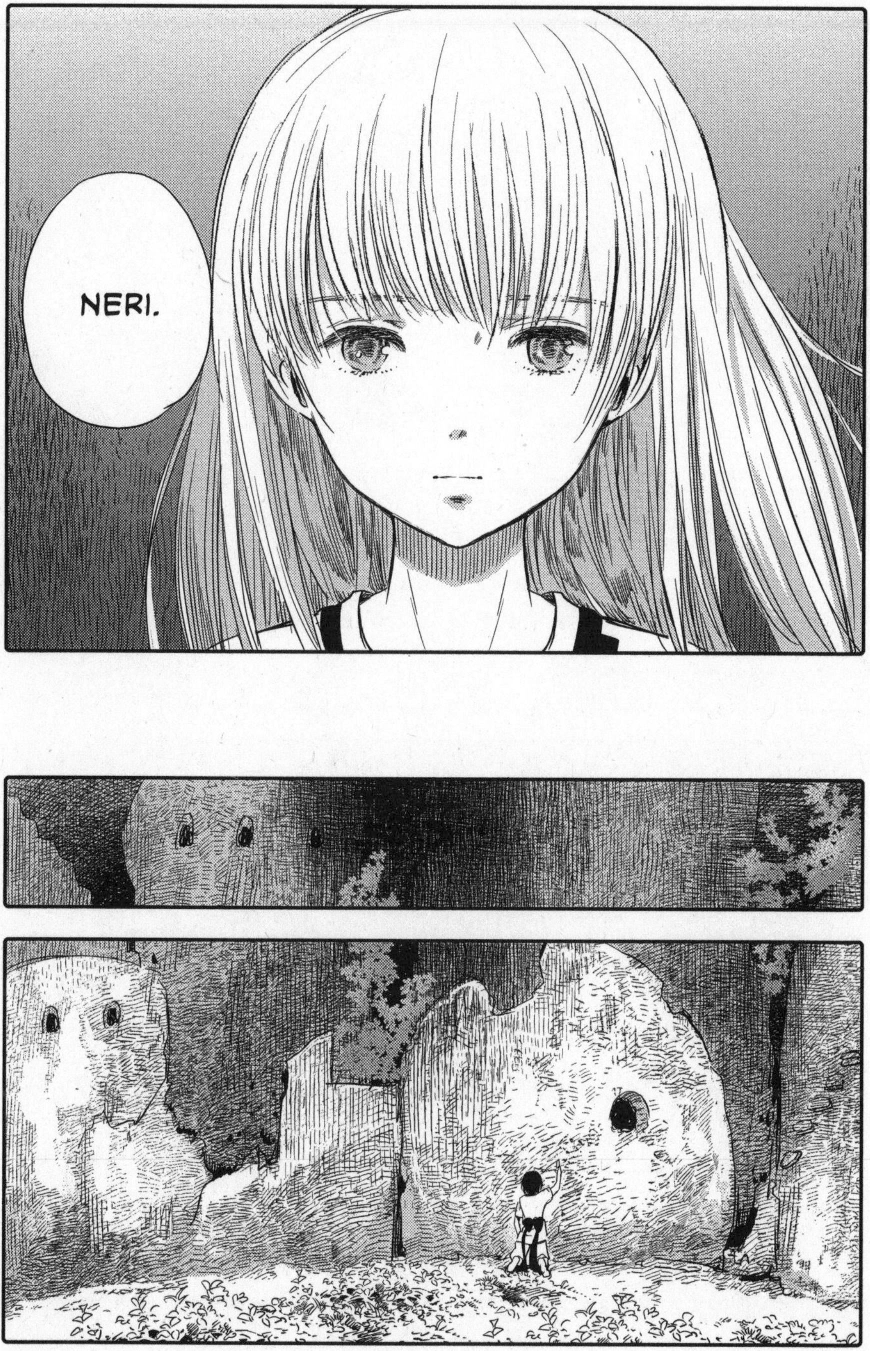
NERI.

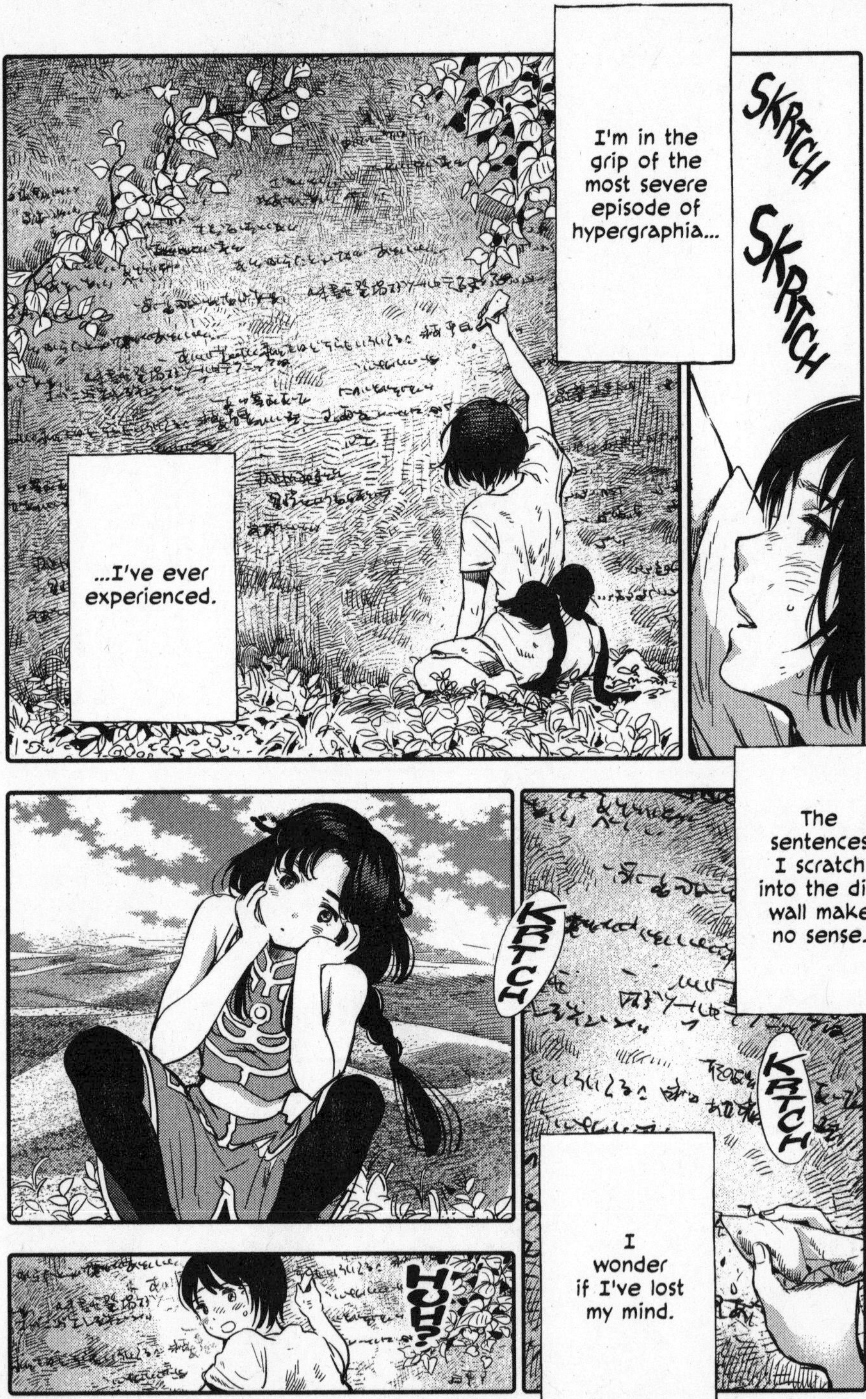
I'm in the grip of the most severe episode of hypergraphia...
SKRTCH
SKRTCH
...I've ever experienced.
The sentences I scratch into the dirt wall make no sense.
KRTCH
KRTCH
I wonder if I've lost my mind.
HUH?!

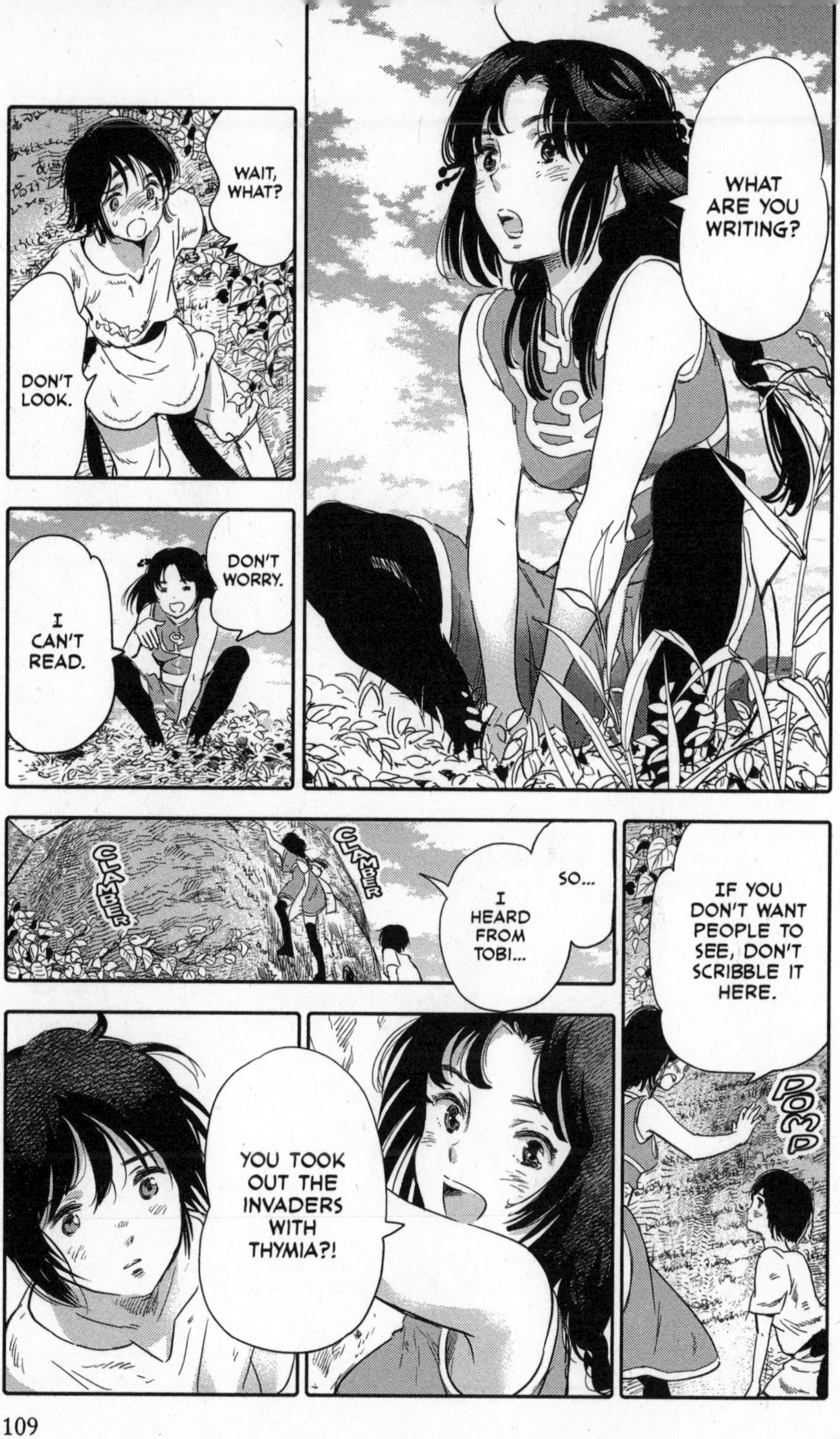
WHAT ARE YOU WRITING?
WAIT, WHAT?
DON'T LOOK.
DON'T WORRY.
I CAN'T READ.
IF YOU DON'T WANT PEOPLE TO SEE, DON'T SCRIBBLE IT HERE.
DOMP
CLAMBER
CLAMBER
SO...
I HEARD FROM TOBI...
YOU TOOK OUT THE INVADERS WITH THYMIA?!

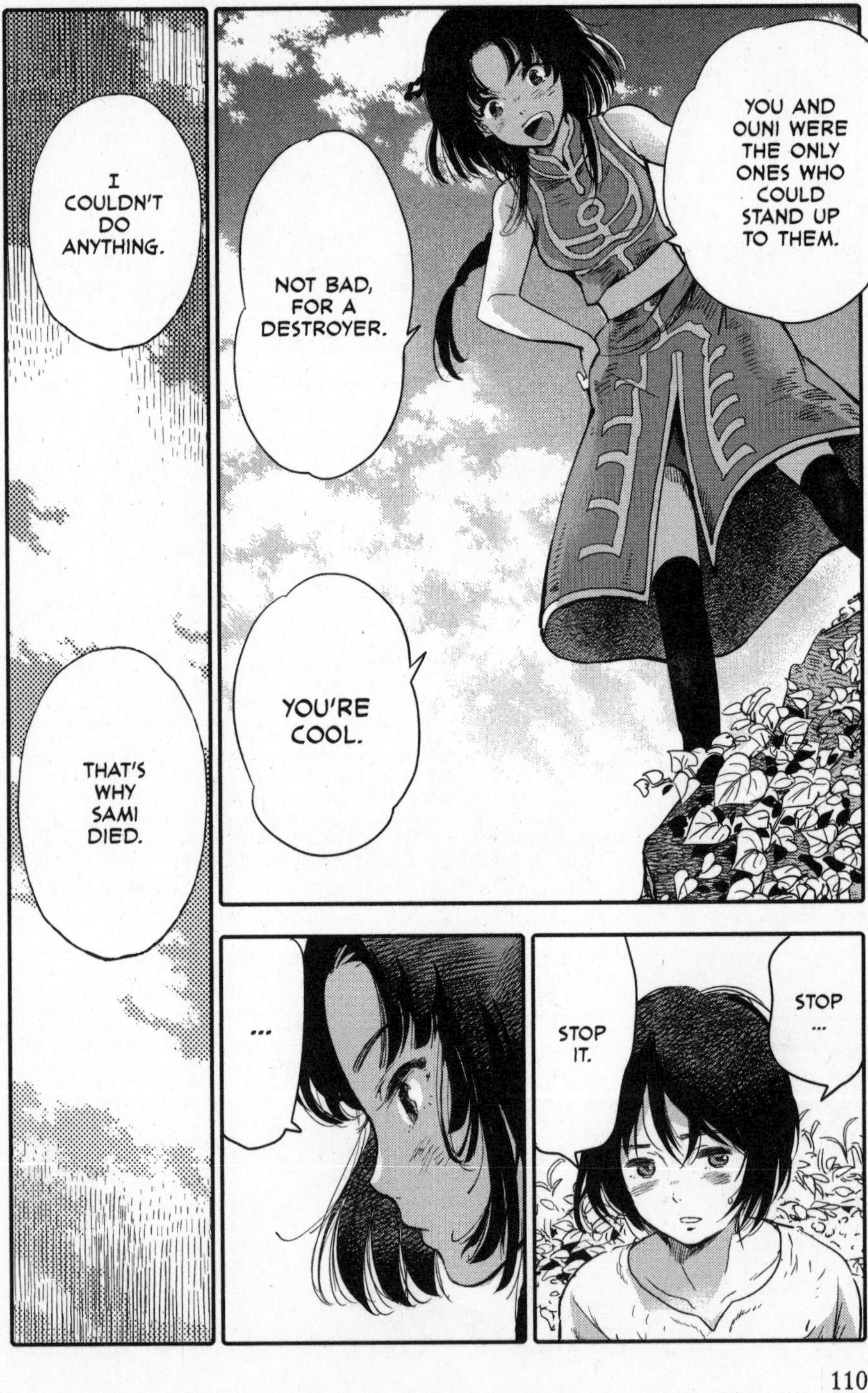
YOU AND OUNI WERE THE ONLY ONES WHO COULD STAND UP TO THEM.
NOT BAD, FOR A DESTROYER.
YOU'RE COOL.
STOP ...
STOP IT.
...
I COULDN'T DO ANYTHING.
THAT'S WHY SAMI DIED.

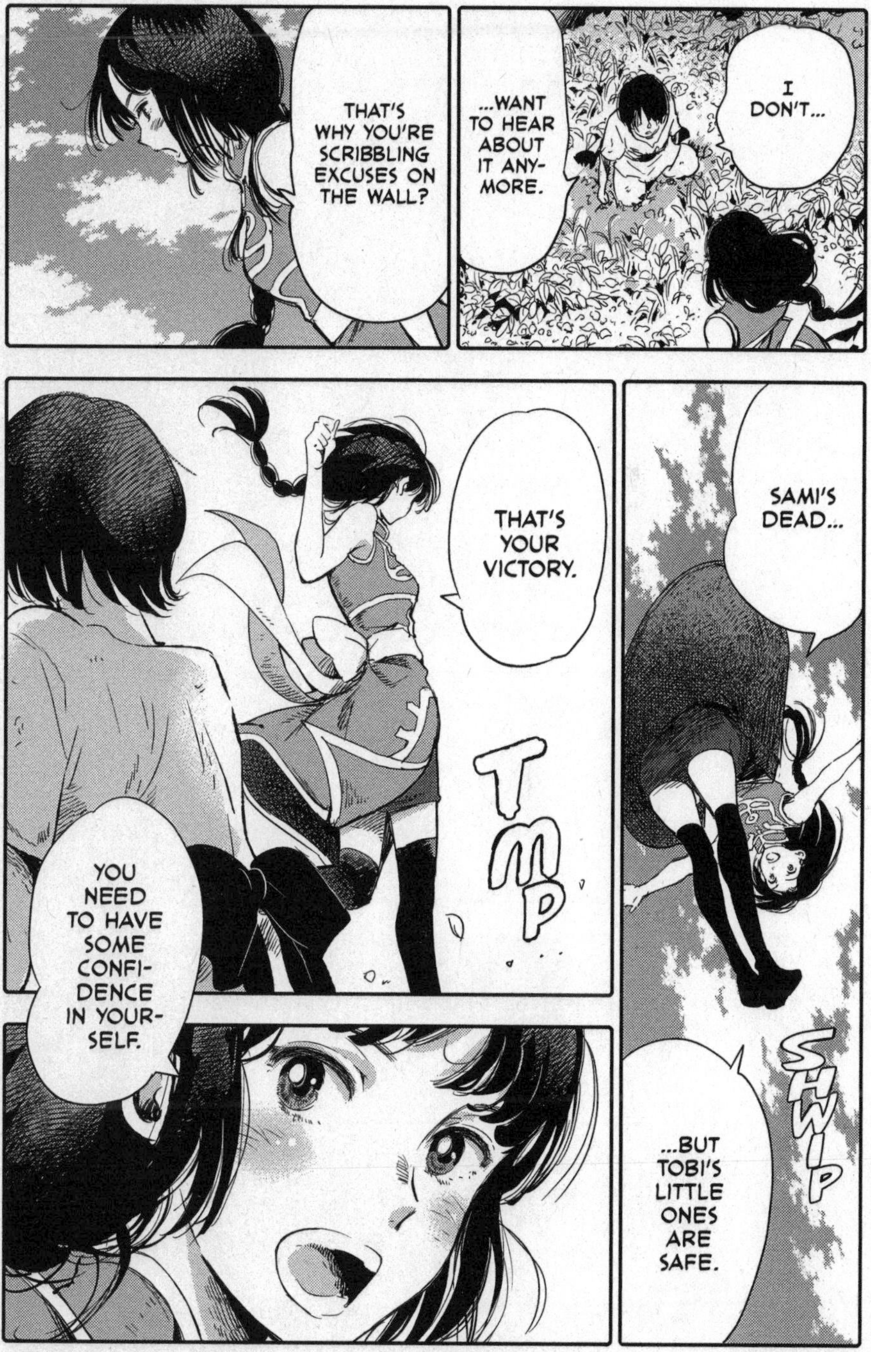
I DON'T...
...WANT TO HEAR ABOUT IT ANYMORE.
THAT'S WHY YOU'RE SCRIBBLING EXCUSES ON THE WALL?
SAMI'S DEAD...
SHWIP
...BUT TOBI'S LITTLE ONES ARE SAFE.
THAT'S YOUR VICTORY.
TMP
YOU NEED TO HAVE SOME CONFIDENCE IN YOURSELF.

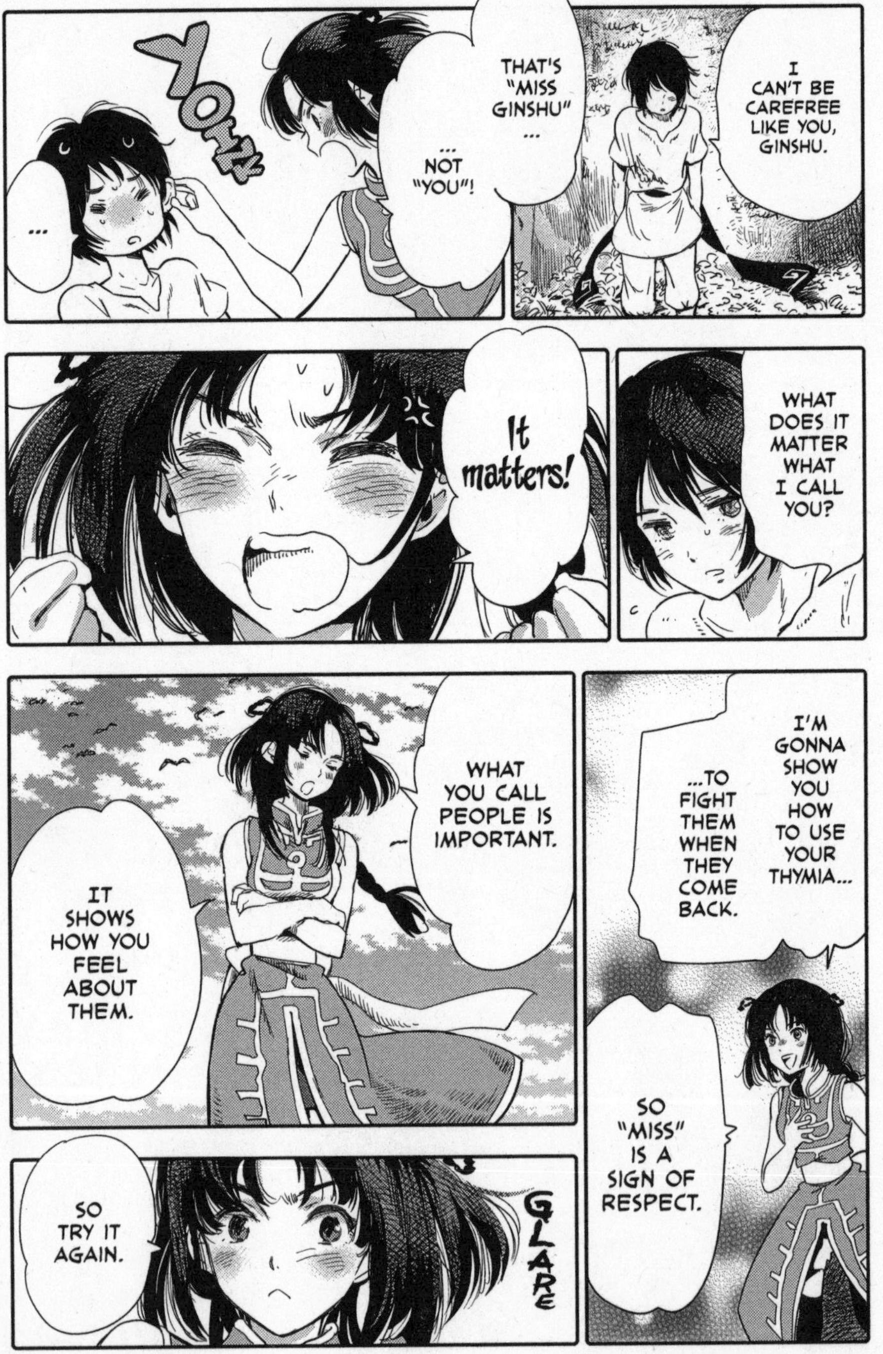
I CAN'T BE CAREFREE LIKE YOU, GINSHU.
THAT'S "MISS GINSHU"...
...NOT "YOU"!
YOINK
...
WHAT DOES IT MATTER WHAT I CALL YOU?
It matters!
I'M GONNA SHOW YOU HOW TO USE YOUR THYMIA...
...TO FIGHT THEM WHEN THEY COME BACK.
SO "MISS" IS A SIGN OF RESPECT.
WHAT YOU CALL PEOPLE IS IMPORTANT.
IT SHOWS HOW YOU FEEL ABOUT THEM.
GLARE
SO TRY IT AGAIN.

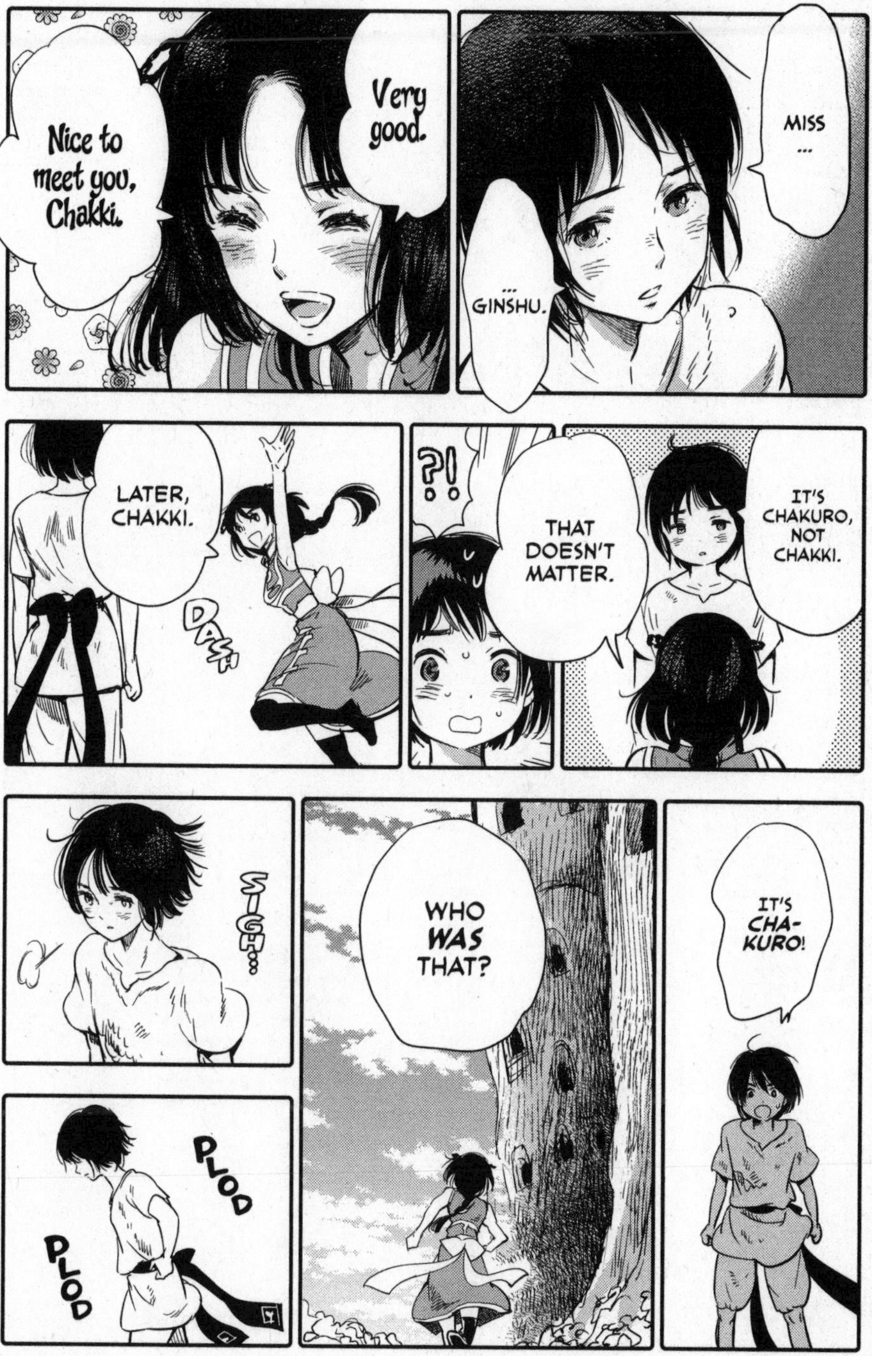
MISS ...
... GINSHU.
Very good.
Nice to meet you, Chakki.
IT'S CHAKURO, NOT CHAKKI.
?!
THAT DOESN'T MATTER.
LATER, CHAKKI.
DASH
IT'S CHA-KURO!
WHO WAS THAT?
SIGH...
PLOD
PLOD

THAT'S YOUR VICTORY.
YOU NEED TO HAVE SOME CONFIDENCE IN YOURSELF.
SHF SHF
WHAT DO YOU WANT ME TO DO?
CHA-KURO.
NERI?
HUFF HUFF

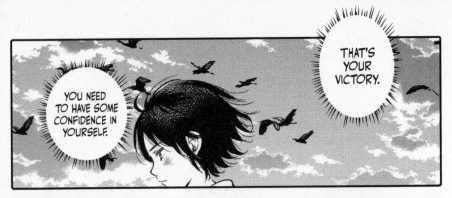

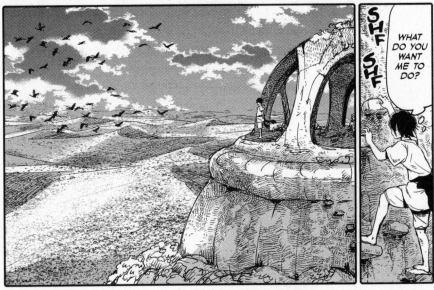

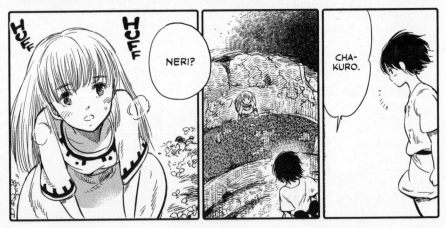

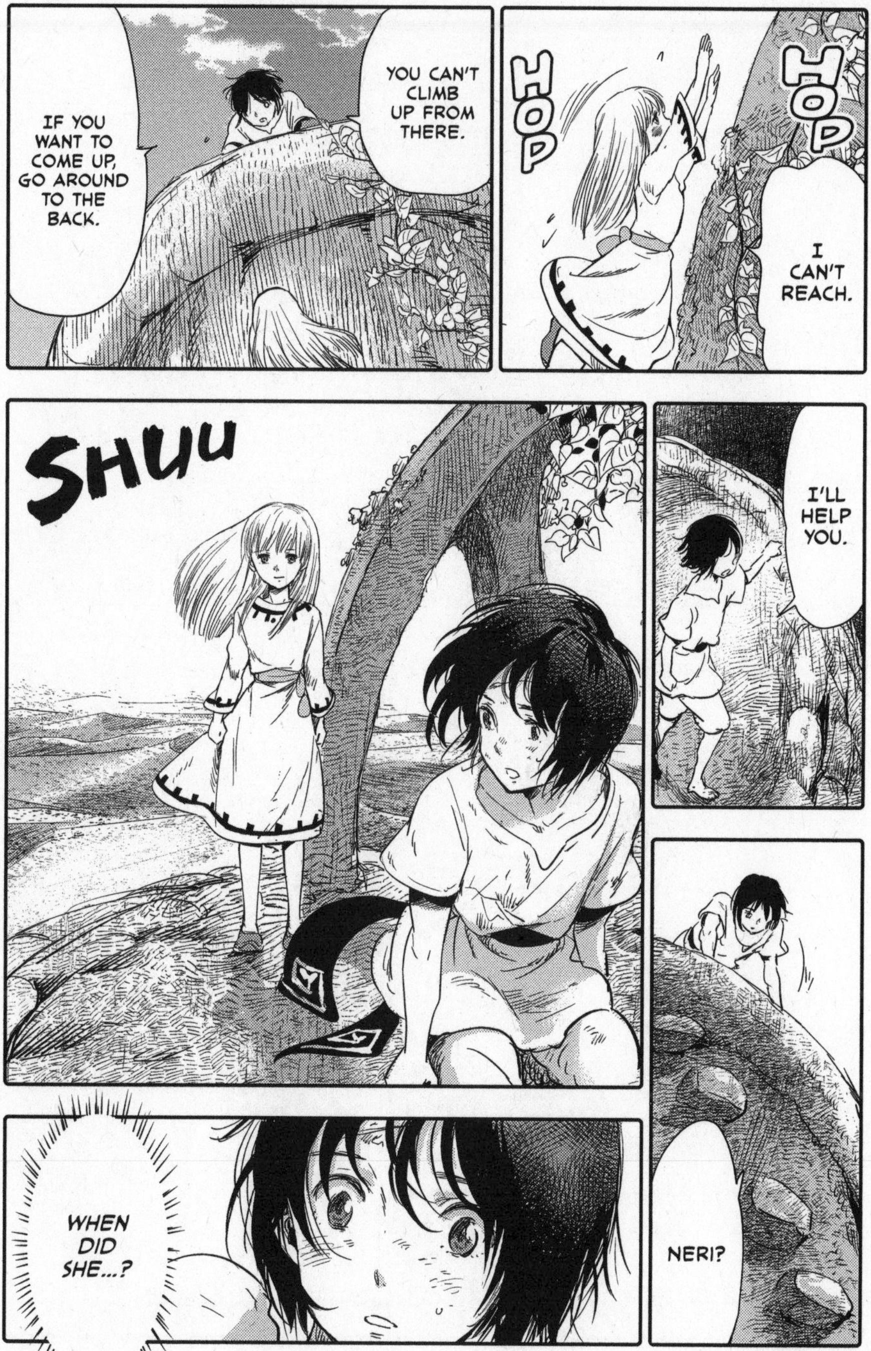
HOP
HOP
I CAN'T REACH.
YOU CAN'T CLIMB UP FROM THERE.
IF YOU WANT TO COME UP, GO AROUND TO THE BACK.
I'LL HELP YOU.
NERI?
SHUU
WHEN DID SHE...?

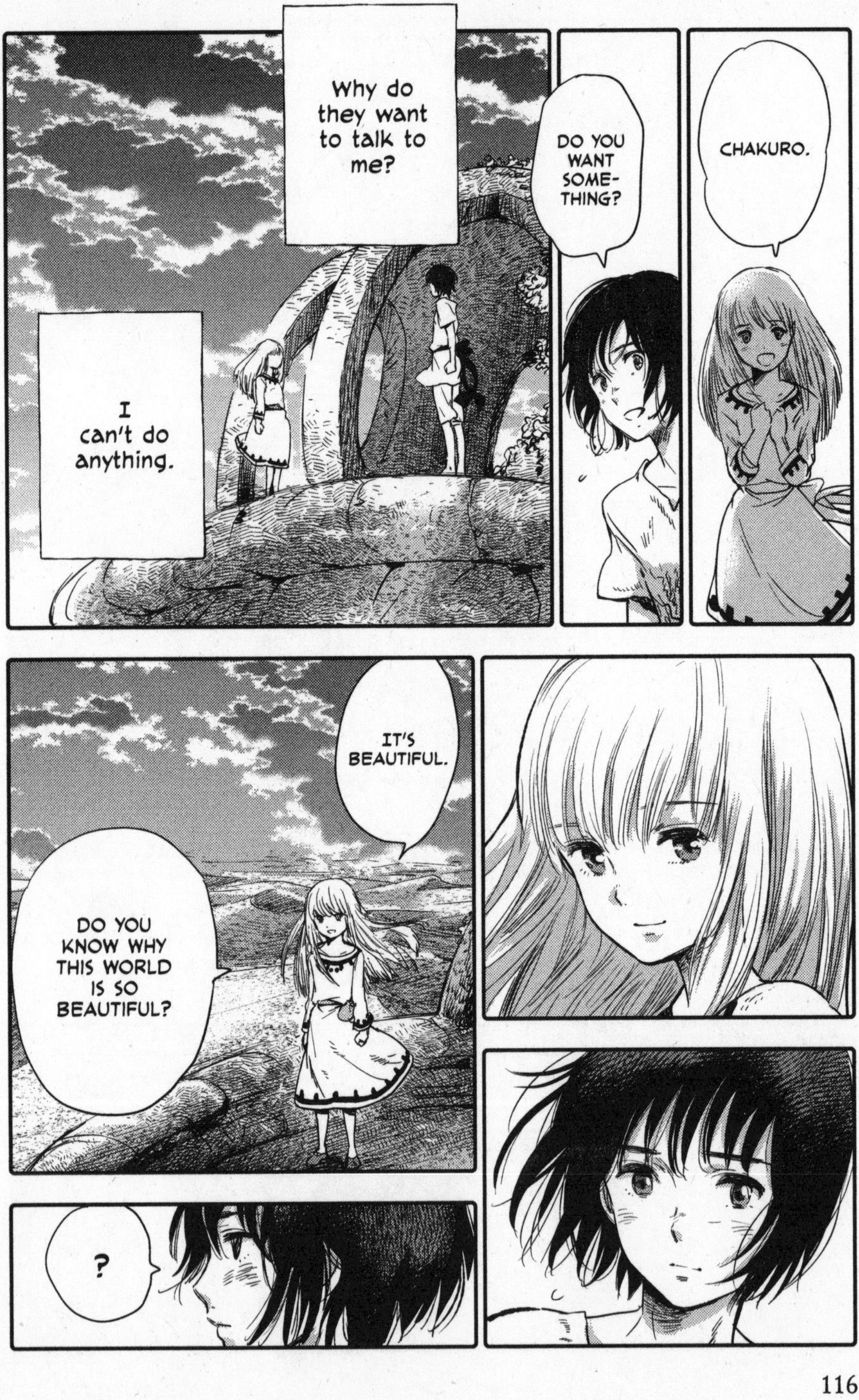
CHAKURO.
DO YOU WANT SOME-THING?
Why do they want to talk to me?
I can't do anything.
IT'S BEAUTIFUL.
DO YOU KNOW WHY THIS WORLD IS SO BEAUTIFUL?
?

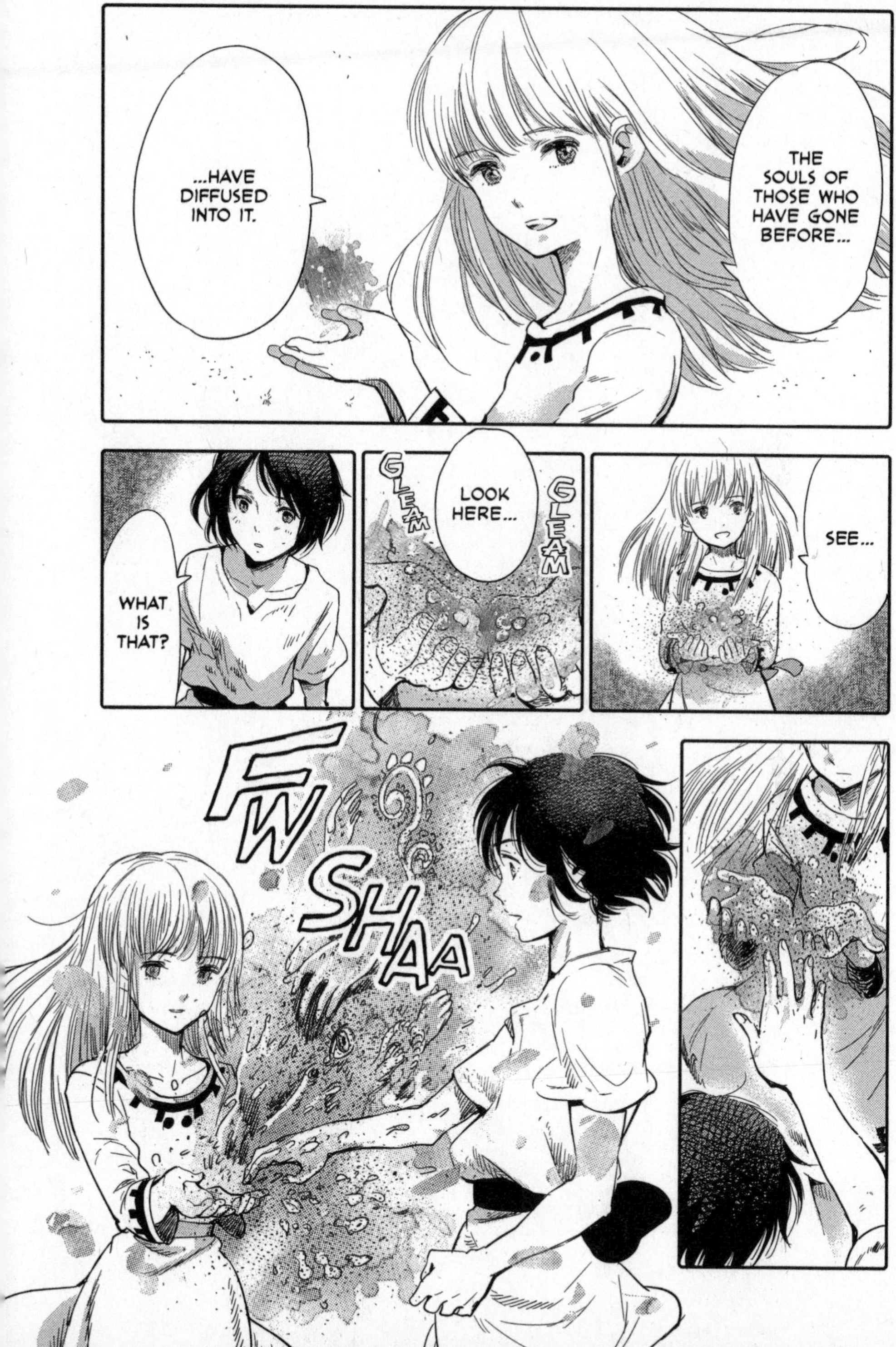
THE SOULS OF THOSE WHO HAVE GONE BEFORE...
...HAVE DIFFUSED INTO IT.
SEE...
GLEAM
LOOK HERE...
GLEAM
WHAT IS THAT?
FWSHAA

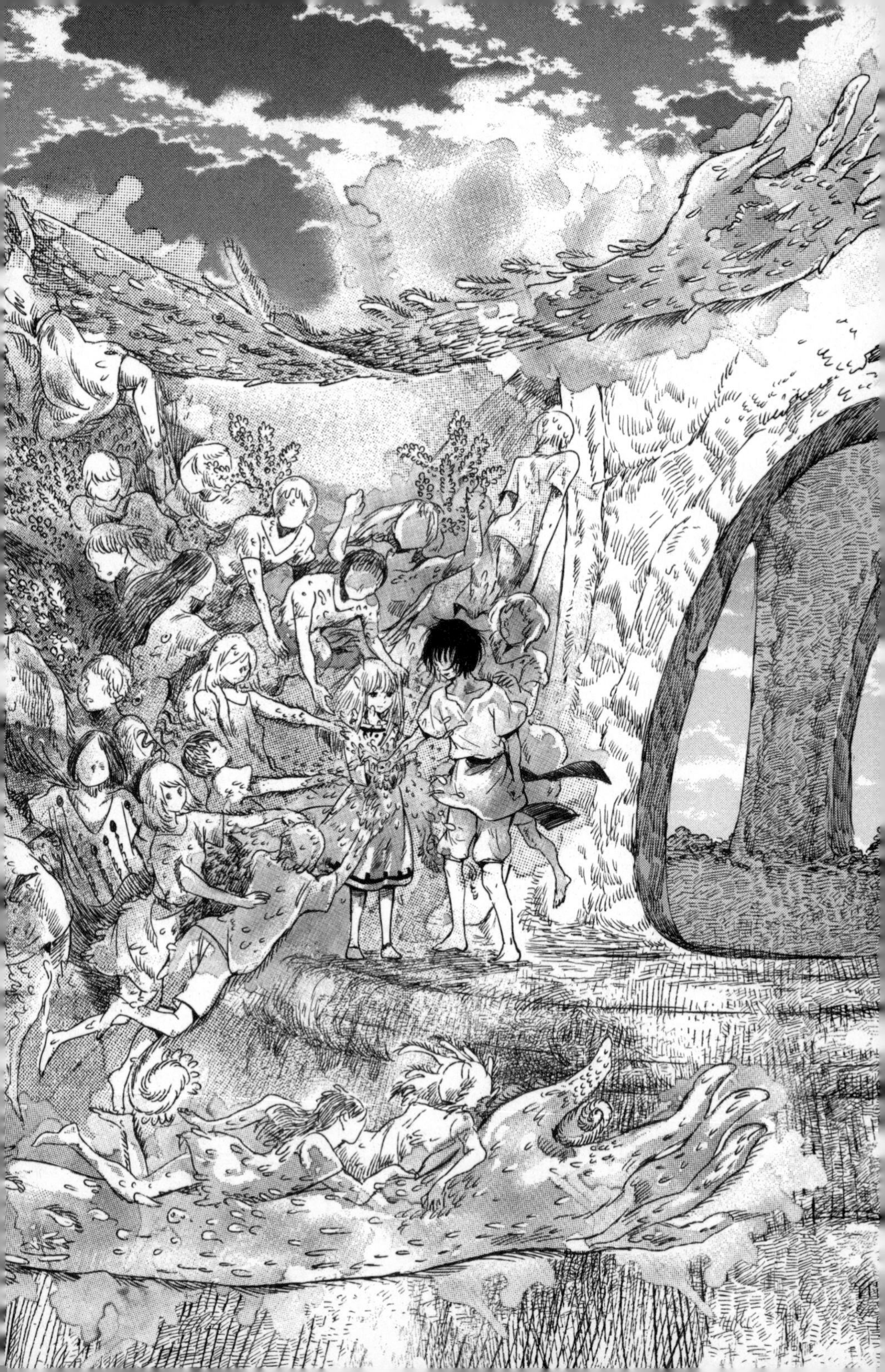

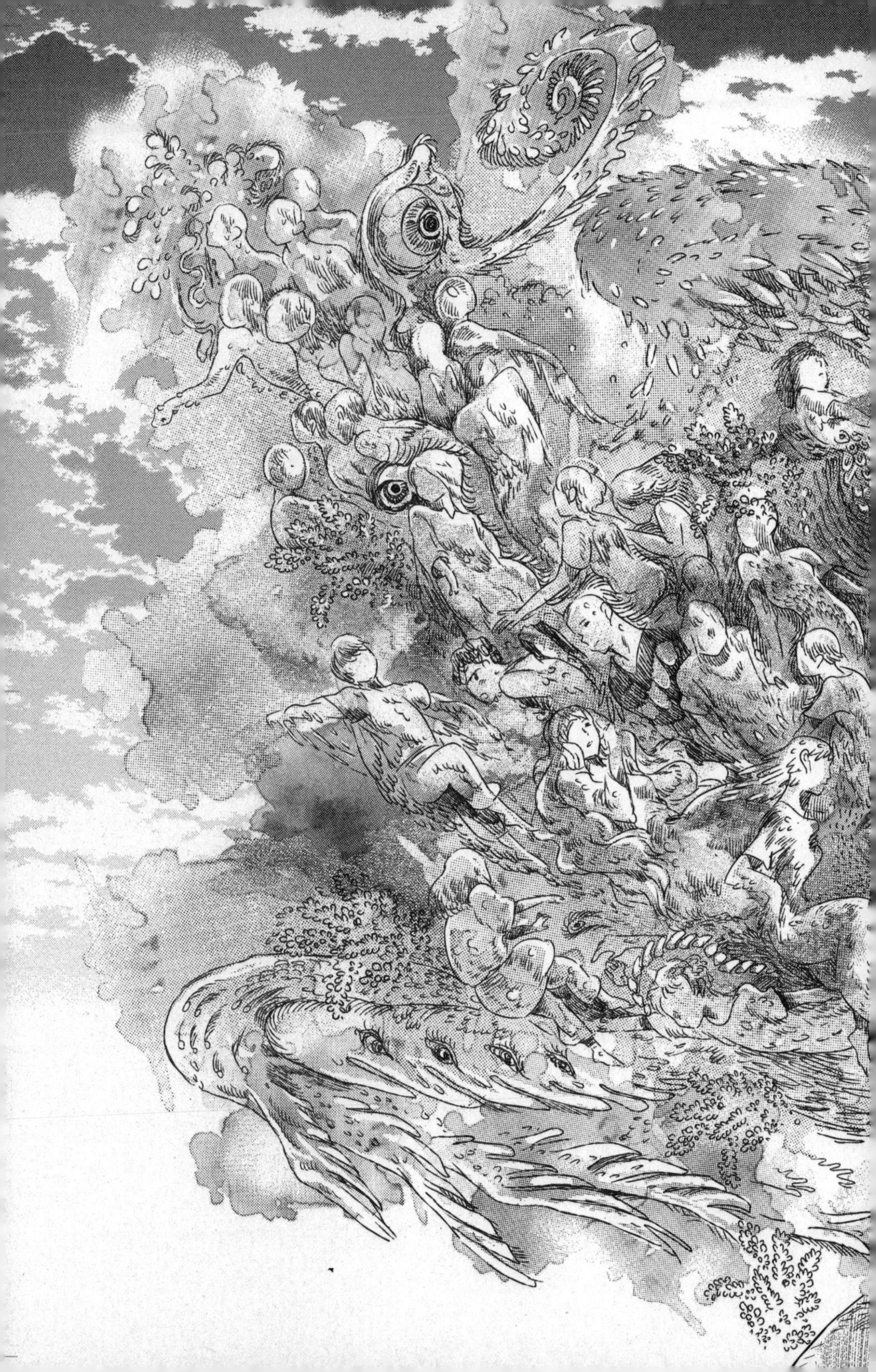

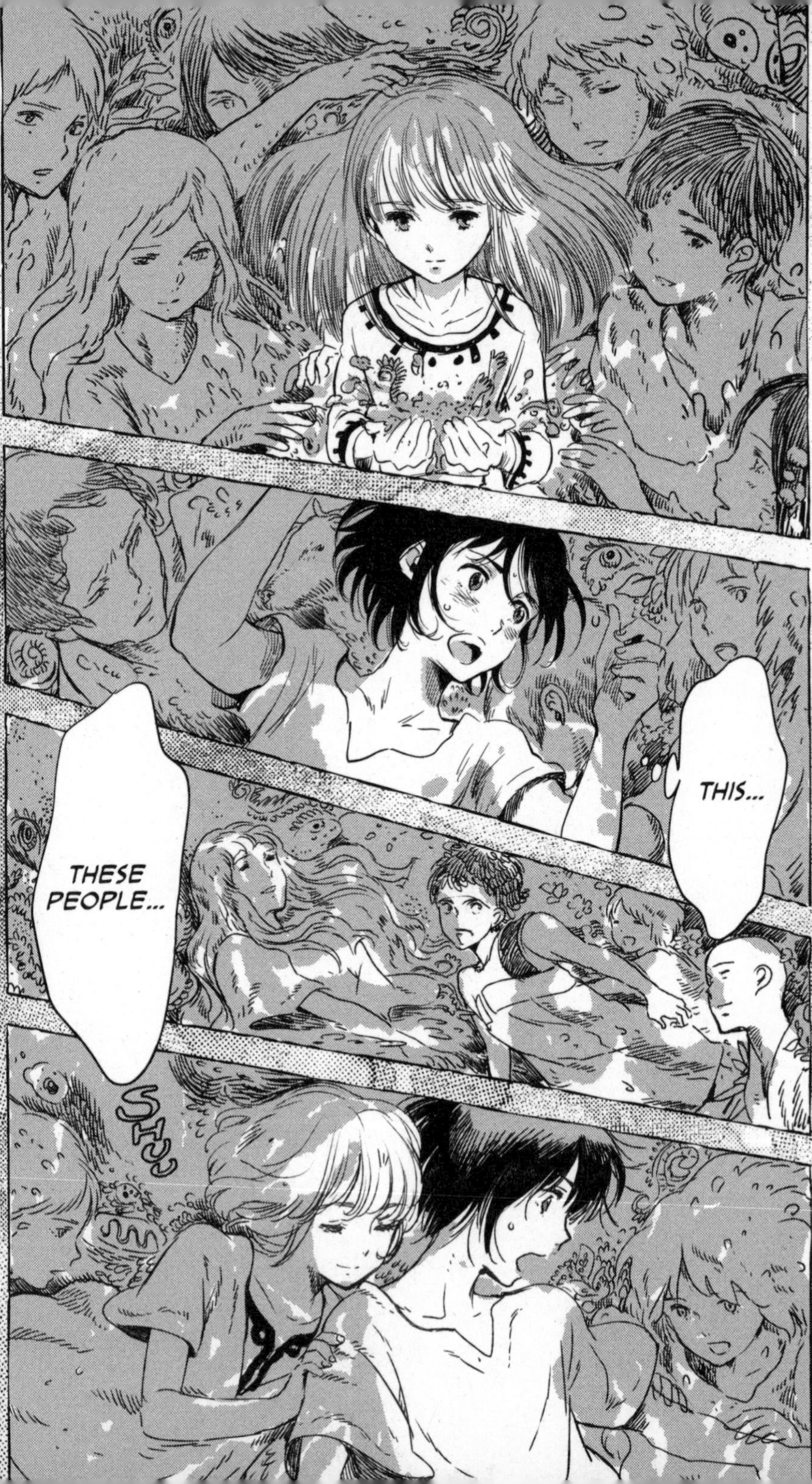
THIS...
THESE PEOPLE...
SHUU

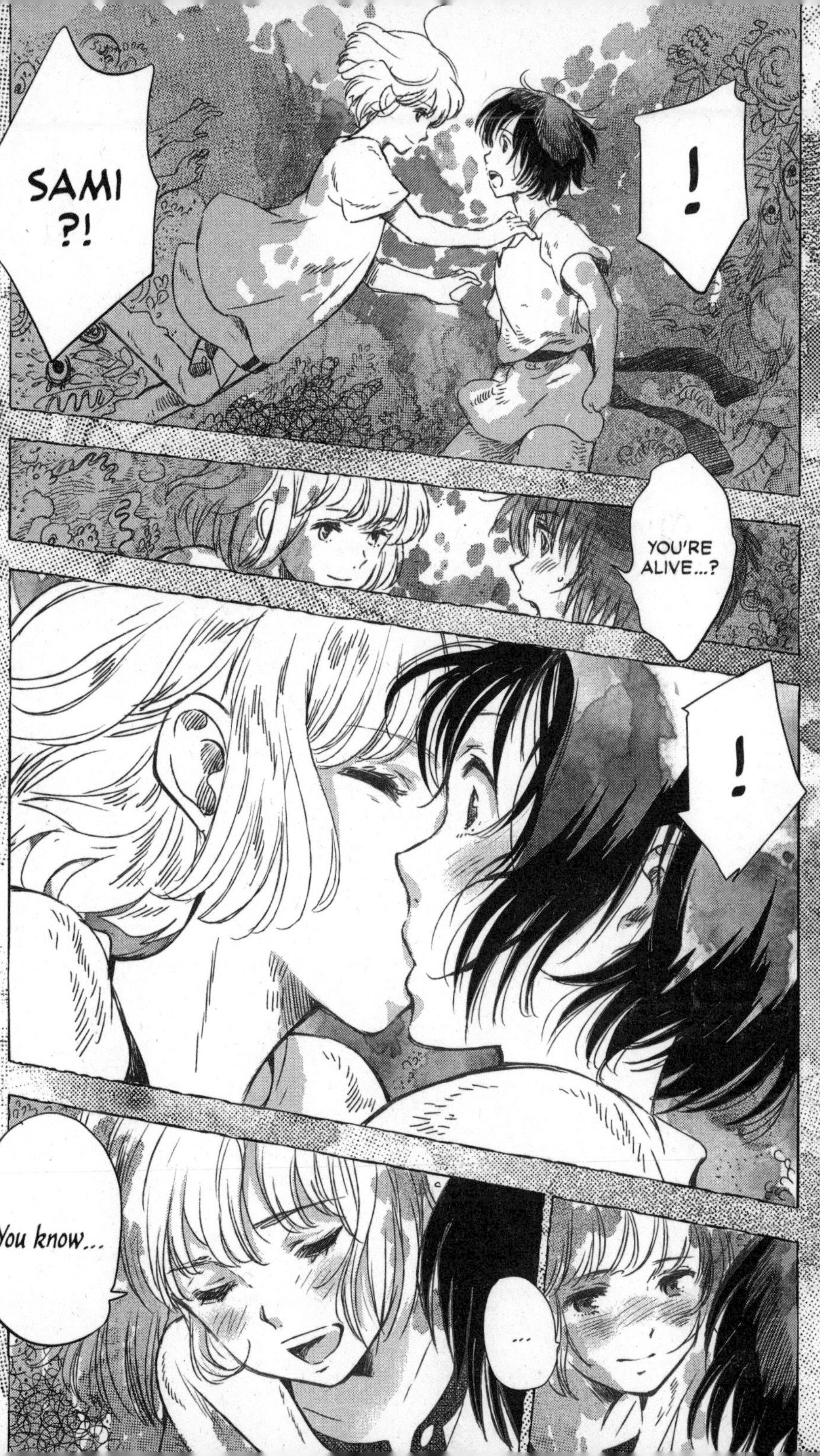
!
SAMI ?!
YOU'RE ALIVE...?
!
...
You know...

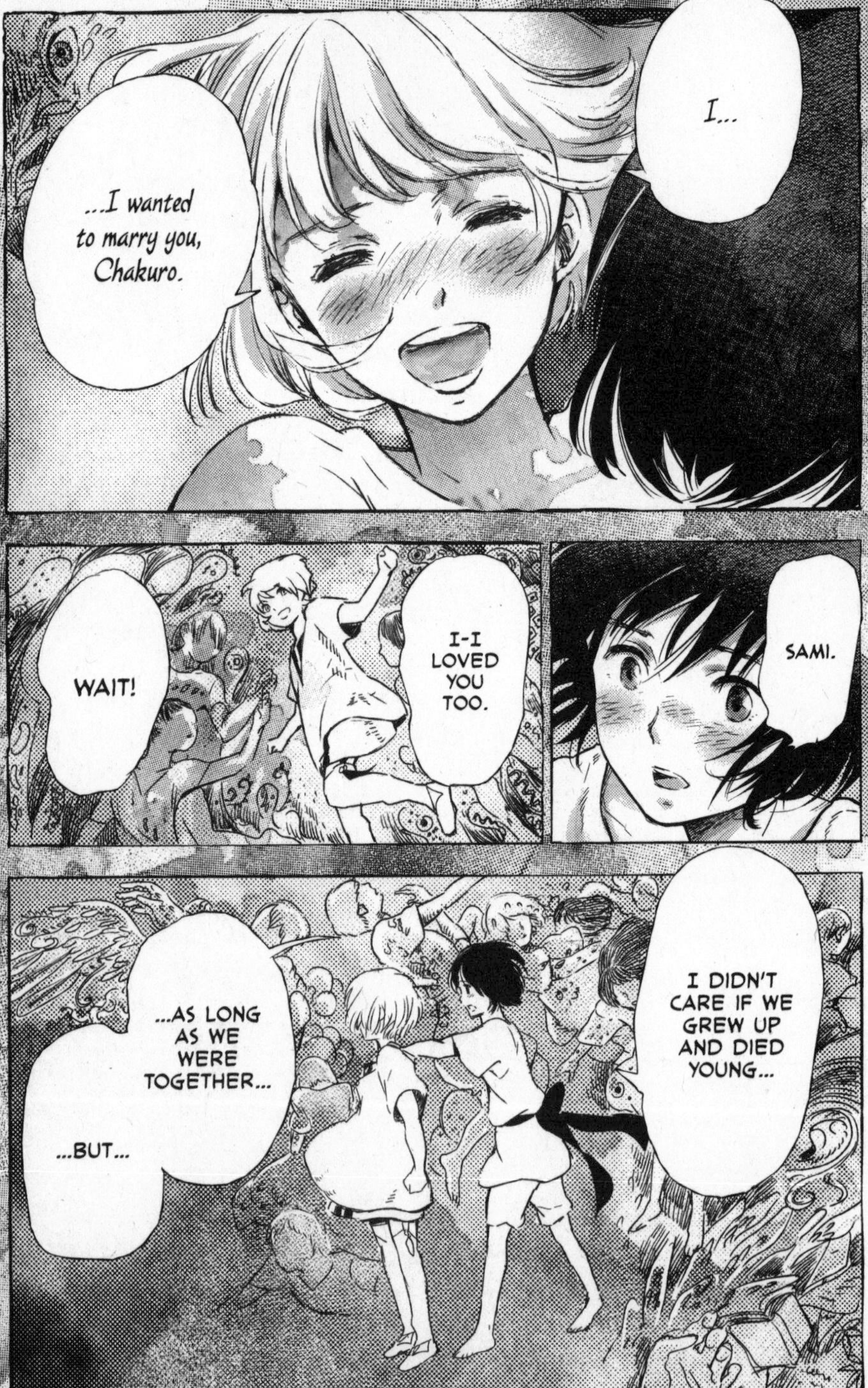
I...
...I wanted to marry you, Chakuro.
SAMI.
I-I LOVED YOU TOO.
WAIT!
I DIDN'T CARE IF WE GREW UP AND DIED YOUNG...
...AS LONG AS WE WERE TOGETHER...
...BUT...

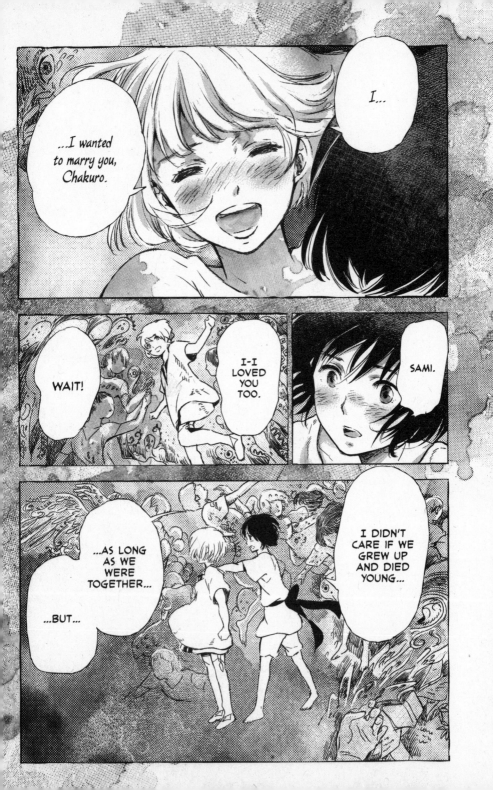

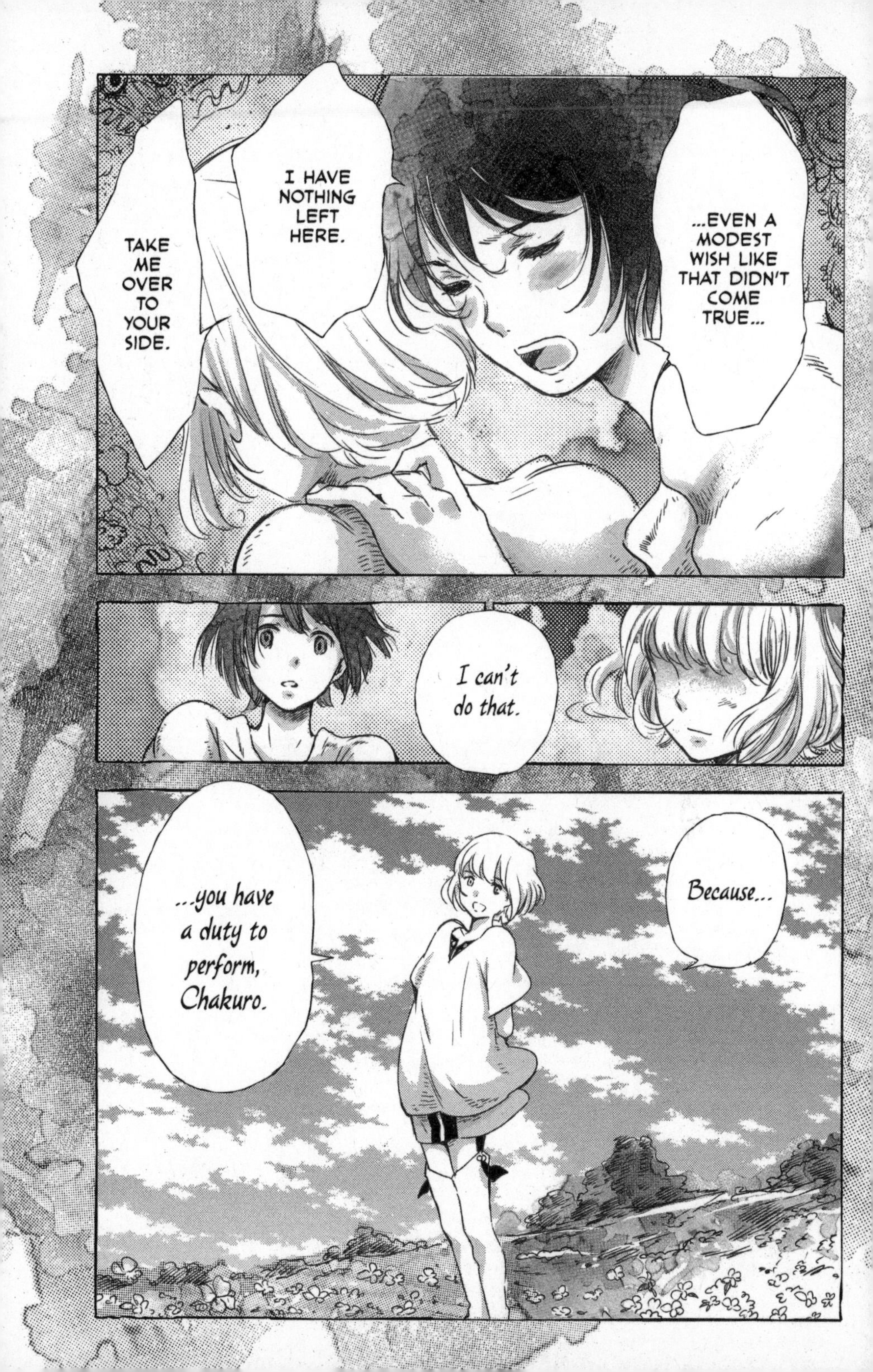
...EVEN A MODEST WISH LIKE THAT DIDN'T COME TRUE...
I HAVE NOTHING LEFT HERE.
TAKE ME OVER TO YOUR SIDE.
I can't do that.
Because...
...you have a duty to perform, Chakuro.

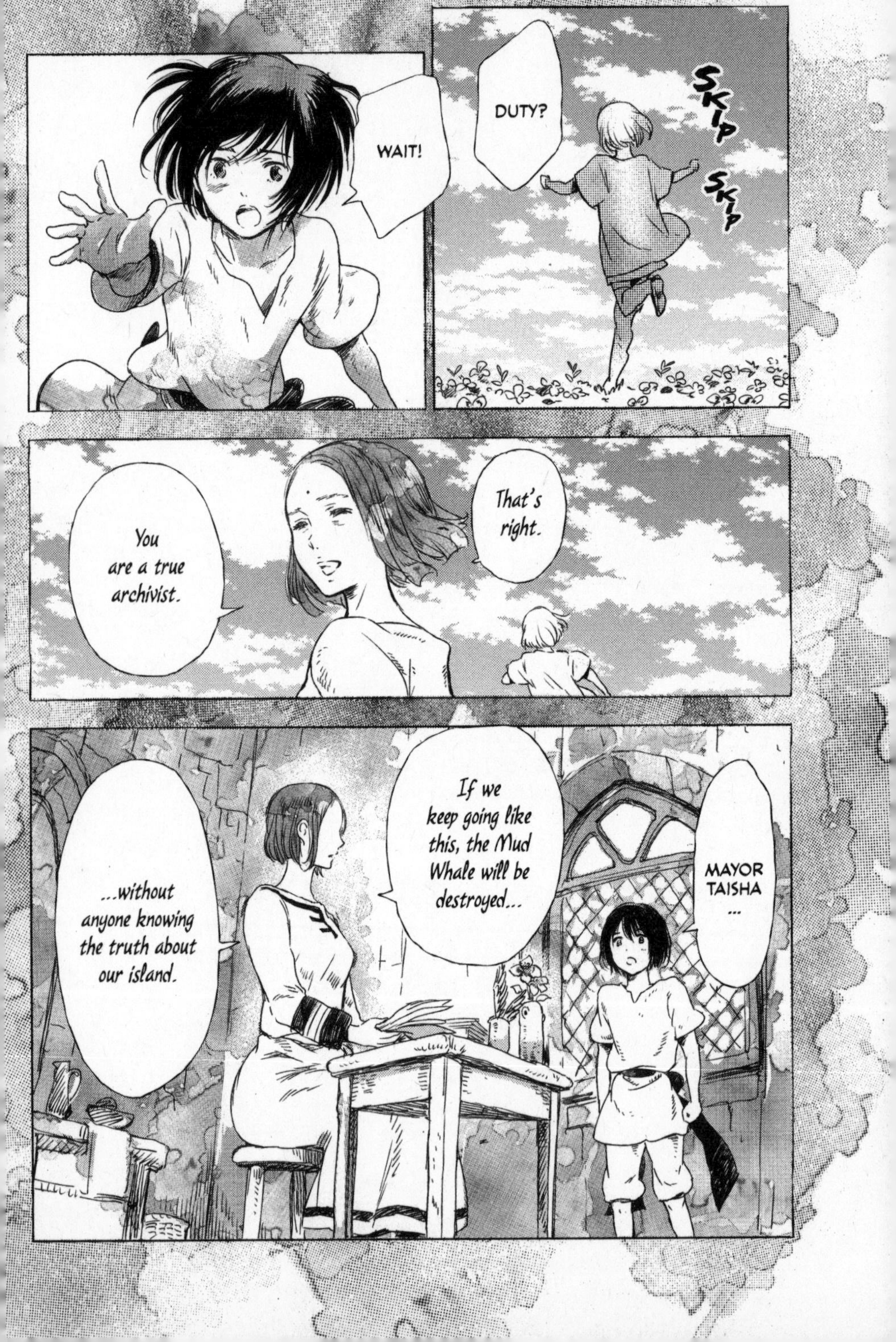
DUTY?
SKIP SKIP
WAIT!
That's right.
You are a true archivist.
MAYOR TAISHA ...
If we keep going like this, the Mud Whale will be destroyed...
...without anyone knowing the truth about our island.

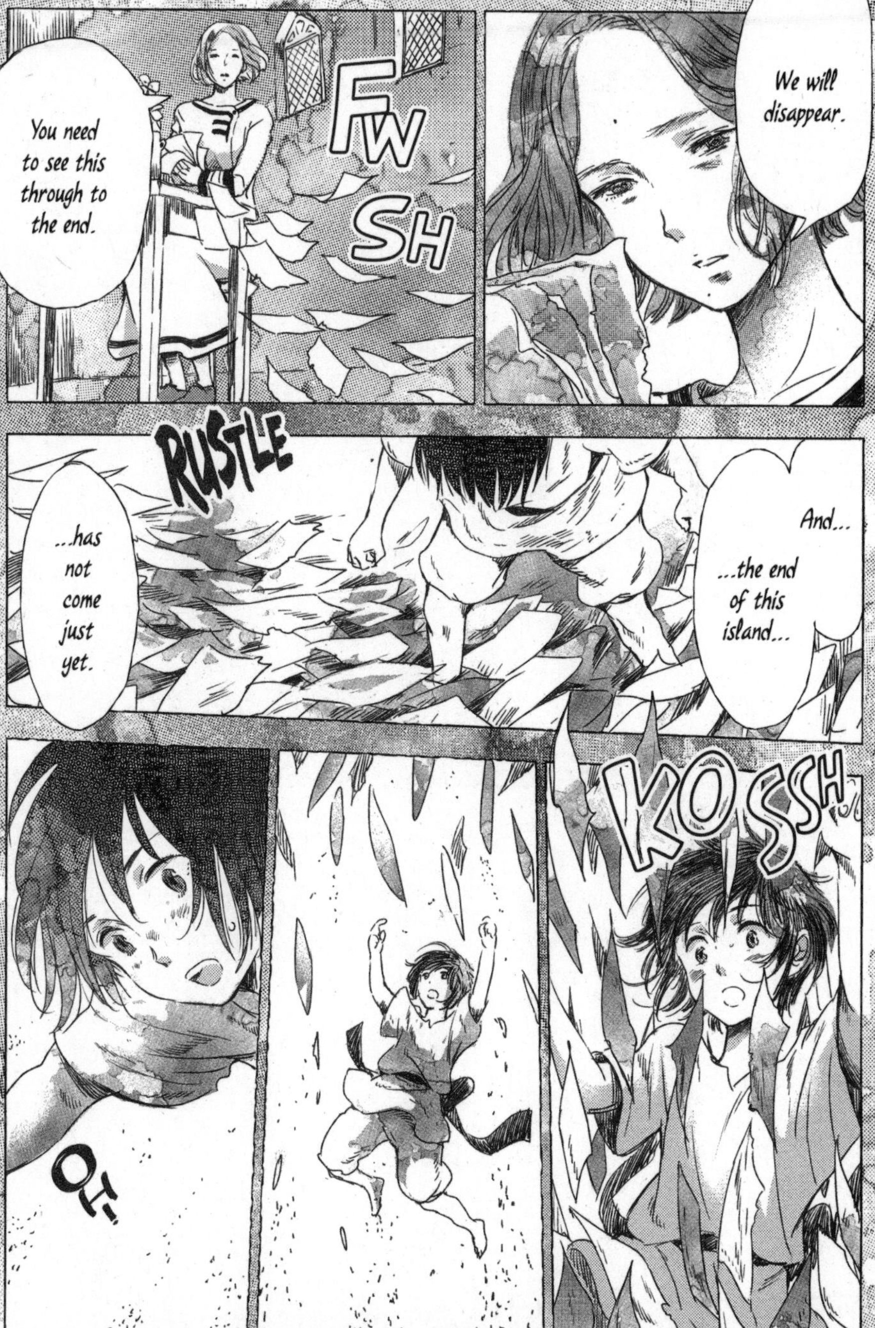
We will disappear.
You need to see this through to the end.
FWSH
And... ...the end of this island...
...has not come just yet.
RUSTLE
KOSSH
OH!

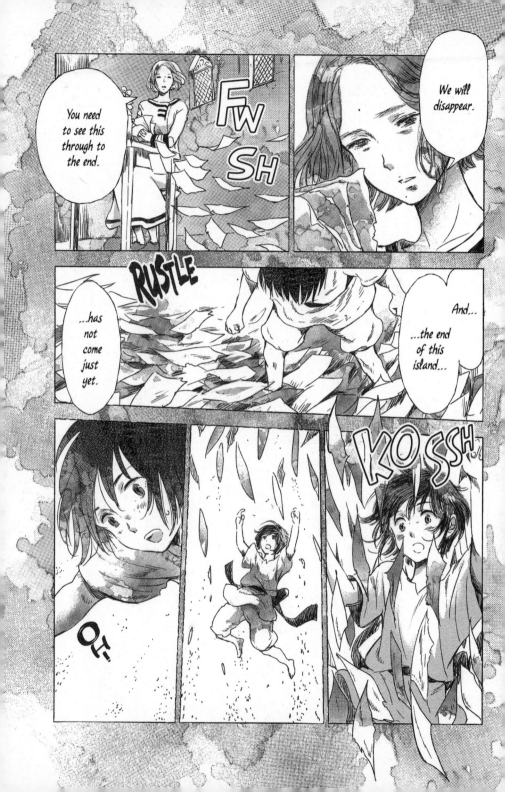

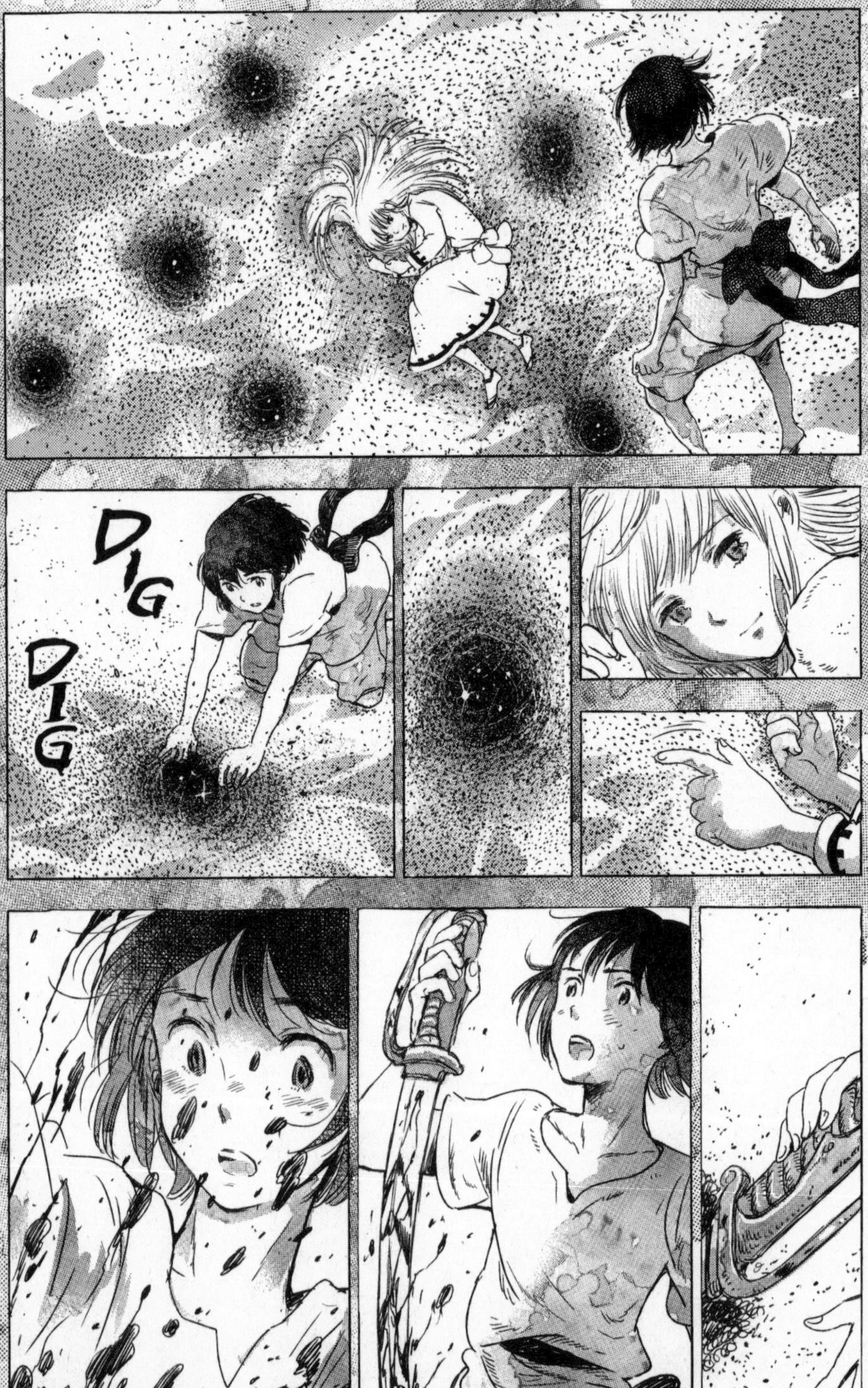
DIG
DIG

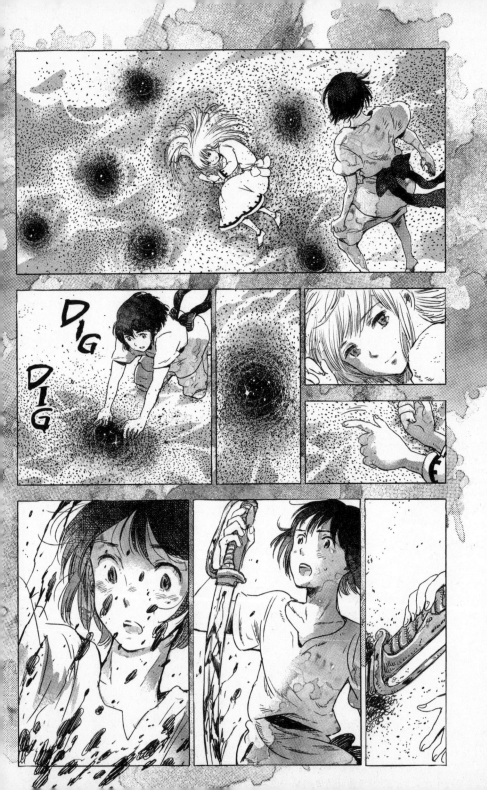

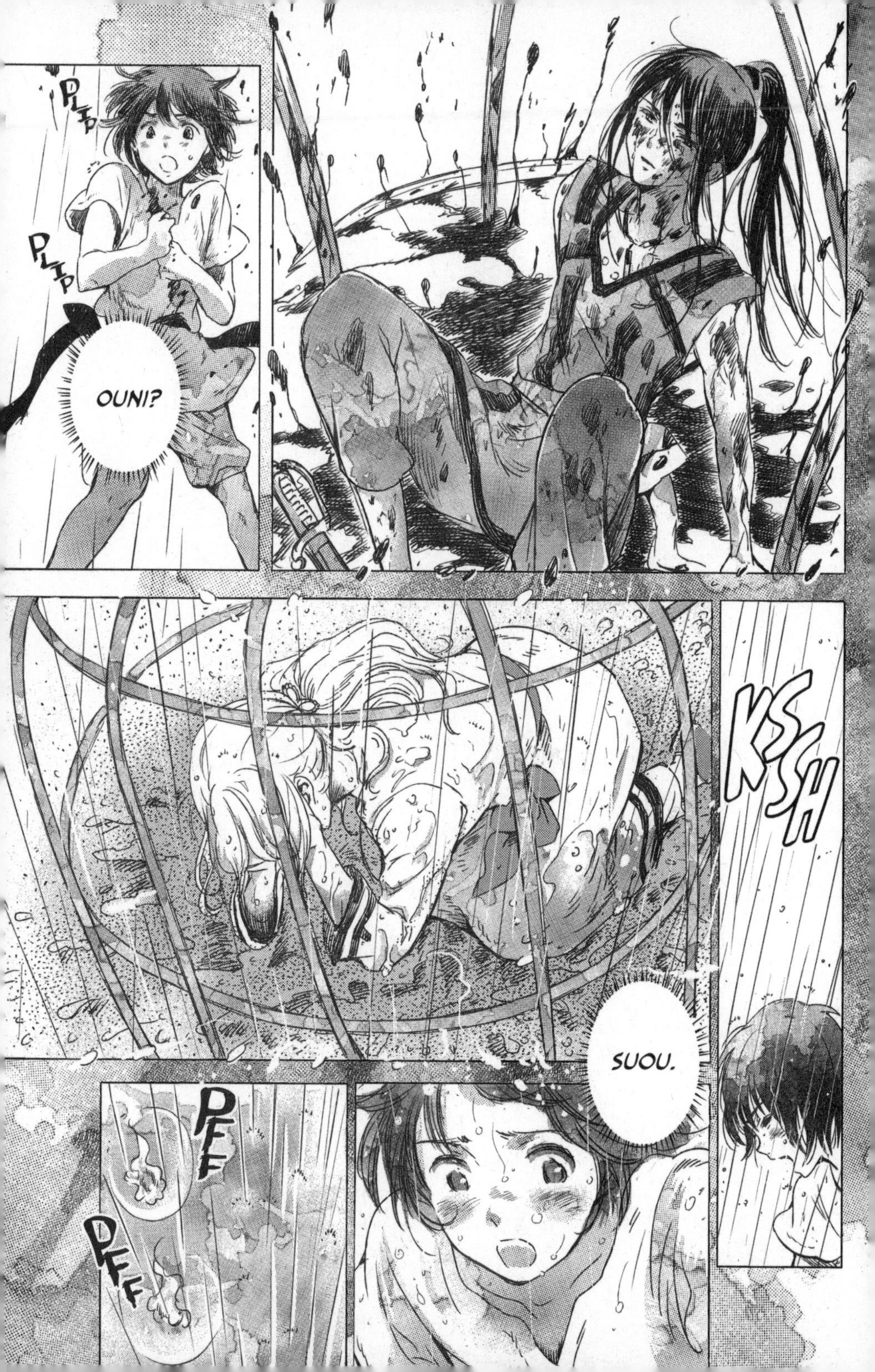
PLIP
PLIP
OUNI?
KSSH
SUOU.
PFF
PFF

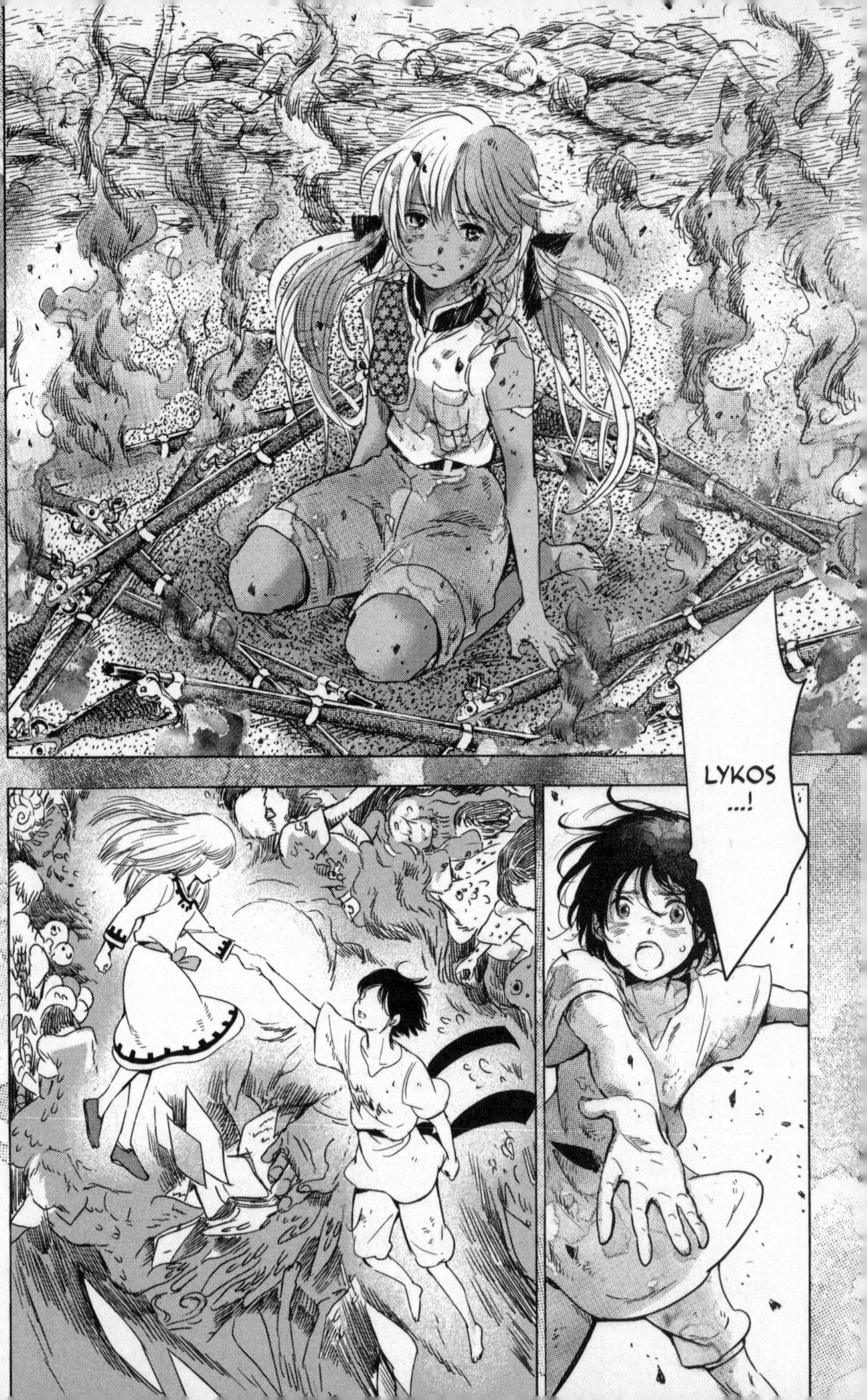
LYKOS ...!

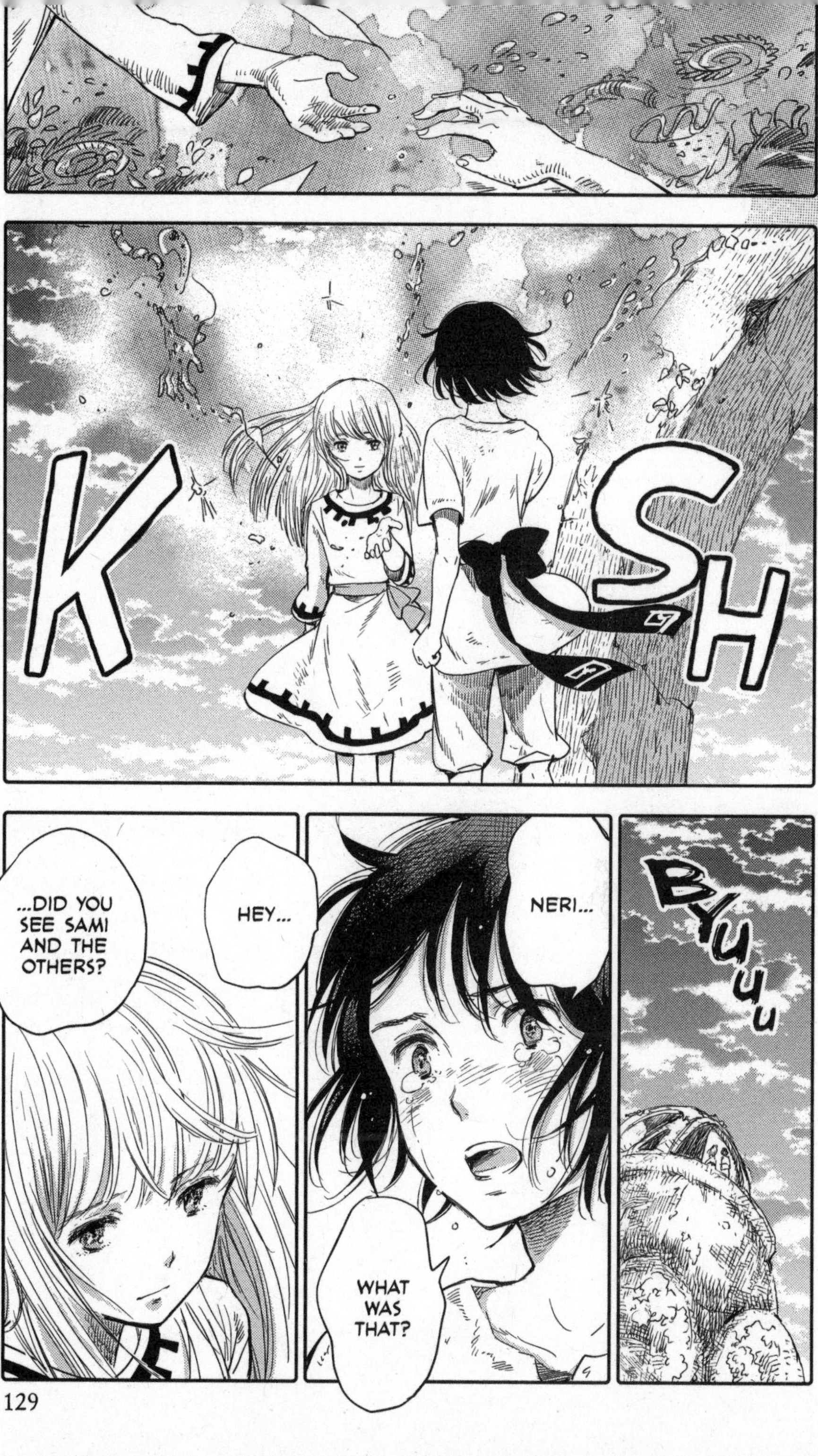
KSH
BYUUU
NERI...
WHAT WAS THAT?
HEY...
...DID YOU SEE SAMI AND THE OTHERS?

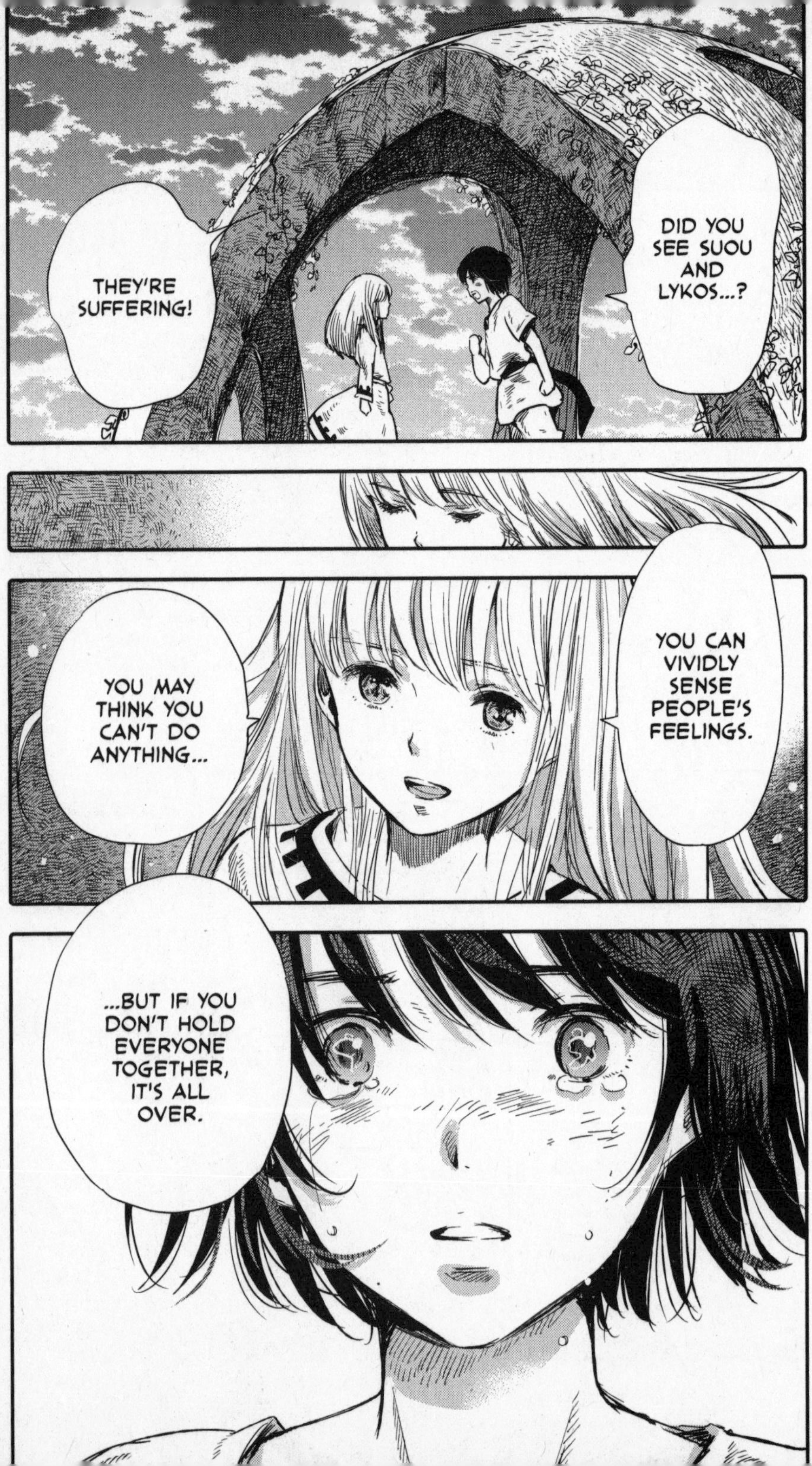
DID YOU SEE SUOU AND LYKOS...?
THEY'RE SUFFERING!
YOU CAN VIVIDLY SENSE PEOPLE'S FEELINGS.
YOU MAY THINK YOU CAN'T DO ANYTHING...
...BUT IF YOU DON'T HOLD EVERYONE TOGETHER,
IT'S ALL OVER.

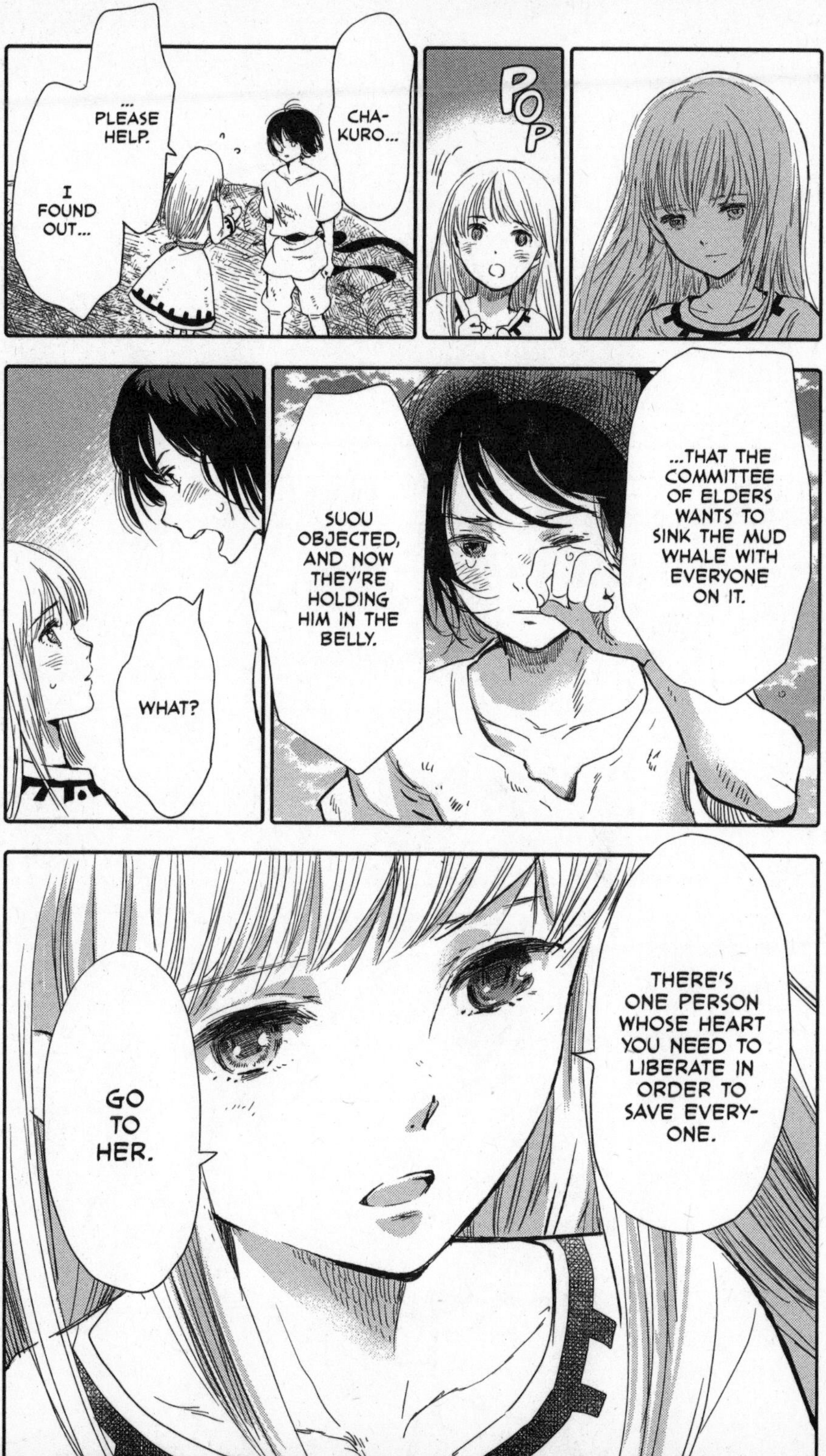
POP
CHA-KURO...
...PLEASE HELP.
I FOUND OUT...
...THAT THE COMMITTEE OF ELDERS WANTS TO SINK THE MUD WHALE WITH EVERYONE ON IT.
SUOU OBJECTED, AND NOW THEY'RE HOLDING HIM IN THE BELLY.
WHAT?
THERE'S ONE PERSON WHOSE HEART YOU NEED TO LIBERATE IN ORDER TO SAVE EVERY-ONE.
GO TO HER.

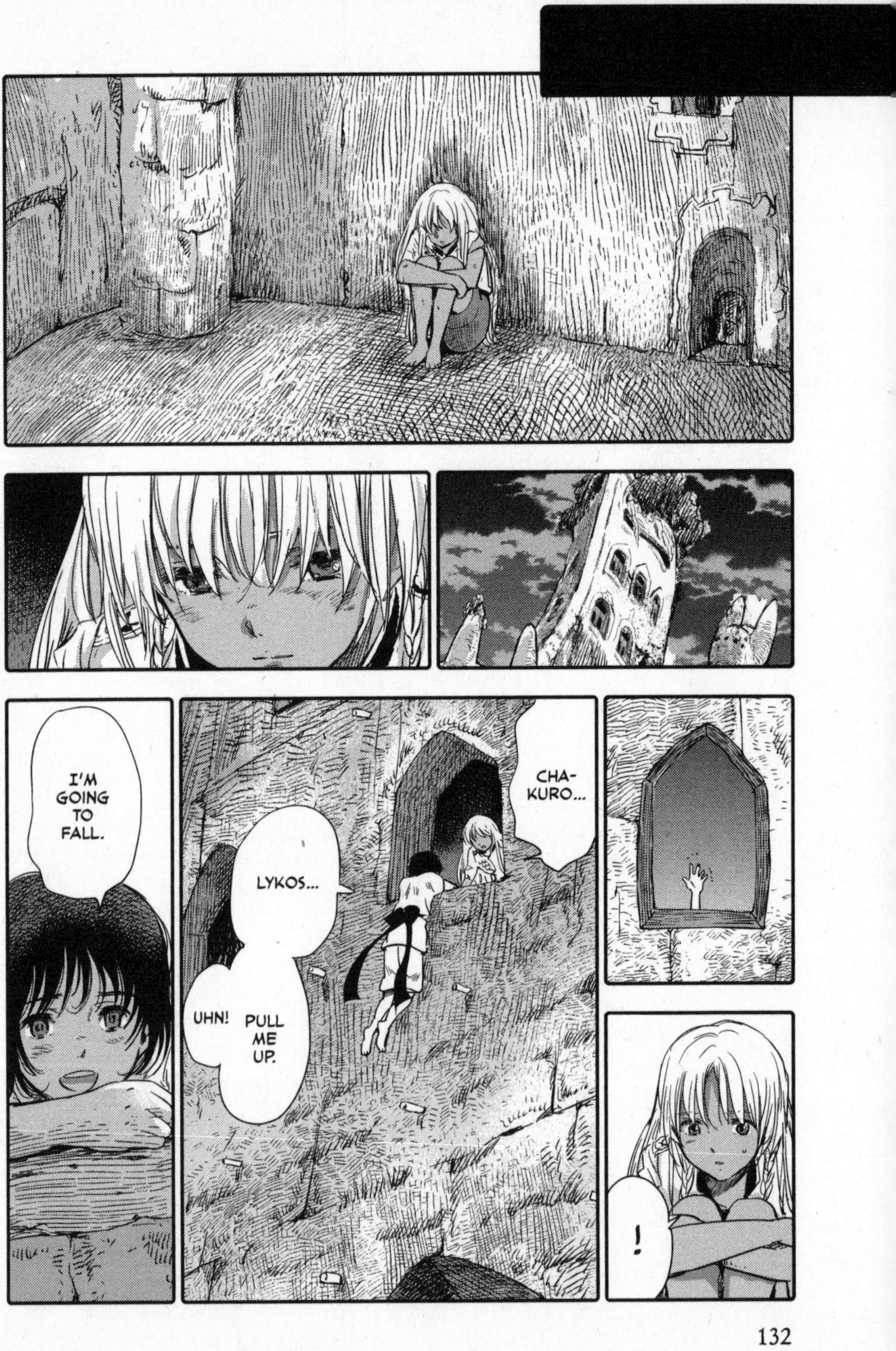
!
CHA-KURO...
LYKOS...
PULL ME UP.
UHN!
I'M GOING TO FALL.

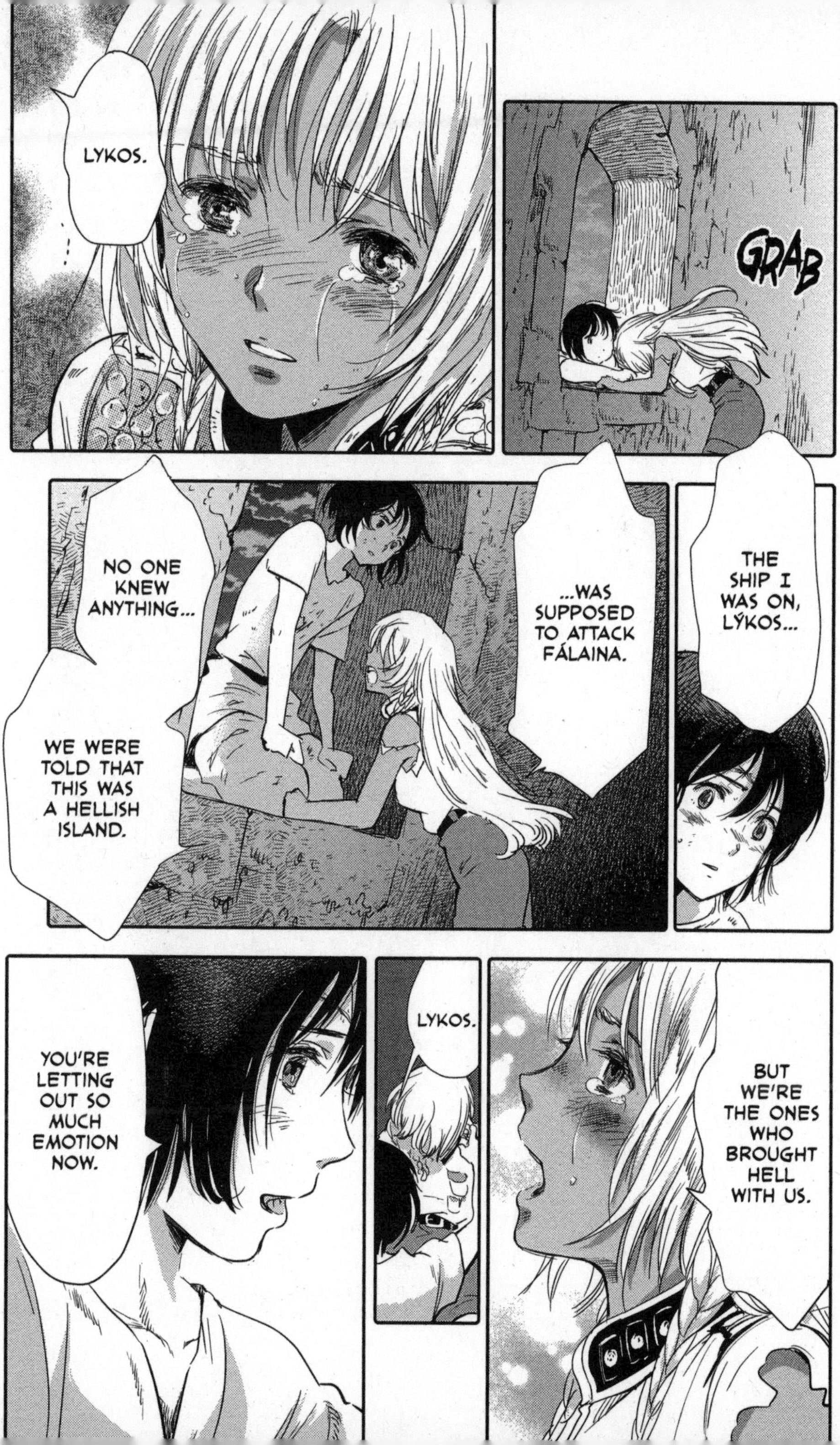
GRAB
LYKOS.
THE SHIP I WAS ON, LÝKOS...
...WAS SUPPOSED TO ATTACK FÁLAINA.
NO ONE KNEW ANYTHING...
WE WERE TOLD THAT THIS WAS A HELLISH ISLAND.
BUT WE'RE THE ONES WHO BROUGHT HELL WITH US.
LYKOS.
YOU'RE LETTING OUT SO MUCH EMOTION NOW.

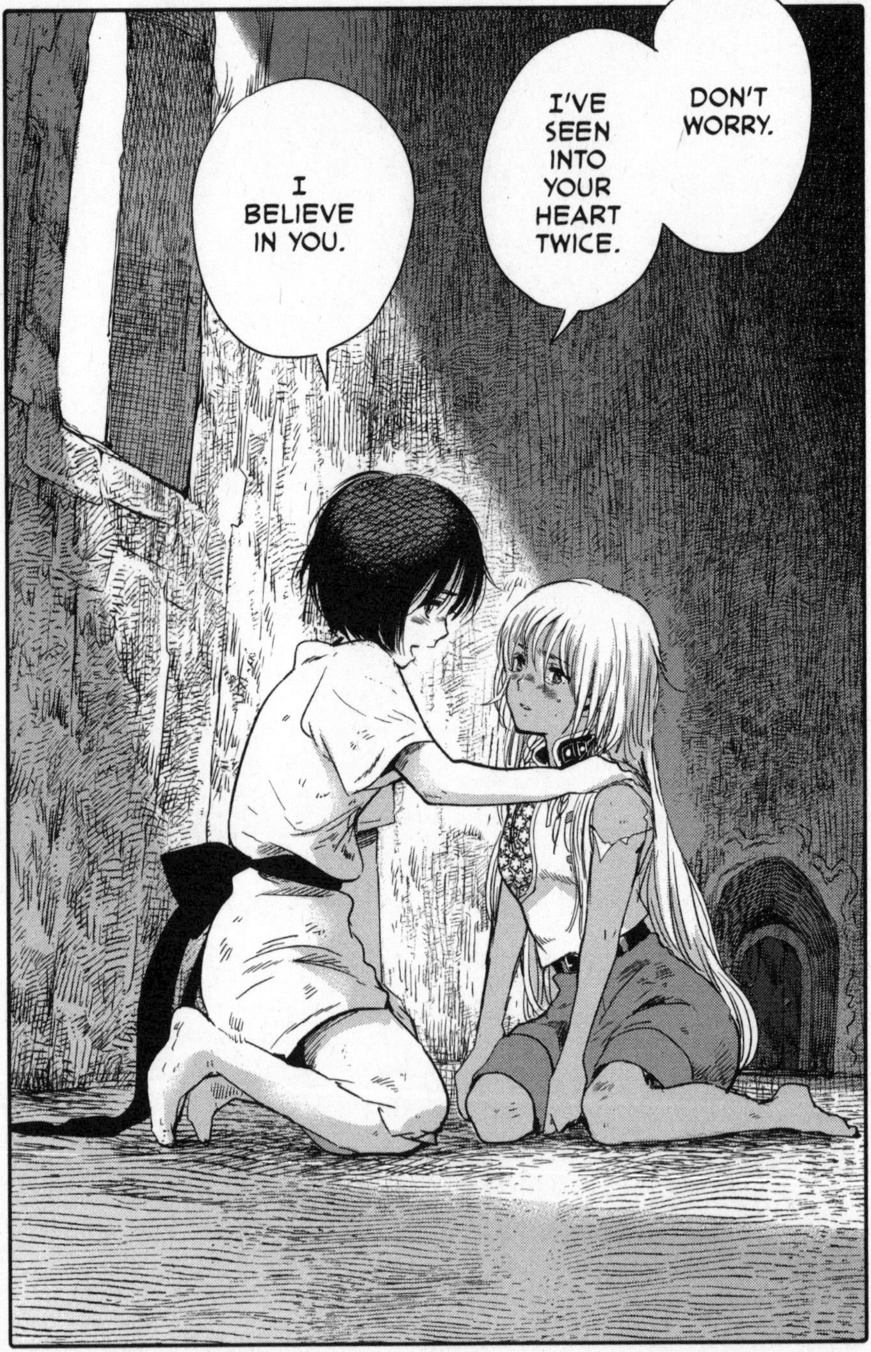
DON'T WORRY.
I'VE SEEN INTO YOUR HEART TWICE.
I BELIEVE IN YOU.

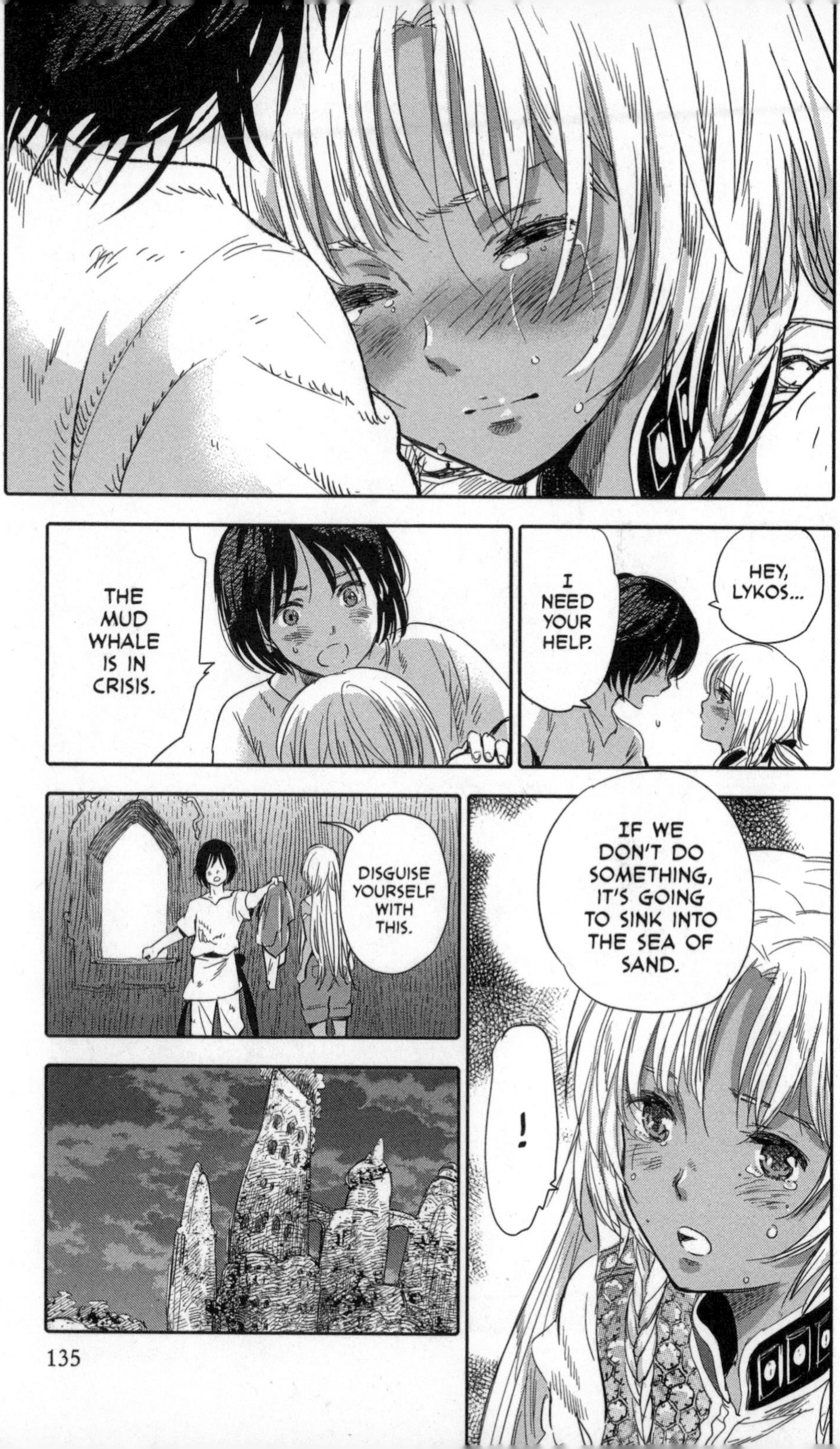
HEY, LYKOS...
I NEED YOUR HELP.
THE MUD WHALE IS IN CRISIS.
IF WE DON'T DO SOMETHING, IT'S GOING TO SINK INTO THE SEA OF SAND.
!
DISGUISE YOURSELF WITH THIS.

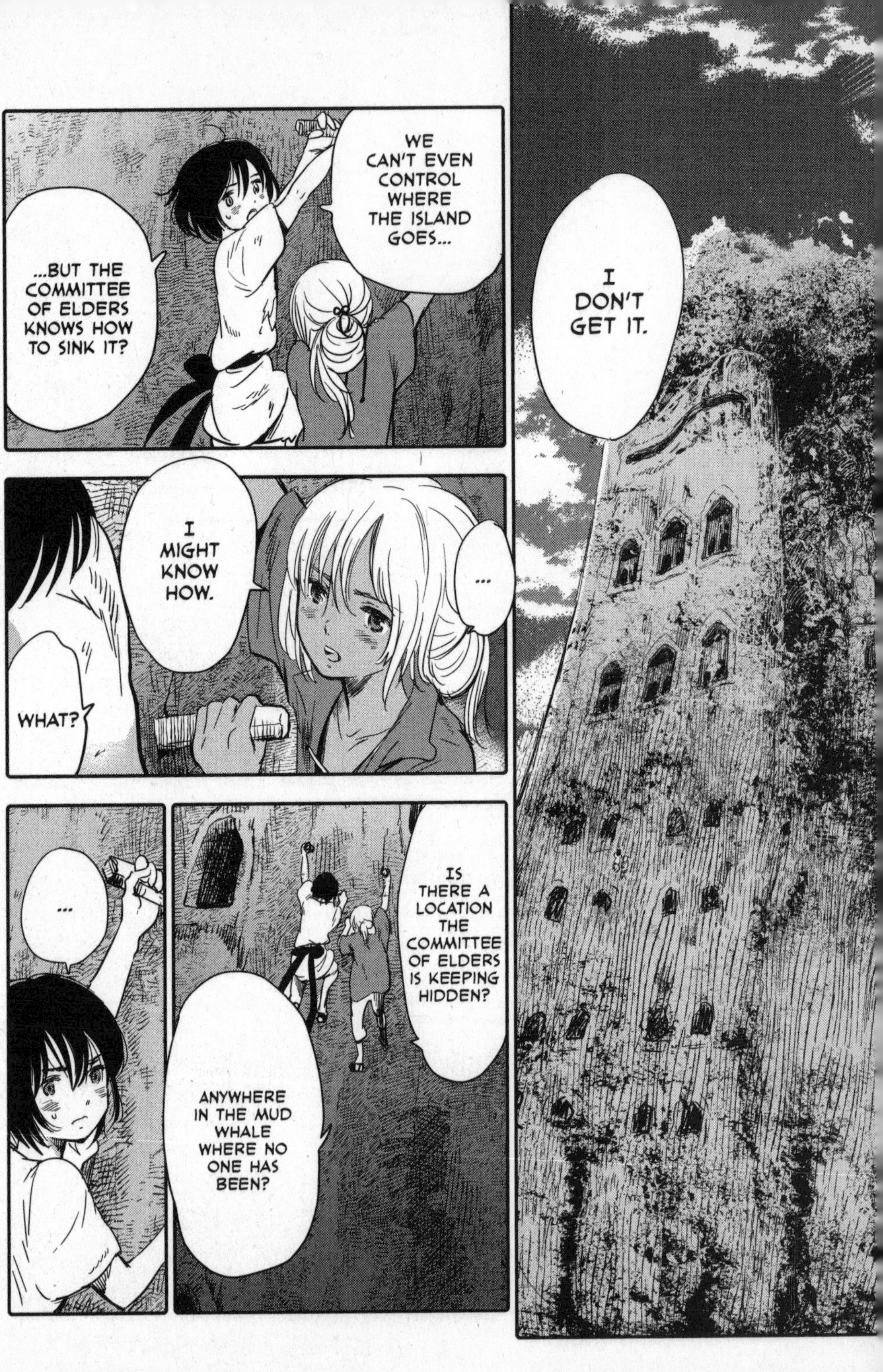
I DON'T GET IT.
WE CAN'T EVEN CONTROL WHERE THE ISLAND GOES...
...BUT THE COMMITTEE OF ELDERS KNOWS HOW TO SINK IT?
...
I MIGHT KNOW HOW.
WHAT?
IS THERE A LOCATION THE COMMITTEE OF ELDERS IS KEEPING HIDDEN?
ANYWHERE IN THE MUD WHALE WHERE NO ONE HAS BEEN?
...

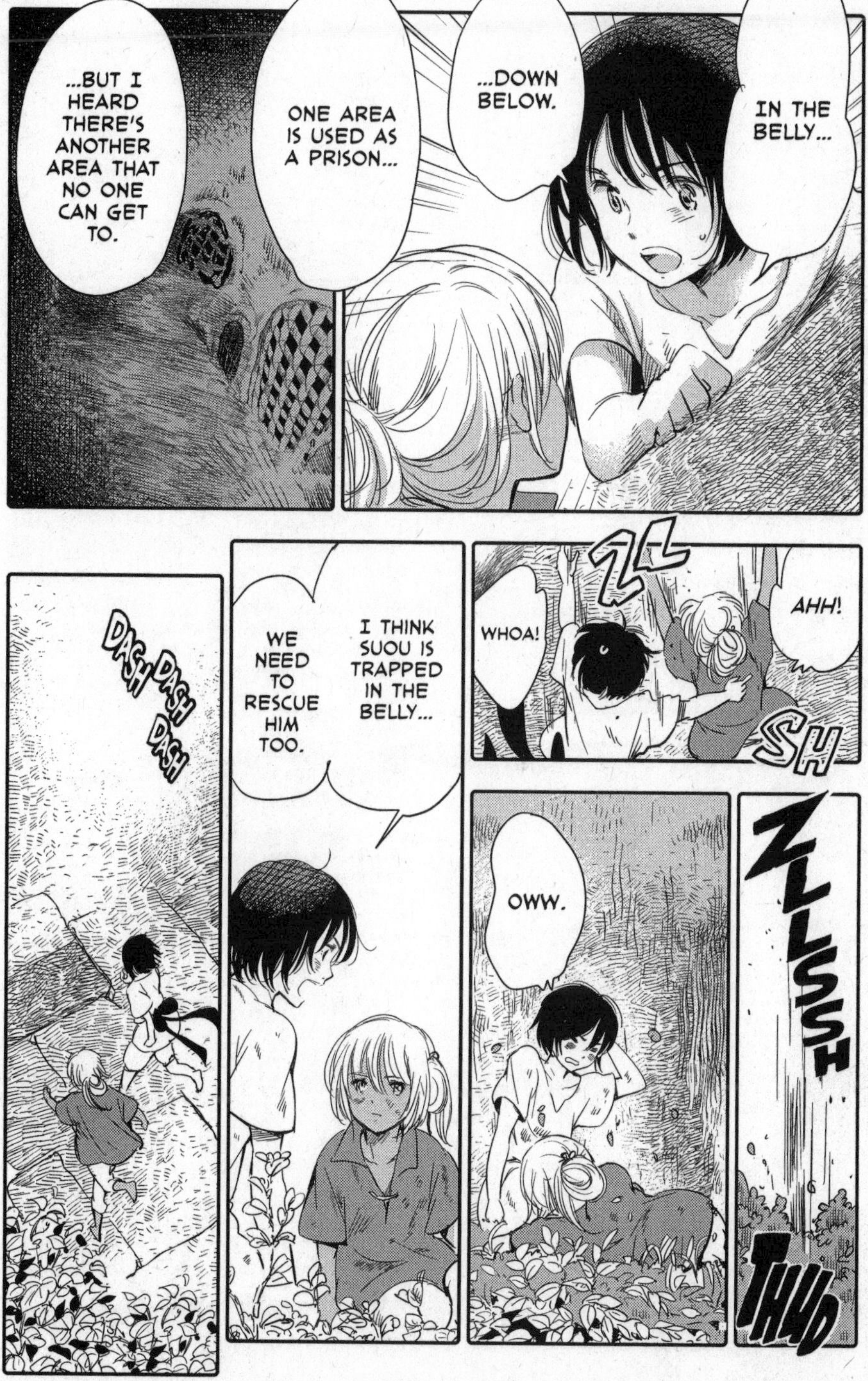
IN THE BELLY...
...DOWN BELOW.
ONE AREA IS USED AS A PRISON...
...BUT I HEARD THERE'S ANOTHER AREA THAT NO ONE CAN GET TO.
ZZ
AHH!
WHOA!
SH
ZZLLSSSH
THUD
OWW.
I THINK SUOU IS TRAPPED IN THE BELLY...
WE NEED TO RESCUE HIM TOO.
DASH DASH DASH

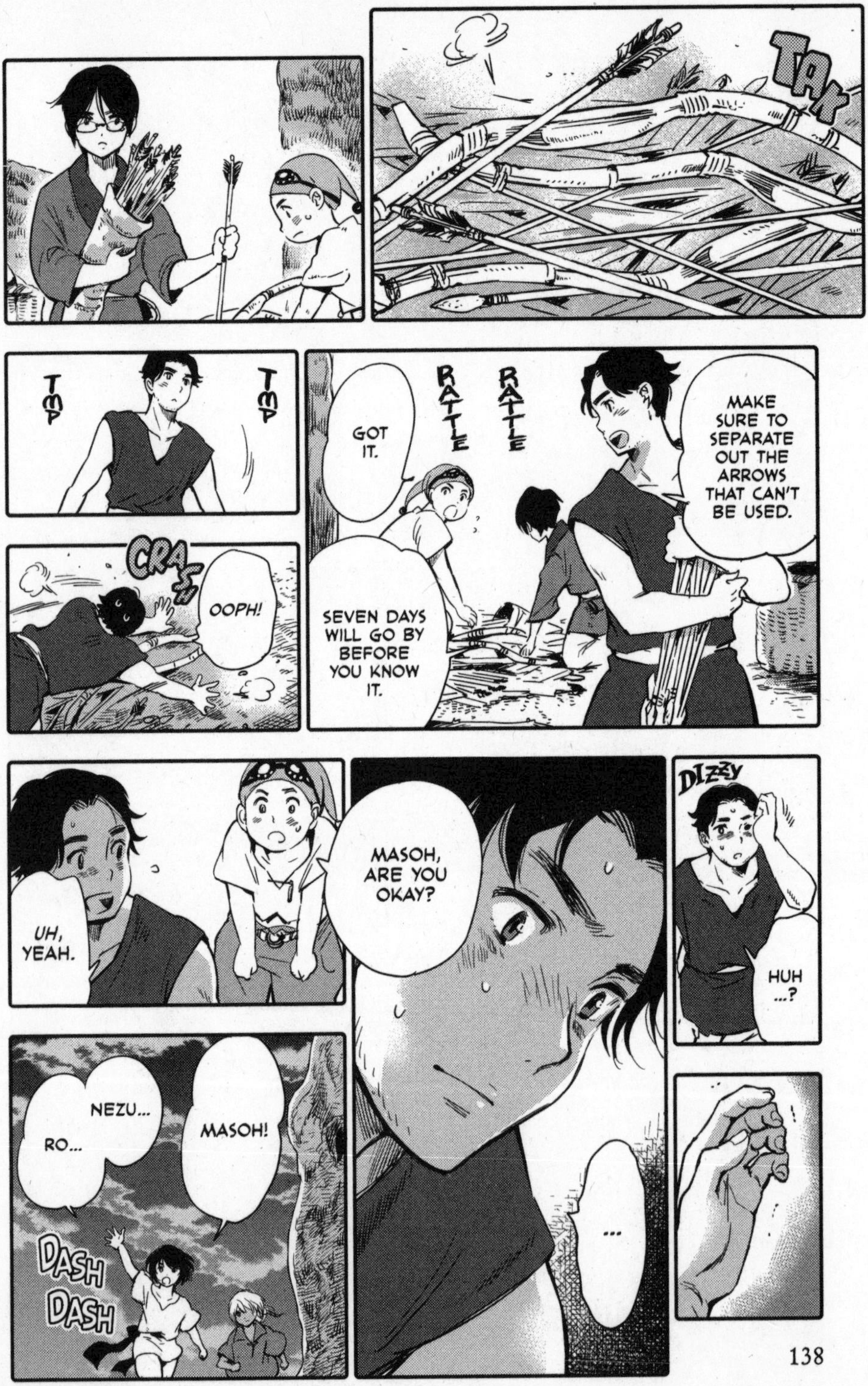
TAK
MAKE SURE TO SEPARATE OUT THE ARROWS THAT CAN'T BE USED.
RATTLE RATTLE
GOT IT.
SEVEN DAYS WILL GO BY BEFORE YOU KNOW IT.
TMP TMP
CRASH
OOPH!
DIZZY
HUH ...?
MASOH, ARE YOU OKAY?
...
UH, YEAH.
MASOH!
NEZU... RO...
DASH DASH

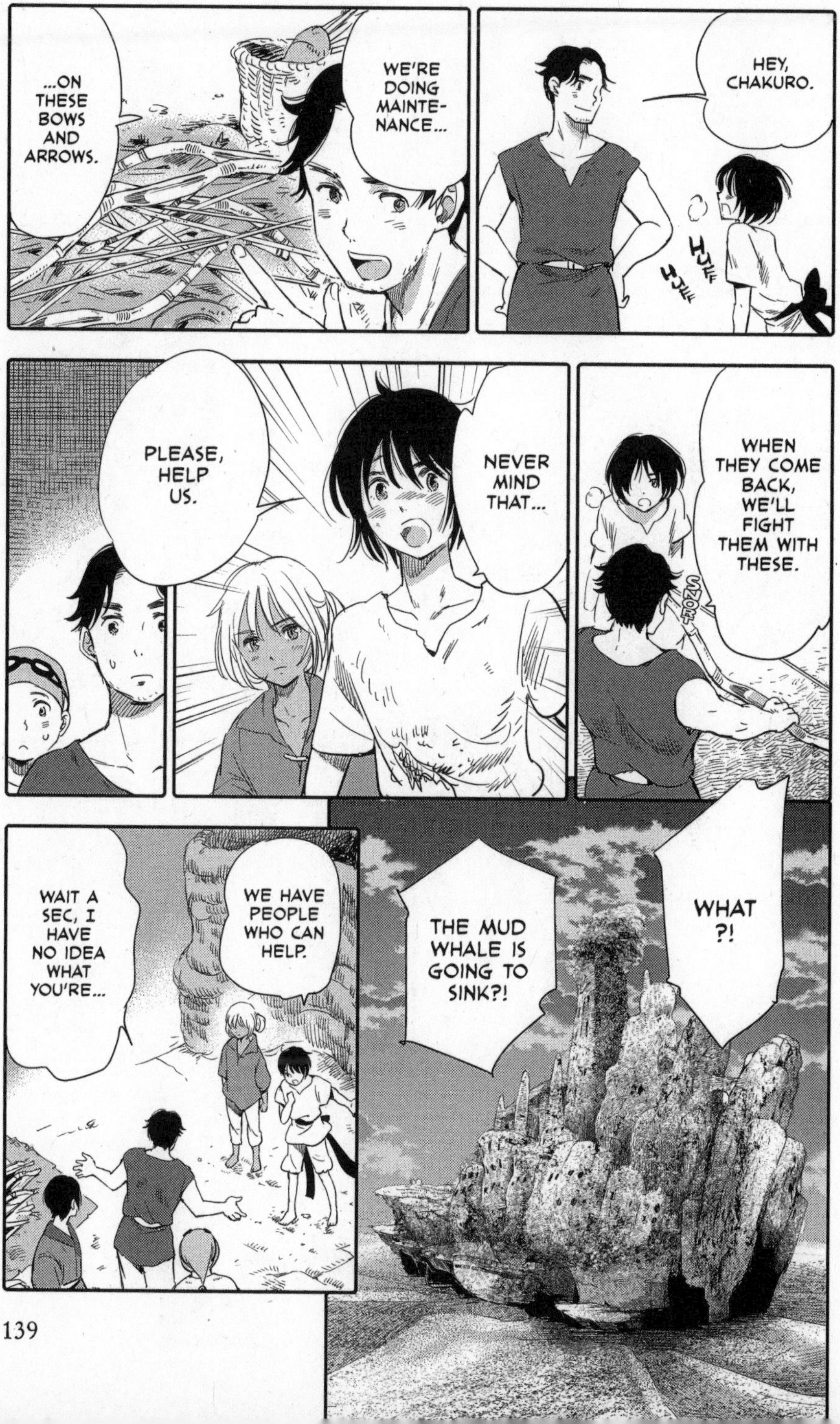
HEY, CHAKURO.
HUFF HUFF
WE'RE DOING MAINTE-NANCE...
...ON THESE BOWS AND ARROWS.
WHEN THEY COME BACK, WE'LL FIGHT THEM WITH THESE.
SNORT
NEVER MIND THAT...
PLEASE, HELP US.
WHAT ?!
THE MUD WHALE IS GOING TO SINK?!
WE HAVE PEOPLE WHO CAN HELP.
WAIT A SEC, I HAVE NO IDEA WHAT YOU'RE...

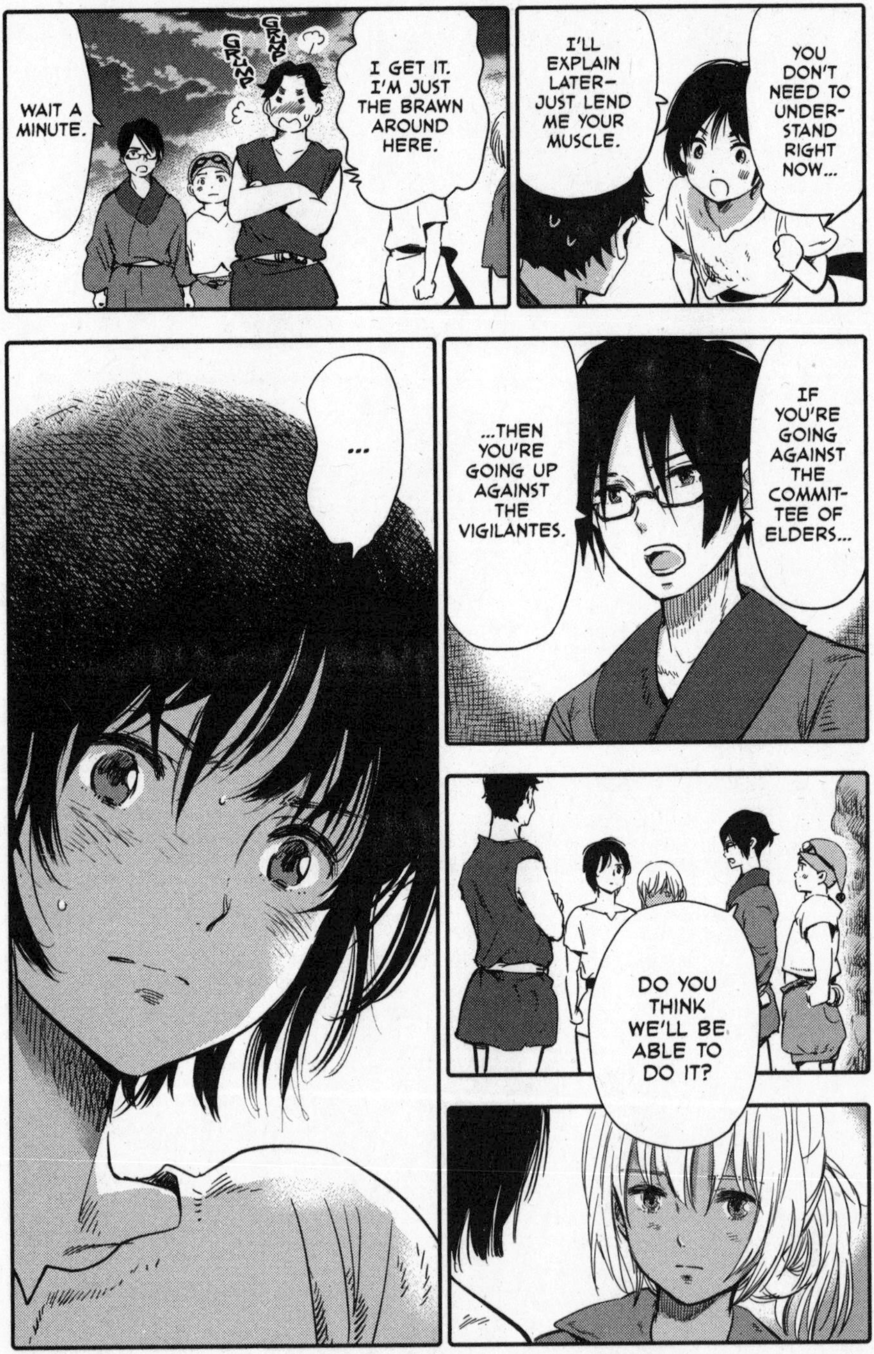
YOU DON'T NEED TO UNDER-STAND RIGHT NOW...
I'LL EXPLAIN LATER— JUST LEND ME YOUR MUSCLE.
I GET IT. I'M JUST THE BRAWN AROUND HERE.
GRUMP
GRUMP
WAIT A MINUTE.
IF YOU'RE GOING AGAINST THE COMMIT-TEE OF ELDERS...
...THEN YOU'RE GOING UP AGAINST THE VIGILANTES.
DO YOU THINK WE'LL BE ABLE TO DO IT?
...

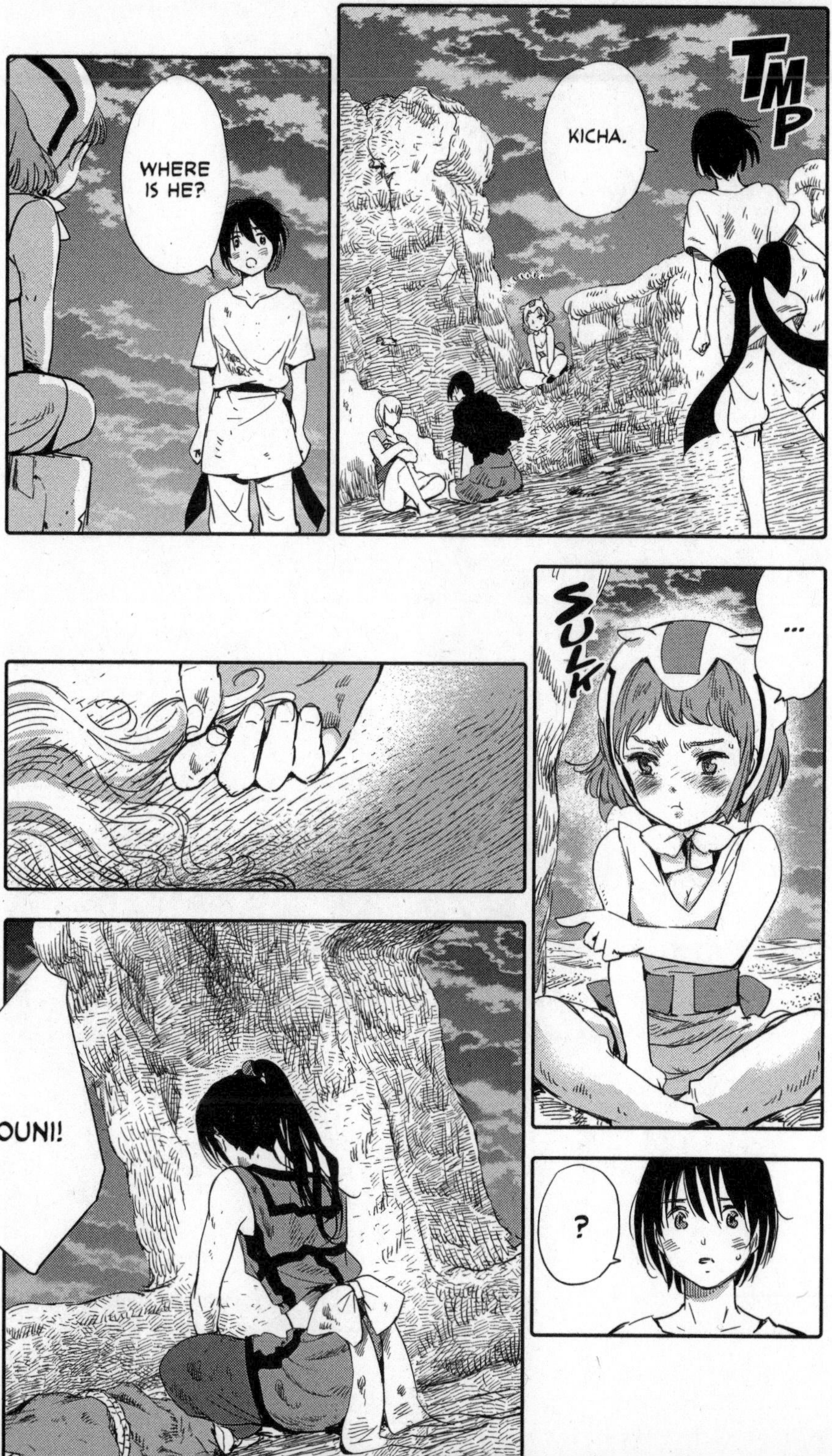
TMP
KICHA.
WHERE IS HE?
SULK
...
?
OUNI!

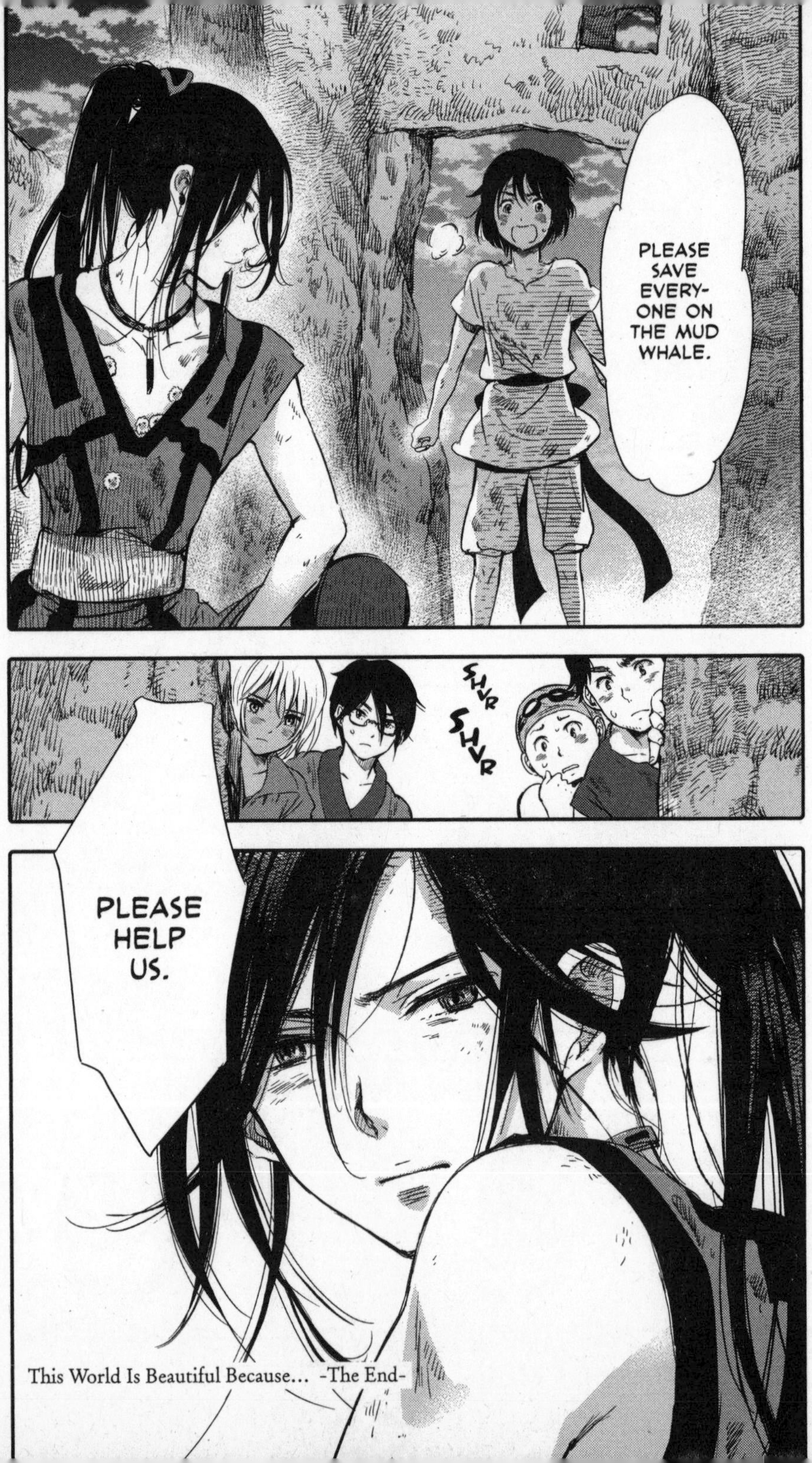
PLEASE SAVE EVERY-ONE ON THE MUD WHALE.
SHVR SHVR
PLEASE HELP US.
This World Is Beautiful Because... -The End-

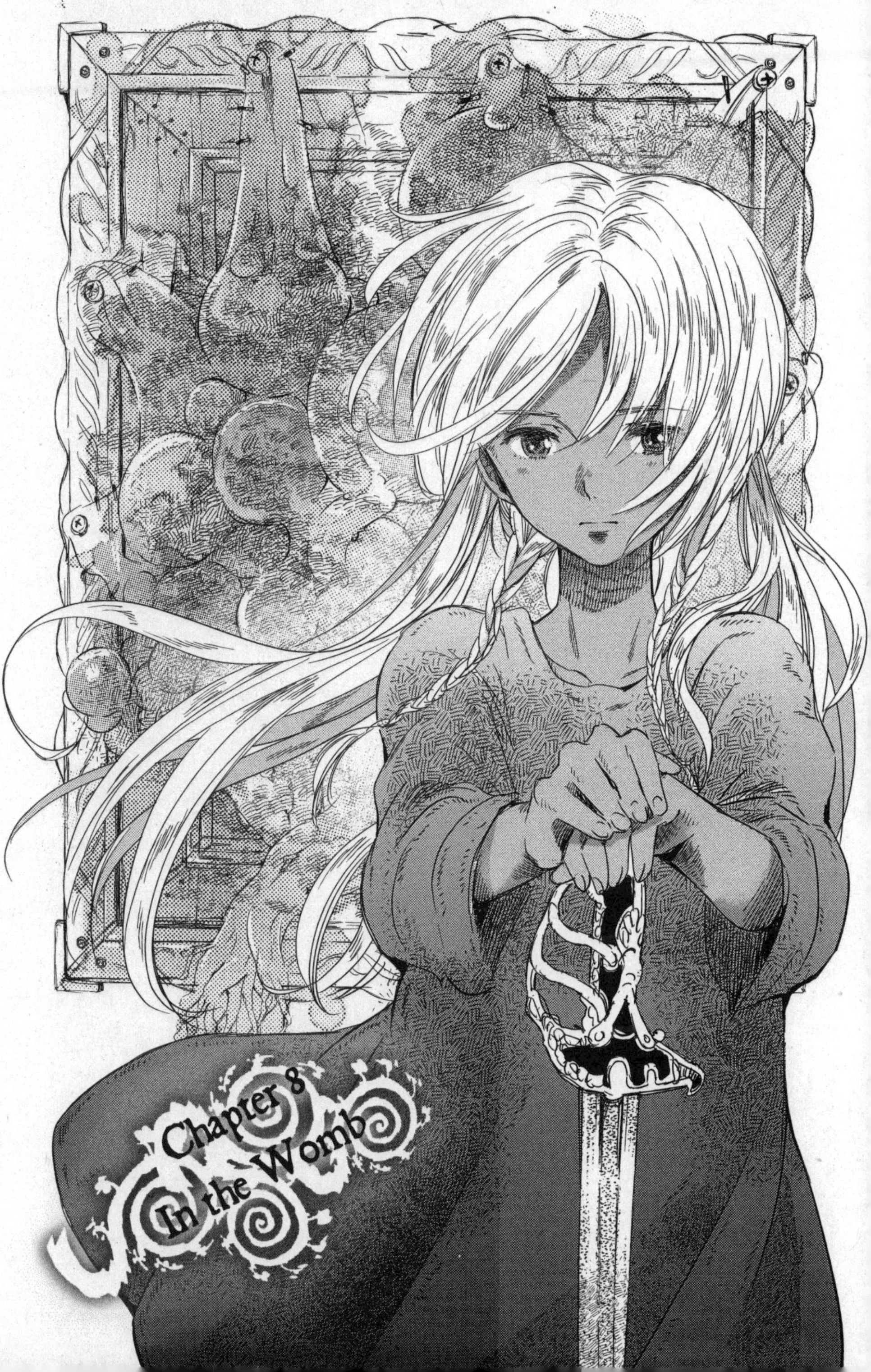
Chapter 8
In the Womb

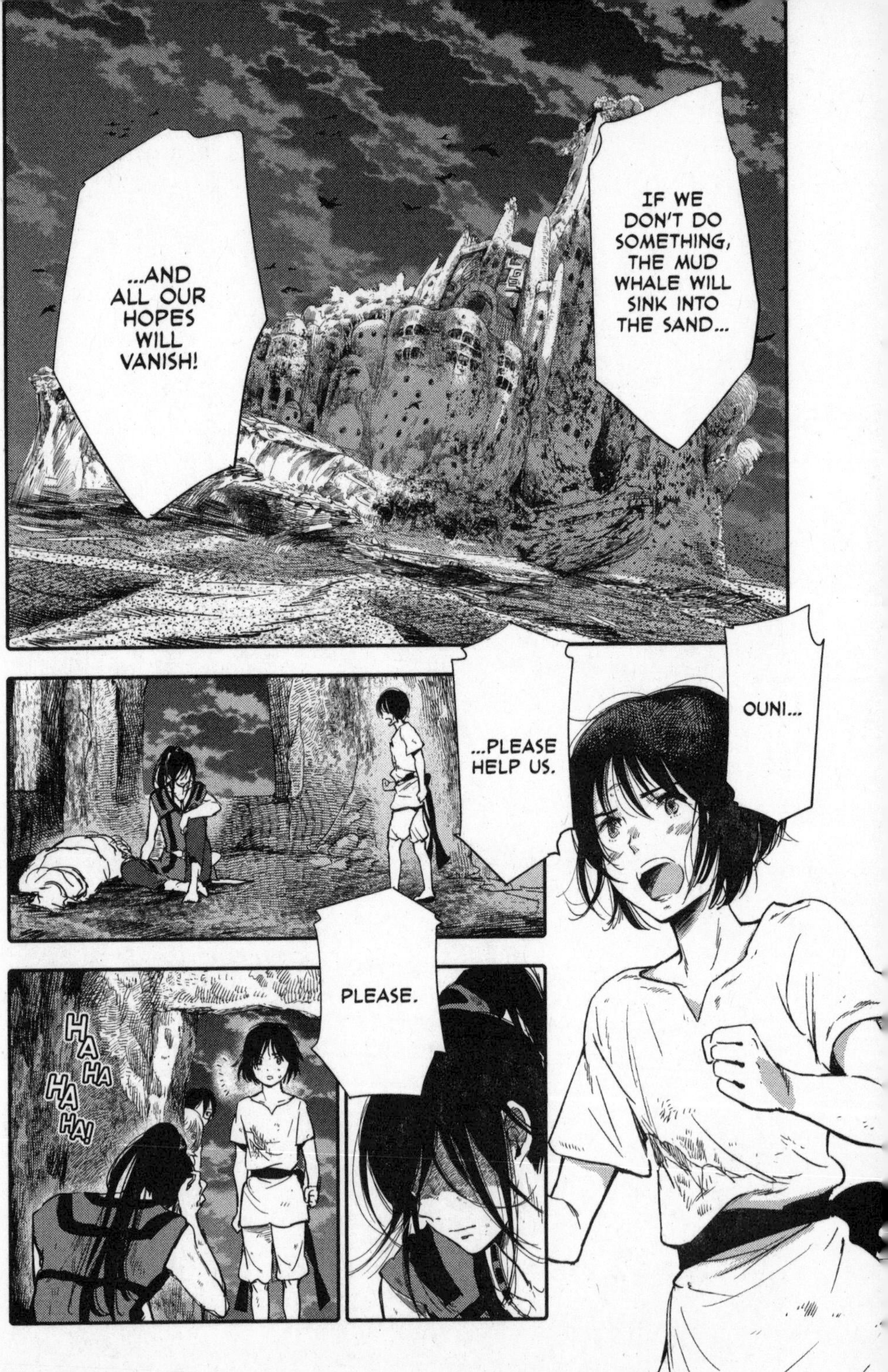
IF WE DON'T DO SOMETHING, THE MUD WHALE WILL SINK INTO THE SAND...
...AND ALL OUR HOPES WILL VANISH!
OUNI...
...PLEASE HELP US.
PLEASE.
HA HA HA HA HA!

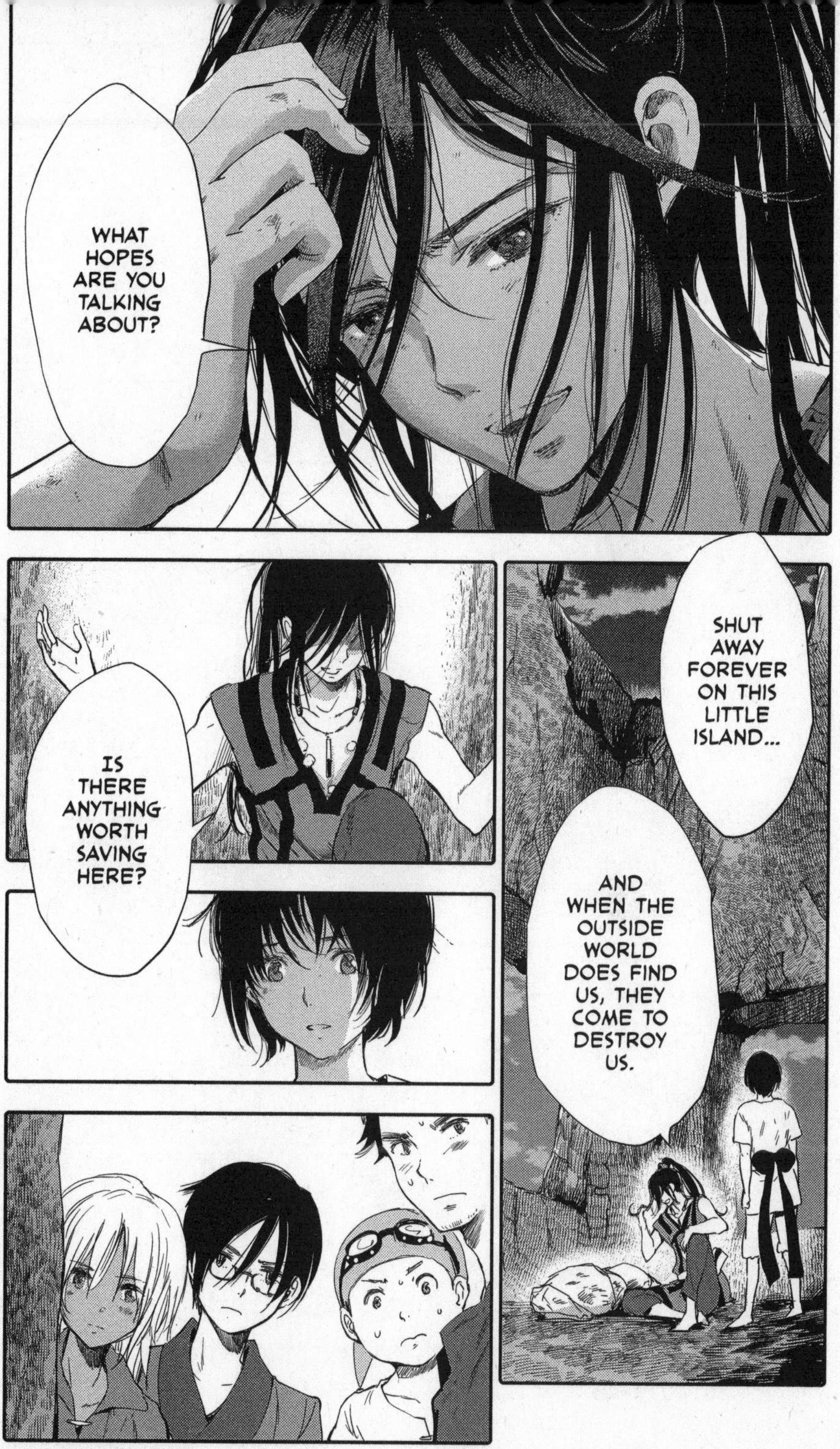
WHAT HOPES ARE YOU TALKING ABOUT?
SHUT AWAY FOREVER ON THIS LITTLE ISLAND...
AND WHEN THE OUTSIDE WORLD DOES FIND US, THEY COME TO DESTROY US.
IS THERE ANYTHING WORTH SAVING HERE?

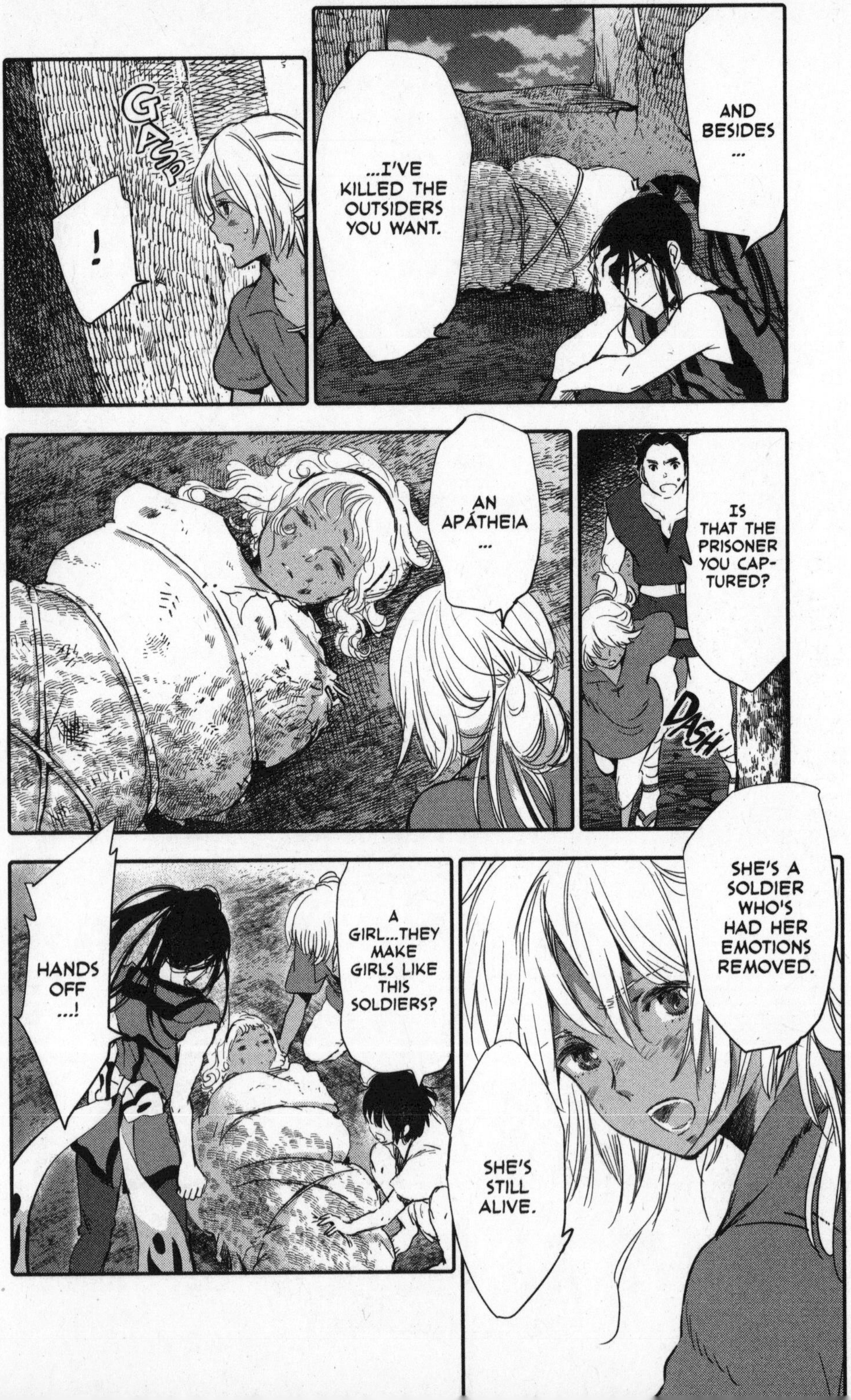
AND BESIDES ...
...I'VE KILLED THE OUTSIDERS YOU WANT.
GASP
!
IS THAT THE PRISONER YOU CAPTURED?
DASH
AN APÁTHEIA ...
SHE'S A SOLDIER WHO'S HAD HER EMOTIONS REMOVED.
SHE'S STILL ALIVE.
A GIRL...THEY MAKE GIRLS LIKE THIS SOLDIERS?
HANDS OFF ...!

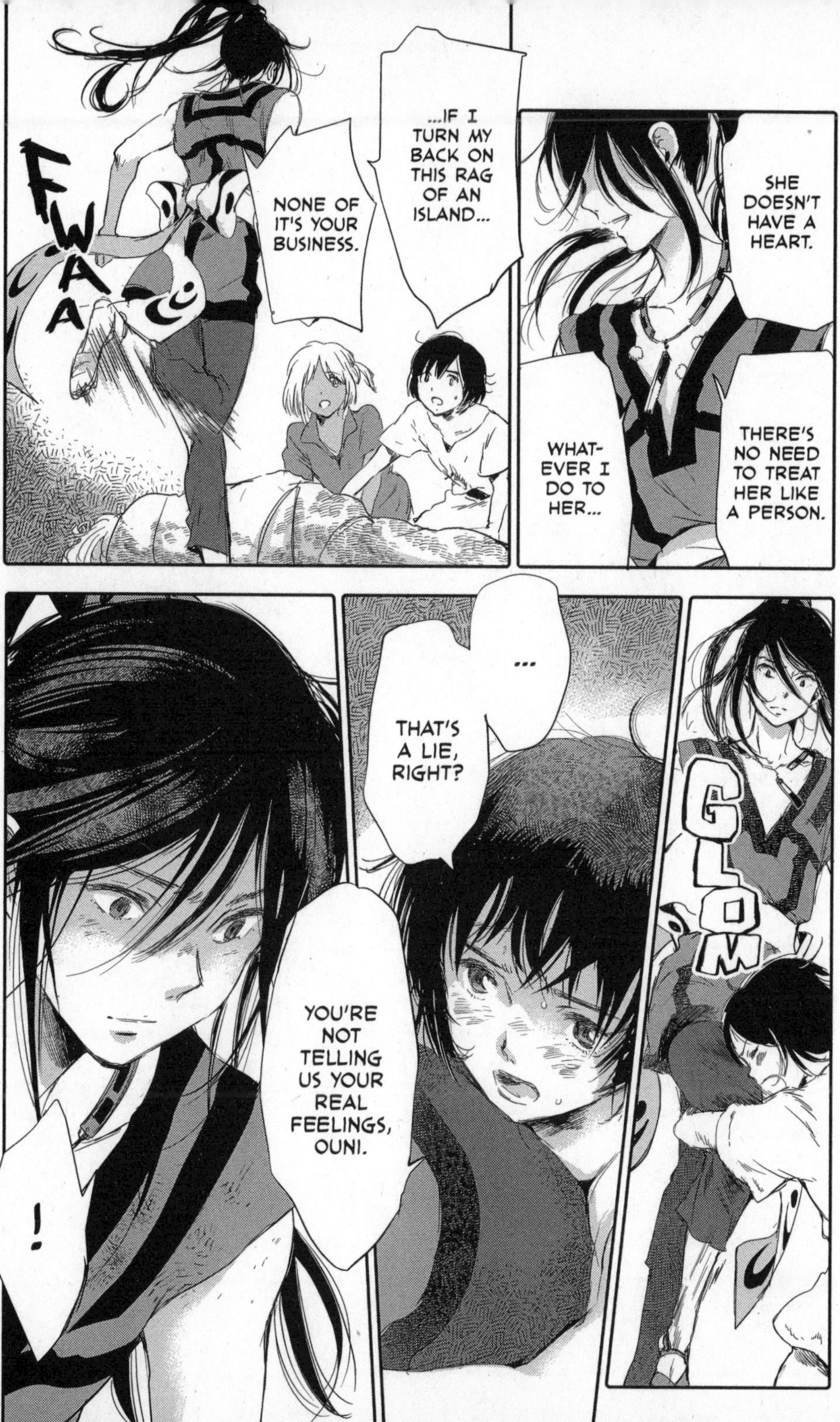
SHE DOESN'T HAVE A HEART.
THERE'S NO NEED TO TREAT HER LIKE A PERSON.
WHAT-EVER I DO TO HER...
...IF I TURN MY BACK ON THIS RAG OF AN ISLAND...
NONE OF IT'S YOUR BUSINESS.
FWAA
GLOM
...
THAT'S A LIE, RIGHT?
YOU'RE NOT TELLING US YOUR REAL FEELINGS, OUNI.
!

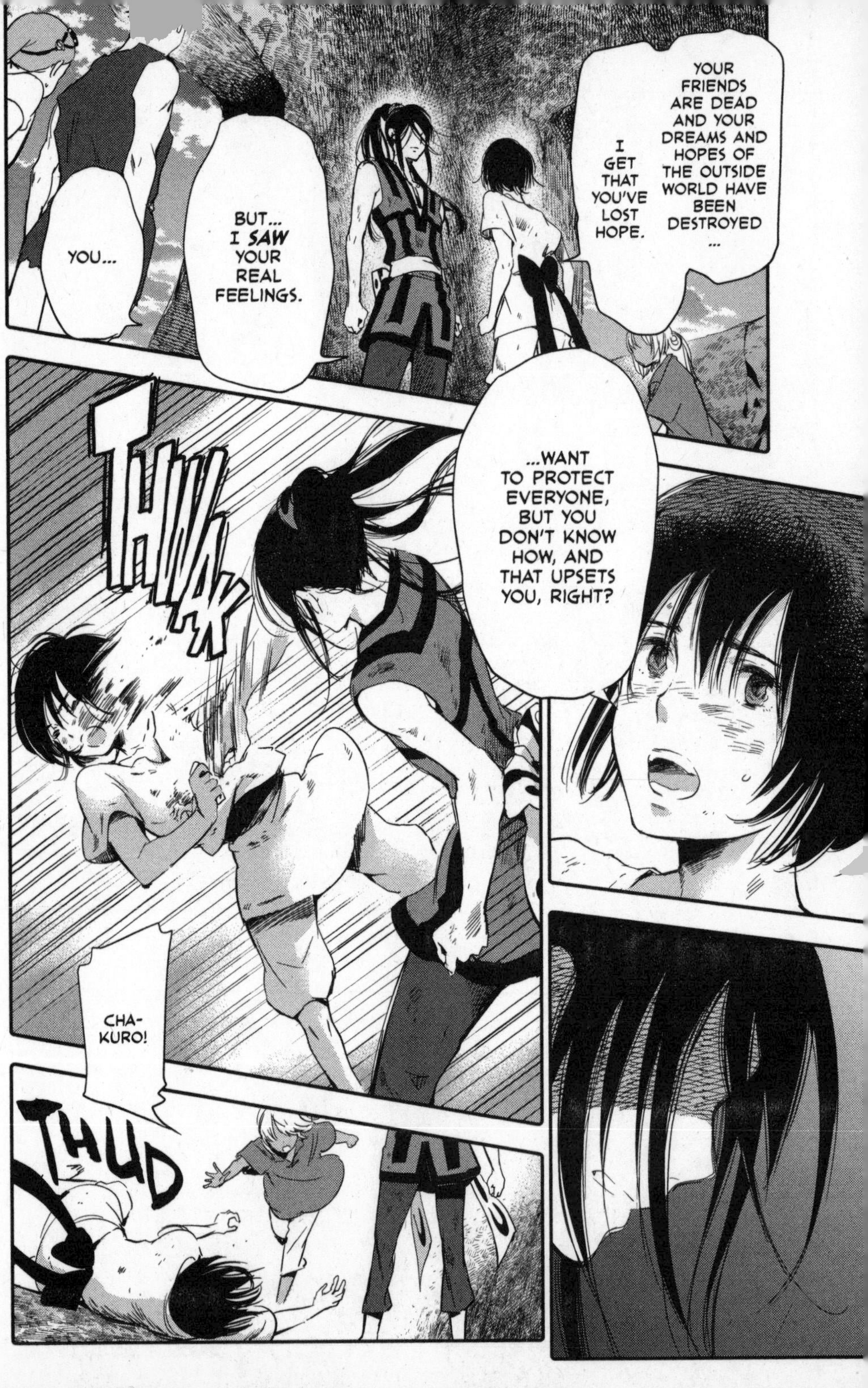
YOUR FRIENDS ARE DEAD AND YOUR DREAMS AND HOPES OF THE OUTSIDE WORLD HAVE BEEN DESTROYED ...
I GET THAT YOU'VE LOST HOPE.
BUT... I SAW YOUR REAL FEELINGS.
YOU...
...WANT TO PROTECT EVERYONE, BUT YOU DON'T KNOW HOW, AND THAT UPSETS YOU, RIGHT?
THWAK
CHA-KURO!
THUD

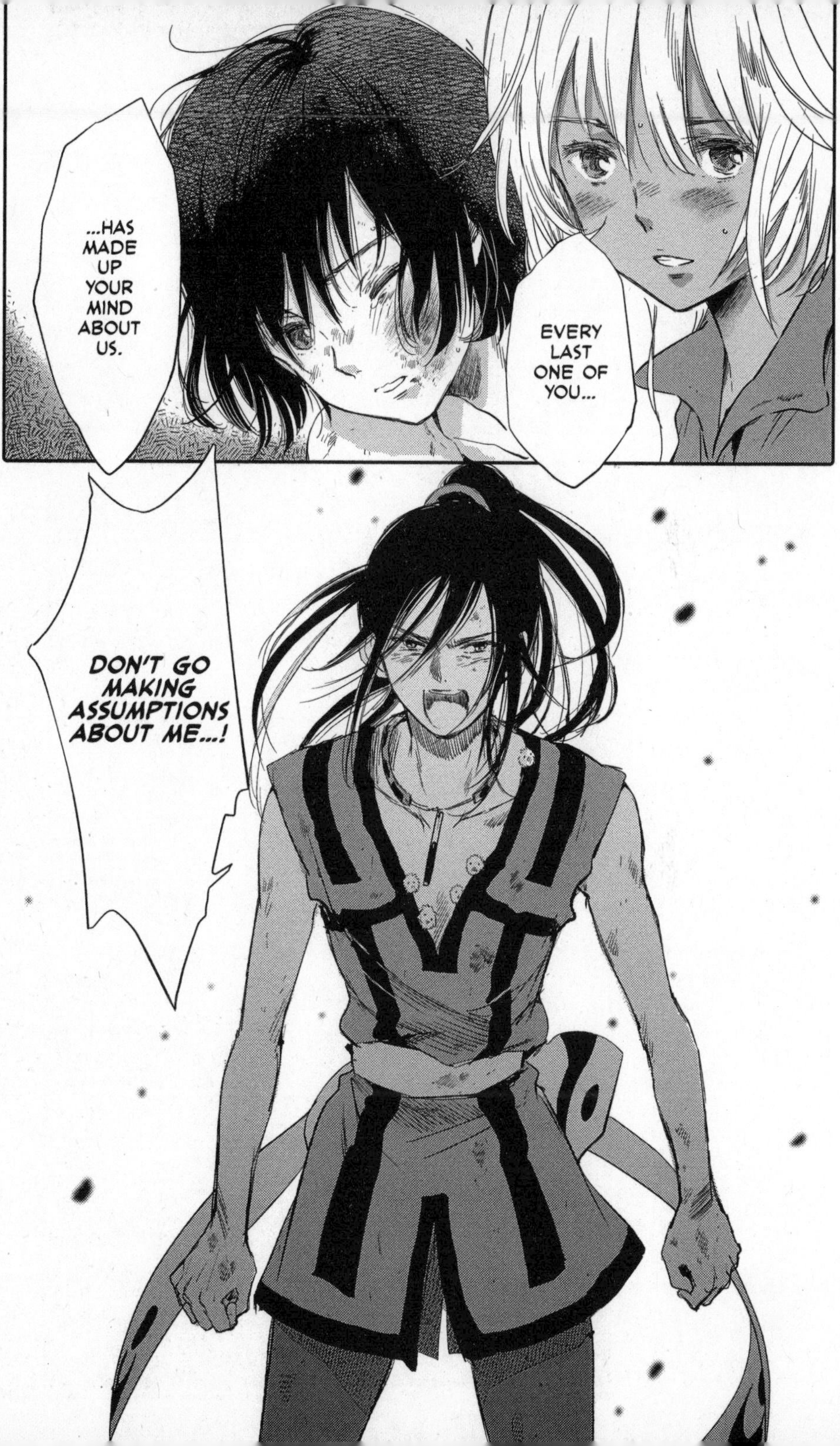
EVERY LAST ONE OF YOU...
...HAS MADE UP YOUR MIND ABOUT US.
DON'T GO MAKING ASSUMPTIONS ABOUT ME...!

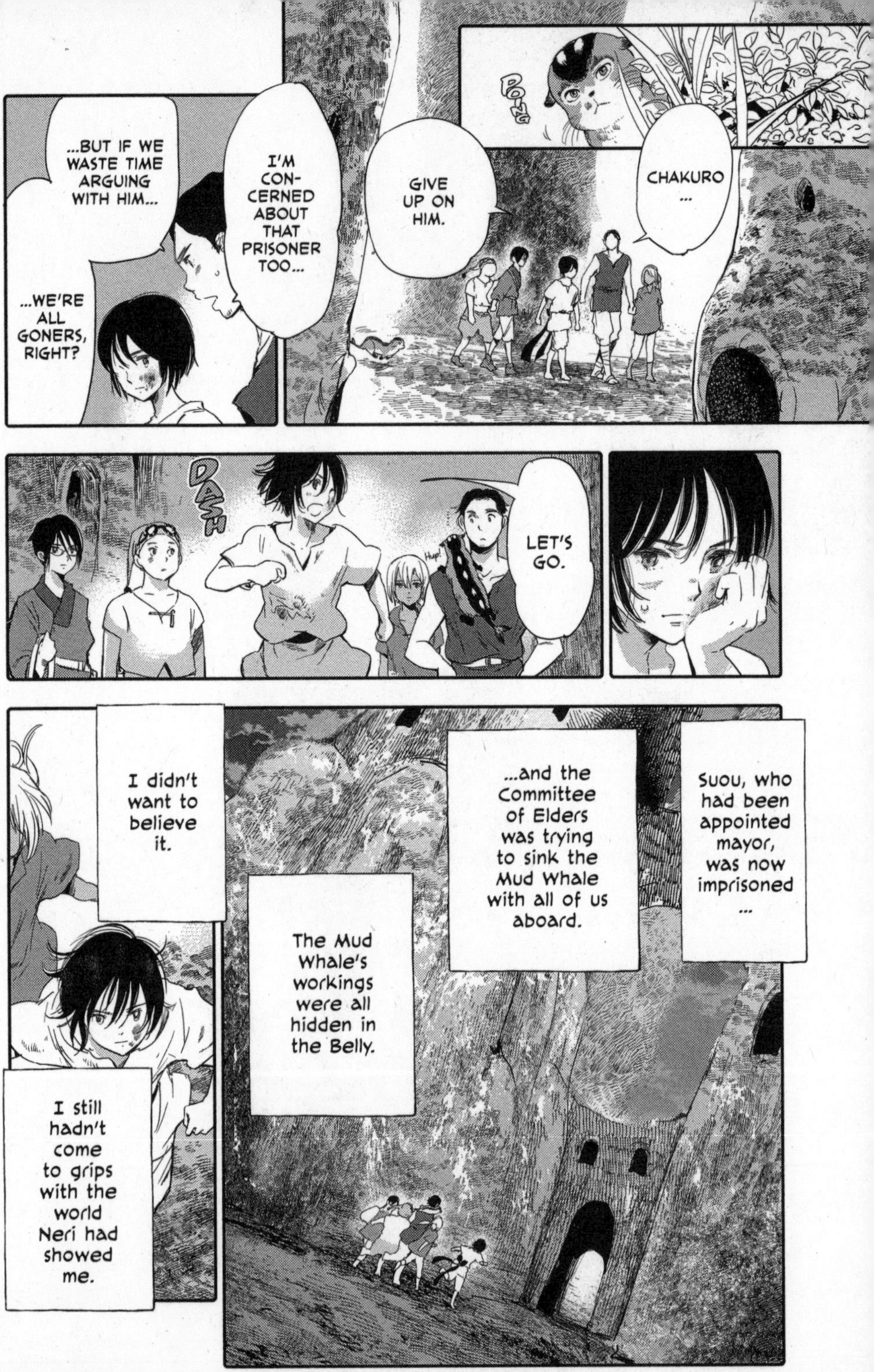
POING
CHAKURO...
GIVE UP ON HIM.
I'M CONCERNED ABOUT THAT PRISONER TOO...
...BUT IF WE WASTE TIME ARGUING WITH HIM...
...WE'RE ALL GONERS, RIGHT?
LET'S GO.
Hup!
DASH
Suou, who had been appointed mayor, was now imprisoned...
...and the Committee of Elders was trying to sink the Mud Whale with all of us aboard.
The Mud Whale's workings were all hidden in the Belly.
I didn't want to believe it.
I still hadn't come to grips with the world Neri had showed me.

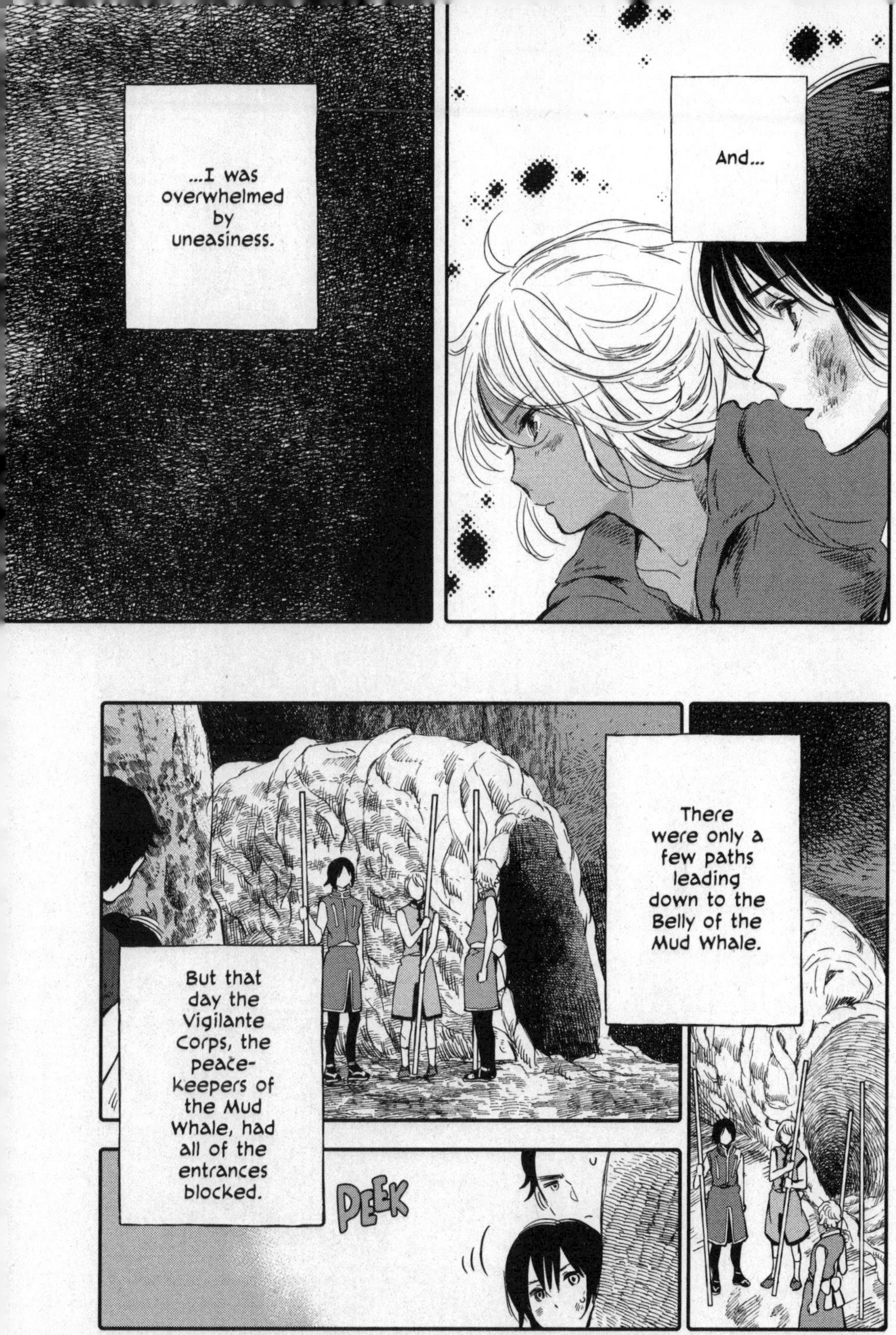
And...
...I was overwhelmed by uneasiness.
There were only a few paths leading down to the Belly of the Mud Whale.
But that day the Vigilante Corps, the peace-keepers of the Mud Whale, had all of the entrances blocked.
PEEK

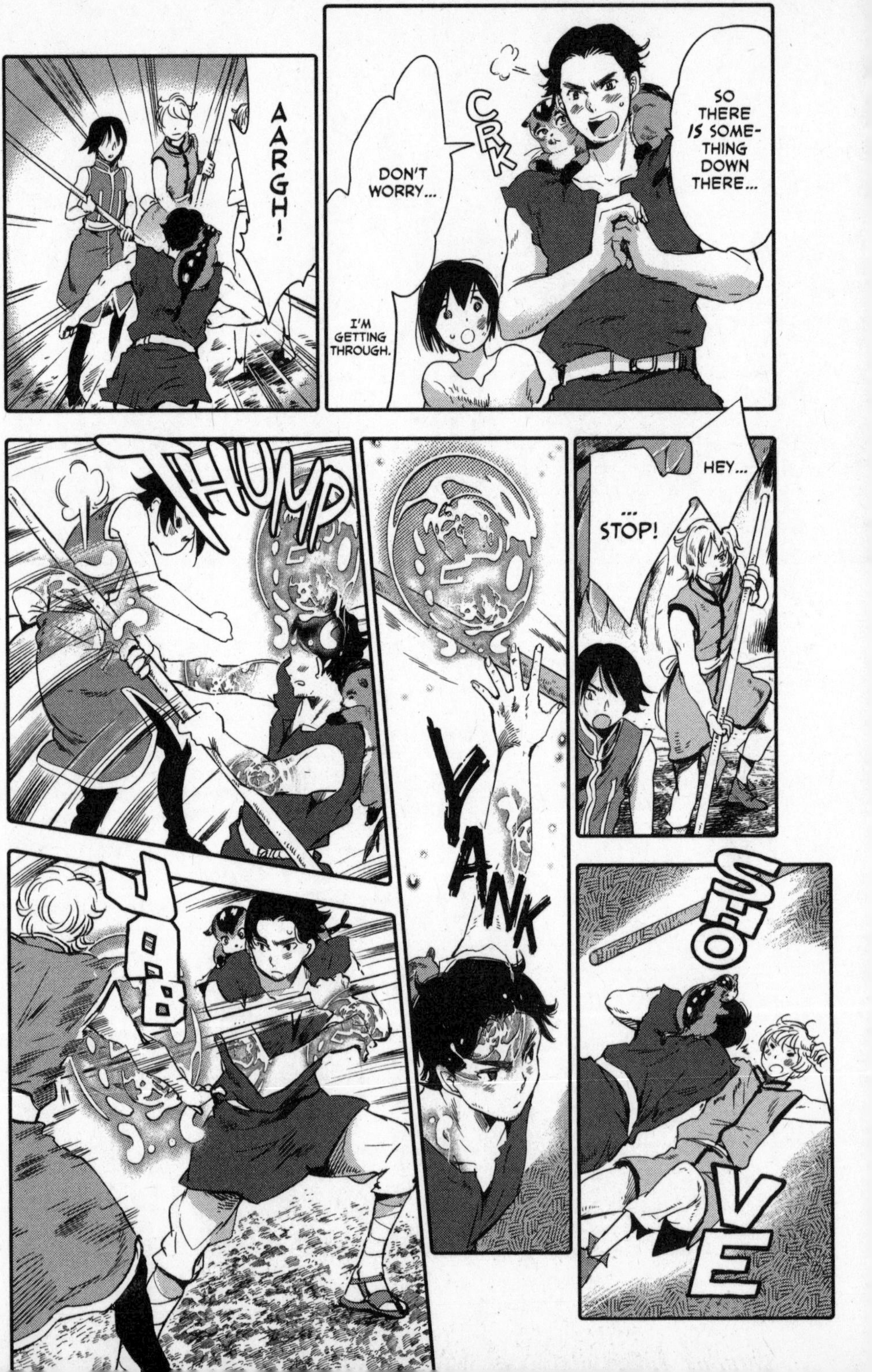
SO THERE IS SOME-THING DOWN THERE...
CRK
DON'T WORRY...
I'M GETTING THROUGH.
AARGH!
HEY...
...STOP!
SHOVE
YANK
THUMP
JAB

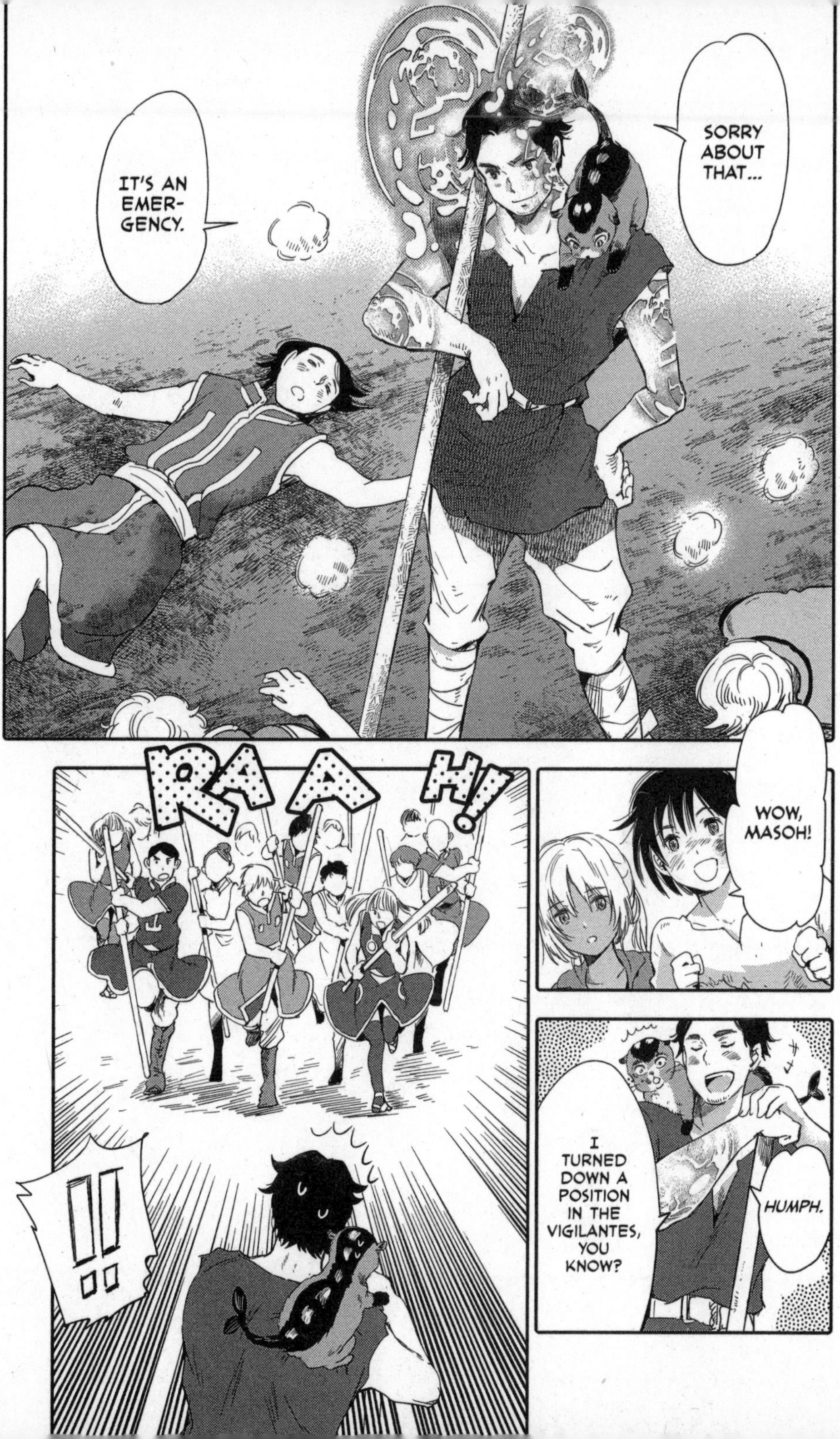
SORRY ABOUT THAT...
IT'S AN EMERGENCY.
WOW, MASOH!
I TURNED DOWN A POSITION IN THE VIGILANTES, YOU KNOW?
HUMPH.
RAAH!
!!

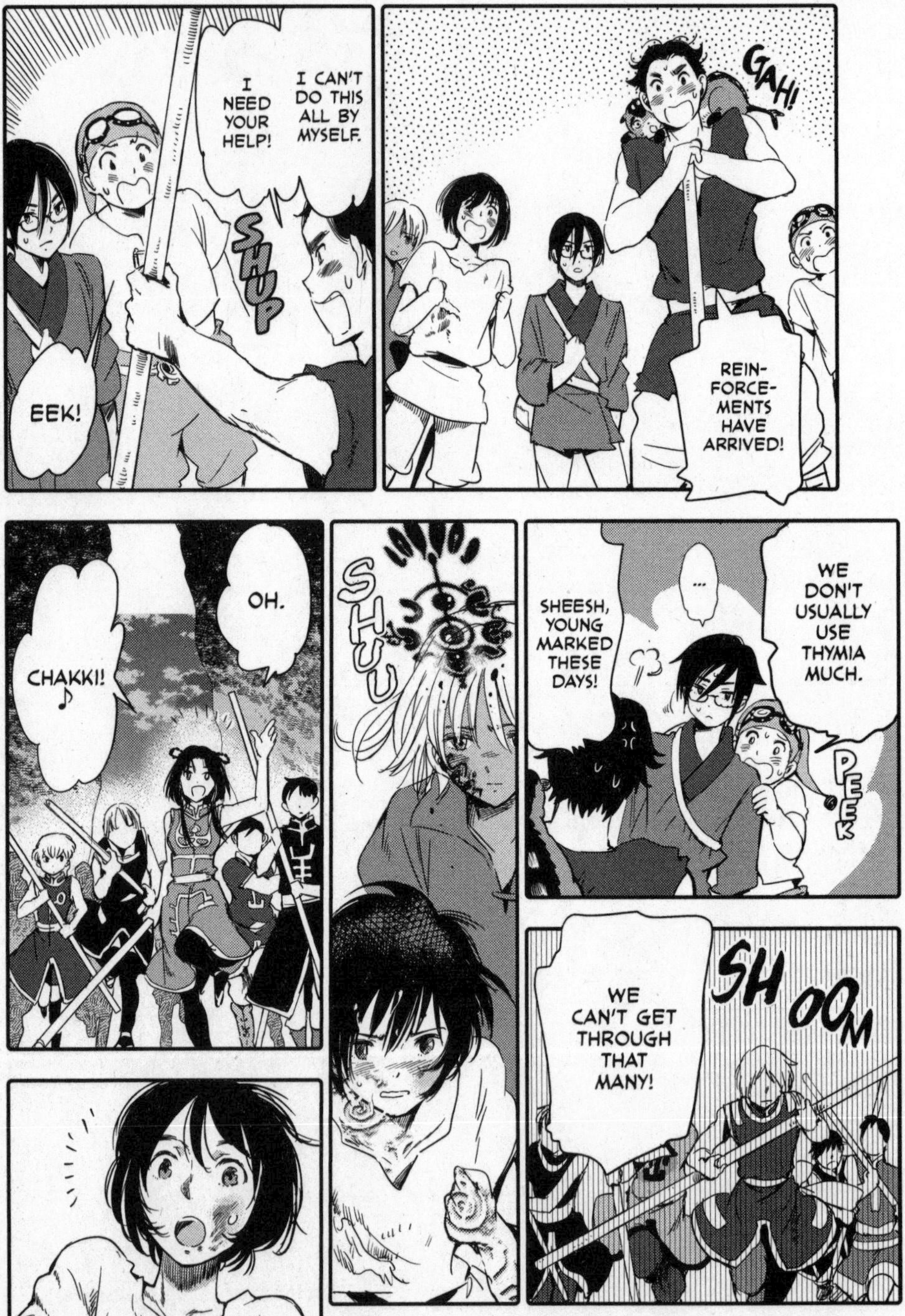
GAH!
REIN-FORCE-MENTS HAVE ARRIVED!
I CAN'T DO THIS ALL BY MYSELF.
I NEED YOUR HELP!
SHUP
EEK!
WE DON'T USUALLY USE THYMIA MUCH.
...
SHEESH, YOUNG MARKED THESE DAYS!
PEEK
WE CAN'T GET THROUGH THAT MANY!
SHOOM
SHUU
OH.
CHAKKI! ♪

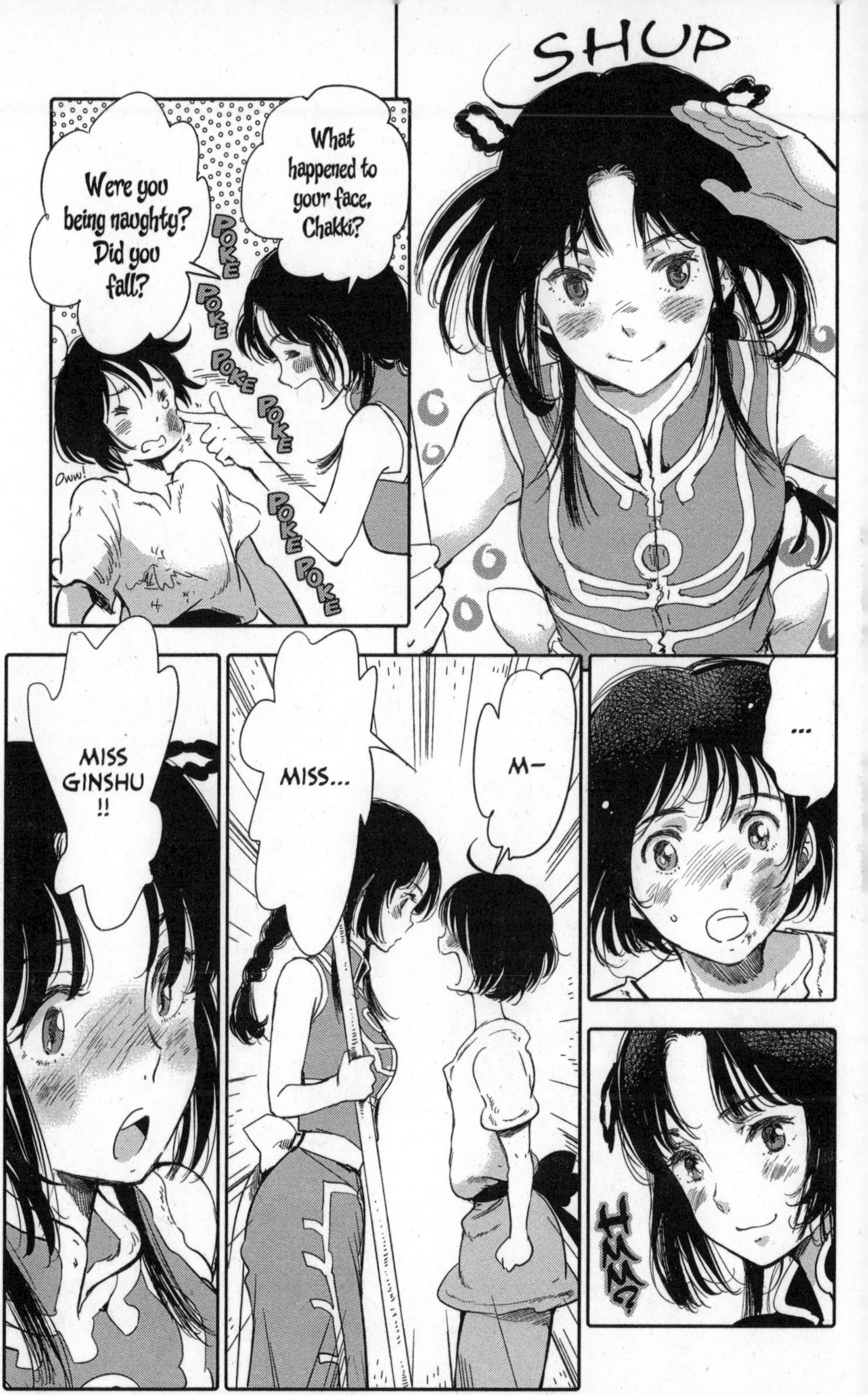
SHUP
What happened to your face, Chakki?
Were you being naughty? Did you fall?
POKE POKE POKE POKE POKE POKE
Oww!
...
HMM?
M–
MISS...
MISS GINSHU !!

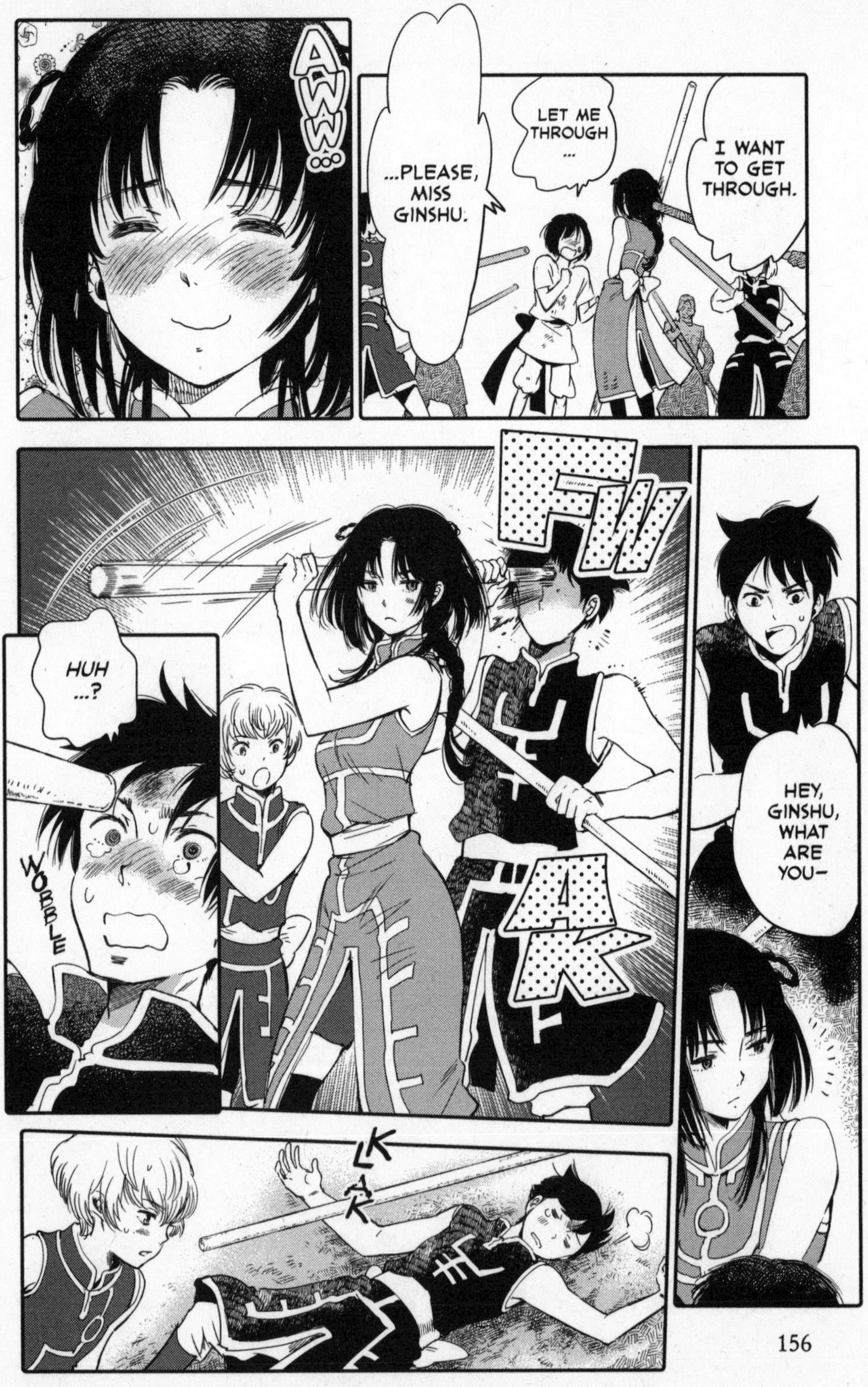

I WANT TO GET THROUGH.
LET ME THROUGH ...
...PLEASE, MISS GINSHU.
AWW...
HEY, GINSHU, WHAT ARE YOU—
FWAK
HUH ...?
WOBBLE
KLAK

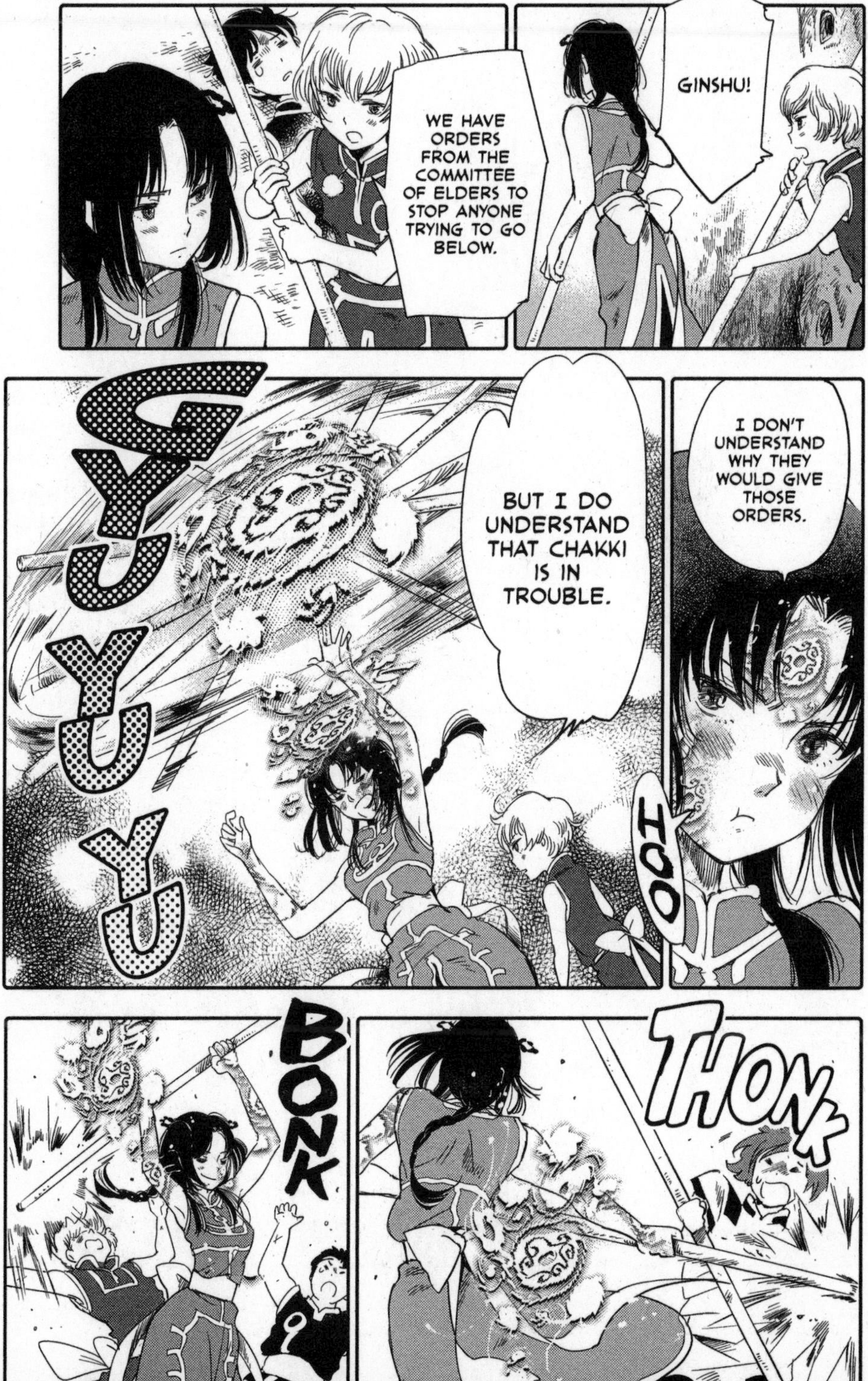
GINSHU!
WE HAVE ORDERS FROM THE COMMITTEE OF ELDERS TO STOP ANYONE TRYING TO GO BELOW.
I DON'T UNDERSTAND WHY THEY WOULD GIVE THOSE ORDERS.
HOO
BUT I DO UNDERSTAND THAT CHAKKI IS IN TROUBLE.
GYUYYUYU
THONK
BONK

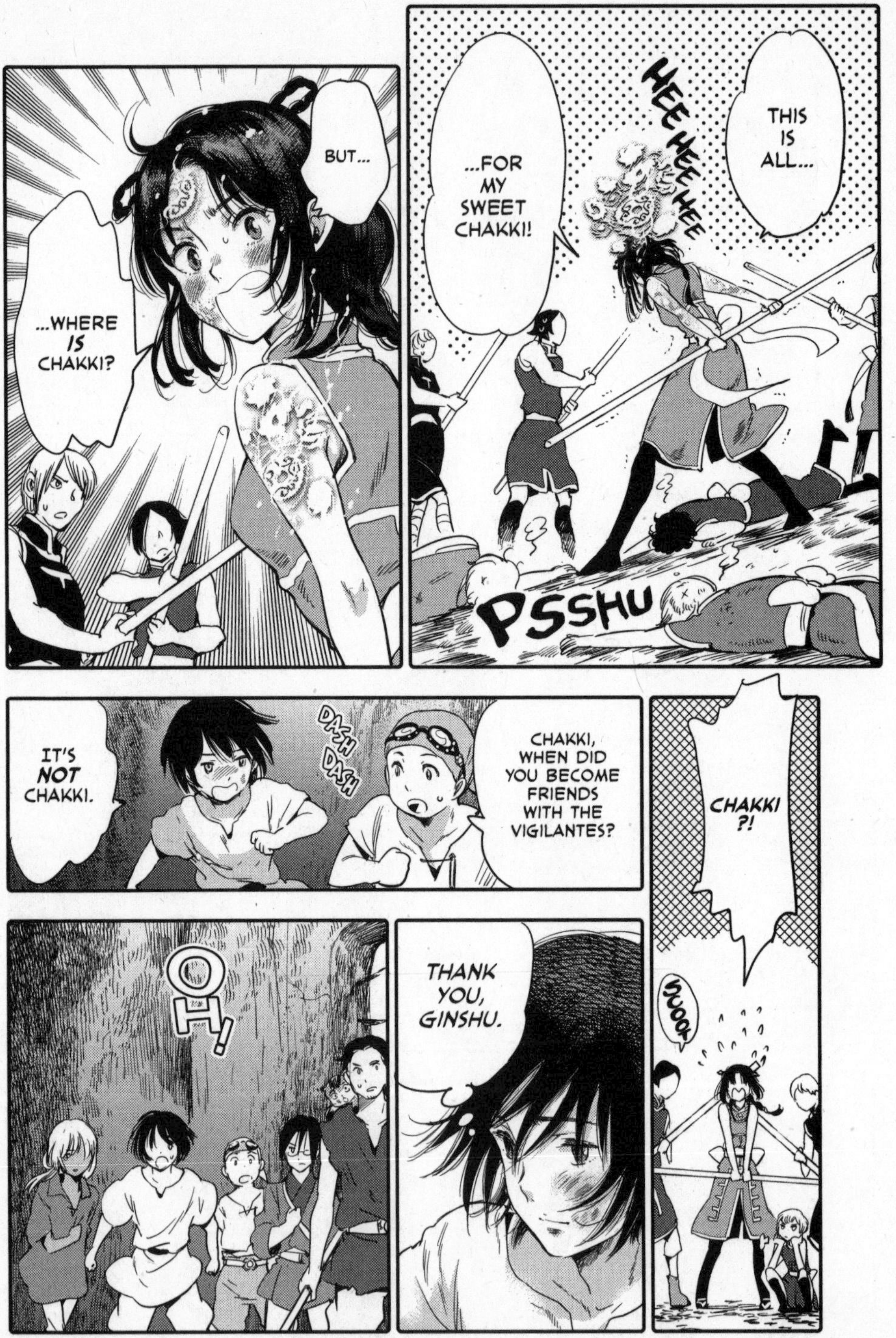
THIS IS ALL...
HEE HEE HEE
...FOR MY SWEET CHAKKI!
PSSHU
BUT...
...WHERE IS CHAKKI?
CHAKKI ?!
CHAKKI, WHEN DID YOU BECOME FRIENDS WITH THE VIGILANTES?
DASH DASH
IT'S NOT CHAKKI.
THANK YOU, GINSHU.
OH!

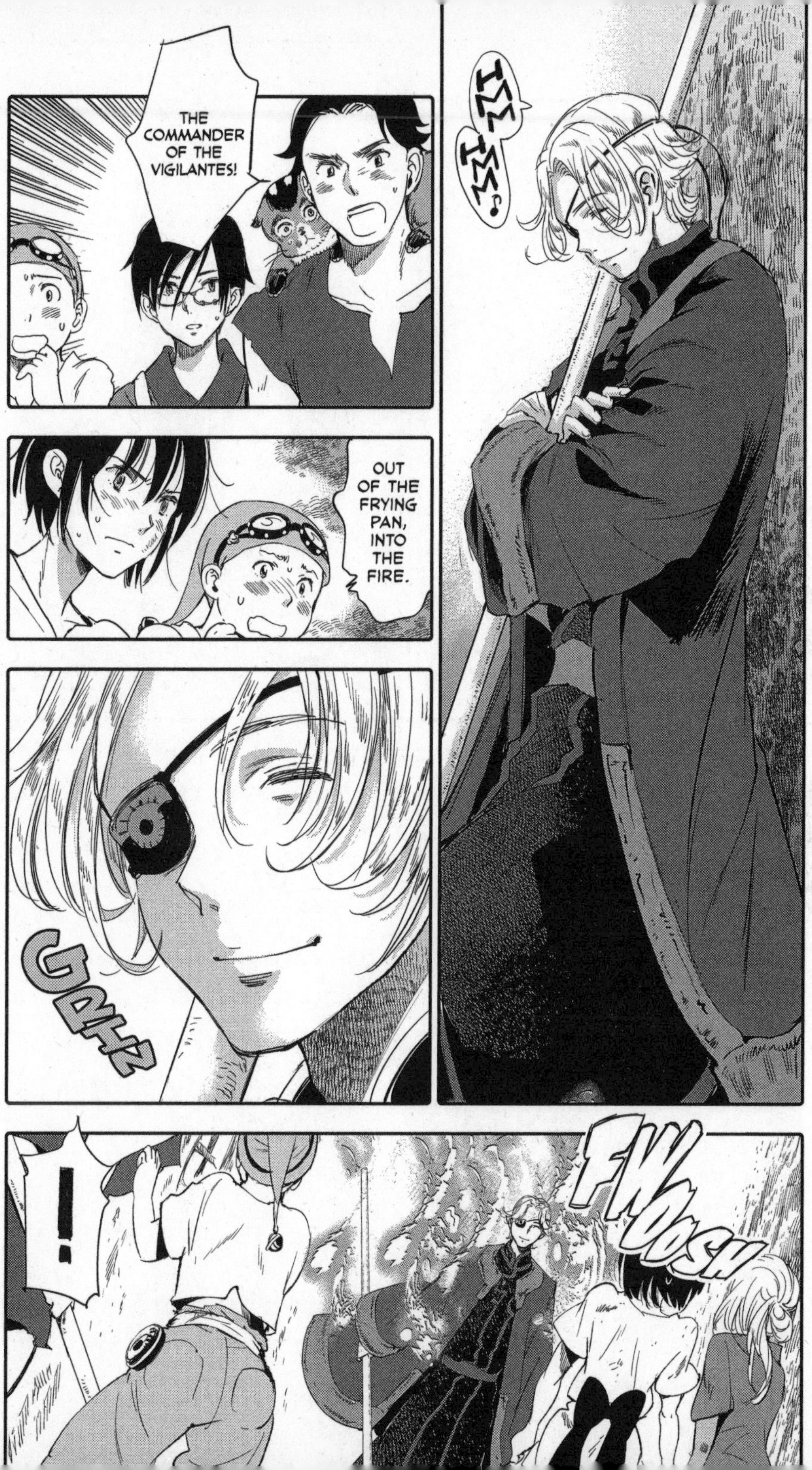
HMM HMM♪
THE COMMANDER OF THE VIGILANTES!
OUT OF THE FRYING PAN, INTO THE FIRE.
GRIN
FWOOSH
!

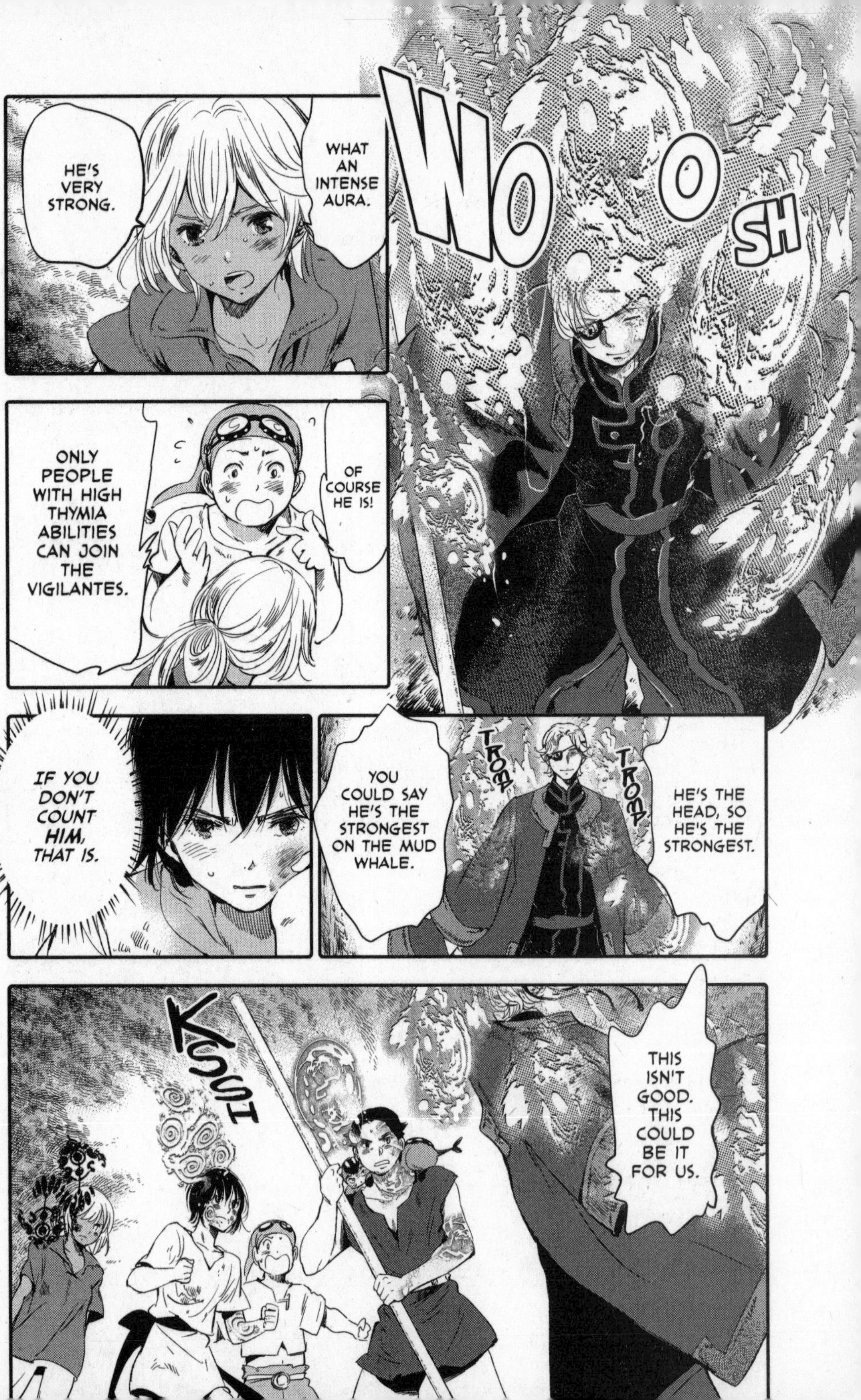
WOOOSH
WHAT AN INTENSE AURA.
HE'S VERY STRONG.
OF COURSE HE IS!
ONLY PEOPLE WITH HIGH THYMIA ABILITIES CAN JOIN THE VIGILANTES.
HE'S THE HEAD, SO HE'S THE STRONGEST.
TROMP
TROMP
YOU COULD SAY HE'S THE STRONGEST ON THE MUD WHALE.
IF YOU DON'T COUNT *HIM*, THAT IS.
THIS ISN'T GOOD. THIS COULD BE IT FOR US.
KSSSH

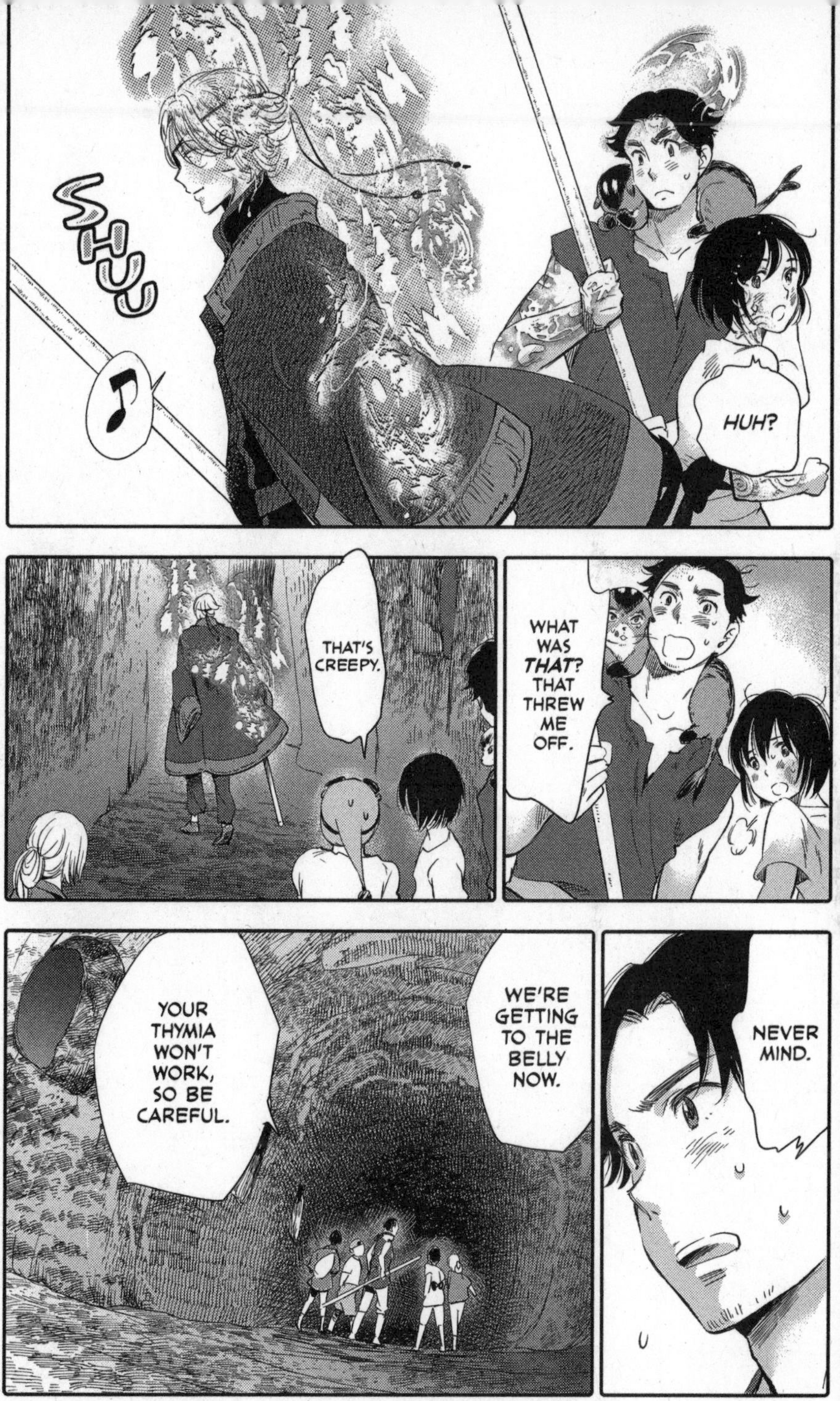
SHUU
♪
HUH?
WHAT WAS *THAT*? THAT THREW ME OFF.
THAT'S CREEPY.
NEVER MIND.
WE'RE GETTING TO THE BELLY NOW.
YOUR THYMIA WON'T WORK, SO BE CAREFUL.

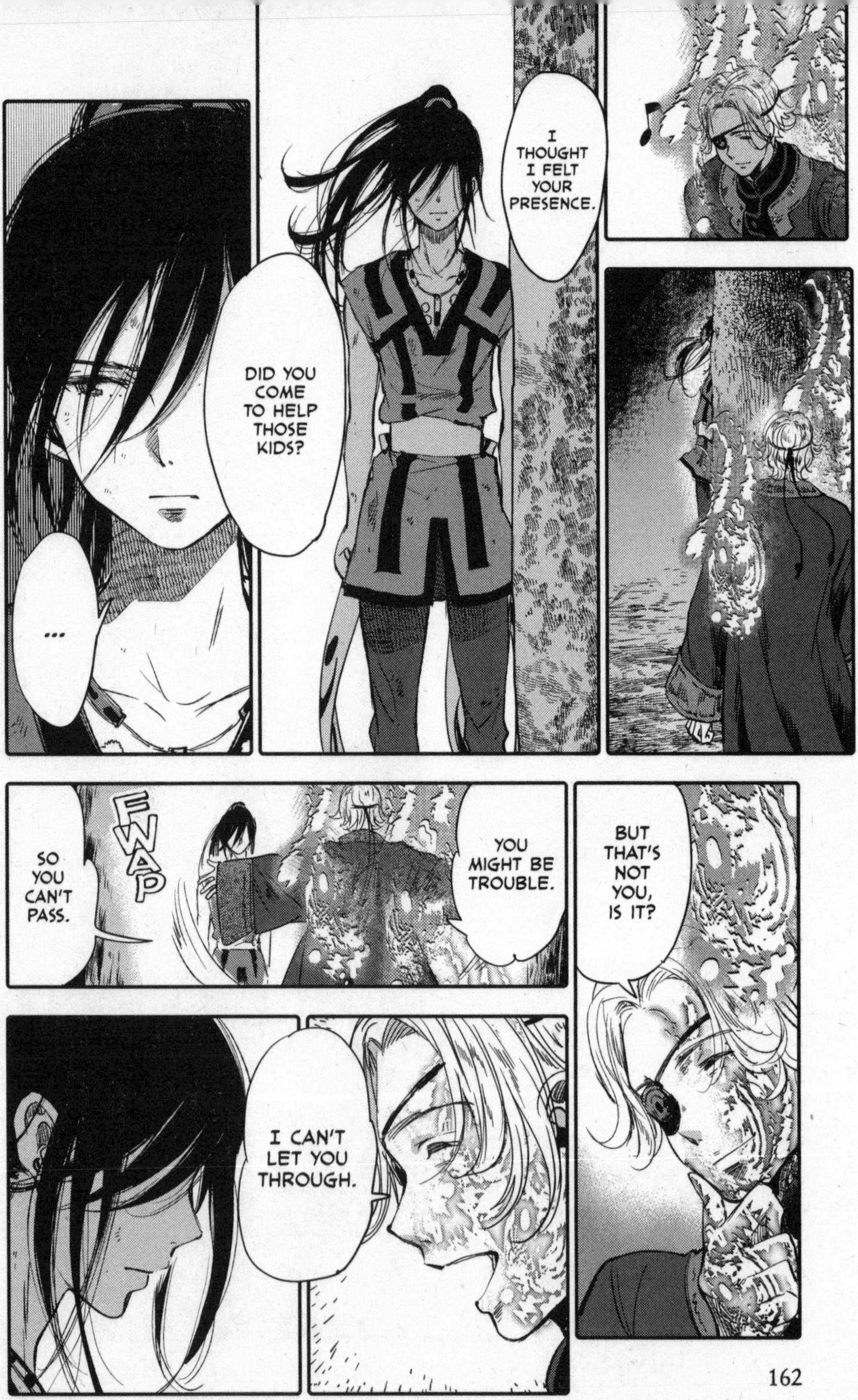
I THOUGHT I FELT YOUR PRESENCE.
DID YOU COME TO HELP THOSE KIDS?
...
BUT THAT'S NOT YOU, IS IT?
YOU MIGHT BE TROUBLE.
FWAP
SO YOU CAN'T PASS.
I CAN'T LET YOU THROUGH.

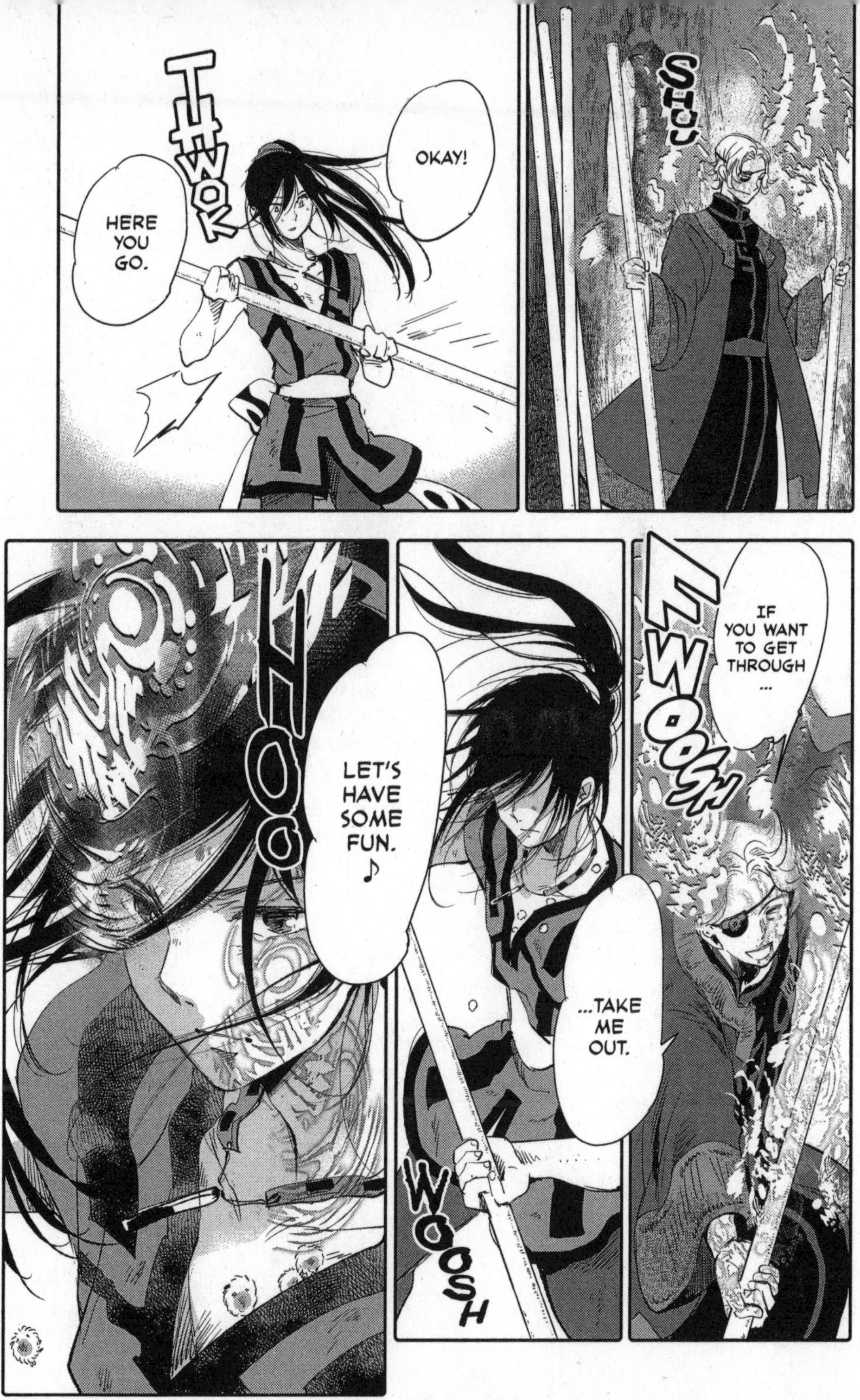
SHUU
OKAY!
THWOK
HERE YOU GO.
IF YOU WANT TO GET THROUGH ...
FWOOSH
...TAKE ME OUT.
LET'S HAVE SOME FUN. ♪
WOOSH

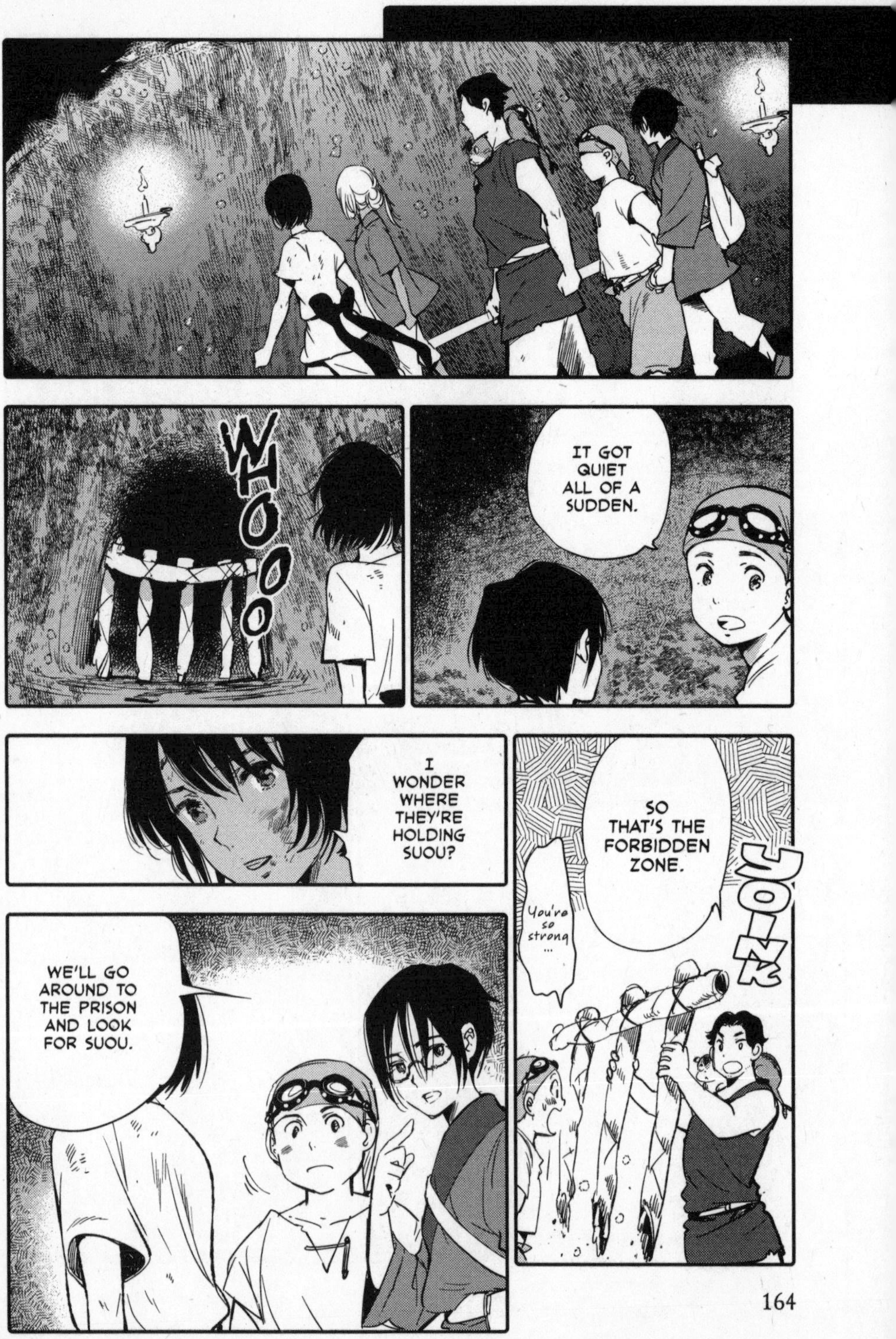
IT GOT QUIET ALL OF A SUDDEN.
WHOOOO
SO THAT'S THE FORBIDDEN ZONE.
YOINK
You're so strong...
I WONDER WHERE THEY'RE HOLDING SUOU?
WE'LL GO AROUND TO THE PRISON AND LOOK FOR SUOU.

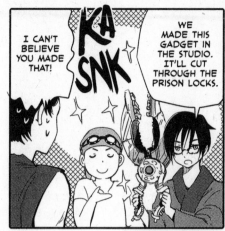

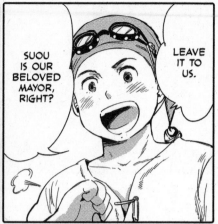

LEAVE IT TO US.
SUOU IS OUR BELOVED MAYOR, RIGHT?
WE MADE THIS GADGET IN THE STUDIO. IT'LL CUT THROUGH THE PRISON LOCKS.
KA SNK
I CAN'T BELIEVE YOU MADE THAT!
OKAY, I'LL LEAVE YOU TO IT.
I THINK THE COMMITTEE OF ELDERS IS IN THE FORBIDDEN ZONE. WE'LL GO THERE FIRST, SO LET'S MEET UP LATER.
YUP!
DASH
TMP TMP TMP

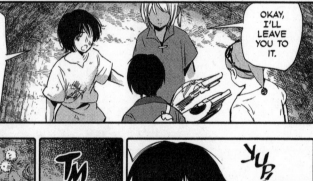

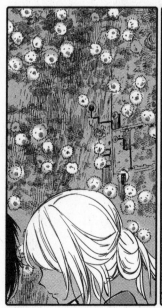

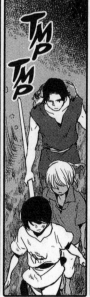

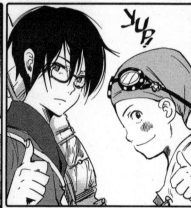

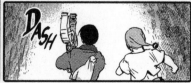

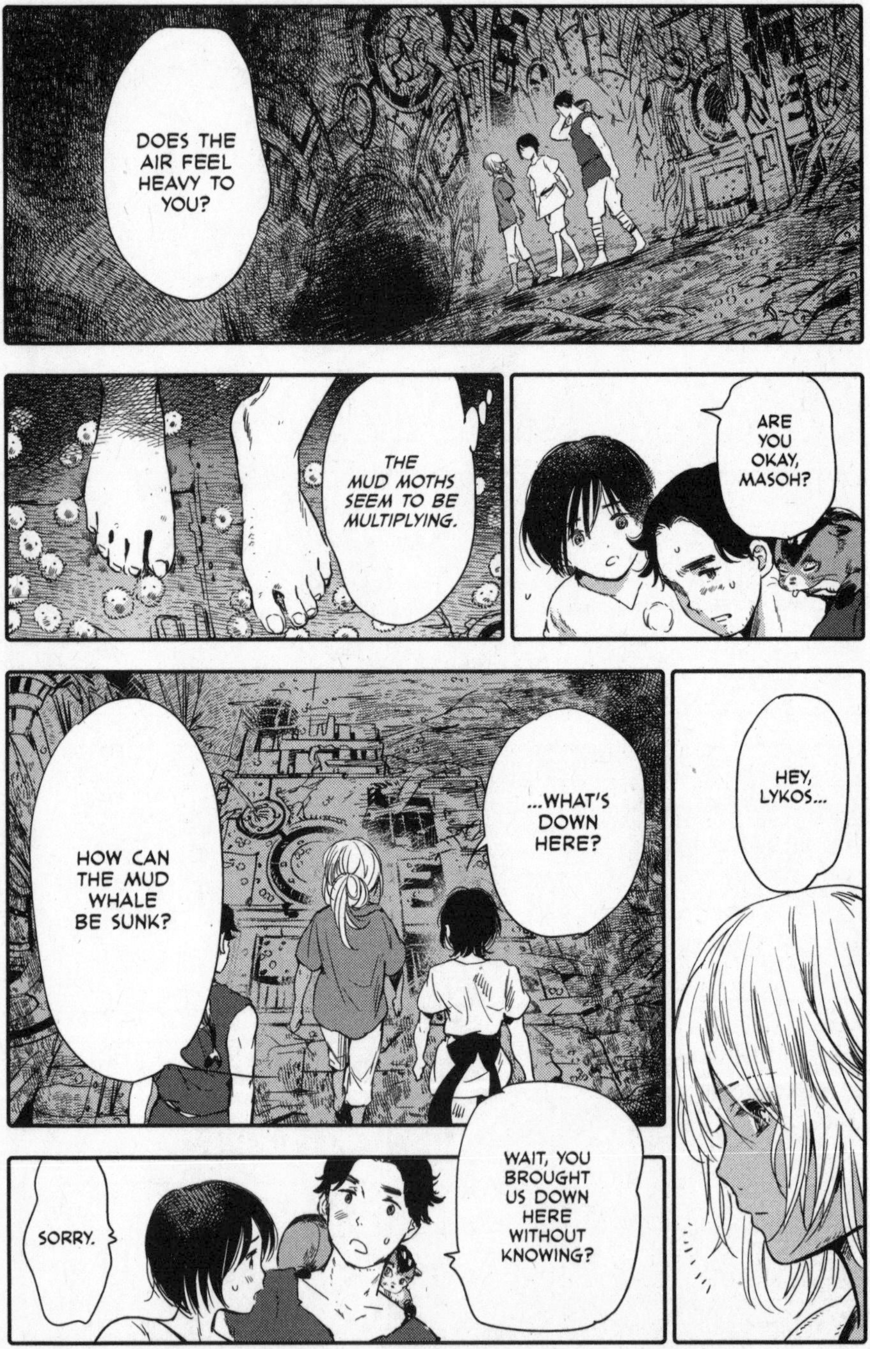
DOES THE AIR FEEL HEAVY TO YOU?
ARE YOU OKAY, MASOH?
THE MUD MOTHS SEEM TO BE MULTIPLYING.
HEY, LYKOS...
...WHAT'S DOWN HERE?
HOW CAN THE MUD WHALE BE SUNK?
WAIT, YOU BROUGHT US DOWN HERE WITHOUT KNOWING?
SORRY.

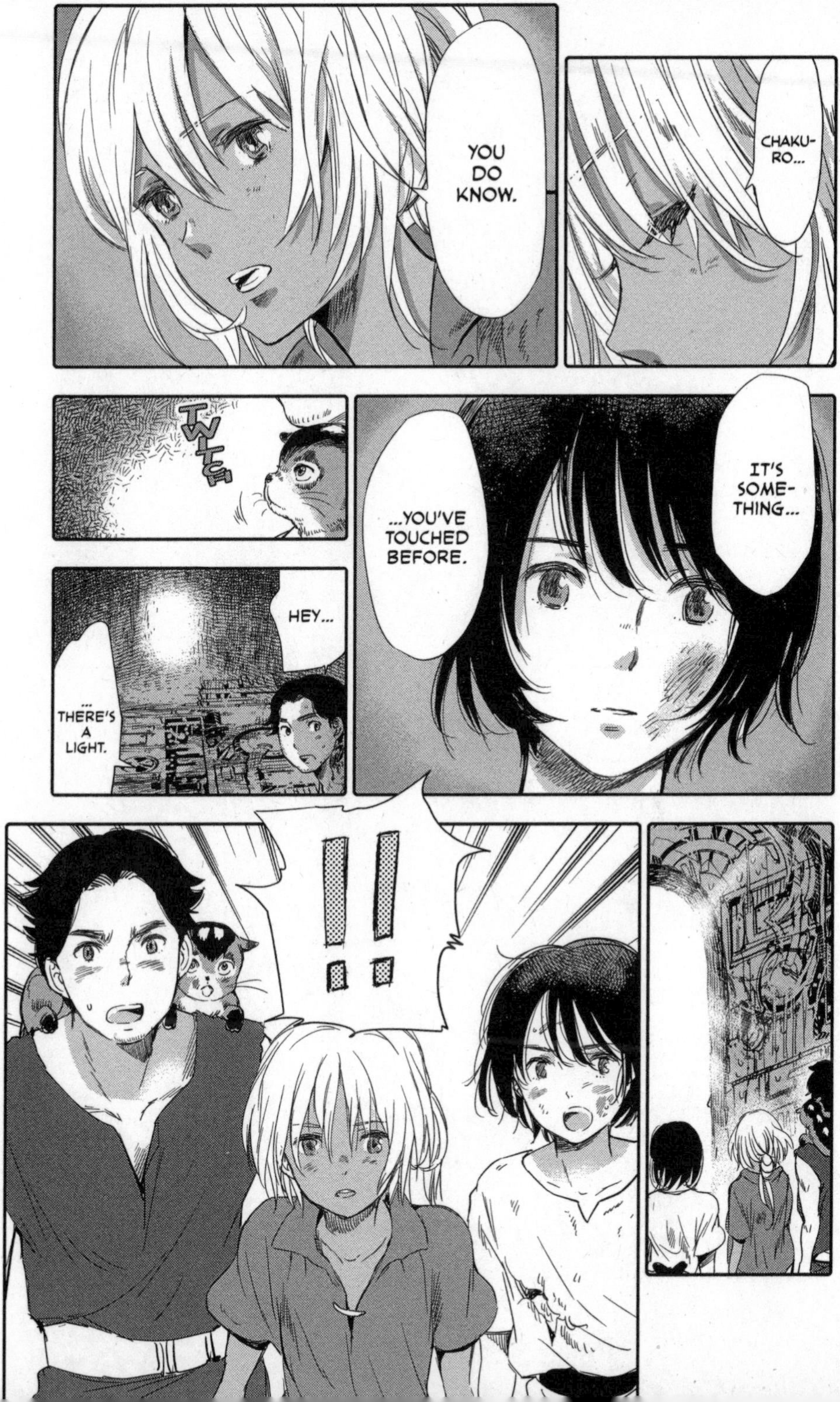
CHAKU-RO...
YOU DO KNOW.
IT'S SOME-THING...
...YOU'VE TOUCHED BEFORE.
TWITCH
HEY...
...THERE'S A LIGHT.
!!

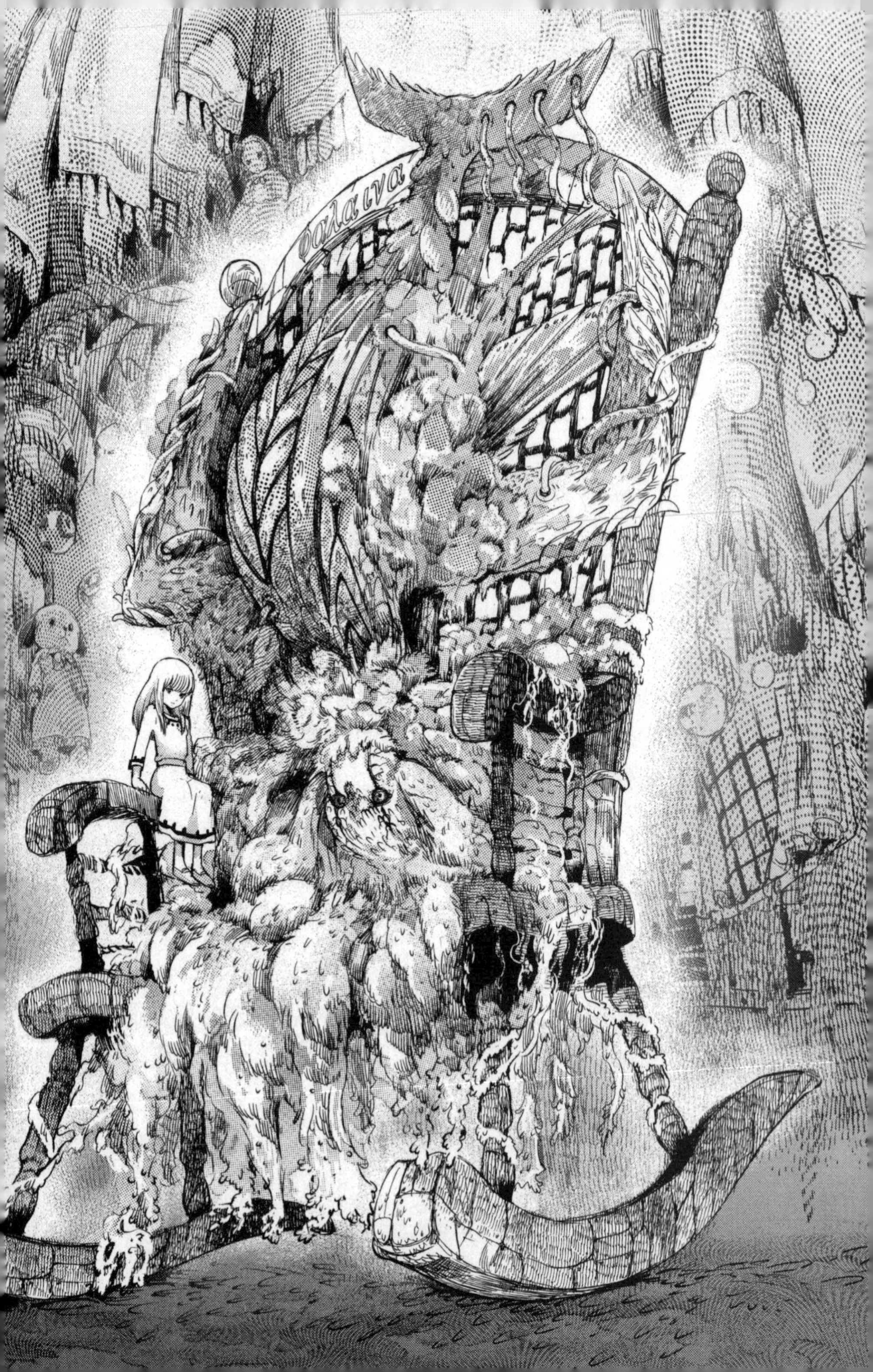
Φαλαινα

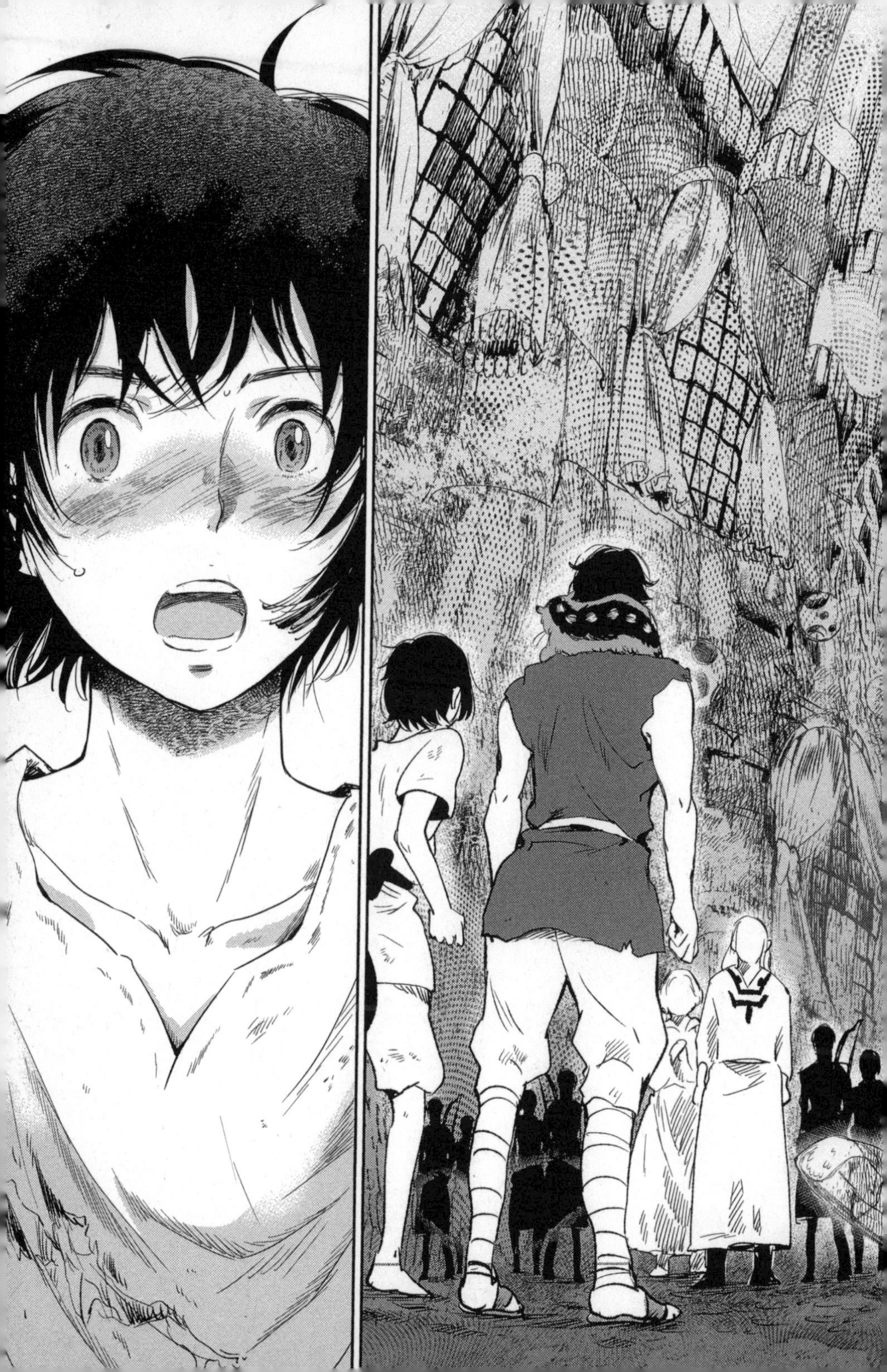

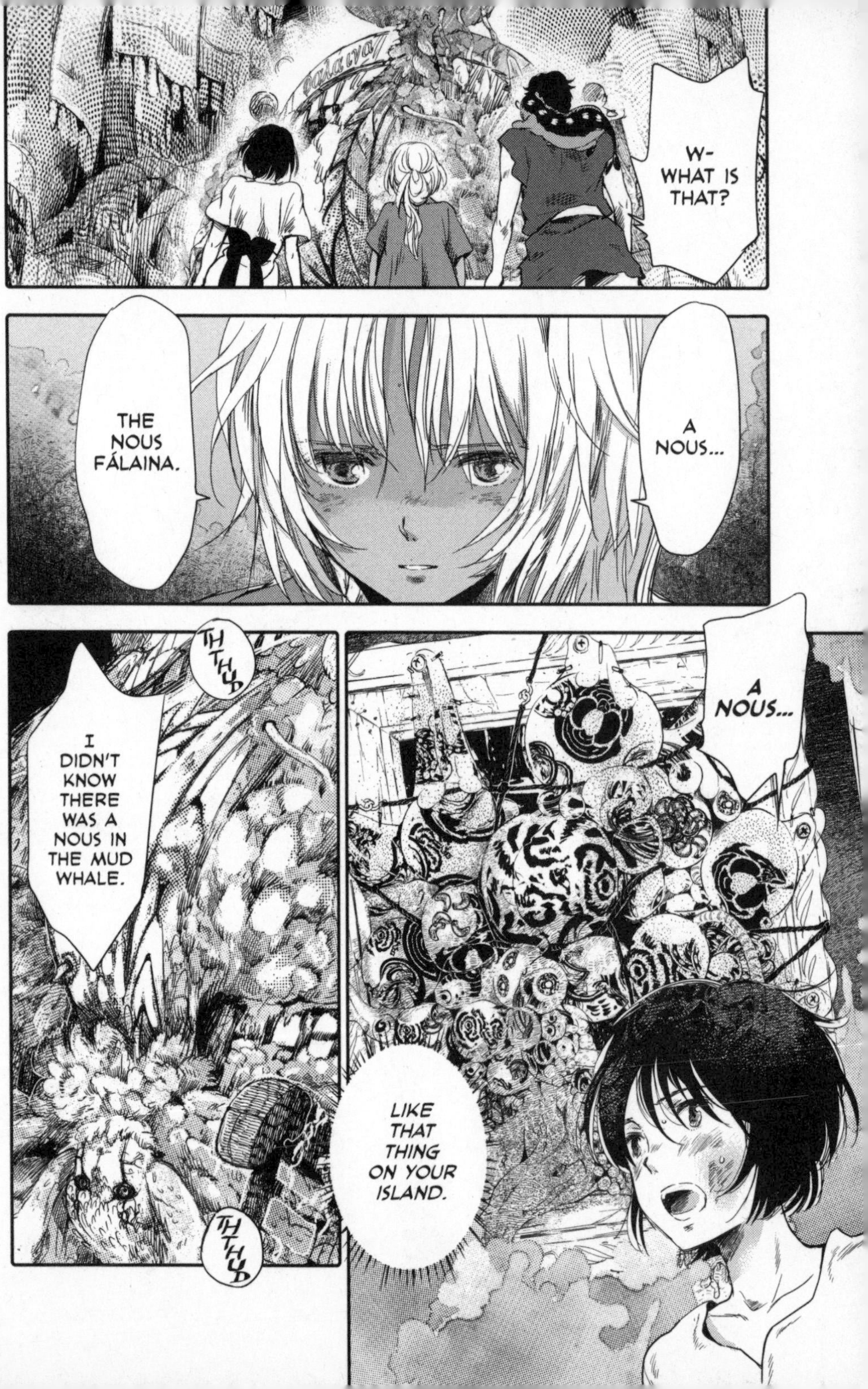
W- WHAT IS THAT?
A NOUS...
THE NOUS FÁLAINA.
A NOUS...
LIKE THAT THING ON YOUR ISLAND.
THTHUD
I DIDN'T KNOW THERE WAS A NOUS IN THE MUD WHALE.
THTHUD

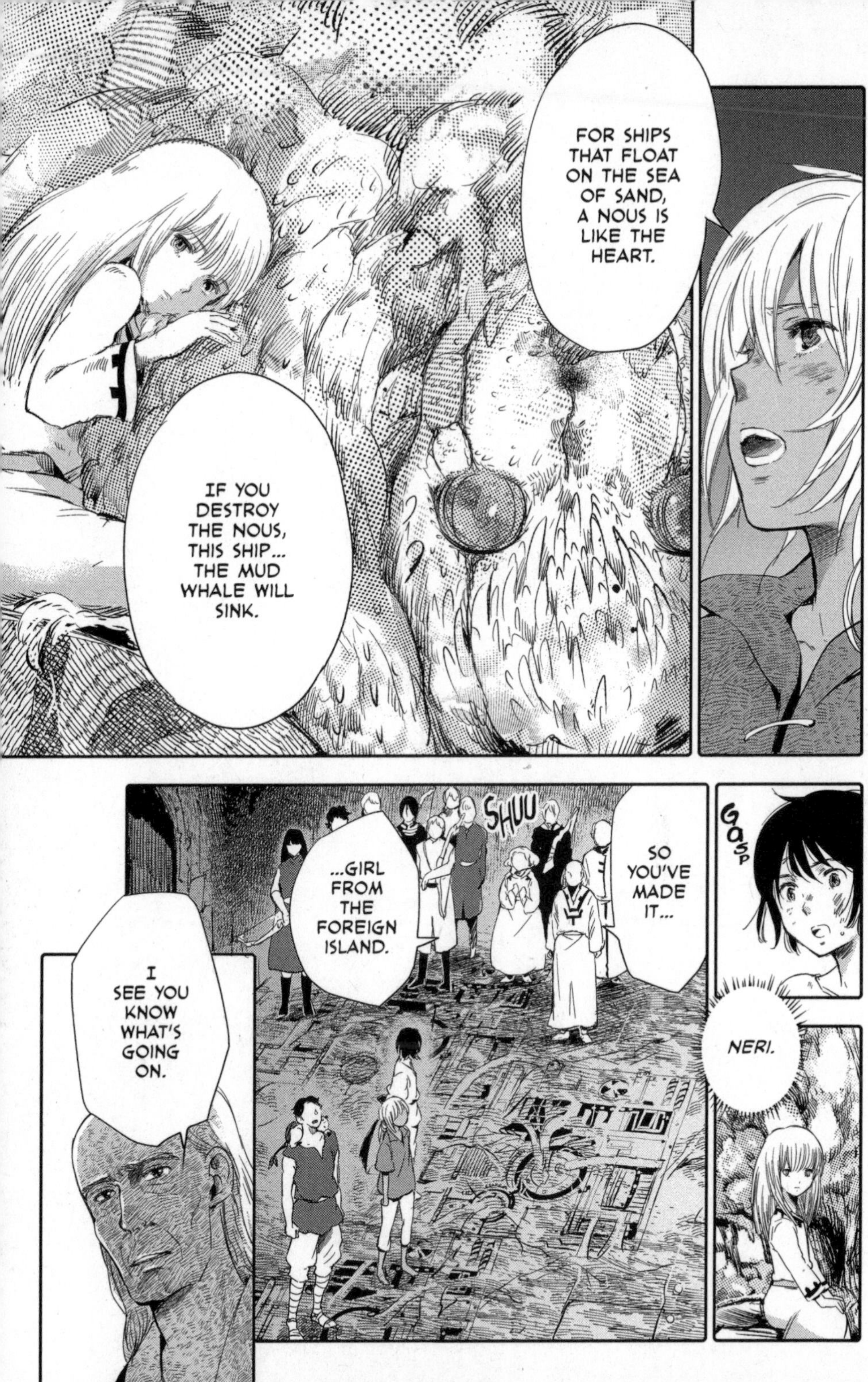
FOR SHIPS THAT FLOAT ON THE SEA OF SAND, A NOUS IS LIKE THE HEART.
IF YOU DESTROY THE NOUS, THIS SHIP... THE MUD WHALE WILL SINK.
GASP
NERI.
SHUU
SO YOU'VE MADE IT...
...GIRL FROM THE FOREIGN ISLAND.
I SEE YOU KNOW WHAT'S GOING ON.

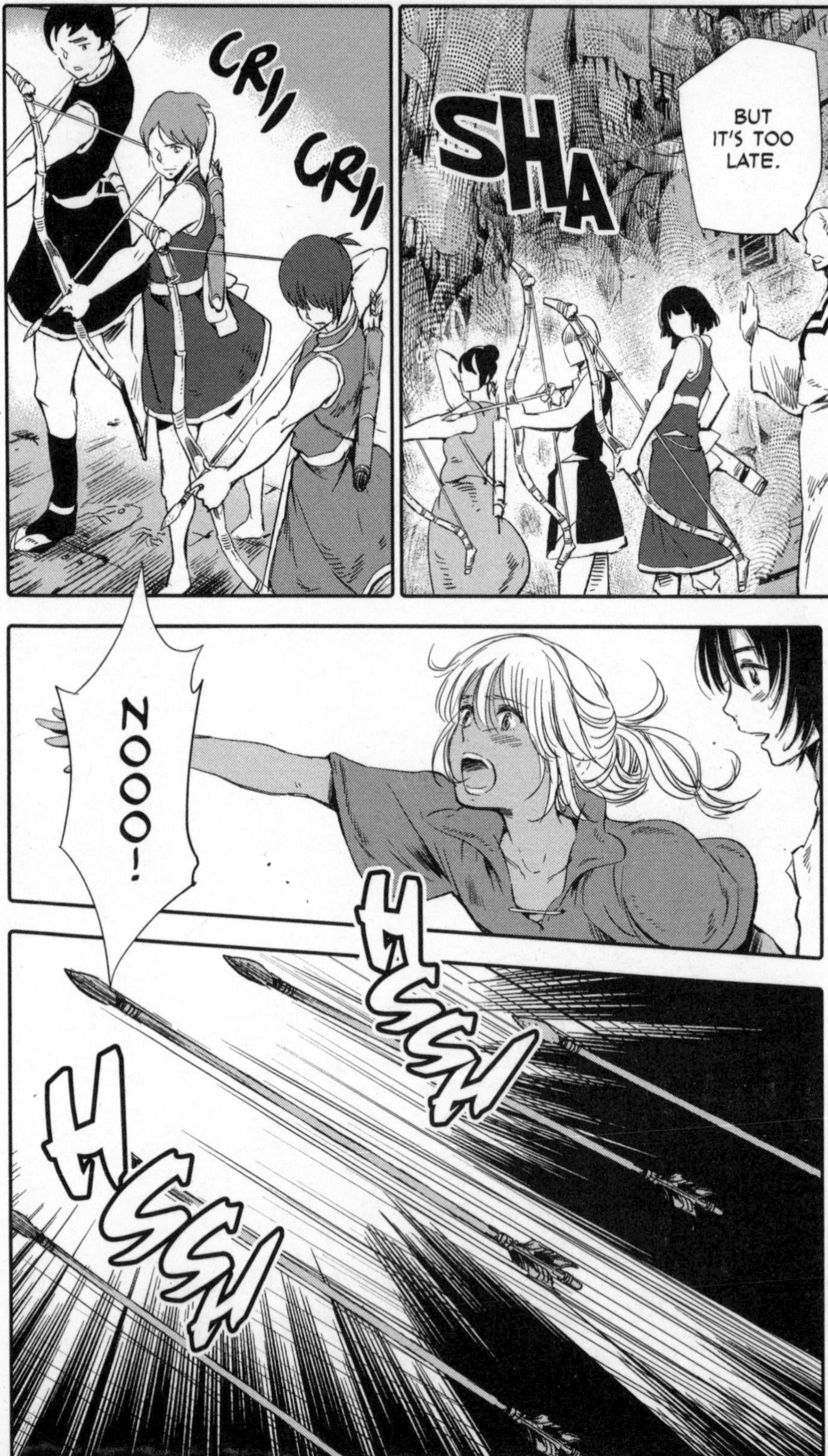
SHA
BUT IT'S TOO LATE.
CRII CRII
NOOOO!
HSSH
HSSH

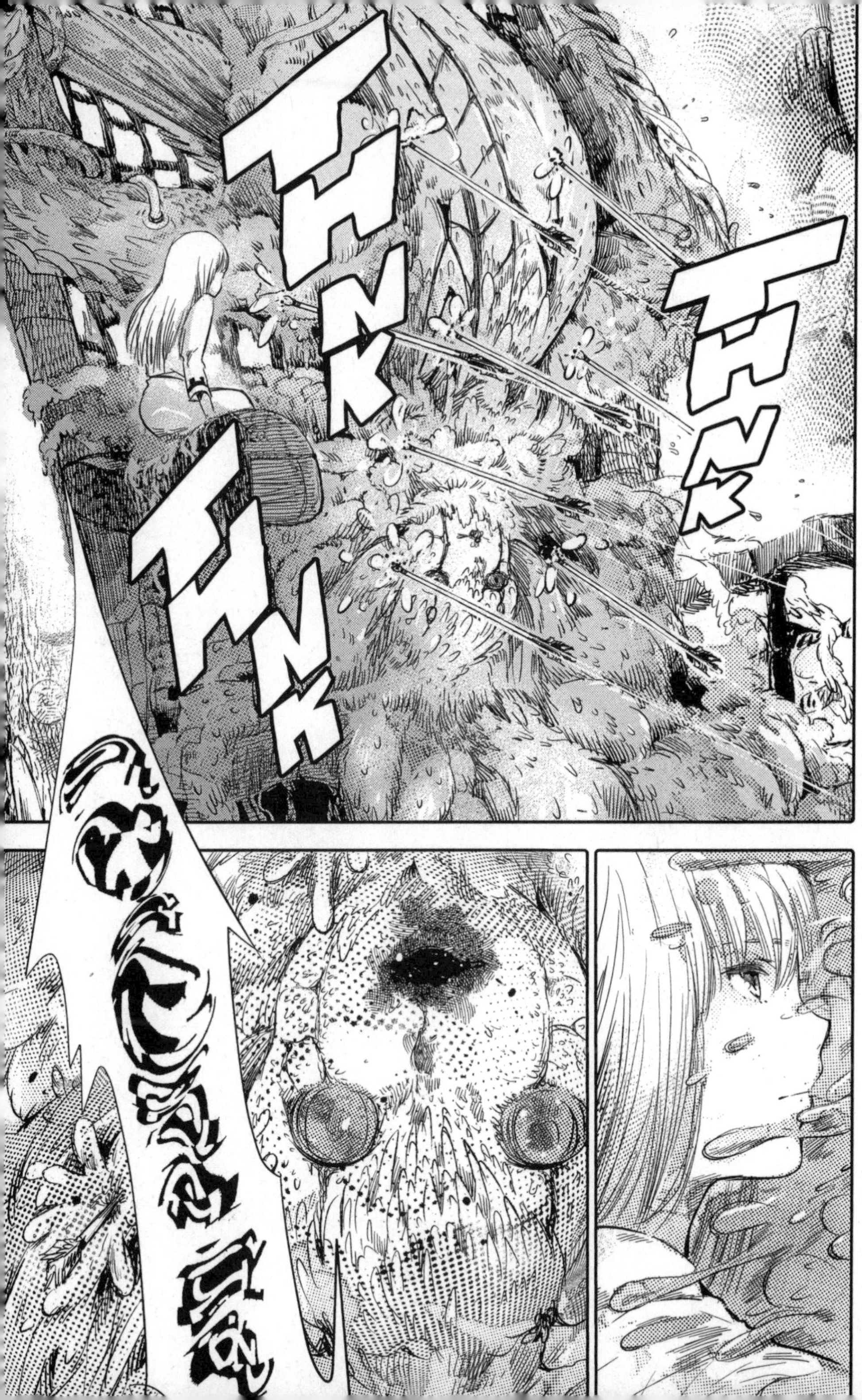
THUNK
THUNK
THUNK

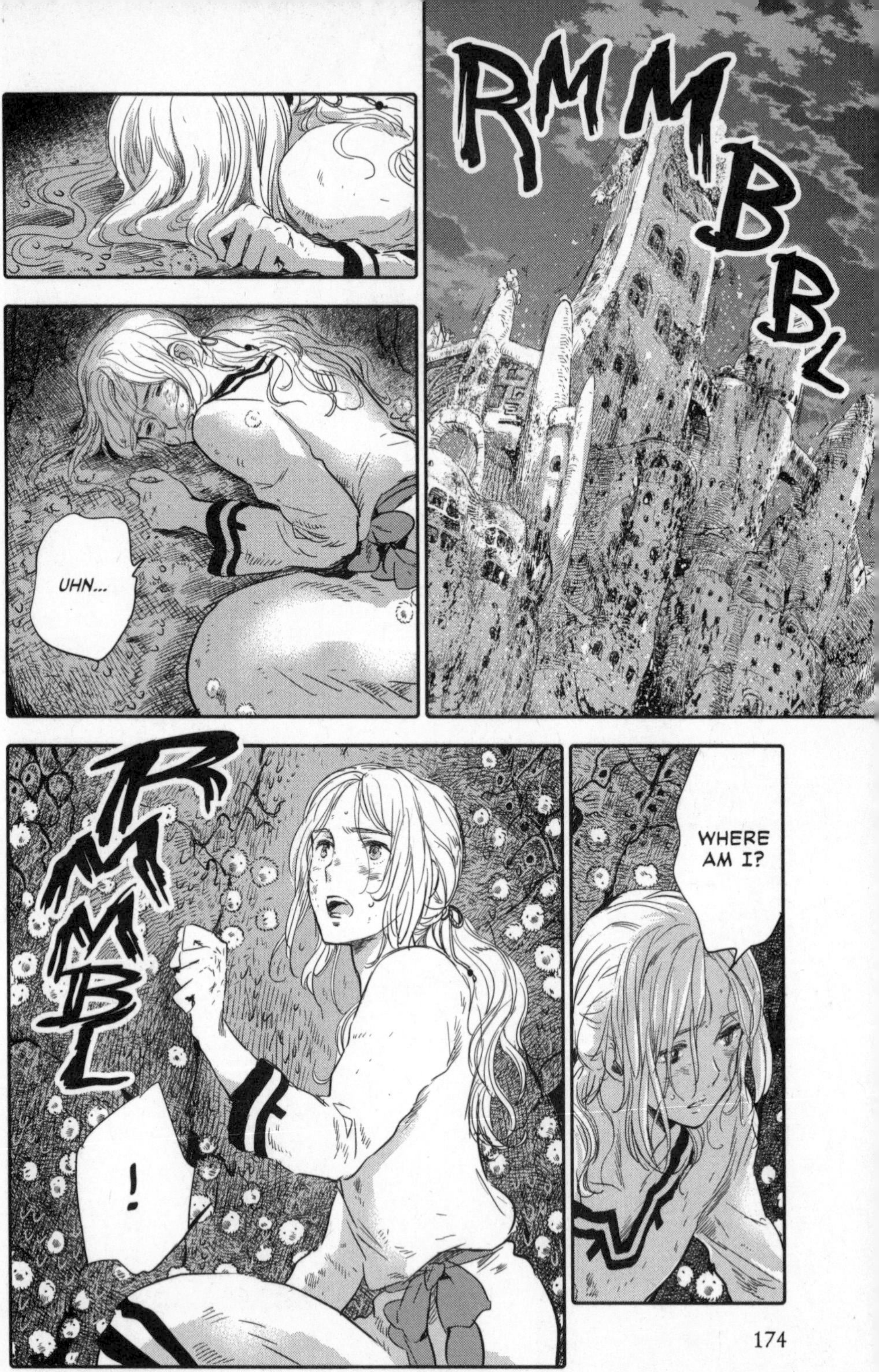
RMMBBL
UHN...
WHERE AM I?
RMMBL
!

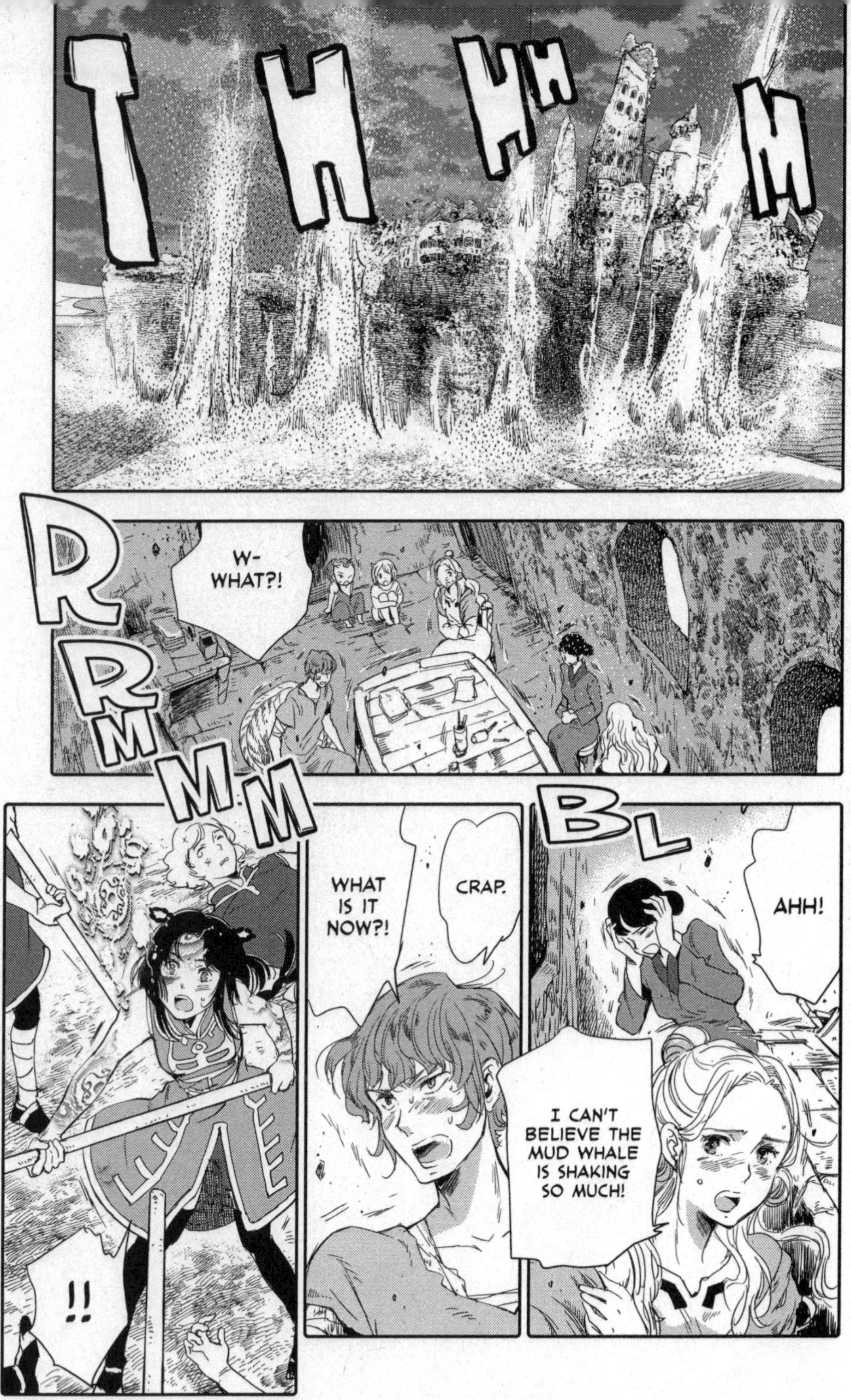
THHHHM
W-WHAT?!
RRMMM
BL
AHH!
I CAN'T BELIEVE THE MUD WHALE IS SHAKING SO MUCH!
CRAP.
WHAT IS IT NOW?!
!!

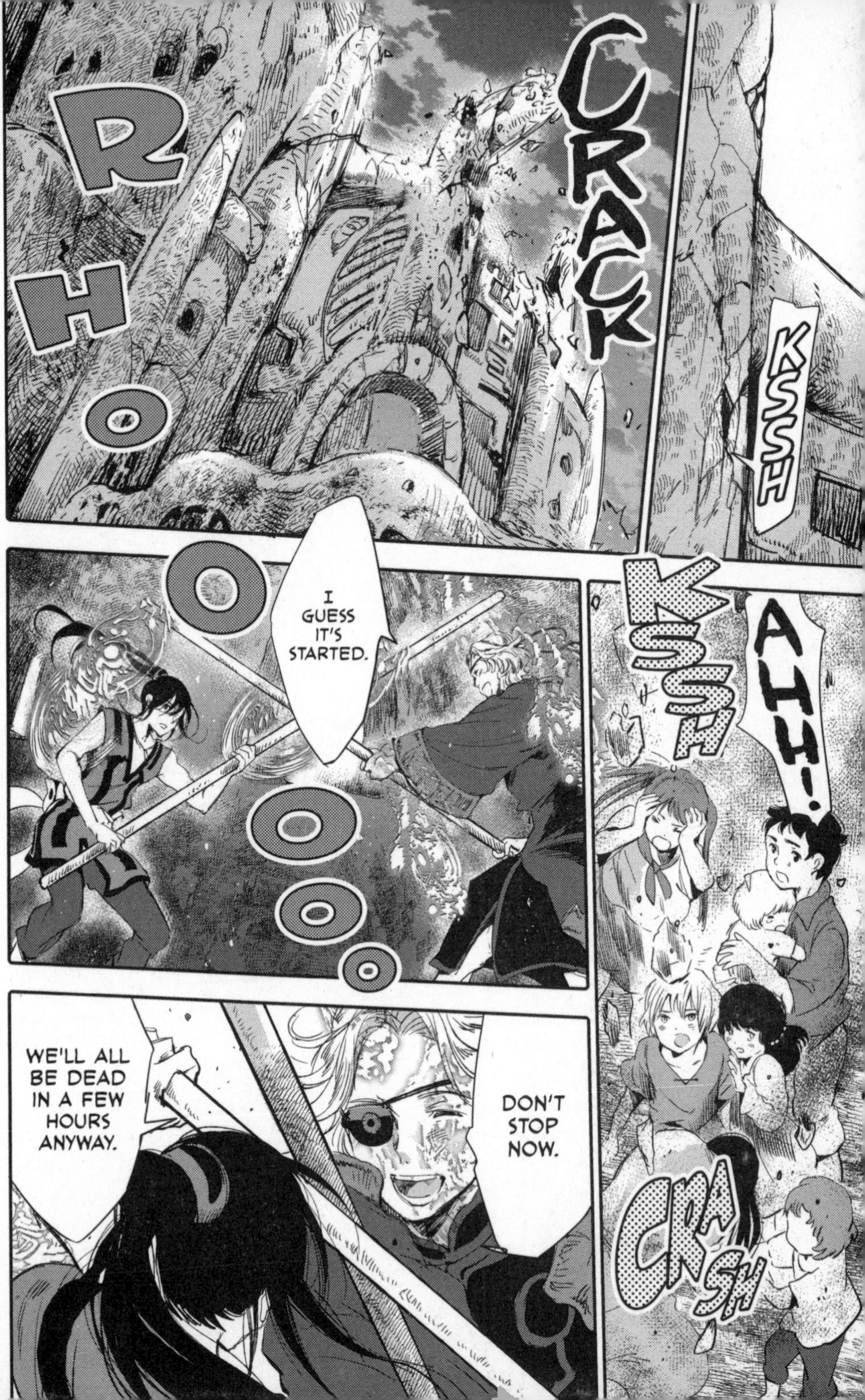
KSSSH
CRACK
RHOOOOO
AHH!
KSSSH
CRASH
I GUESS IT'S STARTED.
DON'T STOP NOW.
WE'LL ALL BE DEAD IN A FEW HOURS ANYWAY.

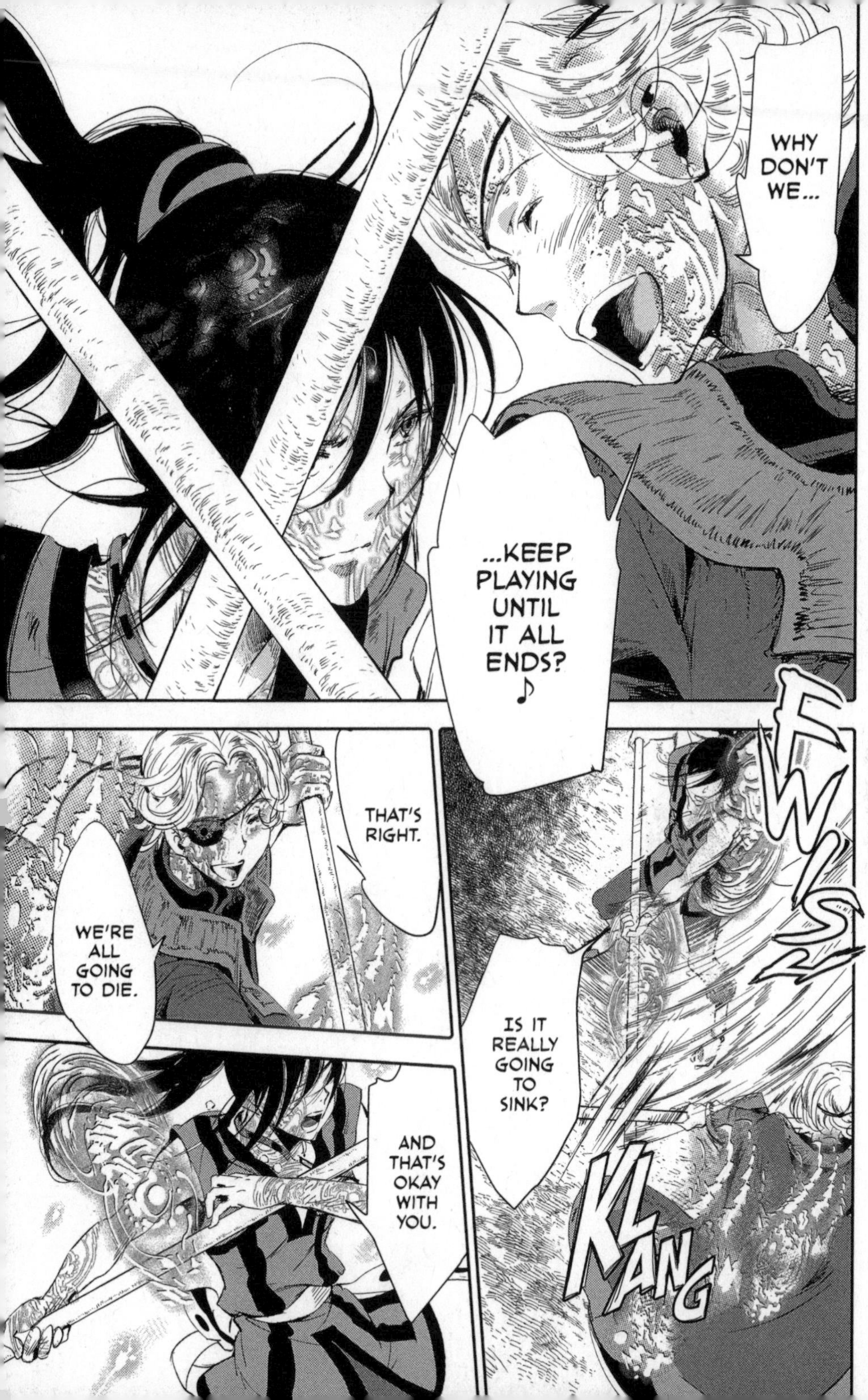
WHY DON'T WE...
...KEEP PLAYING UNTIL IT ALL ENDS? ♪
FWISH
IS IT REALLY GOING TO SINK?
KLANG
THAT'S RIGHT.
WE'RE ALL GOING TO DIE.
AND THAT'S OKAY WITH YOU.

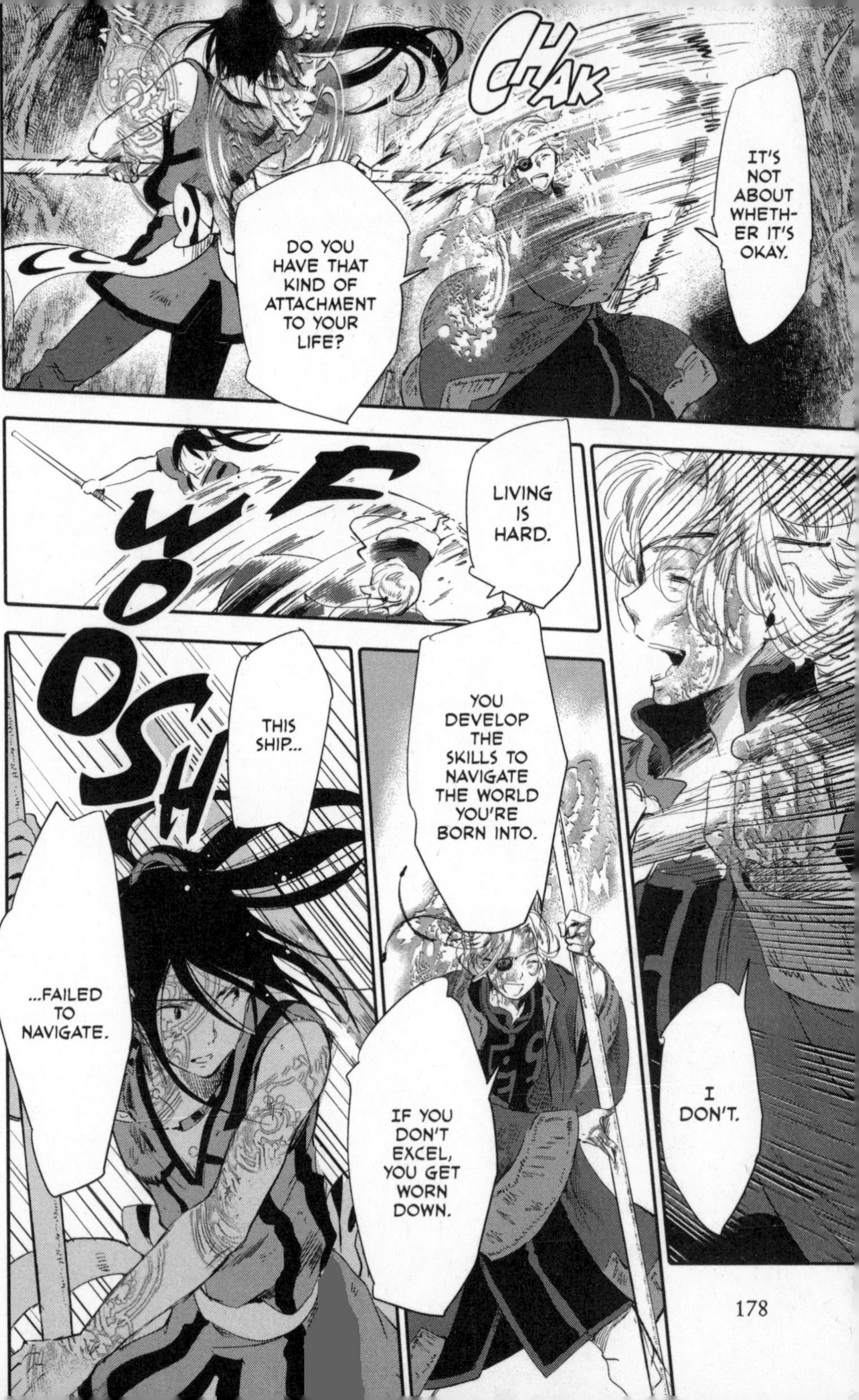
CHAK
IT'S NOT ABOUT WHETHER IT'S OKAY.
DO YOU HAVE THAT KIND OF ATTACHMENT TO YOUR LIFE?
I DON'T.
LIVING IS HARD.
WHOOSH
YOU DEVELOP THE SKILLS TO NAVIGATE THE WORLD YOU'RE BORN INTO.
IF YOU DON'T EXCEL, YOU GET WORN DOWN.
THIS SHIP...
...FAILED TO NAVIGATE.

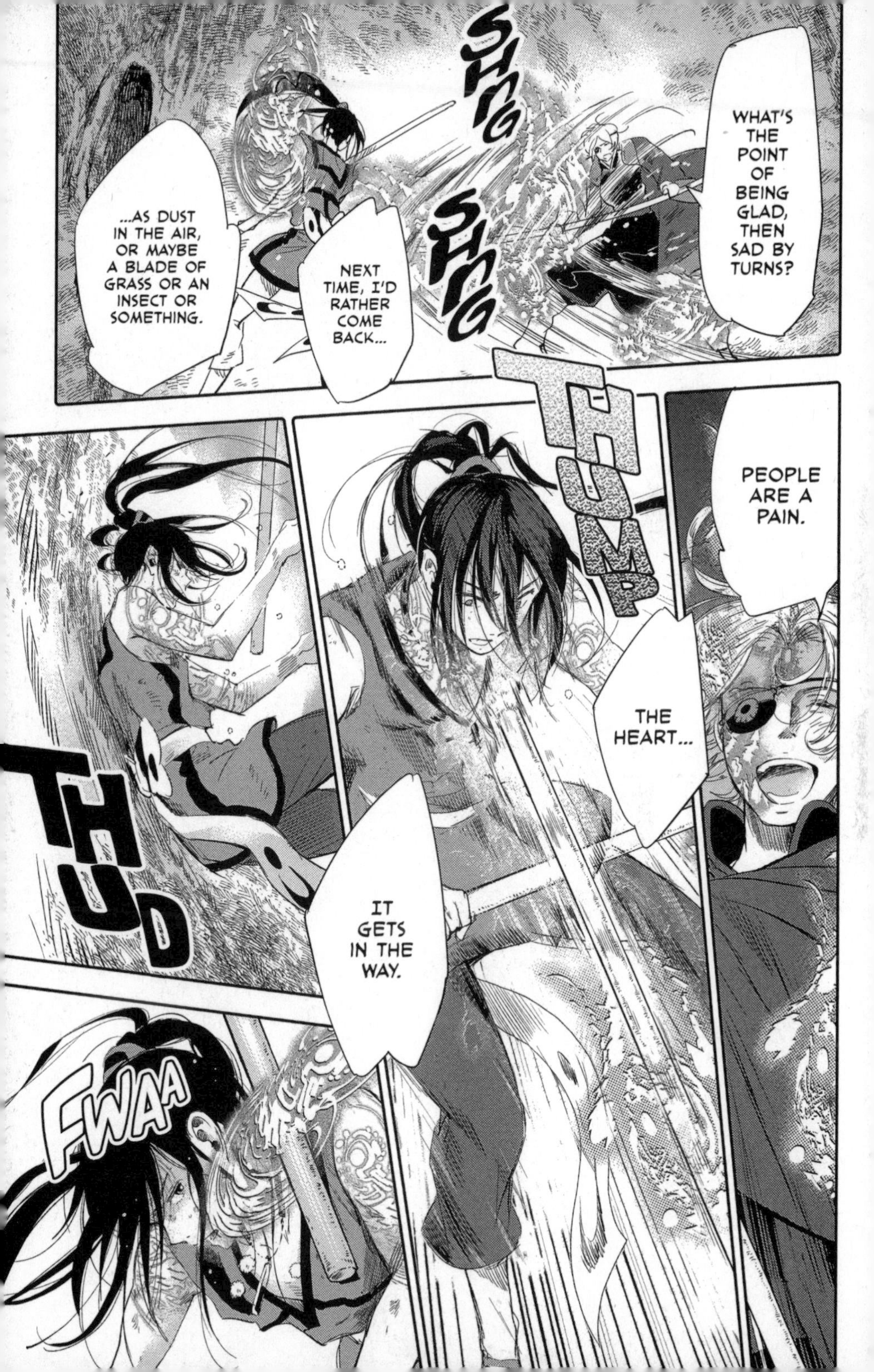
WHAT'S THE POINT OF BEING GLAD, THEN SAD BY TURNS?
SHING
SHING
SHING
NEXT TIME, I'D RATHER COME BACK...
...AS DUST IN THE AIR, OR MAYBE A BLADE OF GRASS OR AN INSECT OR SOMETHING.
PEOPLE ARE A PAIN.
THE HEART...
THUMP
IT GETS IN THE WAY.
THUD
FWAA

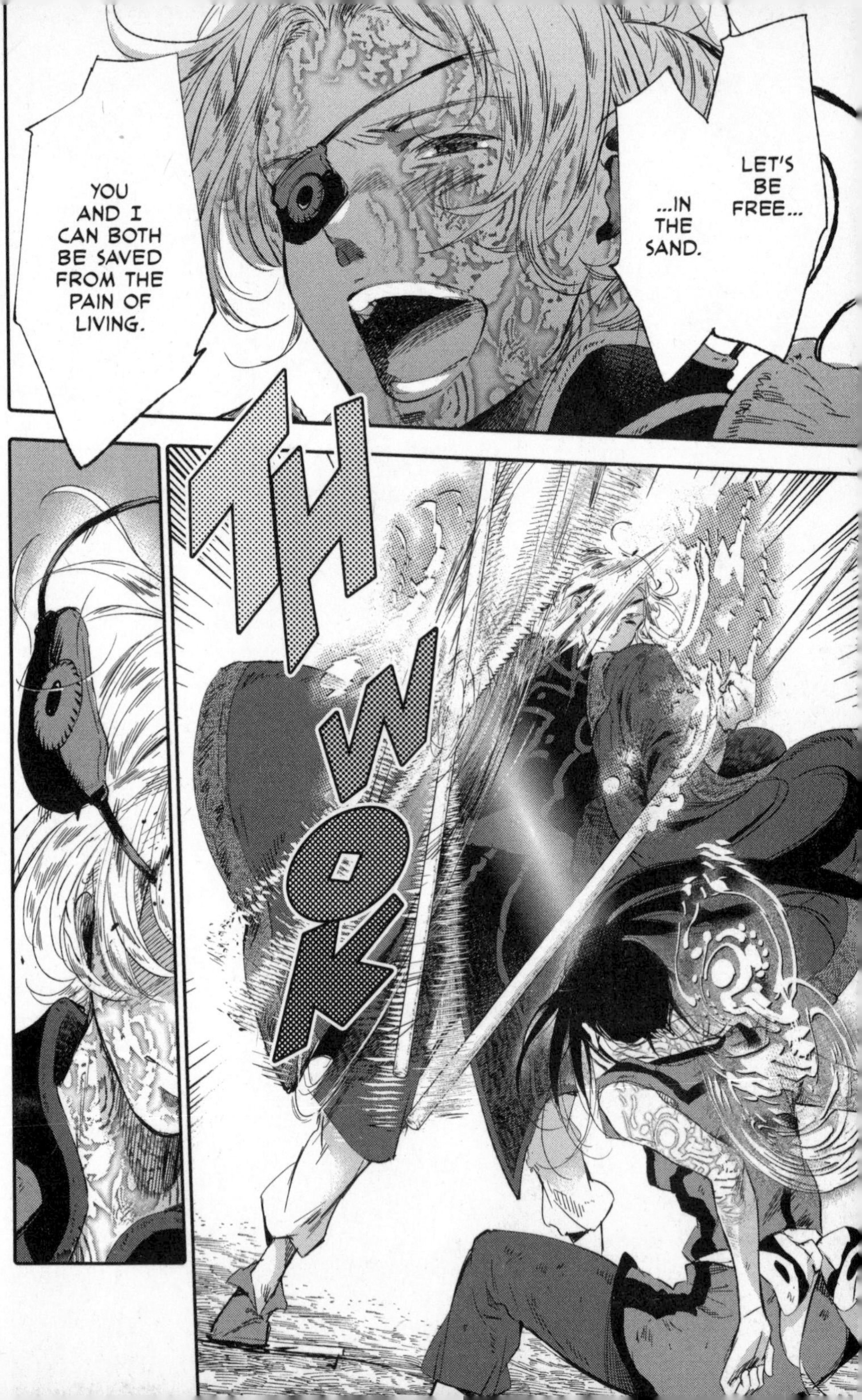
LET'S BE FREE...
...IN THE SAND.
YOU AND I CAN BOTH BE SAVED FROM THE PAIN OF LIVING.
THWOK

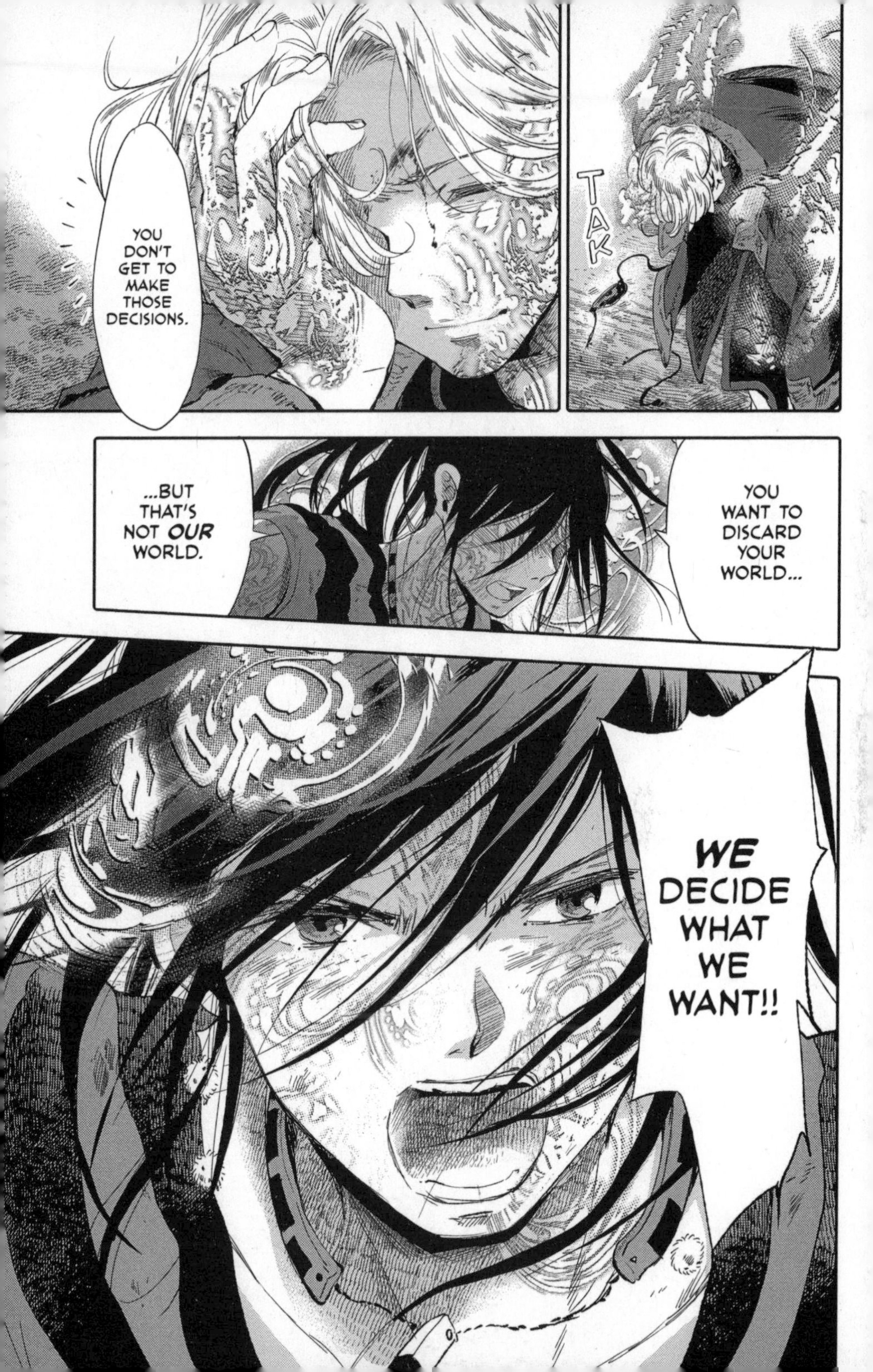
TAK
YOU DON'T GET TO MAKE THOSE DECISIONS.
YOU WANT TO DISCARD YOUR WORLD...
...BUT THAT'S NOT *OUR* WORLD.
WE DECIDE WHAT WE WANT!!

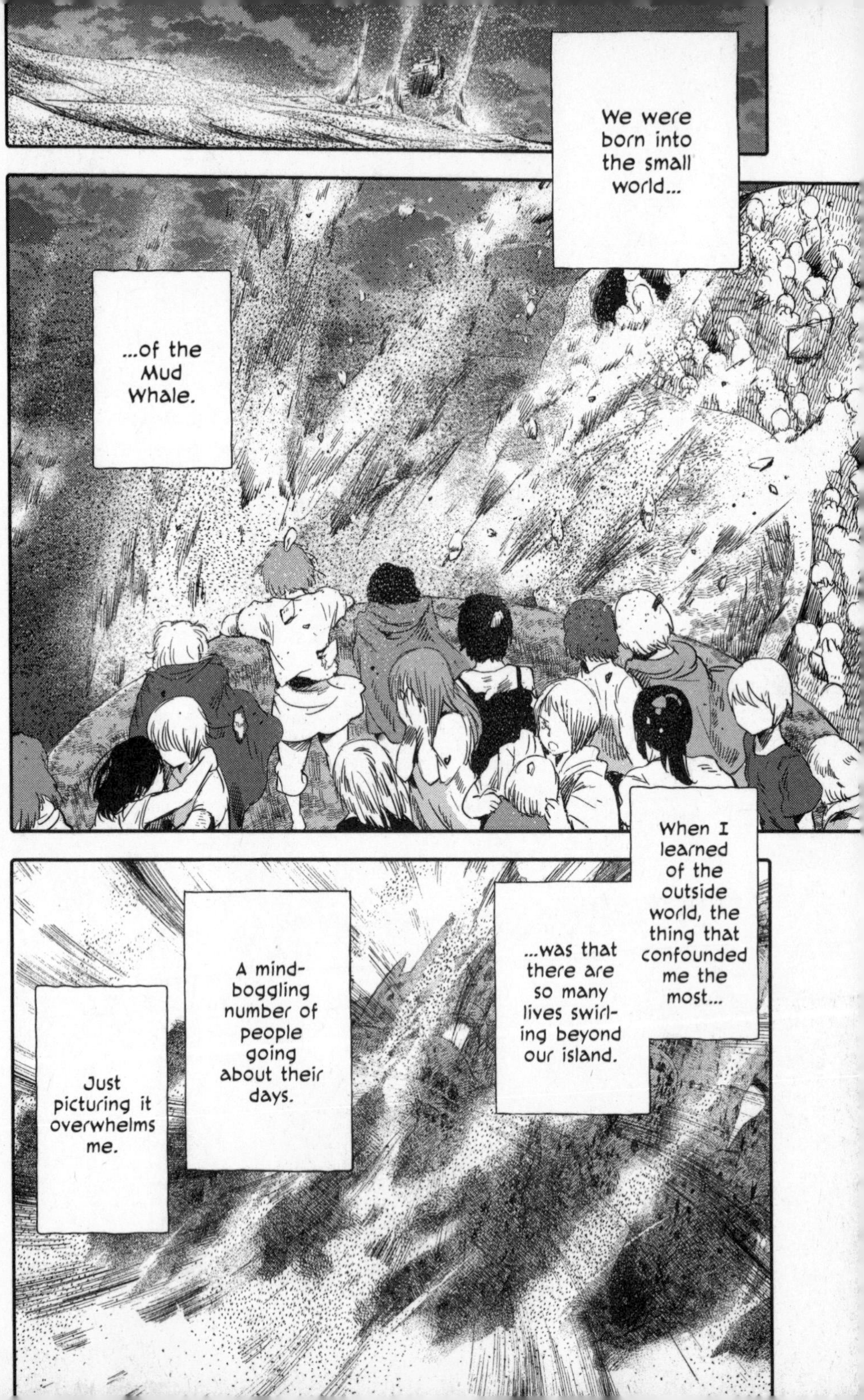
We were born into the small world...
...of the Mud Whale.
When I learned of the outside world, the thing that confounded me the most...
...was that there are so many lives swirl-ing beyond our island.
A mind-boggling number of people going about their days.
Just picturing it overwhelms me.

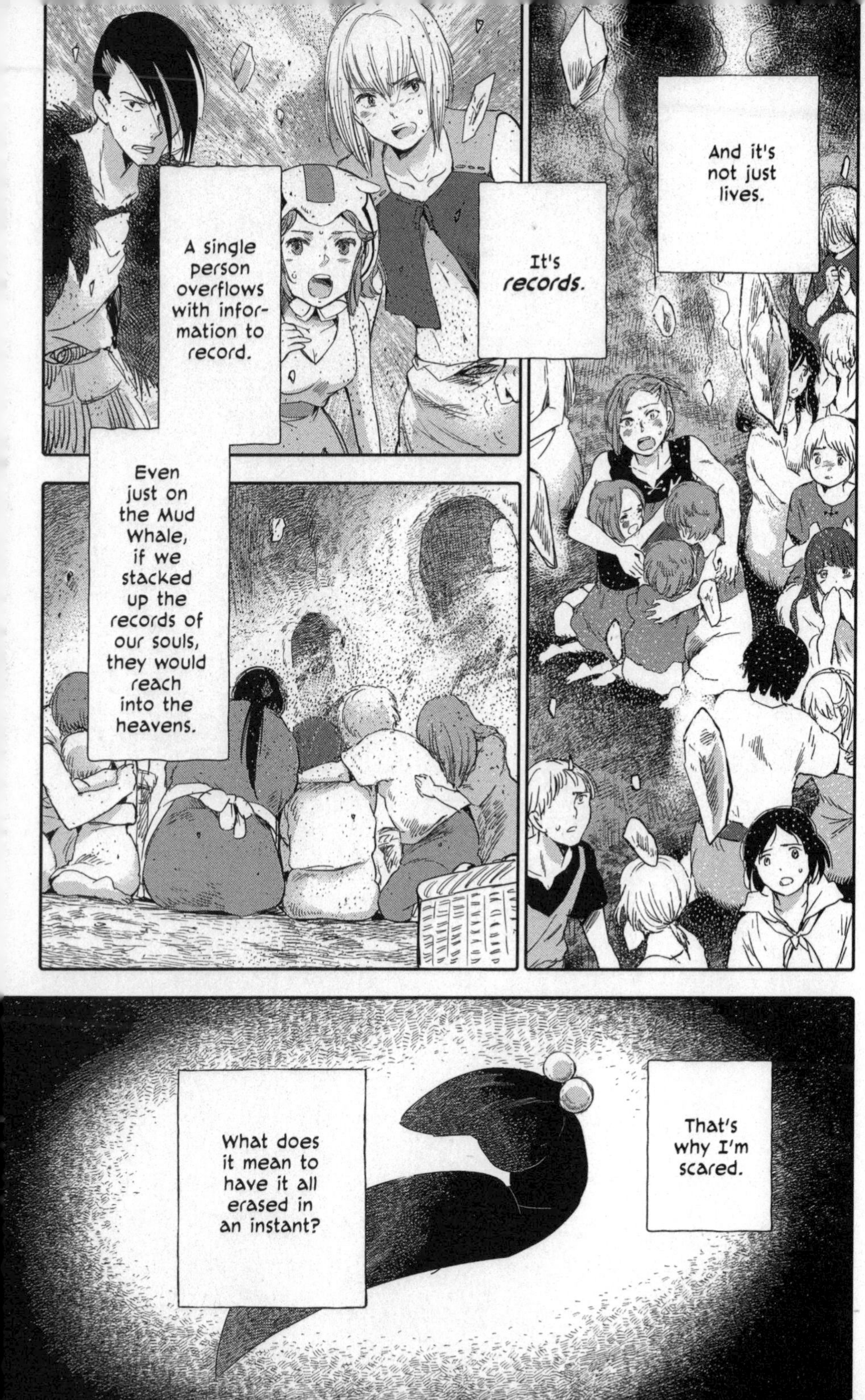
And it's not just lives.
It's *records.*
A single person overflows with information to record.
Even just on the Mud Whale, if we stacked up the records of our souls, they would reach into the heavens.
That's why I'm scared.
What does it mean to have it all erased in an instant?

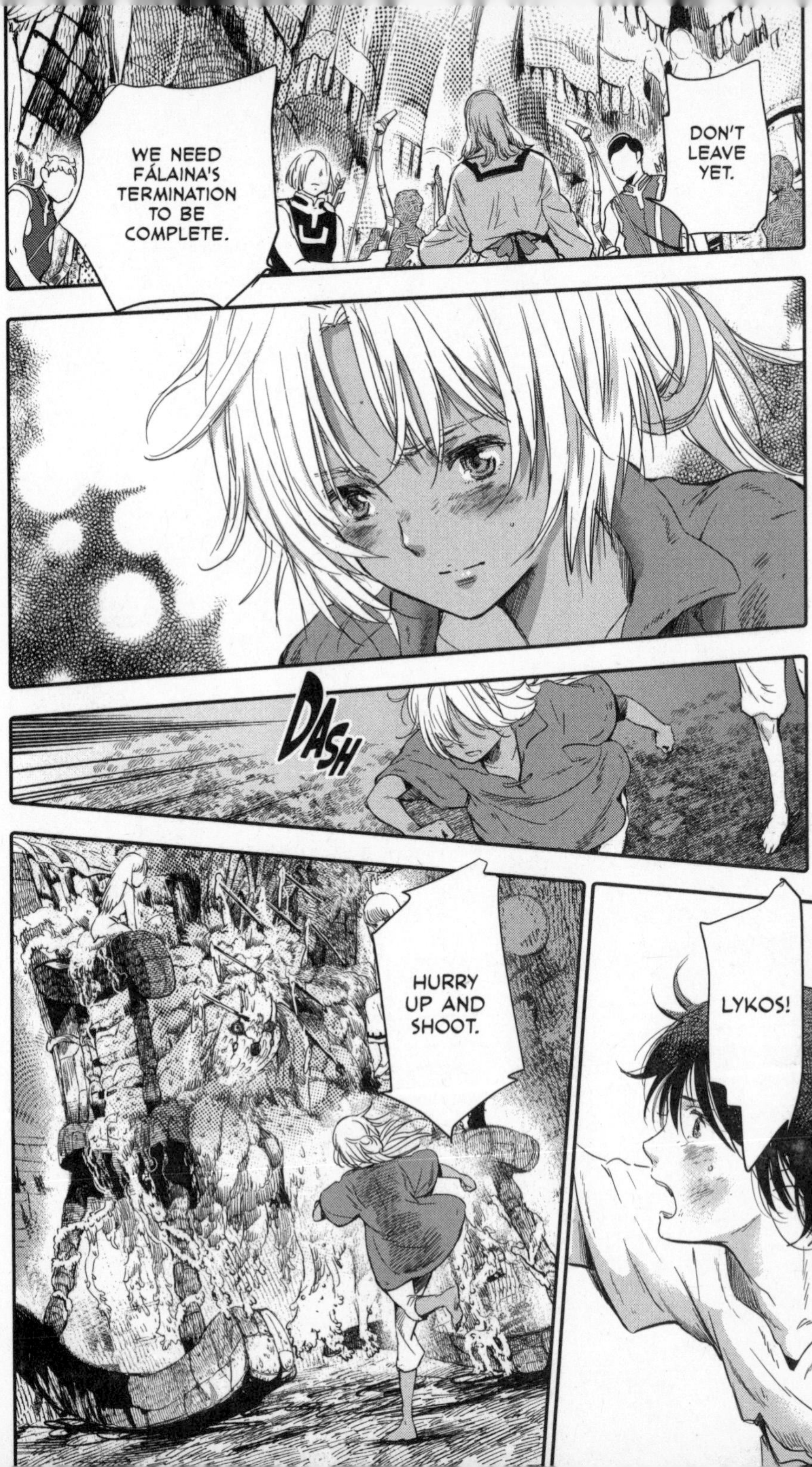
DON'T LEAVE YET.
WE NEED FÁLAINA'S TERMINATION TO BE COMPLETE.
DASH
LYKOS!
HURRY UP AND SHOOT.

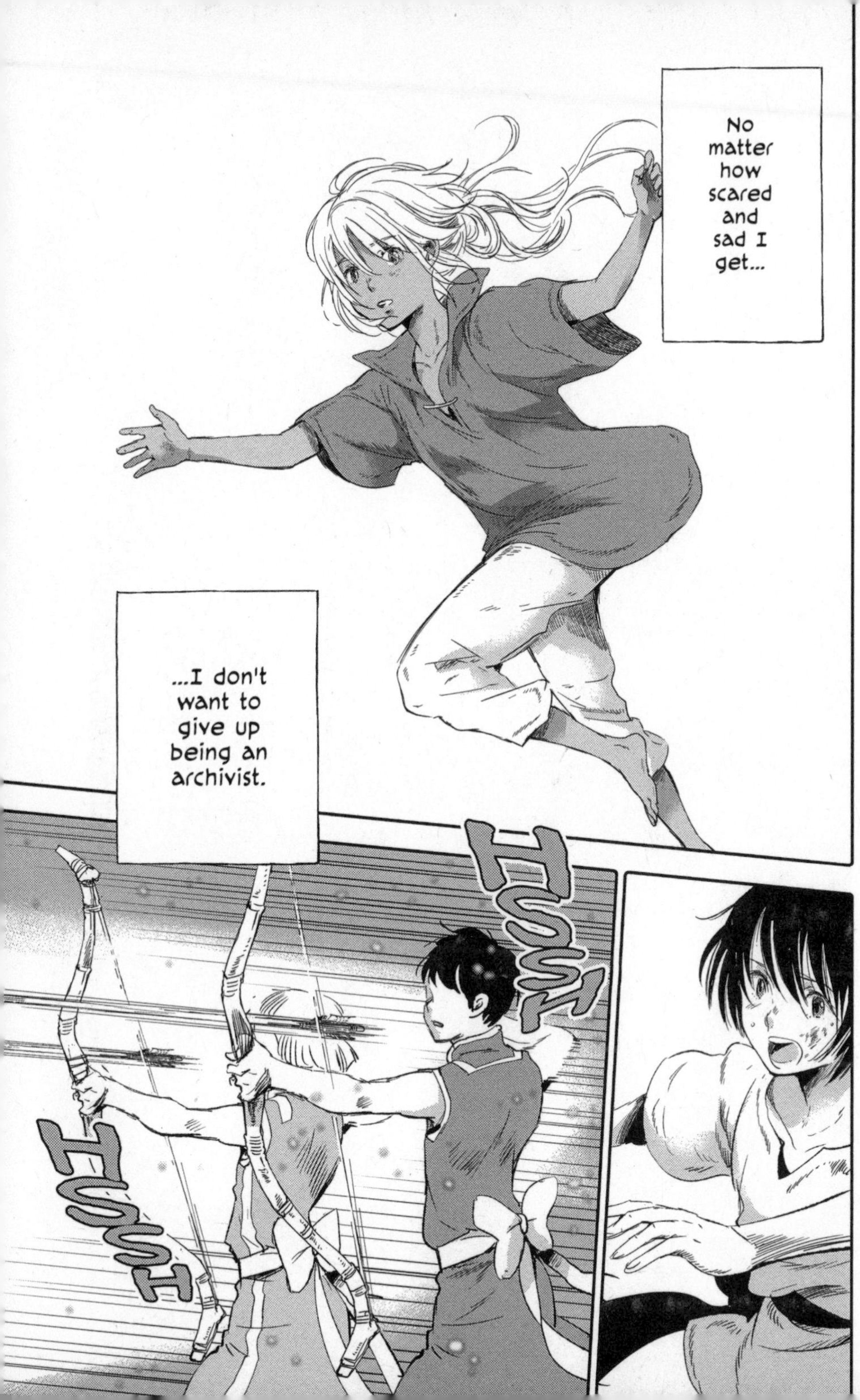
No matter how scared and sad I get...
...I don't want to give up being an archivist.
TSSH
TSSH

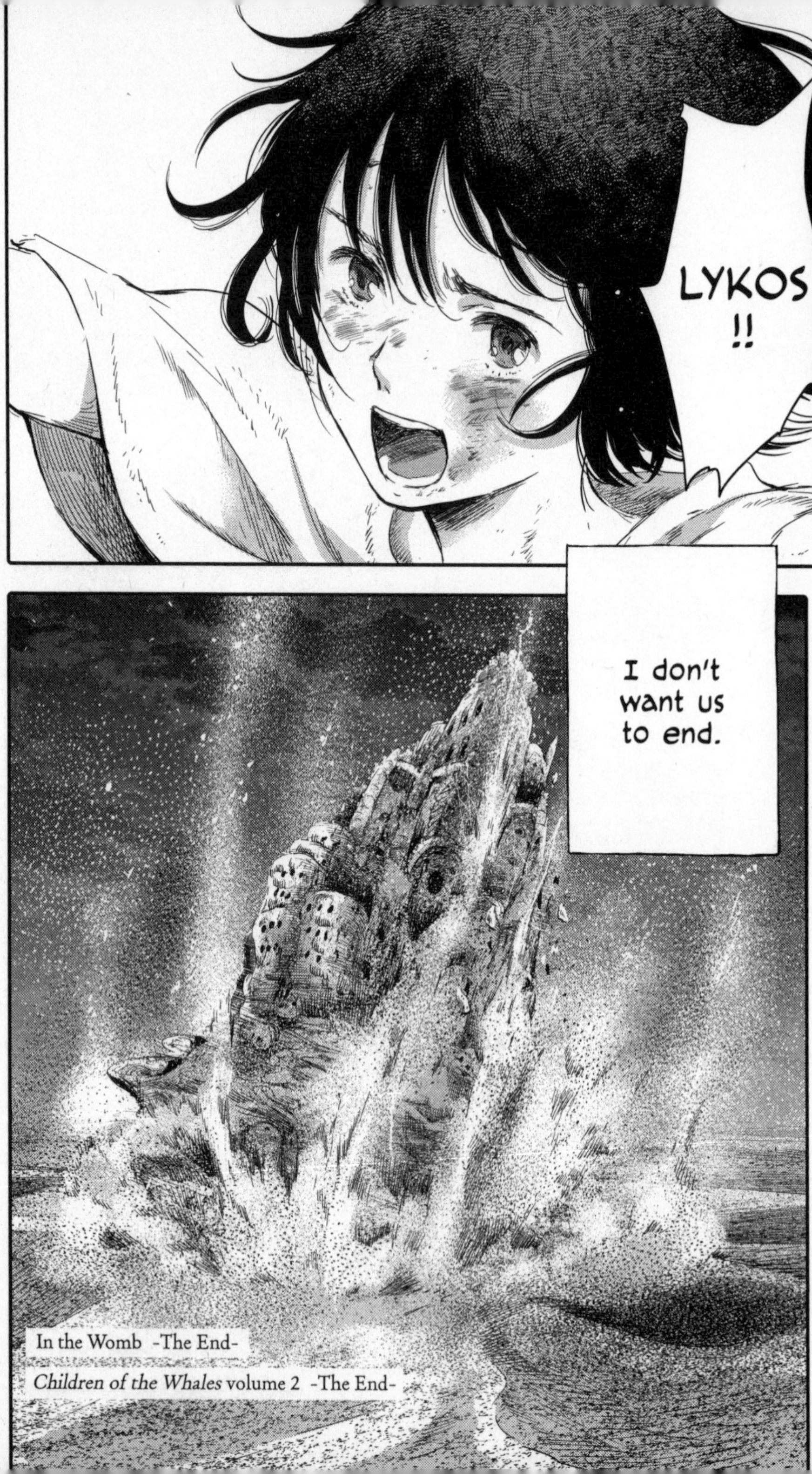
LYKOS !!
I don't want us to end.
In the Womb -The End-
Children of the Whales volume 2 -The End-

Afterward
Looking for Children of the Whales

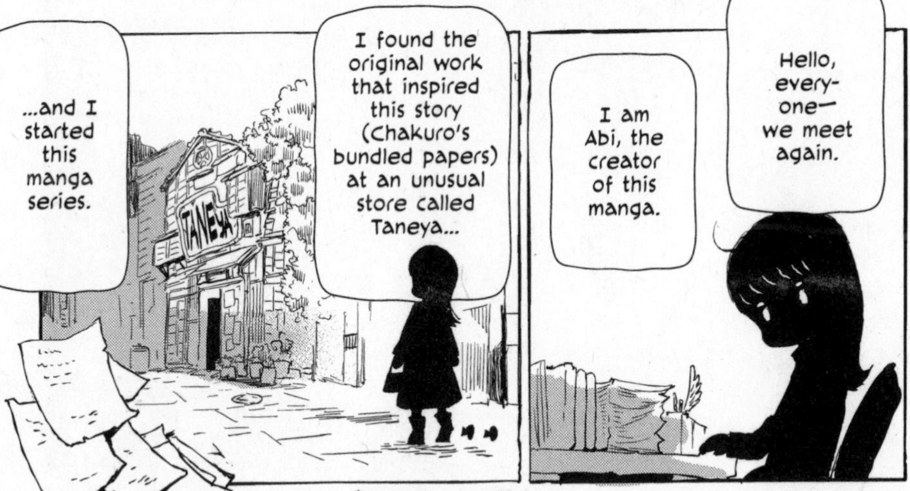
Hello, every-one— we meet again.
I am Abi, the creator of this manga.
I found the original work that inspired this story (Chakuro's bundled papers) at an unusual store called Taneya...
TANEYA
...and I started this manga series.

*See vol. 1, p. 188.

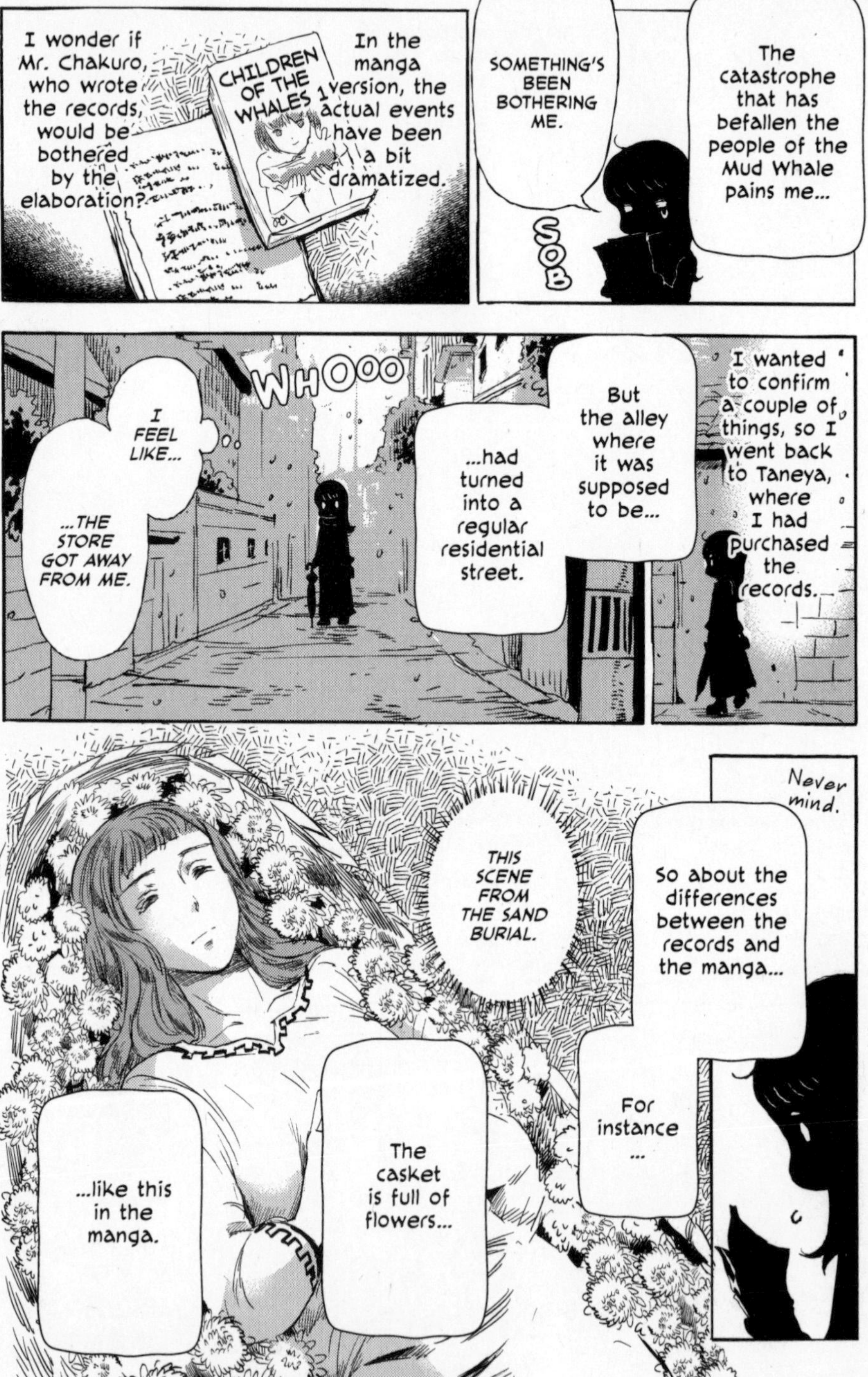
The catastrophe that has befallen the people of the Mud Whale pains me...
SOMETHING'S BEEN BOTHERING ME.
SOB
In the manga version, the actual events have been a bit dramatized.
CHILDREN OF THE WHALES 1
I wonder if Mr. Chakuro, who wrote the records, would be bothered by the elaboration?
I wanted to confirm a couple of things, so I went back to Taneya, where I had purchased the records.
But the alley where it was supposed to be...
...had turned into a regular residential street.
WHOOO
I FEEL LIKE...
...THE STORE GOT AWAY FROM ME.
Never mind.
So about the differences between the records and the manga...
For instance...
THIS SCENE FROM THE SAND BURIAL.
The casket is full of flowers...
...like this in the manga.

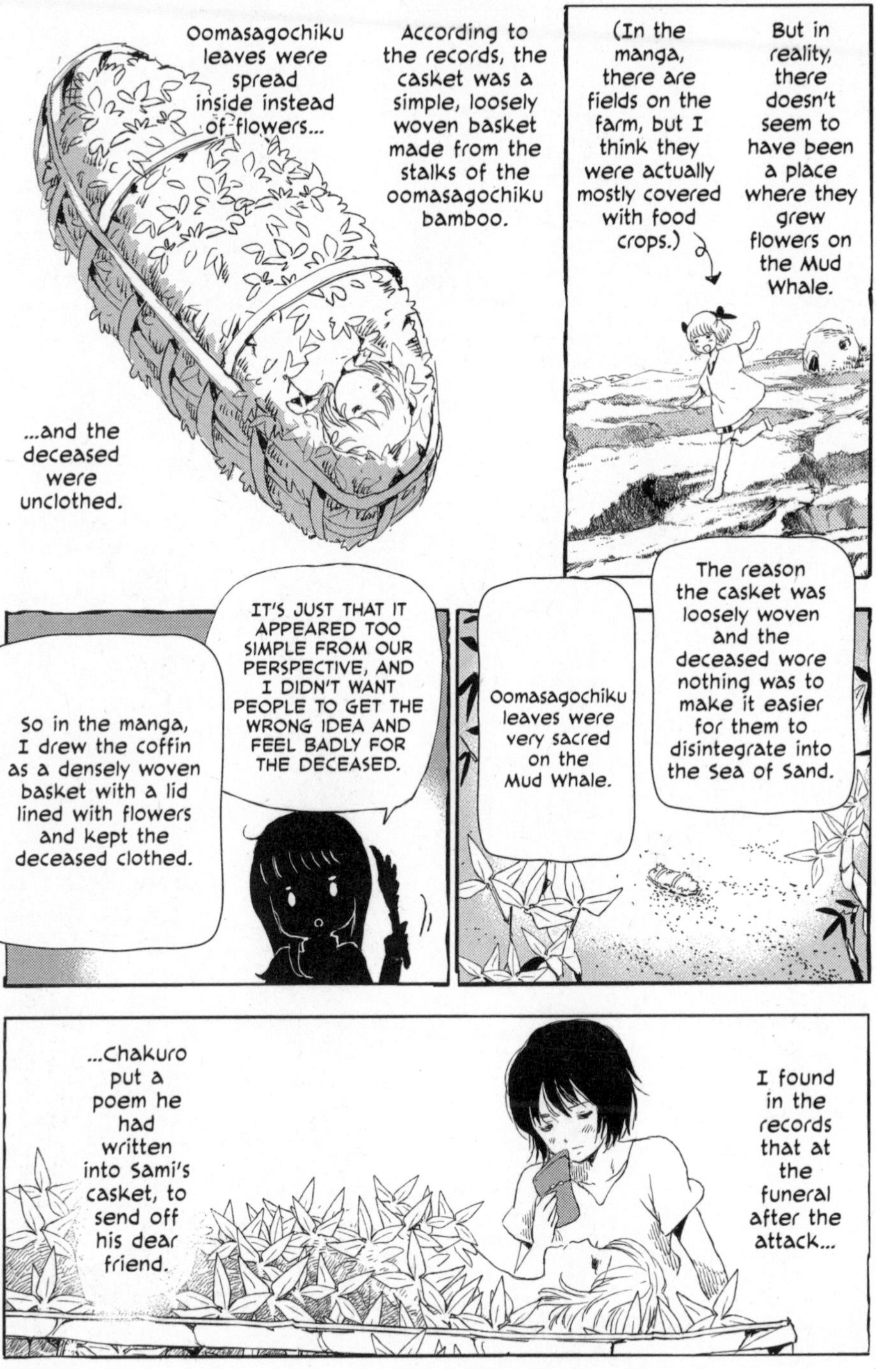
But in reality, there doesn't seem to have been a place where they grew flowers on the Mud Whale.
(In the manga, there are fields on the farm, but I think they were actually mostly covered with food crops.)
According to the records, the casket was a simple, loosely woven basket made from the stalks of the oomasagochiku bamboo.
Oomasagochiku leaves were spread inside instead of flowers...
...and the deceased were unclothed.
The reason the casket was loosely woven and the deceased wore nothing was to make it easier for them to disintegrate into the Sea of Sand.
Oomasagochiku leaves were very sacred on the Mud Whale.
IT'S JUST THAT IT APPEARED TOO SIMPLE FROM OUR PERSPECTIVE, AND I DIDN'T WANT PEOPLE TO GET THE WRONG IDEA AND FEEL BADLY FOR THE DECEASED.
So in the manga, I drew the coffin as a densely woven basket with a lid lined with flowers and kept the deceased clothed.
I found in the records that at the funeral after the attack...
...Chakuro put a poem he had written into Sami's casket, to send off his dear friend.

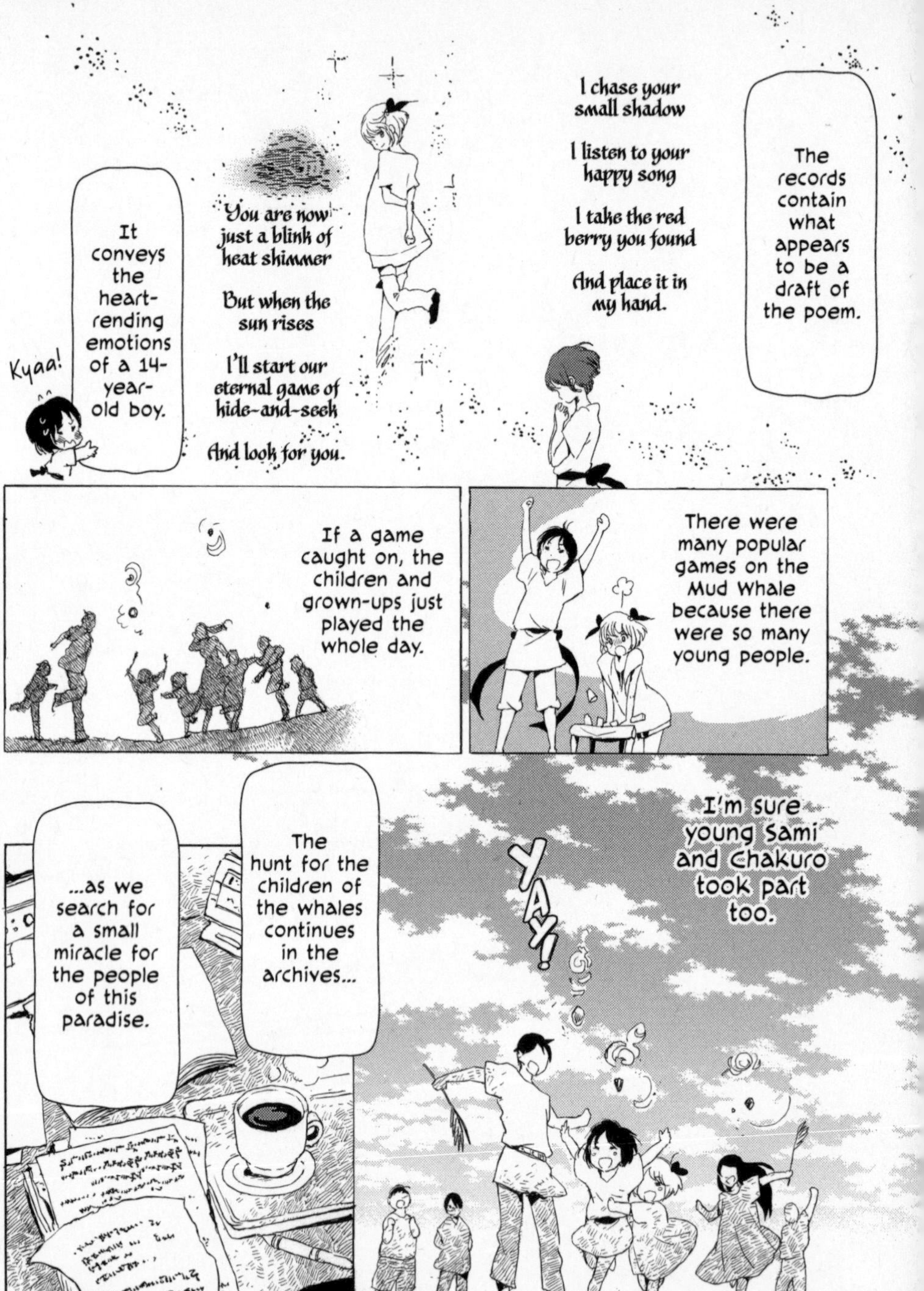
The records contain what appears to be a draft of the poem.
I chase your small shadow
I listen to your happy song
I take the red berry you found
And place it in my hand.
You are now just a blink of heat shimmer
But when the sun rises
I'll start our eternal game of hide-and-seek
And look for you.
It conveys the heart-rending emotions of a 14-year-old boy.
Kyaa!
There were many popular games on the Mud Whale because there were so many young people.
If a game caught on, the children and grown-ups just played the whole day.
I'm sure young Sami and Chakuro took part too.
YAY!
The hunt for the children of the whales continues in the archives...
...as we search for a small miracle for the people of this paradise.

Looking for *Children of the Whales* -The End-

A Note on Names

Those who live on the Mud Whale are named after colors in a language unknown. Abi Umeda uses Japanese translations of the names, which we have maintained. Here is a list of the English equivalents for the curious.

Aijiro	pale blue
Benihi	scarlet
Buki	kerria flower (*yamabuki*)
Chakuro	blackish brown (*cha* = brown, *kuro* = black)
Ginshu	vermillion
Kicha	yellowish brown
Kuchiba	decayed-leaf brown
Masoh	cinnabar
Neri	silk white
Nezu	mouse gray
Nibi	dark gray
Ouni	safflower red
Ro	lacquer black
Sami	light green (*asa* = light, *midori* = green)
Shinono	the color of dawn (*shinonome*)
Suou	raspberry red
Taisha	red ocher
Tobi	reddish brown like a kite's feather

If I could live on the Mud Whale, I would be the cleaner and sweep the mountains of sand every day.

—Abi Umeda

ABI UMEDA debuted as a manga creator with the one-shot "Yukokugendan" in *Weekly Shonen Champion*. *Children of the Whales* is her eighth manga work.

CHILDREN OF THE WHALES

VOLUME 2
VIZ Signature Edition

Story and Art by **Abi Umeda**

Translation / JN Productions
Touch-Up Art & Lettering / Annaliese Christman
Design / Julian (JR) Robinson
Editor / Pancha Diaz

KUJIRANOKORAHA SAJOUNIUTAU Volume 2
© 2014 ABI UMEDA
First published in Japan in 2014 by AKITA PUBLISHING CO., LTD., Tokyo
English translation rights arranged with AKITA PUBLISHING CO., LTD. through
Tuttle-Mori Agency, Inc., Tokyo

The stories, characters and incidents mentioned in this publication are entirely fictional.

Printed in the U.S.A.

Published by VIZ Media, LLC
P.O. Box 77010
San Francisco, CA 94107

10 9 8 7 6 5 4 3 2 1
First printing, January 2018

PARENTAL ADVISORY
CHILDREN OF THE WHALES is rated T+ for Older
Teen and is recommended for ages 16 and up.
Contains violence and death.
ratings.viz.com

viz.com

vizsignature.com

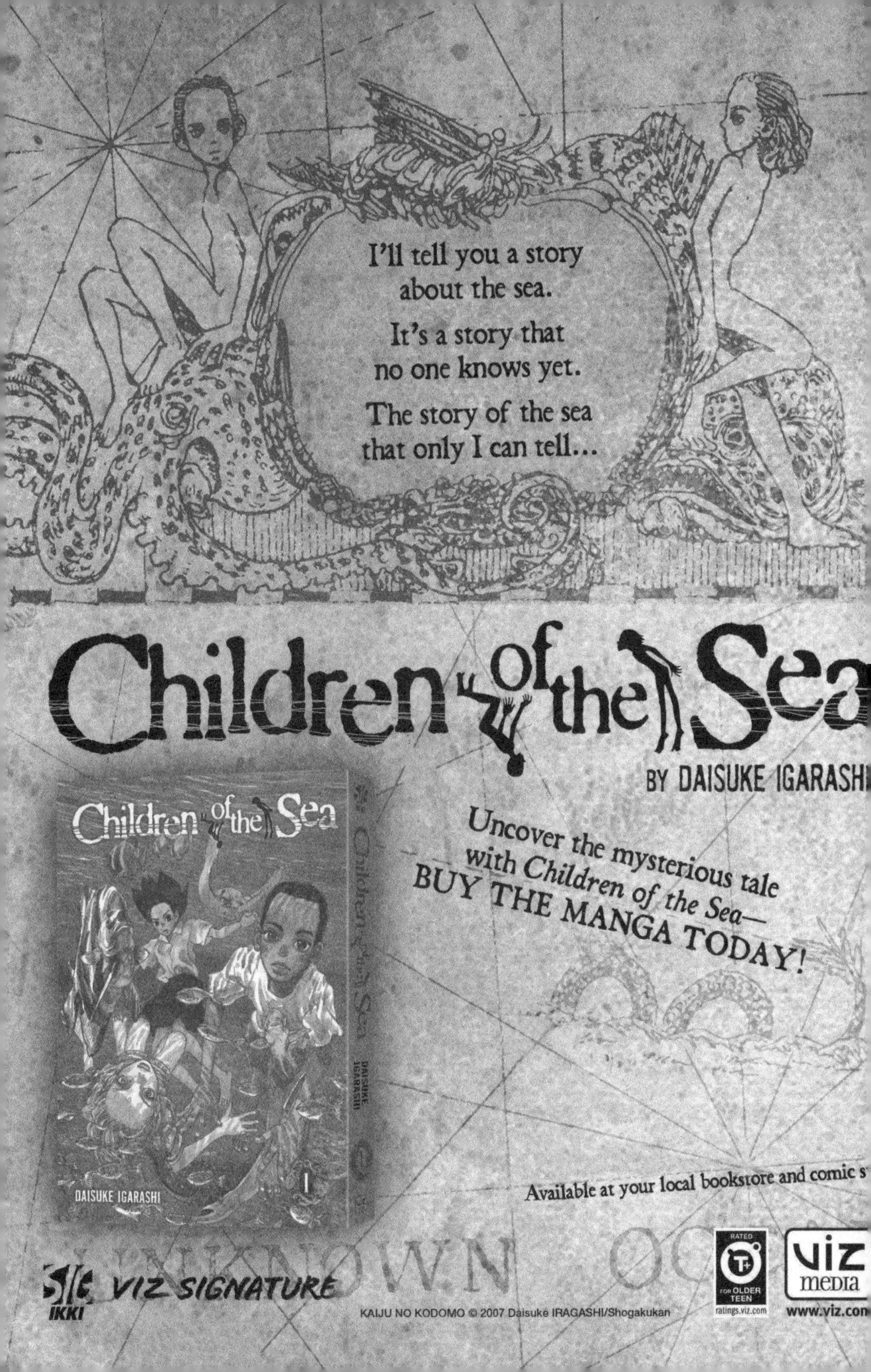
I'll tell you a story
about the sea.
It's a story that
no one knows yet.
The story of the sea
that only I can tell...
Children of the Sea
BY DAISUKE IGARASH
Children of the Sea
DAISUKE IGARASHI
1
Uncover the mysterious tale
with Children of the Sea—
BUY THE MANGA TODAY!
Available at your local bookstore and comic s
VIZ SIGNATURE
IKKI
KAIJU NO KODOMO © 2007 Daisuke IRAGASHI/Shogakukan
RATED T+ FOR OLDER TEEN
ratings.viz.com
VIZ media
www.viz.co

My parents are clueless.

My boyfriend's a mooch.

My boss is a perv.

But who cares? I sure don't.
At least they know who they are.

Being young and dissatisfied
really makes it hard to care
about anything in this world...

solanin

STORY & ART BY INIO ASANO

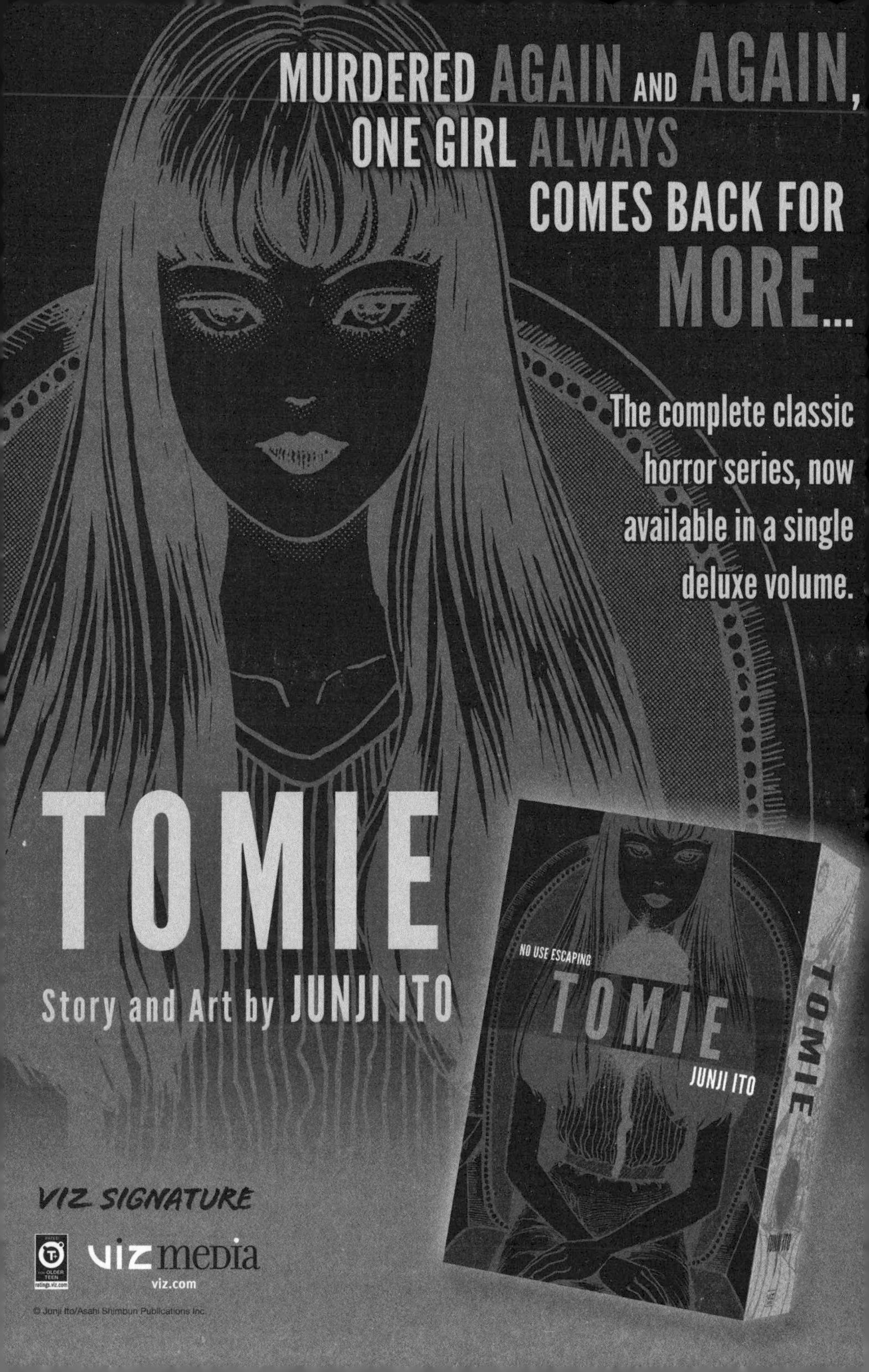
MURDERED AGAIN AND AGAIN,
ONE GIRL ALWAYS
COMES BACK FOR
MORE...
The complete classic horror series, now available in a single deluxe volume.
TOMIE
Story and Art by JUNJI ITO
NO USE ESCAPING
TOMIE
JUNJI ITO
TOMIE
VIZ SIGNATURE
RATED T+ FOR OLDER TEEN
ratings.viz.com
viz media
viz.com
© Junji Ito/Asahi Shimbun Publications Inc.

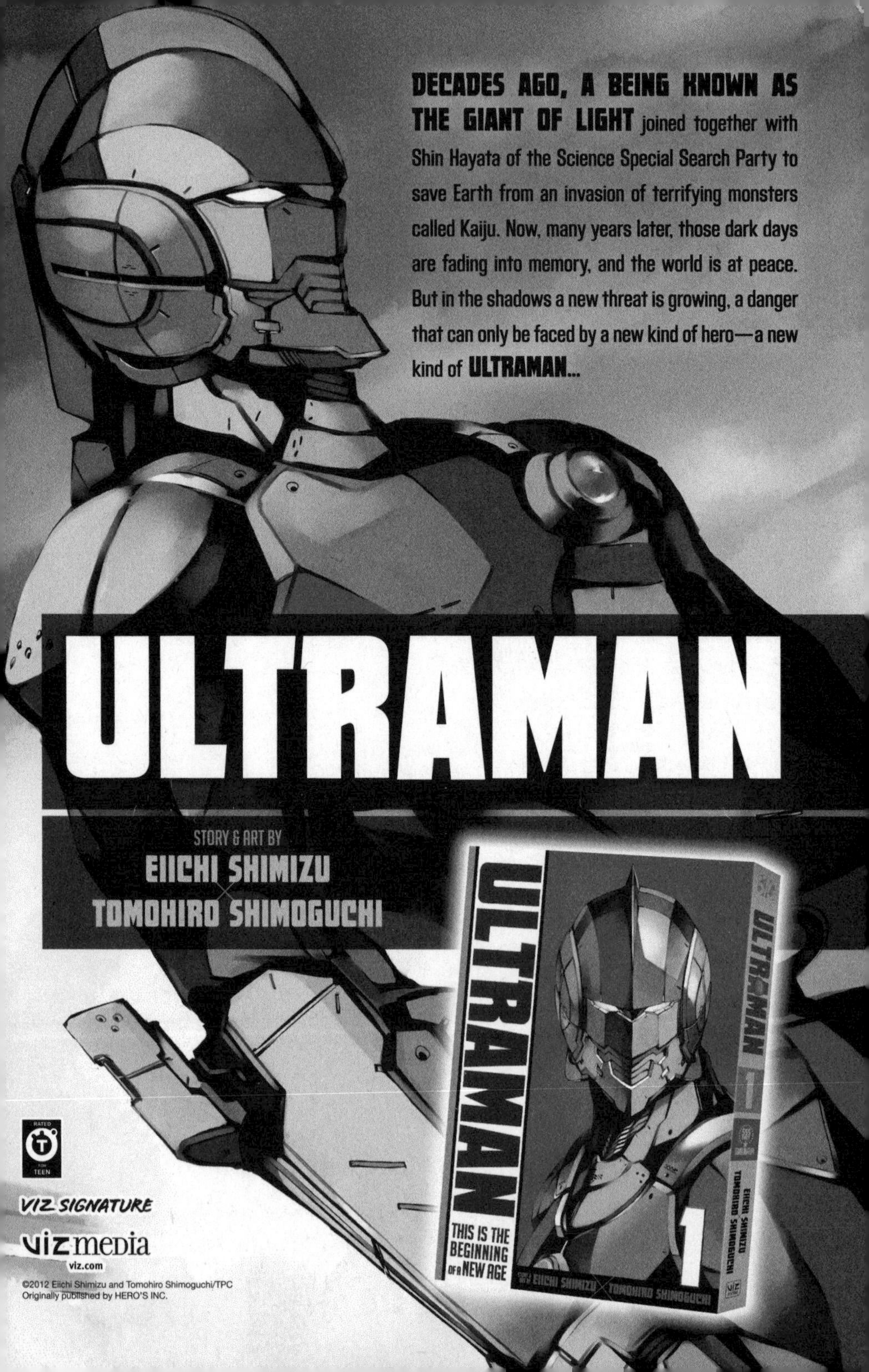
DECADES AGO, A BEING KNOWN AS THE GIANT OF LIGHT joined together with Shin Hayata of the Science Special Search Party to save Earth from an invasion of terrifying monsters called Kaiju. Now, many years later, those dark days are fading into memory, and the world is at peace. But in the shadows a new threat is growing, a danger that can only be faced by a new kind of hero—a new kind of ULTRAMAN...
ULTRAMAN
STORY & ART BY
EIICHI SHIMIZU × TOMOHIRO SHIMOGUCHI
ULTRAMAN
THIS IS THE BEGINNING OF A NEW AGE
1
RATED T FOR TEEN
VIZ SIGNATURE
viz media
viz.com
©2012 Eiichi Shimizu and Tomohiro Shimoguchi/TPC
Originally published by HERO'S INC.

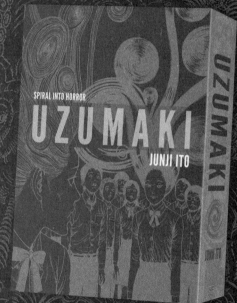

THIS IS THE LAST PAGE!

Children of the Whales has been printed in the original Japanese format to preserve the orientation of the original artwork.